PLAY THERAPY

Virginia M. Axline

D0557473

BALLANTINE BOOKS • NEW YORK

A Ballantine Book
Published by The Random House Publishing Group
Copyright © 1974 by Virginia Mae Axline

Revised edition Copyright © 1969 by Virginia Mae Axline

Published in the United States by Ballantine Books, an imprint of The Random House Publishing Group, a division of Random House, Inc., New York, and simultaneously in Canada by Random House of Canada Limited, Toronto.

Ballantine and colophon are registered trademarks of Random House, Inc.

www.ballantinebooks.com

ISBN 978-0-345-30335-6

Printed in the United States of America

This edition published by arrangement with Houghton Mifflin Company

59 58 57 56 55 54 53 52

First Ballantine Books Edition: March 1969

Photographs of children at play by Richard Boyer.
Photographs of children's artwork by Tony Hirsch.

Preface to the Ballantine Edition

A seven-year-old boy, in the middle of a play-therapy session, cried out spontaneously, "Oh, every child just once in his life should have a chance to spill out all over without a 'Don't you dare! Don't you dare! Don't you dare!' " That was his way of defining his play therapy experience at that moment.

An eight-year-old girl suddenly stopped her play and exclaimed, "In here I turn myself inside out and give myself a shake, shake, shake, and finally I get glad all over that I am me."

In play-therapy experiences, the child is given an opportunity to learn about himself in relation to the therapist. The therapist will behave in ways that she intends will convey to the child the security and opportunity to explore not only the room and the toys but himself in this experience and relationship. He will have the privilege of measuring himself against himself. And as a result of this experience in self-exploration, self-in-relation-to-others, self-expansion, and self-expression, he learns to accept and respect not only himself but others as well, and he learns to use freedom with a sense of responsibility.

There is a frankness, and honesty, and a vividness in the way children state themselves in a play situation. Their feelings, attitudes, and thoughts emerge, unfold themselves, twist and turn and lose their sharp edges. The child learns to understand himself and others a little better and to extend emotional hospitality to all people more generously.

Bit by bit, with extreme caution, the child externalizes that inner self and states it with increasing candor and sometimes with dramatic flair. He soon learns that in this playroom with this unusual adult he can let in and out the tide of his feelings and impulses. He can create his own world with these simple toys that lend themselves so well to projected identities. He can be his own architect and create his castles in the sand, and he can people his world with the folks of his own making. He can select and discard. He can create and destroy. He can build himself a mountain and climb safely to the top and cry out for all his world to hear, "I can build me a mountain or I can flatten it out. In *here* I am big!"

He learns that in his search of self he has opened the door to a broader understanding of all people.

VIRGINIA M. AXLINE

Contents

PART ONE

Introduction

1. Some Children Are Like This   3
2. Play Therapy   9

PART TWO

The Non-Directive Play-Therapy Situation and Participants

3. The Playroom and Suggested Materials   53
4. The Child   57
5. The Therapist   62
6. An Indirect Participant—The Parent or Parent-Substitute   66

PART THREE

The Principles of Non-Directive Play Therapy

7. The Eight Basic Principles   73
8. Establishing Rapport   76
9. Accepting the Child Completely   86
10. Establishing a Feeling of Permissiveness   91

11. Recognition and Reflection
    of Feelings   97
12. Maintaining Respect for the
    Child   106
13. The Child Leads the Way   119
14. Therapy Cannot Be Hurried   125
15. The Value of Limitations   128

PART FOUR

Implications for Education

16. Practical Schoolroom
    Application   139
17. Application to Parent-Teacher
    Relationships   157
18. Application to Teacher-
    Administrator Relationships   161

PART FIVE

Annotated Therapy Records

19. Excerpts from Individual
    Therapy Records   171
20. Excerpts from Group-
    Therapy Records   199
21. Complete Group-Therapy
    Record and Evaluation   209
22. Combined Individual and
    Group-Therapy Contacts   270
23. A Teacher-Therapist Deals
    with a Handicapped Child   327
Index   371

PART ONE

Introduction

1.

Some Children
Are Like This

"It's Fight, Fight, Fight—All Day Long!"

The distraught teacher hurried down to the principal's office a few agitated steps ahead of Tom, who followed with sullen resentment.

"Wait out here," she informed him crisply, while she went in, on a teacher's priority, to present her complaint to the principal. This defiant, disobedient twelve-year-old boy was driving her to distraction. He kept the class in a constant state of turmoil. He was continually reminding her that she was "just a substitute teacher" and remarking that "no one could boss him around."

Tom was bright enough to do satisfactory school work, but he refused to apply himself to the assignments. If he had his way he would read all the time. He resented criticism He was antagonistic toward the other children—complained that they "picked on him."

And now the group had just come in from recess and there had been another fight. Tom said the boys had all ganged up on him; and the boys said that Tom had spit on the American flag. When they had returned to the classroom, Tom showing signs of having been severely beaten by the gang, the teacher had reprimanded them for fighting on the playground. The other boys had said they were sorry and had related the flag episode. But Tom had glared at her in defiance, had swept his book off his desk with a gesture of utter contempt and anger, and had said, "I'll do as I please! *They* started it. *They* ganged up on me. I hate the whole bunch of them. I hate their very guts and I'll get even. Damn them all!" His black eyes blazed. His voice trembled. Yes, he even cried—big hulk that he was—and scenes like this were so upsetting to the class and made her so nervous she was all shaky and could just cry! She couldn't stand it much longer. She just couldn't!

Then, after she had finished her complaint, Tom was summoned into the inner sanctum.

"Miss Blank tells me you've been fighting again."

"Well, they ganged up on me."

"She tells me you were disrespectful to the American flag."

"I *really* didn't spit on it. I just said that."

"She says you were disrespectful in class, threw your book down on the floor, and swore."

"I can't stand this place any longer!" Tom cries out—and once again the tears come to his eyes. "Everybody picks on me and lies about me and——"

"That's enough! I'm getting pretty tired of all this trouble we have with you. Every day you are brought down to the office. Every day you are reported for undesirable behavior. It's fight, fight, fight—all day long. Words don't seem to do you any good. Well, perhaps this will!" The principal gets out his strap and applies it wearily, despairingly, but effectively, where he thinks it will do the most good.

Tom and his teacher return to the classroom. The principal goes on about the business of being a principal. In the afternoon the teacher reports that Tom is absent. The principal calls Tom's home. His mother does not know where he is. She thought he had returned to school. He is truant from home and school for three days.

Everyone concerned with the case feels futile and inadequate. This does not seem to be the solution to this type of problem, but what can a person do? There must be order and discipline and control or the place would soon become a bedlam. Tom is certainly a difficult problem child.

II

"So You're Goin' Home, Are You?"

The matron of the Children's Home stood on the side porch of one of the cottages and watched Emma and the other children standing out in the yard. Emma was dressed to leave the grounds. She had her small overnight bag packed and waiting on the porch. The other children were standing apart from Emma. They made faces at her and she made faces at them. There was a tenseness— almost a grimness about her bearing as she waited there. Her handkerchief was twisted into a string. She stood first on one foot and then on the other.

"Ole Emma thinks she's smart 'cause she's going away," calls one of the children in a taunting voice.

"Shut up your sass," Emma retorts, "you stinky old polecat. You filthy, old, moldy-faced, double-jointed rat!"

"Don't you call me names!" angrily shouts the first child.

Emma leans toward her tormenters.

"Yah! I'll spit on you, see!" She does. There is an immediate clash.

"Children! Children!" calls the matron. They draw apart. Emma tosses her head defiantly. She watches the road eagerly for an approaching car. Her mother has promised to come after her and take her away for a short vacation.

The cottage door opens and out comes another matron. The two women talk together for a few minutes and then the first matron picks up Emma's suitcase and calls to her.

"Emma. Emma, dear. Your mother just called. She won't be able to come for you this week-end."

Emma turns toward the matron as though electrified. Her green eyes seem to be on fire. She glares at the matron.

"Come on, Emma. Take off your good clothes."

The other children shriek with glee.

"Yah! Yah! Smarty! So you're goin' *home*, are you?"

"Children! Children!" cry both matrons.

Emma turns and with the fleetness of a deer runs across the grounds until she comes to an isolated spot. She flings herself face down on the ground and lies there tense and silent. The matron finds her there and finally coaxes her back to the cottage. This has all happened so many, many times before. The mother promises to come for Emma and take her away. She disappoints the child and never keeps her promise.

Back in the cottage Emma cannot eat, cannot sleep, cannot even cry. She becomes sick and is placed in the hospital room. When she recovers—as she soon does—and goes out among the other children, she is hateful and mean and sullen. She, too, is a problem child.

III

"THIS BOY DOESN'T NEED MEDICINE"

Timmy and Bobby hadn't felt solid ground under their feet since their mother and father had separated and the children had been placed in a foster home.

When his mother had come to take him home for a short visit, Timmy had been reluctant to go with her, but she had insisted. Timmy had been having trouble eating and retaining what he ate. It didn't seem natural for an eight-year-old boy to be without an appetite and to be so babyish. He cried easily, was difficult to get along with, fought with his younger brother, Bobby. He seemed tense and nervous.

Timmy's mother took him to the doctor and the doctor diagnosed it as a "case of nerves."

Timmy nibbled his fingernails as his mother discussed his case with the doctor. Then, in a moment of silence, Timmy exclaimed rapidly, in a high, shrill voice, "I saw my daddy yesterday. He came to the house. They're going to get a divorce. They're not going to live together any more. My father doesn't love my mother and my mother doesn't love my father and maybe he's going to be married again and we won't hardly ever see him, mother said, because she said she wouldn't let him have me and Bobby ever and he said that he would show her!"

"All this was discussed before Timmy, I suppose?" the doctor asked.

"Well," the mother said defensively, "he'll have to know about it sooner or later. He might as well know it now!"

"Bobby and me are living in —— now," Timmy said. He was screaming at the doctor. "We live with Mother R. We *like* it there!"

"Can't you give me a prescription—or something?" Timmy's mother said. "He doesn't sleep well at night. He vomits almost everything he eats. The woman he stays with says he is nervous and acts so wild."

"I'll give you a precription," the doctor replied, "but this boy doesn't need *medicine*."

In disgust, the physician wrote a prescription. He added caustically, as he handed it to the mother, "He needs a home and congenial parents more than he needs a nerve sedative."

Timmy returned to the foster home. He sought out Bobby. "Mom and Daddy are going to get a divorce, and she said he couldn't ever have us if she could help it and——"

Timmy and Bobby are problem children.

Tom and Emma and Timmy and Bobby are all described as "problem children." They are tense, unhappy, thoroughly miserable youngsters who sometimes find their lives almost too much to bear. Those who are interested in the personal adjustment of such children regard them with genuine concern. The environmental forces are unfavorable, and little help can be expected from parents or others who are responsible for them. What, if anything, can be done to help them to help themselves?

There is a method of helping such children to work out their own difficulties—a method which has been used successfully with Tom and Emma and Timmy and Bobby and with many other children like them. This method is called play therapy. It is the purpose of this book to explain just what play therapy is and to present the theory of personality structure upon which it is based, to describe in detail the play-therapy set-up and those who participate in the therapeutic process, to present the principles which are fundamental to the successful conduct of play therapy, to report case records which show its effectiveness in helping so-called problem children to help themselves in making their personal adjustments, and, finally, to point out the implications of play therapy for education.

2.

Play Therapy

*A Method of Helping
Problem Children
Help Themselves*

PLAY THERAPY is based upon the fact that play is the child's natural medium of self-expression. It is an opportunity which is given to the child to "play out" his feelings and problems just as, in certain types of adult therapy, an individual "talks out" his difficulties.

Play therapy may be directive in form—that is, the therapist may assume responsibility for guidance and interpretation, or it may be non-directive: the therapist may leave responsibility and direction to the child. It is with the latter type of play therapy that we shall be concerned.

However, before we proceed further with the actual description of play therapy, it may be well to formulate the point of view regarding the potentials within each individual; that is, the theory of personality structure upon which it is based.

There are many sources of information regarding the basic personality structure of the individual, because this is one of the most intriguing, if baffling, aspects of the human being. Many theories of personality have been advanced, discarded, re-examined, altered, and studied again. Attempts have been made to "test" personality, to "predict" personality traits, and to explain "personality structure." However, the whole subject is still wide open, and the theories that have been advanced to date do not seem entirely adequate to explain satisfactorily all that has been observed regarding the inner dynamics of the individual.

Therefore, in order to set up a frame of reference within which to proceed, the following explanation of personality structure is advanced as a tentative theory, open to criticism and evaluation, but based upon observation and study of both children and adults during and after a non-directive therapeutic experience.

The Theory of Personality Structure upon Which Non-directive Play Therapy is Based

There seems to be a powerful force within each individual which strives continuously for complete self-realization. This force may be characterized as a drive toward maturity, independence, and self-direction. It goes on relentlessly to achieve consummation, but it needs good "growing ground" to develop a well-balanced structure. Just as a plant needs sun and rain and good rich earth in order to attain its maximum growth, so the individual needs the permissiveness to be himself, the complete acceptance of himself—by himself, as well as by others—and the right to be an individual entitled to the dignity that is the birthright of every human being in order to achieve a direct satisfaction of this growth impulse.

Growth is a spiraling process of change—relative and dynamic. Experiences change the individual's perspective and focus. Everything is constantly evolving. interchanging, and assuming varying degrees of importance to the individual in the light of the reorganization and integration of his attitudes, thoughts, and feelings.

The impact of the forces of life, the interaction of individuals, and the very nature of a human being bring about this constantly changing integration within the individual. Everything is relative and the pattern is a changing, reorganizing sort of thing—like the pattern one sees in a kaleidoscope, a tube in which you look, through a tiny peep-hole, down upon odd-shaped pieces of colored glass; as you turn the tube, the pattern falls apart and reorganizes itself into something quite different. As different parts of the design touch, they form a new configuration. No matter how the tube is turned, the design maintains balance, the difference being in the design itself, which is sometimes compact and indicative of strength and sometimes spread out and seemingly frail and without much body. There is always rhythm and harmony in the design. Each pattern is different from every other, and the difference is caused by the way the light shines through and by the steadiness of the hand that holds the kaleidoscope, as well as by the interchanging positions of the bits of colored glass.

So, it seems, is personality. The living organism has within it the "bits of colored glass" and the personality is "structured" by the organization of these "bits."

The dynamics of life are such that every experience and attitude and thought of every individual is constantly changing in relation to the interplay of psychological and environmental forces upon each and every individual, so that what happened yesterday does not have the same meaning for the individual today as it had when it happened because of the impact of the forces of life and the interaction of individuals; likewise, the experience will be integrated differently tomorrow.

This characteristic of change applies also to behavioral responses. Responses that seem fairly similar day after day are sometimes referred to as habits, but habits seem to disappear suddenly into thin air when the individual no longer feels a need for them or when a more satisfying type of behavior is discovered.

It is this observable flexibility of the personality and behavior of the individual that has opened the door to admit the element of hope and a positive way of looking at the individuals who seem to have three strikes against them from the beginning. When the individual becomes aware of the part he can play in directing his own life— and when he accepts the responsibility that goes with the freedom of this inner authority—then he is better able to sight his course of action with more accuracy.

Why does Emma hope and hope and hope again in the face of continual disappointments and rebuffs? What feeds her faith and buoys her up after each shattering experience? Could it be this accumulation within her of "wisdom" and "experience" plus a growing awareness of her own ability to meet this situation? Is she gaining faith in her ability to withstand disappointments and to stand on her own feet? Is she gradually building up an acceptance of her mother that enables her to go forth to meet her each time the call comes through with a compelling faith in humanity?

A child is usually quick to forgive and to forget those experiences which have been negative. Unless conditions are extremely bad, he is accepting of life as he finds it, and accepting of the people with whom he lives. He manifests in every way an eagerness, a curiosity, a great love of life that thrills and delights him in its simplest pleasures. Normally, a child loves growing up and strives for it constantly—sometimes outreaching himself in his eagerness. He is both humble and proud, courageous and afraid, dominant and submissive, curious and satisfied, eager and indifferent. He loves and hates and fights and makes peace, is delightfully happy and despairingly sad. Why? Some psychologists might explain these reactions as examples of responses to given stimuli. The writer prefers to explain them as the reactions of a child who is growing—growing—growing—growing in experience, growing in understanding, growing in his acceptance of himself and of his world. He is assimilating all the ingredients that become integrated into the configuration that is uniquely his. It is called his "personality."

It has been said many times that there are certain basic needs within each individual and that the organism is striving constantly to satisfy these needs. When there is a relatively direct satisfaction, the individual is said to be well adjusted. When the seeking-effort to satisfy the needs is blocked, devious paths are taken to bring about satisfaction, and the individual is said to be maladjusted This is a very simple explanation of adjustment and maladjustment. It does not seem adequate to explain the complex achievements of the human organism. Certainly there is little in such an explanation of human behavior to justify the terms "respect for the individual" and the "dignity that is the birthright of man." In fact, one is inclined to admire the "maladjusted type of behavior" because it seems more complex, more ingenious, and more selective than that which is based on direct satisfaction of needs.

Personality seems to defy classification, stereotyping, and

compartmentalizing. An individual who is rigid and fearful in a particular situation or with a particular person often reacts quite differently under other circumstances and in other relationships. The behavior of the individual at all times seems to be caused by one drive, the drive for complete self-realization. When this drive is blocked by pressures from without, the growth toward this objective does not stop, but continues with increased momentum because of the generative force of the tensions that are created by the frustrations.

When an individual reaches a barrier which makes it more difficult for him to achieve the complete realization of the self, there is set up an area of resistance and friction and tension. The drive toward self-realization continues, and the individual's behavior demonstrates that he is satisfying this inner drive by outwardly fighting to establish his self-concept in the world of reality, or that he is satisfying it vicariously by confining it to his inner world where he can build it up with less struggle. The more it is turned inward, the more dangerous it becomes; and the further he departs from the world of reality, the more difficult it is to help him.

The outward behavior manifestations are dependent upon the integration of all past and present experiences, conditions, and relationships, but are pointed toward the fulfillment of this inner drive that continues as long as there is life. Possibly the difference between well-adjusted behavior and maladjusted behavior could be explained as follows: When the individual develops sufficient self-confidence to bring his self-concept out of the shadow land and into the sun and consciously and purposefully to direct his behavior by evaluation, selectivity, and application to achieve his ultimate goal in life—complete self-realization—then he seems to be well adjusted.

On the other hand, when the individual lacks sufficient self-confidence to chart his course of actions openly, seems content to grow in self-realization vicariously rather than directly, and does little or nothing about channeling this drive in more constructive and productive directions, then he is said to be maladjusted.

The various types of maladjusted behavior, such as

daydreaming, withdrawal, compensation, identification, projection, regression, repression—and all the other so-called mechanisms of maladjusted behavior—seem to be evidences of the inner self's attempting to approximate a full realization of this self-concept. But this realization is achieved in an "underground" manner. The individual's behavior is not consistent with the inner concept of the self which the individual has created in his attempt to achieve complete self-realization. The further apart the behavior and the concept, the greater the degree of maladjustment When the behavior and the concept of self are consistent and the self-concept that is built up within the individual finds adequate outward expression, then the individual is said to be well adjusted. There is no longer a split focus There is no longer inner conflict.

For example, Emma wants to be an individual who is respected and recognized as someone of importance. She wants to feel that she is a lovable person, that she is worthwhile and capable. Her environment places her in a situation where she is denied the conditions necessary to demonstrate outwardly this inner drive to establish selfhood or conscious personality. Therefore she tries to acquire it vicariously. She lies and fights and withdraws into the world of her dreams where she can realize her own self-concept. The same is true of Tom and Timmy and Bobby. It seems as though these children—and every other child- -must have a feeling of self-esteem. This feeling is sometimes created in the child by love and security and a sense that he belongs. but these factors seem to be evidences to the child that he is being accepted as an individual of value rather than just the satisfaction of his need of love for love's sake and security for security's sake. The children whose records appear in this book were in many instances without relationships that supplied love, security. and belongingness, and yet, through the process of therapy. they acquired the necessary feeling of personal worth, a feeling that they were capable of self-direction, a growing awareness that they had within themselves the ability to stand on their own two feet, to accept themselves. to assume the responsibility for their conscious personalities, and by so doing synchronize the two projections of their personalities—what the individual *is* within himself and how he outwardly manifests this inner self.

The individual reacts as he does because of the total configuration of all his experiences. His reaction is a complex, weighted sort of thing that calls for clarification, objectivity, acceptance, and the responsibility to do something about it.

Non-directive Therapy

Non-directive therapy is based upon the assumption that the individual has within himself, not only the ability to solve his own problems satisfactorily, but also this growth impulse that makes mature behavior more satisfying than immature behavior.

This type of therapy starts where the individual is and bases the process on the present configuration, allowing for change from minute to minute during the therapeutic contact if it should occur that rapidly, the rate depending upon the reorganization of the individual's accumulated experiences, attitudes, thoughts, and feelings to bring about insight, which is a prerequisite of successful therapy.

Non-directive therapy grants the individual the permissiveness to be himself; it accepts that self completely, without evaluation or pressure to change; it recognizes and clarifies the expressed emotionalized attitudes by a reflection of what the client has expressed; and, by the very process of non-directive therapy, it offers the individual the opportunity to be himself, to learn to know himself, to chart his own course openly and aboveboard—to rotate the kaleidoscope, so to speak, so that he may form a more satisfactory design for living.

When one is faced with Tom and Emma and Timmy and Bobby and there are visible evidences that these children are developing "warped" personalities, one is challenged to do something to help each one to understand himself, to free himself from his tensions and frustrations, to realize fully the powerful forces within himself that are striving continuously for growth, maturity, and fulfillment.

Play Therapy

Non-directive play therapy, as we have said before, may be described as an opportunity that is offered to the child to experience growth under the most favorable conditions. Since play is his natural medium for self-expression, the child is given the opportunity to play out his accumulated feelings of tension, frustration, insecurity, aggression, fear, bewilderment, confusion.

By playing out these feelings he brings them to the surface, gets them out in the open, faces them, learns to control them, or abandons them. When he has achieved emotional relaxation, he begins to realize the power within himself to be an individual in his own right, to think for himself, to make his own decisions, to become psychologically more mature, and, by so doing, to realize selfhood.

The play-therapy room is good growing ground. In the security of this room where the *child* is the most important person, where he is in command of the situation and of himself, where no one tells him what to do, no one criticizes what he does, no one nags, or suggests, or goads him on, or pries into his private world, he suddenly feels that *here* he can unfold his wings; he can look squarely at himself, for he is accepted completely; he can test out his ideas; he can express himself fully; for this is *his* world, and he no longer has to compete with such other forces as adult authority or rival contemporaries or situations where he is a human pawn in a game between bickering parents, or where he is the butt of someone else's frustrations and aggressions. He is an individual in his own right. He is treated with dignity and respect. He can say anything that he feels like saying—and he is accepted completely. He can play with the toys in any way that he likes to—and he is accepted completely. He can hate and he can love and he can be as indifferent as the Great Stone Face—and he is still accepted completely. He can be as fast as a whirlwind or as slow as molasses in January—and he is neither restrained nor hurried.

It is a unique experience for a child suddenly to find adult suggestions, mandates, rebukes, restraints, criticisms, disapprovals, support, intrusions gone. They are all replaced by complete acceptance and permissiveness to be himself.

No wonder the child, during his first play contact, often expresses bewilderment. What is this all about? He is suspicious. He is curious. All his life there has been someone to help him live his life. There may even have been someone who was determined to live his life for him. Suddenly this interference is gone and he is no longer living in the shadow of someone who looms larger than he on his horizon. He is out in the sun and the only shadows are the ones which he himself wishes to cast.

It is a challenge. And something deep within the child responds to this clearly felt challenge to *be*—to exercise this power of life within himself, to give it direction, to become more purposeful and decisive and individual.

He tries it out—gingerly at first—then, as he feels the permissiveness and security in the situation, he sets forth more boldly to explore the possibilities of this arrangement. He is no longer blocked by exterior forces and so the drive within him for growth has no barriers to go around. The psychological resistance that he has formerly met is gone.

The presence of an accepting, understanding, friendly therapist in the playroom gives him a sense of security. The limitations, few as they are, add to this feeling of security and reality. The participation of the therapist during the therapy contact also reinforces the child's feeling of security. The therapist is sensitive to what the child is feeling and expressing through his play and verbalization. She reflects these expressed, emotionalized attitudes back to him in such a way as to help him understand himself a little better. She respects the child and his ability to stand on his own two feet and to become a more mature and independent individual if he is given an opportunity to do so. In addition to helping the child gain a better understanding of himself by the reflection of his emotionalized attitudes, the therapist also conveys to him the feeling that she is understanding him and accepting him at all times regardless of what he says or does. Thus, the therapist gives him the courage to go deeper and deeper into his innermost world and bring out into the open his real self.

To the child, therapy is indeed a challenge to this drive
within him that is constantly striving for realization. It is a
challenge that has never been ignored in the writer's experience with children. The speed at which they utilize
this opportunity varies with the individual, but the fact
that varying degrees of growth do take place during a
play-therapy experience has been demonstrated many
times.

To the therapist, it is an opportunity to test out the
hypothesis that, given a chance, the child can and does
become more mature, more positive in his attitudes, and
more constructive in the way he expresses this inner drive.

The writer believes that it is the same inner drive
toward self-realization, maturity, fulfillment, and independence that also creates those conditions which we call
maladjustment, which seems to be either an aggressive
determination on the part of the child to be himself by one
means or another or a strong resistance to the blocking of
his complete self-expression. For instance, when Tom is
scorned by his parents and teachers and friends because
his attitude and behavior have made him unacceptable to
them, then he is determined to maintain his way before
them, though they slay him. He will fight them. He will
sulk. He will defy them. He will pretend to spit on the
flag. And, in his complete frustration and conflict, he will
weep with despair. This also seems to be true of the other
children who are mentioned in this book. They are all
fighting for maturity, independence, and a right to be
themselves. If the reader will examine all the illustrative
material in this book with the question in mind— What
really happened to the child during this therapy hour?—
the answer seems to jump out at the reader. The child was
given the opportunity to channel this inner growth into a
constructive and positive way of life. He eagerly seized the
opportunity. He is capable of solving his own problems,
making his own choices, taking the responsibility for himself in many more ways than he is usually permitted to
do.

Quotations of what children have actually said in describing the play-therapy experience as the remarks came
out spontaneously are more indicative of what it means to
the child than anything the therapist can say.

Three boys, aged eight, were experiencing group-therapy sessions.[1] During the eighth interview, Herby suddenly asked the therapist, "Do you *have* to do this? Or do you *like* to do this?" Then he added, "I wouldn't know *how* to do this." Ronny asked, "What do you mean? You play. That's all. You just play." And Owen agreed with Ronny. "Why, sure you do," he said. But Herby continued the discussion. "I mean I wouldn't know how to do what she does. I don't even know what she does. She doesn't seem to do anything. Only all of a sudden, I'm free. Inside me, I'm free." (He flings his arms around.) "I'm Herb and Frankenstein and Tojo and a devil." (He laughs and pounds his chest.) "I'm a great giant and a hero. I'm wonderful and I'm terrible. I'm a dope and I'm so smart. I'm two, four, six, eight, ten people, and I fight and I kill!" The therapist said to Herby, "You're all kinds of people rolled up in one." Ronny added, "And you stink, too." Herby glared at Ronny, and replied, "I stink and you stink. Why, I'll mess you up." The therapist continued to speak to Herby— "You're all kinds of people in here. You're wonderful and you're terrible and you're dopey and you're smart." Herby interrupted exultantly, "I'm good and I'm bad and still I'm Herby. I tell you I'm wonderful. I can be anything I want to be!" Apparently Herby felt that during the therapy hour he could express fully all of the attitudes and feelings that were an expression of his personality. He felt the acceptance and permissiveness to be himself. He seemed to recognize the power of self-direction within himself.

Another boy, aged twelve, commented during a first therapy session: "This is all so different and so strange. In here you say I can do what *I* want to do. You don't tell me what to do. I can mess up a picture if I want to. I can make a clay model of my art teacher and let the crocodile eat her." He laughed. "I can do anything. I can be me!"

Five-year-old Billy always referred to himself in the second and third person. When he wanted to do something like taking off his coat, for example, he would say, "You will take off your coat," instead of "I will take off my coat." Or, "You will paint" instead of "I will paint."

---

[1] Group therapy will be discussed further on in this chapter.

Gradually, during the therapy sessions, Billy became *"I"* and at the conclusion of one session said, "I found the sand interesting today." During the sixth contact he finally got into the sand box and sat down and ran his hands through the clean white sand and said with a note of wonderment in his voice, "Today *I* got into the sand box. Little by little, I got into the sand." This was so true. Week by week he had gotten a little closer to the sand, and finally, as he said, "Today I got into the sand box."

Feeling their way, testing themselves, unfolding their personalities, taking the responsibility for themselves— that is what happens during therapy.

Dozens of similar examples could be cited. Every therapy experience demonstrates this one consistent manifestation: the child gains the courage to move ahead, to become a more mature and independent individual.

Since the element of complete acceptance of the child seems to be of such vital importance, it is worth a more penetrating study. Acceptance of what? The answer seems to be that it is acceptance of the child and a firm belief that the child is capable of self-determination. It seems to be a respect for the child's ability to be a thinking, independent, constructive human being.

Acceptance seems also to imply an understanding of that never-ceasing drive toward complete self-realization— or complete fulfillment of himself as an individual that is psychologically freed so that he can function at his maximum capacity. An adjusted person seems to be an individual who does not encounter too many obstacles in his path—and who has been given the opportunity to become free and independent in his own right. The maladjusted person seems to be the one who, by some means or other, is denied the right to achieve this without a struggle. Examination of the records indicates this again and again. Sometimes the individual is rejected and brushed aside. Sometimes he is smothered by supportive care that makes it difficult for him to break through the barrier. It seems as though the individuals would not manifest the behavior symptoms that they do unless they were striving to achieve individual status. The ways in which they attempt to do this are varied and many, but there always seems to be some manifestation of the individual's resistance to the blocking of his maturity and independence. Even the dominated child who becomes rigidly dependent seems to be achieving a controlling independence in that way. The "babied" child, who refuses to learn to read when sent to school, at first glance seems to be fighting independence and maturity. It could be that it is the most effective way that he has discovered to control the situation and is therefore a satisfaction to him because it is an expression of his power to direct and individualize himself. This is a very controversial hypothesis and is presented as an interpretation of the play-therapy records' primary manifestation—that of growth within the individual at all times, unfolding sometimes in an unbelievably short time, but always present in greater or lesser degree.

Many cases seem to prove that the only need of the individual is the need to be unshackled, to be freed, to be permitted to expand into a complete self without a frustrating and warping struggle to satisfy this inner drive. This does not mean that he becomes so self-centered that the rest of the world ceases to exist for him. It means that he achieves the freedom to fulfill this inner drive naturally, without its becoming necessary to make it the central issue of his whole existence, and to channel all of his energies into an onslaught against the barriers that are preventing his maturity and that turn the individual's attention inward.

When this inner drive is satisfied naturally and constantly—because growth is a continuous process as long as there is life—it is an outgoing thing. The individual is achieving physical maturity and must achieve psychological maturity in order to strike a balance.

Just as an individual utilizes increasing physical independence to extend the boundaries of his physical capacities, so he uses the increasing psychological independence to extend the boundaries of his mental capacities.

The child who can run can go farther than the baby who can only crawl. The child who has learned to talk can communicate more effectively than the baby who can only coo and gurgle. With maturity comes the expansion of the individual to encompass the world as far as he can incorporate it in his scheme of life. And so it is, all through life. The child who is psychologically freed can achieve far more in a creative and constructive manner than can the individual who spends all his energies in a frustrating, tense battle to achieve this freedom and status as an individual.

He *will be* an individual. If he cannot achieve it by a legitimate way, then he will get it by some substitute action. Thus, the child has tantrums, teases, sulks, daydreams, fights, and tries to shock others by his behavior. Teachers have many times said, when trying to "manage" a show-off, "Give him a legitimate reason to show off. Let him take a part in a play. Give him some responsibility in the classroom!"—and have used other such devices to meet the child's need to be recognized as a person of value. Similarly, during the play-therapy hour the child is given the opportunity to realize this power within himself to be himself.

The toys implement the process because they are definitely the child's medium of expression. They are the materials that are generally conceded to be the child's property. His free play is an expression of what he *wants* to do. He can order this world of his. That is why the nondirective therapist does not direct the play in any way. The therapist renders unto the child what is the child's— in this case the toys and the undirected use of them. When he plays freely and without direction, he is expressing his personality. He is experiencing a period of independent thought and action. He is releasing the feelings and attitudes that have been pushing to get out into the open.

That is why it does not seem to be necessary for the child to be aware that he has a problem before he can benefit by the therapy session. Many a child has utilized the therapy experience and has emerged from the experience with visible signs of more mature attitudes and behavior and still has not been aware that it was any more than a free play period.

Non-directive play therapy is not meant to be a means of substituting one type of behavior, that is considered more desirable by adult standards, for another "less desirable" type. It is not an attempt to impose upon the child the voice of authority that says, "*You* have a problem. *I* want you to correct it." When that happens, the child meets it with resistance—either active or passive. He does not want to be made over. Above all things he strives to be himself. Behavior patterns that are not of his own choice are flimsy things that are not worth the time and effort required to force them upon him.

The type of therapy which we are describing is based upon a positive theory of the individual's ability. It is not limiting to any individual's growth. It is outgoing. It starts where the individual *is* and lets that individual go as far as he is able to go. That is why there are no diagnostic interviews before therapy. Regardless of symptomatic behavior, the individual is met by the therapist where he is. That is why interpretation is ruled out as far as it is possible to do so. What has happened in the past is past history. Since the dynamics of life are constantly changing the relativity of things, past experience is colored by the interactions of life and is also constantly changing. Anything that attempts to shackle the individual's growth is a blocking experience. Taking the therapy back into the individual's past history rules out the possibility that he has grown in the meantime and consequently the past no longer has the same significance that it formerly had. Probing questions are also ruled out for this same reason. The individual will select the things that to him are most important *when he is ready to do so*. When the nondirective therapist says that the therapy is client-centered, he really means it, because, to him, the client is the source of living power that directs the growth from within himself.

During a play-therapy experience, that sort of relationship is established between the therapist and the child that makes it possible for the child to reveal his real self to the therapist, and, having had it accepted--and, by that very acceptance, having grown a bit in self-confidence—he is more able to extend the frontiers of his personality expression.

The child lives in a world of his own and very few adults really understand him. There is such a rush and pressure in modern times that it is difficult for a child to establish the intimate, delicate relationship with the adult that is necessary to enable him to lay bare his innermost secret life. Too many people are tempted to exploit his personality, and so he defends his identity. He keeps himself apart, reveling in the things that to him are so vastly important and interesting.

Bent intently over some simple thing, the child indulges his insatiable curiosity and sensory interests, and the adult is prone to laugh or belittle him when he announces, with the thrill of a true discoverer in his voice, "Why, this sand is gritty and sharp and it tastes like nothing. Is *this* what *nothing* tastes like?" Or, "This finger paint oozes through— oozes through—like red mud or green mud—oozy, oozy mud." Or the observation, "People going home from work—home from work—home from work. Going east when they go home from work—going to their suppers. Then tomorrow they will come again. They will come again. They will come again west. Come west in the morning and come back to work." Or, as in the case of the little five-year-old, looking out the window at a large church near-by, "There is the church--the big, big church. The church that goes up into the sky. The church that makes music. The church that chimes one, two, three, four, when it is four o'clock. A big church with bushes of sticks around it and where people go." Then, after a long pause, he added, "And sky! So lots of sky—away up there. And a bird. And airplane. And smoke." Another long, long pause—then, "And Dibs standing by a little window—looking out—at the bigness."

"It looks like a big, big world to you from here," said the therapist, very quietly.

"That's right," he said softly. "Bigness. Just bigness."

"Everything seems so very, very big," said the therapist.

Dibs turned away from the window. He sighed. "But not Dibs," he said. "Dibs isn't church-size."

There are rhythm and poetry and keenness in that observation. Adults are sometimes in so much of a hurry that they cannot take the time to appreciate the child. The little five-year-old who made the above observations during his therapy time had been "peculiar, queer, slow, unable to communicate with others," three months before.

Our culture superimposes dependence upon the child— but he continues to grow in independence within his inner world. In the therapy hour—once the child has established confidence in the therapist and has accepted the therapist even as she has accepted him—he shares his inner world with her and, by the sharing, extends the horizons of both their worlds.

Non-directive Group Therapy

So far in our discussion we have spoken only of individual therapy. Actually, the techniques of non-directive play therapy may also be applied to groups. Group therapy is a non-directive therapeutic experience with the added element of contemporary evaluation of behavior plus the reaction of personalities upon one another. The group experience injects into therapy a very realistic element because the child lives in the world with other children and must consider the reaction of others and must develop a consideration of other individuals' feelings. However, the group which partakes of non-directive group therapy is not thought of as a "club," a "recreational group," or an "educational group"; nor is it considered as a substitute for a "family situation."

It is obvious that, in cases where the child's problems are centered around social adjustments, group therapy may be more helpful than individual treatment. On the other hand, in cases where the problems are centered around a deep-seated emotional difficulty, individual therapy seems to be more helpful to the child. Since it is often impossible to determine just what is the basis of a child's problems, perhaps the best policy is to offer him both individual and group contacts where such an arrangement is possible.

The problems of group therapy are discussed further in Part Three, where the application of non-directive principles is discussed in detail, also in Chapter 18, where a complete group-therapy record is presented and evaluated, and in Chapter 19, where the combined individual and group contacts with Emma are recorded.

Similarity to Non-directive Counseling

The principles of non-directive play therapy which are discussed in this book are based upon the non-directive counseling technique which has been developed by Doctor Carl R. Rogers and is explained in detail in his book *Counseling and Psychotherapy.*[1] Non-directive counseling is really more than a technique. It is a basic philosophy of human capacities which stresses the ability within the individual to be self-directive. It is an experience which involves two persons and which gives unity of purpose to the one who is seeking help—that of realizing as completely as possible his self-concept and of becoming the kind of a person that satisfies the self, that merges into an integrated whole any conflicting concepts between the *I* and the *me,* or between the inner self-concept and the outer self-behavior.

Because primary emphasis is placed upon the active participation of the self in this growth experience, the term non-directive seems inadequate. While this term does accurately describe the rôle of the counselor, in that he maintains sufficient self-discipline to restrain any impulses which he might have to take over the client's responsibility, it is certainly inaccurate when applied to the rôle of the client. Instead, self-directive therapy seems to be a more accurate and more honestly descriptive term.

The relationship that is established between the counselor and client in this type of therapy is an outgrowth of basic attitudes on the part of the counselor which make it possible for him to accept without reservation the inalienable rights of the individual to be self-directive. Such attitudes are not put on and taken off like a coat, but are an integral part of the personality of the counselor.

Based upon such attitudes on the part of the counselor, the structure of this self-directive therapy process embraces complete acceptance of the client as he is and permissiveness to use the counseling hour in any way that he sees fit. He is the one who directs the way in which the interview is to go. He selects the things that to him are important. He assumes the responsibility for making the decisions. He does the interpreting. And as he works through his problem in the atmosphere of mutual respect which characterizes this relationship, he charts his course

[1] Boston: Houghton Mifflin Company, 1942.

of action—a positive course of action that correlates with his inner drive toward maturity.

Although we emphasize the part of the client, the counselor is not a passive agent in this experience. He is the precipitant, so to speak, that enables the client to separate out his emotionalized attitudes and, by evaluating them intellectually, either to discard or to accept them in the reorientation of his frame of reference. The counselor achieves this result by developing an understanding of his client which sensitizes him to the emotionalized attitudes being expressed by the client. By accurate and selective clarification of these expressed attitudes, he precipitates them out of the flood of emotions in such a way that the client can identify them and know them for what they are: and consequently construct a consistent code of values which gives him the strength to be himself and the stability to maintain an honest relationship with others.

The counselor is humble in his rôle and does not at any time precede his client, since he knows full well that the client is the master of his own self and that the client's will, not the counselor's, is the determining factor in his behavior.

In the warm and friendly relationship which the counselor establishes, the client is enabled to face himself squarely, feeling secure in this genuinely co-operative relationship, experiencing an absolute togetherness in this effort to achieve complete self-understanding and self-acceptance. As a result of a successful non-directive counseling experience, the client seems to acquire a consistent philosophy of life which can be summed up as follows: He gains respect for himself as an individual of value. He learns to accept himself, to grant himself the permissiveness to utilize all of his capacities, and to assume responsibility for himself. And in turn he applies this philosophy in his relationships with others so that he has a real respect for people, an acceptance of them as they are, and a belief in their capacities so that he grants them the permissiveness to utilize their capacities and lets them assume responsibility for making their own decisions. It is a real belief in the integrity of the individual. It places emphasis on a positive and constructive way of life.

When the non-directive, or self-directive, techniques are

applied to the treatment of children, the results are extremely significant. If a little child, rejected, insecure, without love, without success, without a feeling of belongingness, can meet this challenge to realize more fully the capacity within himself, can withstand the "slings and arrows of outrageous fortune," and can show positive signs of more mature and responsible behavior, then educators and social workers and industrialists might find it profitable to re-examine the adequacies of their contributions to the development of the individual and to recognize the potential ability within the individual to reciprocate by making a contribution for the improvement of all human relationships. Here, too, the individual's responsibility to others is in direct proportion to the amount of freedom that is entrusted to him.

When the individual learns to know himself completely, then he becomes the master of himself and is truly a free man. If non-directive counseling—or psychotherapy (call it what you will)—is one means of freeing the individual so that he can become a more spontaneous, creative, and happy individual, then it is well worth further study and more extensive application. If it seems to be a way of extending emotional hospitality to a troubled and confused child, then it seems only just that it be tried.

Now that we have a general introduction to play therapy, before we take up a detailed study of the play-therapy situation and the principles which govern its conduct, let us turn to an actual case to see how non-directive play therapy works. We shall take the case of Tom, the difficult problem child whom we met in Chapter 1.

How Does Play Therapy Work?

THE CASE OF TOM

Tom was twelve years old, above average in intelligence, nice-looking, but seriously maladjusted both at home and at school. He was referred for play therapy because he was antisocial, aggressive, and insisted that everyone blamed him unfairly for the trouble in which he usually found himself. Tom had a step-father, also a half-sister who was much younger than he, and who was the darling of the family.

Tom had spent most of his life with his grandmother, but two years previous to the time when he was referred for therapy, his mother had taken him back to live with her and the step-father and the half-sister. Tom did not get along at all well with them. Nor did he get along with the children in school, for he had never been permitted to play with other children until he started to school and had difficulty in adjusting to other personalities.

In this case the reader will note how quickly and graphically Tom played out his problem, mainly through the use of puppets. It is interesting to notice how the same puppets were used for different characters that were alike in their relationship to him. The father and school principal represented dictatorial authority to Tom. His ambivalent feeling toward his father seemed to be shown by the two parts the puppets played, first beating up the father and then defending him. The boy's play certainly seemed to be definitely correlated with his feelings and attitudes and problems.

FIRST CONTACT

Tom came into the room, wearing his hat and coat, and sat down at the table. He had a little tin whistle in his hand and twisted the mouthpiece off and on as he sat there. His expression was very serious. He avoided the therapist's eyes.

Tom: Well, here I am. I just came because ... out of curiosity, you know. I couldn't understand what Mother was talking about. She said that you would help me with my problems, but I don't have any problems.

Therapist: You don't think you have any problems, but your curiosity made you look into this.

Tom: Oh yeah! I'm curious. Always stickin' my nose in everything. Thought I'd come and see.

Therapist: You would like to see what counseling is like.

Tom: Counseling. That's the word I couldn't remember. Yeah. Only I haven't any problems (*Pause*). Except that ... well ... a ... my dad ... *step*-dad, really ... I can't stand him and he can't stand me, and when he's home and when I'm home there's trouble, trouble, trouble. I make too much noise. I'm in the way. I put my feet up on things. We can't stand each other. The only time I can bear to be around the house is when he is gone.

Therapist: You and your father don't get along well together.

Tom: My *step*-father.

Therapist: Your *step*-father.

Tom: But I don't have any problems.

Therapist: Even though you and your step-father don't get along, you don't feel that that is any problem.

Tom: Nope. And all the kids pick on me. They don't like me. (*Pause.*) I can't think of anything to say. Mother said I was to talk about my problems, but I don't have any problems.

Therapist: Let's forget what your mother said to talk about. Just talk about anything you want to bring up. Or don't talk at all, if you'd rather not.

Tom: Like that flag episode last week? You want to hear about that? They all ganged up on me. 'Cause I said "I spit on the flag." And I said, "Heil Hitler!" They all ganged up on me. But I really didn't spit on the flag. I just did it to get their goats. Believe me, I did, too.

Therapist: You wanted to get their goats and you certainly did. To say something shocking like that got their attention right away.

Tom: I don't know why I did it, though. I really wouldn't spit on the flag. I'm a good American. I have too much respect for the flag to spit on it. But that's what I did. They ganged up on me and beat me up. I was outnumbered.

Therapist: You can't understand why you sometimes do things like that.

Tom: Not because I got beat up, either. I just—— But I haven't got any problems.

Therapist: You don't like to admit that you have problems.

Tom (laughing): That's about the size of it. I really have more than my share of problems. My step-dad. And our substitute teacher. Gosh, she's mean. And nobody likes me. I don't know why. I don't think there is a person alive who doesn't have problems.

Therapist: You really believe that everybody has problems then, and that you are really no different from anyone else.

Tom: Only I'll admit that I've got problems. Some people won't admit it.

Therapist: You're ready to start by admitting that you've got problems.

Tom: My life is no picnic.

Therapist: You're not very happy.

Tom: Would anybody ever know what I say? My mother or anybody? Are you writing what I say down?

Therapist: I'm making some notes; but no one will ever be told what you say during this time.

Tom (with deep sigh): You know this is a mighty peculiar situation. Are you writing this down?

Therapist: Some of it. Just for my own information.

Tom: Yeah. *(Long pause.)*

Tom: Teachers don't care what happens. No one cares what happens to a guy, and here it is after school and you're not even my teacher and I don't bother you. I don't get in your hair. And yet——*(shrugs shoulders).*

Therapist: You didn't think other people cared enough about what happens to a guy and yet . . .

Tom: I was *curious.*

Therapist: You were *curious.*

Tom: Of course! I— Well, there isn't anything that really bothers me. Not really, I mean. I don't let it.

Therapist: You think you have things pretty well under control.

Tom: Well, yeah. Only I—— Well, I can't think of anything to say. I haven't got anything to say.

Therapist: If you haven't anything to say, you haven't anythin to say. *(Pause.)* If you care to come back next Thursday, I'll be here. If you don't care to, I would appreciate it if you would let me know by three o'clock next Thursday.

Tom: Yeah. I sure would.

Therapist: If you care to go now, you may. Or if you care to stay longer, you may. Use this time as you see fit.

Tom: Yeah. *(He removes his hat and coat.)* I'm in no hurry.

Therapist: Think you might like to stay a little longer.

Tom: Yeah. I like to look around in here. You don't care, do you?

Therapist: Look around if you like.

Tom (looking at everything in the room): I bet the kids like to paint.

Therapist: You think they do?

Tom: I do, too. Only in my room at school . . . Say. If I ever got a problem it's that sub. She sure could furnish all the crab meat in the world. Only you'd probably get indigestion and die.

Therapist: You don't like the sub.

Tom: You catch on. *(He examines the clay.)* This would be fun, too. *(Picks up the puppet.)* I could make up plenty of funny plays about the fixes I get in. Just my autobiography would bring tears to their eyes.

Therapist: You think your life is sad.

Tom: Well. I mean it is certainly full of something. I'm always in trouble. *(Tom puts puppet on his hand.)* Now see here. I'll *murder* you if you don't do as I say. See? *(Voice is completely changed—low, deep, threatening.)*

Therapist: He feels like murdering someone.

Tom: I do, too, sometimes. Only of course *(laughs)* I don't. Respect for the law and all that, you know. But tell you what. Next time I come I'll put on a play. Episode One: My life and troubles.

Therapist: All right. Next time you come you present your life and troubles.

Tom (playing with the different puppets): I'm sure I could make some of these.

Therapist: Think you might even be able to make some puppets. *(He continues to play with them.)* Your time is up for today, Tom.

Tom: Well, so long. I'll see you tomorrow.

From then on, Tom used the puppets for the major part of his therapy periods. He acted out his family problems and worked out his aggressive feelings toward the father, sister, and school.

EXCERPT FROM SECOND CONTACT

Tom comes in and arranges the puppet theater for a puppet play. He picks up the boy puppet.

Tom (holding up the puppet): This is Ronny, the bad boy. Boy! is he bad! He is now at home in bed. His *father* is downstairs. He wants him to get up. Ronny's father is always bossing him around. *(Laughs.)* But he doesn't get very far as you shall see.

Tom addresses this preliminary speech to the therapist. During the play he manipulates all the puppets and changes his voice completely each time a different one speaks.

> *Father (ugly tone of voice):* "Ronny. Get out of bed."
> *Ronny (sleepily):* "Don't want to."
> *Father:* "You hear me? You get out of bed or I'll——"
> *Ronny:* "Or you'll what?"
> *Father:* "I'll come up there and I'll make you."
> *Ronny:* "Don't brag so."
> *Father:* "You get ready and go to school."
> *Ronny:* "I don't want to go to school. I don't like school. Besides——I—I—I—I got a stomach ache."
> *Father:* "A stomach ache? You *are* a liar. And you're dumb. You don't learn a thing in school."
> *Ronny:* "Why don't I?"
> *Father:* " 'Cause you're dumb. You're the dumbest white boy I ever knew."
> *Ronny:* "I'm not dumb. I'll show you. I'll—I'll—I'll— Well, I'll——" *(Father spanks Ronny.)*
> *Ronny:* "Ow! Ow! Oh, you mean, mean man!"
> *Father:* "Now, you do what I say."
> *Ronny·* "I'll run away from home. I will. Wheeee——" *(Puppet shoots off stage.)*
> *Father:* "Why you little pup. I'll go after him." *(Father disappears.)*
> *(The clown meets Ronny.)*
> *Clown:* "Hello. Where you going? I'm Dopey, the Clown."
> *Ronny:* "And I'm Ronny, the Bad Boy. I'm running away from home."
> *Clown:* "Oh. Come with me. We'll find some real fun."
> *(Little girl puppet comes up in clown's place. The little girl is bawling loudly.)*
> *Girl:* "I want my mamma. I've lost my mamma."
> *Ronny:* "Go away. I don't like brats."
> *Girl:* "I lost my mamma."
> *Ronny:* "Ain't that just too bad! That is a calamity." *(Girl bawls louder than ever.)* "Where do you live?"
> *Girl:* "I—I—I—don't know."

Ronny: "What's your mamma's name?"

Girl: "Mamma."

Ronny: "First name?"

Girl: "Mamma."

Ronny: "Middle name?"

Girl: "Mamma."

Ronny: "Last name?"

Girl: "Mamma."

Ronny: "Now I wonder who is dumb." (*Girl screams and cries. Ronny disappears. Father enters.*)

Father: "What's the matter? What's the matter?"

Girl: "That boy hit me." (*Girl disappears. Ronny reappears.*)

Ronny: "I did not. I wish I had. I might of. But I hadn't yet."

Father: "What is your name?"

Ronny: "Ronny."

Father: "Ronny what?"

Ronny: "Ronny Gooseberry."

Father: "Are you a smart alec!"

Ronny: "Am I a smart alec? I just hate myself for being a smart alec."

Father: "Listen you!"

Ronny: "Listen *you!*"

Father: "Why, I'll murder you."

Ronny: "Oh yeah! We'll see about that."

(*Father and Ronny fight. Ronny beats up the father, who begs for mercy.*)

Father: "I'll send my son after you."

(*Ronny disappears, then comes up again, this time as the son.*)

Ronny: "Want me, Pop?"

Father: "You go fix that boy. He beat me all up." (*Father leaves. Another boy puppet comes up in Father's place.*)

Ronny (to boy): "You beat up my father. I'll mop the world up with you." (*Terrific fight. Ronny wins.*) "This sure is tiresome."

(*Girl comes up again. Ronny hits her. Girl bawls and disappears. Father comes back.*)

Father: "Hello, Ronny, Old Pal. If you hit her again I'll spank you."

Ronny: "I'll bet you can't."

Father: "Want to see me try?"

(*Father does. Ronny yells. Father then disappears.*)

Ronny: "Maybe I should have gone on to school. I'm hungry. Besides, sometimes, I think school is safer."

Clown: "Hamburgers. Hamburgers. Ten cents. Hamburgers."

Ronny: "I only got a nickel."

Clown: "I'll sell you an extra short one for a nickel."

(Tom pops up and interrupts puppet play at this moment.)

Tom: They are hot dogs now. This gets out of control every once in a while. *(Tom disappears again.)*

Ronny: "I'll go home. I better not go home. My pop, he'll murder me. I'll sneak up to my room."

Clown: "Hamburgers. Ten cents."

Ronny: "Here give me one."

Clown (yells): "Why you ... You counterfeiter you! I want good money." *(Ronny hits the clown.)* "Oh, you hit my nose, my beautiful nose." *(Bawls.)*

Ronny: "This is a very puzzling fact." *(Ronny disappears.)*

(Off stage there are sounds of choking and drowning.)

Ronny: "There goes the school bell. I wonder if I should go."

Father: "Ronny!"

(Tom again pops up.)

Tom: This time this puppet is the principal.

Ronny: "Yes, sir."

Principal: "Where was you this morning?"

Ronny: "A ... A ... A ... I ... I had a stomach ache this morning."

Principal: "How did you get a—— Say! Did you take those apples from my orchard?"

Ronny: "Can you prove I did?"

Principal: "No."

Ronny: "Then I won't admit it."

Principal: "I'll beat you up."

Ronny: "You will?"

Principal: "Why don't you go home to your pop?"

Ronny: " 'Cause I don't want to."

Principal: "You better."

Ronny: "I'm playing hooky today."

Principal: "You better not."

Tom: Swoosh! *(Puppets disappear.)*

(Off-stage yells and moans.)

Voice, off stage: "Oh! I fell in the lake! Oh, help me! Oh! Help! Oh!"

(Father and Ronny reappear.)
Ronny: "Hello, Pop."
Father: "What happened?" *(Ronny knocks Father down.)*
Tom (again sticking head up: Ha! He landed right in a mud puddle.
Father (sneezing and coughing): "I caught a cold. I really got sick. Oh!" *(Father disappears.)*
Ronny: "Ha, ha, ha."
(Girl re-enters.)
Girl: "I want my mommy."
Ronny: "You again." *(Ronny knocks her down. Beats her up.)*
Girl (yelling): "Wait 'til I tell my poppy on you!"
Ronny: "I just *can't* wait!" *(Puppets disappear.)*
Tom (popping his head up again): That's all, folks. To be continued tomorrow!

THIRD INDIVIDUAL CONTACT

Tom presented his puppet plays to an audience of six-year-old children. In an individual contact which followed, Tom evaluated the group experience. This is an excerpt from the third individual contact.

Tom: How about me fixing some of these toys for the little kids? See these broken ones.
Therapist: If you want to.
Tom: It would please the little kids.
Therapist: You want to do something for the little ones.
Tom: Yeah. You know I've got a little sister at home. Her name is Rose Marie. But there is no Rozy around our house. No, sir! It's Rose Marie. *(Long pause.)* Sometimes I call her Rozy. *(He starts to fix the wheels on a little car in the sand table.)* Sometimes I call her Rozy. I just do it to aggravate my parents. I tease them, just for the heck of it.
Therapist: You tease them——
Tom (interrupting): Know what? Guess I'm spoiled. I lived with my grandmother for so long. And I'm not used to my step-father. He's not used to me, either. I guess it's six of one and half a dozen of another. I sometimes think if I had been with my step-father from the beginning—— I don't know.
Therapist: You think it spoiled things between your step-

father and you because you didn't live with your parents from the beginning.

Tom: Grandma spoiled me. She let me have my own way all the time. I grew up selfish.

Therapist: You think it made you selfish, having your own way all the time.

Tom: Unhuh. *(He tinkers with the bus.)* There. That is fixed now. Let's see about this here fort. I'll fix this. *(He takes it over to the workbench and hammers it together.)* You know, I've been thinking. Do you think the play was too strong for the little kids the other day?

Therapist: What do you mean?

Tom: When the father was knocked over the cliff and was killed. They seemed to like it when Ronny knocked his father over the cliff. But afterward, I wondered.

Therapist: You thought it was pretty strong.

Tom: Well, yeah. I wouldn't want them to go home and knock their fathers over the cliff.

Therapist: You think they might want to try what Ronny did?

Tom: The thing that surprised me——— Well, I thought I was the only one who felt like that about my father because he was a step-father, but theirs are real fathers and they acted glad he was killed.

Therapist: You were surprised to even think that other children might feel like you sometimes do about your step-father.

Tom: Yeah. I don't know. You know when I went back to my room that day I wrote a letter to my father. My real one. He's in the navy. And I told mother. She said she didn't think he would want to hear from me, but I don't believe her. I don't think he's got another son. I think she just said that."

Therapist: It upset you when your mother said she didn't think your own father would want to hear from you.

Tom: And that he had another son.

Therapist: You don't want him to have another son.

Tom: I don't believe her. I think she just said that. *(Long pause. He hammers away at the fort.)* You know, I used to have a paper route, but I lost it.

Therapist: You did?

Tom: They took it away from me. They threw me out of the station. The dirty gyps owe me five dollars. You see I was late a few times and I missed a few customers and I lost my route. But I don't care.

Therapist: They beat you out of five dollars because you were late a few times and missed a few customers and you lost the route, but you don't care.

Tom: Yeah. *(Long pause.)* I say that, see? What I do mean is that I'm mad as hops about it and I just say I don't care. I always say I don't care, no matter how much I do care.

Therapist: You don't want people to know how you really feel about things.

Tom: Yeah. I don't want to give them anything to crow over.

Therapist: You think others might crow over you if you let them know how you feel.

Tom: Sure. They would. I know. I been around.

Therapist: That's the way it has seemed to you.

Tom: That's the way it *is.*

Therapist: You think that's the way it is.

Tom: Well, is there any difference between what you *know* is and what you *think* is? Hmm. Why sure. Hm. *(Very long silence. He works on the game he is fixing and hums under his breath.)* So that's the way the world goes around.

Therapist: Hmm?

Tom: I said so that's the way the world goes around.

Therapist: What way?

Tom: Oh, I don't know. I was just thinking. *(He finishes the game.)* Now I'll take these tools back. *(Leaves the room to return the tools he has been using. Returning.)* I'll be seeing you tomorrow, and how about me bringing some more kids with me next time?

Therapist: You would like it better if you had some of your friends with you?

Tom: I wouldn't say I had any friends. Let's say some of the chumps in my room.

Therapist: You're not sure you've got any friends. Well, if you want to bring some of the chumps in your room, all right. But try to keep the size of the group down to six.

Tom: How about three boys and three girls?

Therapist: I'll leave that up to you.

Tom: I'll ask Joe. He's a nice kid. Maybe he would be a good influence. And I'll ask Tommy, 'cause he's worse than I am. You see I don't want to be the worst guy here.

Therapist: All right, bring them next time, if you want to.

Tom: Know what? I think the little kids like me.

Therapist: You think the little kids like you.

Tom: Yeah. And it's a novel experience for me. People as a general rule don't like me.

Therapist: You don't think people like you?

Tom: No. They don't seem to. But the little kids run up to me out there in the yard and they speak and they act glad to see me. They seem to like my puppet plays, too.

Therapist: It makes you feel good when they act like that toward you.

Tom: Suppose so. Well, time for me to go. I'll be seeing you tomorrow.

This excerpt seems to illustrate several factors that were therapeutically significant in this case. The reader will notice how flexible the therapy hour was. Although Tom was in the playroom and was busying himself with the play materials, he was not using them as a medium for self-expression. This was a straight counseling interview. Tom had given his puppet plays before a group of six-year-old children in the school and their expressions of delight in his plays had impressed him. He, of course, thought that they were identifying Ronny's father with their own fathers. At this point it seems that Tom put his finger on one of the values of a group experience when he said that he was surprised to discover that other children with apparently less reason to do so reacted favorably to the father-beating. The realization that his was not a unique problem would certainly seem to dispel guilt feelings and lessen the weight of his problem, since sharing a problem seems to have some therapeutic value.

The appreciation which the six-year-old children demonstrated to Tom built up his self-esteem to the point where he could look more or less objectively at his problems. He relates, also, that after disposing of the puppet-father he attempted to establish a relationship with his own father. The reported reaction of the mother is indicative of a possible cause for Tom's behavior. Tom's request to bring some friends ("I wouldn't say I had any friends. Let's say some of the chumps in my room.") seems significant. He had been a lone child up to this point, content to go his lonely way. His asking to bring along other children seems to indicate that positive forces were already at work within him. He takes the initiative in tackling the problem of what to do about getting friends. The following day he appeared with almost the entire sixth-grade class. They all wanted to join his group. When told that he would have to confine his choice to six children, he chose three boys and three girls. His plan of selecting the boys—one for a good influence and one because he was worse than Tom—is thought-provoking. The idea of letting the child bring in his own group rather than having it selected for him seems to have value, too. If the therapy is truly child-centered, the child-chosen group should be more valuable to the child choosing the group than a group chosen by the therapist. This seems to imply that one child is in for treatment and the others are there for the fun of it. In the case of Tom, this was initially true. The therapist felt that a group experience was what he needed more than anything else. When he requested it, then it seemed more important than ever. The other children whom Tom invited looked at him with a new interest and he became one of them. He achieved status with the group. This seemed to the therapist in this particular case to be a significant part of the therapy and more meaningful than it would have been had the therapist done the grouping. Of course, permeating all these values is the release of feelings that Tom achieved through his plays and his talks.

First Group Contact

Tom's first group experience, with his six chosen friends, is recorded here.

Tom: This will be a sort of club for us. We'll be puppeteers.

Theda: Yeah. We'll sit here, huh? Oh, look, clay.

Jean: I never worked with clay.

Martha: What shall we do?

Tom: Miss A., you take care of the girls. I'll handle the boys. *(Boys laugh.)*

Joe: We'll handle *you.*

Tom (singing): Maybe we'll just get along together. Miss A., you tell 'em what to do.

Therapist: Suppose we plan it this way. You may come here on Thursdays from three-fifteen until four. You may use that time as you wish—and use any of the materials over here.

Tom: Okay. Freedom at last.

Therapist: You like the idea of making your own choices.

Tom: I should say that I do.

(The girls sit down at the table and begin to work with the clay.)

Martha: Well, Tom said we would make puppets. I think we should follow the plan. You tell us how.

Therapist: You want me to tell you what to do.

Martha: Well, you're the teacher.

Therapist: Forget that I'm the teacher. Now, do you still want me to tell you what to do?

Martha: Well, Tom said we were to make puppets.

Tom: All right. So I said make puppets. And she says you can use your own brain and you howl. What's your brain for, anyway?

Martha: Well, I like to do what I'm supposed to do.

Therapist: It's important to you to do what you think people want you to do.

Martha: Well, yes. I think it's important. People won't like you if you don't.

Tom: And you want people to like you. You want everybody to be crazy about you. Bah! *(Getting out the doll family.)* Look, they could be puppets, too. Look. *(Takes out girl doll, jerks her hair off.)* Oh! I'll fix it. It was half off. I couldn't resist the temptation. Anyone could see she was a brat. *(Laughs.)*

Therapist: You don't like the brat.

Tom: That's the truth. *(Boys gather around and look at the dolls. Tom grabs out the father.)* I am happy to report that the father has one leg missing. I shall nevertheless fix him for the kids.

Therapist: As far as you are concerned, you don't care if the father does have one leg missing, but you'll fix him for the other children.

Tom: Yeah. *(Fixes doll.)* I won't be able to stay full time tonight. I've got an ice-cream route now.

Joe: Last night he almost got killed. Some fellow down there almost ran over Tom. He did it deliberately.

Therapist: Think he tried to hit you with his car?

Tom: Yes. But it was my fault.

Joe: Your fault! Why, you said upstairs today that it was all his fault. Now you say . . .

Tom: Yeah! *All* my fault. I teased him into it.

Tommy: But you said in class today . . .

Tom: Down here I'm honest. See? It was my fault. I really cause most of my own trouble.

Therapist: Honest down here and able to admit that maybe you do cause most of your own trouble?

Tom: You don't nag. I don't get in so much trouble any more.

(Girls comment on puppet theater.)

Martha: What is that thing?

Tom: *My* puppet theater.

Joe: Ha, that is good.

Tom: Well, the school's and mine.

Tommy: Not the school's and not yours.

Tom: Then Miss A.'s and mine.

Joe: That's getting warm.

Tommy: Miss A.'s and not yours.

Tom: Mine partly, because I use it. I give plays here. I *am* the puppets and the puppets are me.

Tommy: Oh.

(Long pause.)

Tom: I didn't come down with a puppet play today nor yesterday.

Tommy: Why not?

Tom: Oh, I hadn't anything to give out with. You see I just extemporaneously give out just what occurs to me at the moment. There is no planning, no hashing it over, no preliminaries. That's the beauty of it. You just pick up a puppet and give out.

Joe: Like what?

Tom: You just let yourself float away and you change into the puppets.

Tommy: Show us.

(Tom gets puppets. His voice changes completely.)

Tom: "Now, see here, folks. I'm tough, see? I'm Ronny, the bad boy."

Goofus: "Hello, there. Where do you think you're going?"

Ronny: "Ah—ah—ah choo." *(Blows Goofus away.)*

Goofus (head only appears—the head is detachable): "Where is my body? Where is my body?"

Ronny: "I'll knock the living daylights out of you." *(The puppets fight.)* "See, folks. That's the kind of guy I am. And the little kids just love it. The more fights and slamming around there is, the better they like it."

(Girl puppet appears. Her voice is sticky-sweet.)

Girl: "Hello. I want my . . ."

Ronny: "You want your mommy. But you know what you are going to get instead? Well, this."

(There is a terrific fight and Ronny is victorious.)

Tom: Well, my time is up now. I gotta go now or I won't be able to take the wagon out. And I want to make good on this job.

Therapist: You really want to make good on this job and you want to follow the rules.

Tom: So long. I'll see you tomorrow and especially next Thursday.

(Tom leaves. The other boys come over and work with the clay at the same table with the girls. They start to make clay heads.)

Martha: He isn't nearly so bad in school any more.

Jean: He really is funny.

Theda: Yeah. He really is. He was singing under his breath all day today.

Tommy: Just about drove the teacher crazy. When she asked him what was the matter with him, he said he was happy, glad that it was Thursday, and was there any law against being happy? *(The children giggle.)* That's Tom. Always says what he thinks.

Joe: He makes his own trouble.

Theda: Yeah. He knows it, too.

Joe: Tom is plenty smart. That was a good play.

This illustrates the dynamics of a group relation. Martha reveals a feeling of insecurity. The therapist attempts to reflect Martha's feeling back to her so that she might gain insight into her behavior. So often the type of behavior that Martha exhibits is not considered undesirable behavior. Martha's problem is as different from Tom's as it could be, and yet both Martha and Tom are helped in the same group. Groups chosen by a child often include withdrawn and insecure children who would not always be recommended for therapy because they are not troublesome children. Criteria for maladjusted behavior sometimes overlook the child who is not a bother to adults. This implies that conformity to socially approved standards is not necessarily an indication of adjustment Group therapy often brings out this factor, and the withdrawn, approval-seeking child gets an opportunity for self-appraisal by comparison with others that is frequently helpful to him.

Tom's identification with the puppets is interesting and his explanation of how he picks up a puppet and "extemporaneously gives out" is illuminating. His example of a puppet play immediately centers around his problem of aggression toward the little sister. The surprise that he expressed about the little children enjoying the fight continued to dispel his feelings of guilt and, in the opinion of the writer, gave him the courage to bring out even deeper feelings. Tom felt the acceptance and permissiveness of this therapy situation.

It is significant that Tom differentiates between the therapy situation and the class situation. "Here," says Tom, "I'm honest, see?" And, when he examines his behavior honestly, he adds, "I really cause most of my own trouble."

What is therapy if not an examination and re-examination of the self in an effort to reorient one's values and by honest introspection achieve insight into ways of satisfying the drive for complete self-actualization and to achieve the strength and courage to be himself?

SECOND GROUP CONTACT

In the second group meeting, which followed the presentation of three more puppet plays to the six-year-olds, the group worked on puppet heads made out of powdered asbestos and paste and water. An excerpt from this contact follows.

Jean (to Tom): You're so mean.

Tom: It's nice to know what's the matter with me.

Jean: You don't do anything about it.

Tom: Still it's nice to know. Then, if I wanted to improve, I could.

Jean: If you improved, you wouldn't always be in trouble.

Tom: Sure. But if she (teacher) wasn't picking on me, it might be you. Did it ever occur to you that I really give an unusual service to the rest of you guys? I'm blamed for everything. The *wind* blows the papers off the old crab's desk and *I* get the blame for it. Now do I look like the wind?

Joe: She didn't say you did it.

Tom: She looked at me *first*, then she looked at the wind.

Tommy: She looked at the wind!

Martha: But you eventually did something.

Tom: As usual, *I* got the blame, but as I saw it there were a few others that might well have spent the afternoon on the stairs with me. *(To therapist)* Know what? I spent the entire afternoon on the stairs. Am I getting an education, I ask you? I miss all my work.

Therapist: You don't think you were the only one to blame and you didn't like missing your education.

Joe: She forgot you.

Tom: So she forgot me! Well, I didn't care. I just looked out the window and I thought.

Jean: Tom said he was taking a sun bath.

Tom: Sure. Taking a sun bath. Spending the day on the stairs. Was I gypped out of my education!

Martha: I don't see why—if you don't like getting blamed—why you keep doing things all the time.

Tom: She's got to have someone to blame. That's my special service. Tom, the blame-taker! *(He laughs and seems to have enjoyed the attention he got by his defiance.)*

Joe: When anyone left the room, Tom said he was taking his sun bath.

Martha: Yes. He didn't seem to mind at all.

Tom: The only thing I minded was getting gypped out of my education.

Therapist: You really didn't like getting gypped out of your education.

Tom: No. *(Silence. The children worked with the asbestos material.)* Know what? This stuff feels like dead flesh.

Jean: I wouldn't know. I never felt dead flesh.

Tom: Well, this is what it feels like.

Jean: How do you know?

Tom: Why, I got an imagination.

(Silence. All work on the heads.)

Tom: I'm going to make Hitler. Then we can have a fight and I can beat up Hitler.

Martha: Oh, no! Let's don't make Hitler. Make funny ones, then let them fight.

Tom: I said Hitler.

Martha: But the other kids——Well, for them——I don't think it would be right to make Hitler and then——

Tom: It wasn't right to make Hitler in the first place.

Martha: But I don't think——

Tom: I know you don't think. I'm going to make Hitler and then I'm going to destroy him.

Martha: Well, go ahead, then. Make your old Hitler. But *I* wouldn't.

(Silence.)

Tom: Look. His mouth down at the corners. This guy never smiles.

Jean: No, of course not. He's hateful.

Martha: Here, let me stab his eyes out. *(She gouges her pencil in Hitler's eyes.)*

Tom: Hey! You quit that. You'll ruin him.

Martha: I *want* to ruin him.

Tom: Well, this happens to be mine, see?

Theda (jeeringly): See?

(Tom goes up in back of the puppet theater and takes the puppets. His voice changes completely, becomes hard and tough.)

Ronny: "Now, look here. See. I'll murder you guys if I don't get my way, see? I'm narrow-minded, see?" *(Others laugh delightedly.)* "I'll start something, see? I'll just mess up somebody and I'll start something."

Another boy puppet: "Is that so? Is that so? You big bag of wind. What makes you think you can mess up somebody?"

Ronny: "You misunderstand me. Sorry. So sorry. I didn't mean it. Please don't look at me like that."

Second puppet: "Well!" *(Turns back on first puppet, which sneaks up and beats up the second puppet. Howls and screams as they fight.)*

First puppet: "We'll see. It just doesn't pay to fool with me."

(Tom tosses the puppets up in the air. He comes out from behind the puppet theater.)

Tom: I'll make me something out of clay.

Martha: So will I.

Tom: I'll make me a black-jack.

(They all make black-jacks out of clay. A sham battle

ensues. Tom hits Jean over the head. It obviously does not hurt her, but she yells at him.)

Jean: That's the trouble with you. You're so mean.

Tom: Yes, I'm mean. We were just playing, and you know it.

Jean: That's just it. You can't play fair. You're so mean you've just got to hurt someone.

Tom: I didn't hurt you. You didn't fall over unconscious, did you?

Jean: You're mean. That's what causes all your trouble. You are just the meanest person I ever knew.

Tom: Well, it's nice to know what causes all my trouble. But, offhand, I'd say it was people like you who cause all my trouble. You play around and then some little accident happens and you start squawking. What do you play for if you're scared of your own shadow?

(Jean hits Tom on the head with her clay black-jack.)

Tom (mockingly): Oh, you mean thing! Oh, that's what causes all your trouble. You *hurt* me! *(The girl laughs at him. Tom laughs. Then he gets out his Hitler head.)* Come on, everybody. Free for all. Who wants to stab Hitler?

(The group attacks the asbestos head of Hitler and in a short time it is reduced to a mass of shapeless material. When the therapist announced that the time was up they put the materials away. As Tom left, he said to the therapist, "Well, so long. I'll be seeing you. And I'm making good on that ice cream route, too. I'm doing all right.")

In this contact the therapist said very little. The interplay between the children seemed to be the element that clarified Tom's feelings.

Excerpts from Later Contacts

At the next individual contact, Tom commented to the therapist, "You know, it's a funny thing, but I've discovered that people don't understand me."

Therapist: You don't think people really understand you.

Tom: No. Now like last Thursday. She said I was just being mean and I wasn't really being mean at all. I was honestly just playing.

Therapist: She didn't understand that you were just playing. She thought you deliberately hurt her.

Tom: Yes. And really that's the way it is most of the time. I do something and people don't realize I don't mean to hurt them.

Therapist: You do things that sometimes hurt others and they can't understand that you didn't mean to hurt them.

Tom: Yes. (*Long silence. Tom buries his chin in his hands.*) I'll have to do something about that.

Therapist: Think you'll have to do something about that.

Tom: Yep. I'll have to give it a good think. (*Tom reaches over and picks up the puppet.*) What'll I do, Ronny?

Ronny: "What do you care? Smack 'em down. Smack 'em down!"

Tom: Think real hard, Ronny. Tell me what to do.

Ronny: "Kick 'em in the teeth."

Tom (*tossing the puppet down on the table*): He's no help. He's as bad as I am. In fact, he is *me*.

Therapist: He's one side of you. You think you ought to do something about it, but he wants to keep on fighting his way through things.

Tom: Yeah. Well, I gotta go now. (*Gets up.*) Good-bye.

Apparently the therapist's last remark was too critical, attempting to force the change, because Tom abruptly terminated the interview half an hour before the time was up. However, this interview indicates that Tom used the group reaction for a measurement of his own adjustment. He was honestly trying to straighten out his problem. Tom's puppet plays began to taper off. The girl puppet, the mother, the father, and Ronny continued their battles. Then one day the fight between the puppets was "according to rules." One excerpt showing this is as follows:

Ronny: "This is going to be a clean fight."

Clown: "Yes. We want this to be a fair fight."

(*Sounds of fighting.*)

Ronny: "This is a boxing match. This will be according to rules." (*Clown runs away.*) "Quit your running." (*Fight.*) "Now listen. I'm getting tired of this."

Clown: "Listen. I'll squeeze you."

Ronny: "Oh. My nose. My beautiful nose. My nice long nose. Now I can't stick it into other people's business. Didn't

I tell you this was a clean fight? *(Fight.)* This is a boxing match. This is according to rules."

And then in one of the later contacts this excerpt:

Ronny: "I feel like fighting somebody."

Girl puppet: "I'm going to tell on you."

Ronny: "I'm not going to hurt you, sister. You're just a baby. You don't know any better. I just feel like fighting—like a prize-fight—according to rules."

Clown: "You want me?"

Ronny: "Do you want to fight?"

Clown: "I love to fight."

Ronny: "Then let's have a fight—a good, clean fight, according to rules."

Clown: "Okay. According to rules." *(Puppets fight.)*

Tom (standing up with the puppets): That's all, folks. The fight is all over. Now you two shake hands. *(Puppets are made to shake hands.)* That's right. According to rules.

SUMMARY

In the early therapeutic contacts, Tom needed the anonymity of the puppets to bring out his feelings. Secure in the knowledge that he could not be blamed for what the puppets said, he could delve deeply into the very complex problem of his family relationships and at the same time maintain his dignity and self-respect. The therapist, in this instance, did not interrupt to reflect back to Tom any feelings that he expressed. It seemed that he had chosen the medium that would give him the most protection. He was giving a play. He was out of sight. The feelings were flowing freely. It was a legitimate outlet for his remarks. For the therapist to interrupt at such a time would have been an invasion of his isolation. Out of respect for his ability to run this by himself, the therapist's remarks were not intruded. It seemed adequate for Tom's clarification to play them out.

As the therapy progressed, the puppet plays became shorter and occurred less frequently, then finally stopped all together. Incidentally, they lost all their appeal for the six-year-old audience when they were carried on "according to rules."

The last group meeting was spent by the group in presenting a puppet play which was nothing more than entertainment. The puppets sang songs, played hide-and-seek, and in back of the puppet theater Tom played the drum and other rhythm band instruments. Tom had solved his problem of adjustment. According to a check-up six months later, Tom had become a well-adjusted leader in his class.

The treatment which Tom received was a combination of individual and group contacts. The therapist felt, however, that, while one supplemented the other, the therapy was successful on several counts because of the group experience. Tom had never before been accepted as a member of a group. At the conclusion of the therapy, he had found his place in the group; he understood himself better; he became a leader. Although he still has occasional difficulties, he seems to have achieved the necessary insight to maintain a place in the group and to have overcome the need to retain defensive, antisocial behavior.

PART TWO

The Non-Directive Play-Therapy Situation and Participants

3.

The Playroom
and
Suggested Materials

IN OUR DISCUSSION of play therapy and in the report of Tom's therapy contacts, we have frequently mentioned the playroom and have discussed briefly the importance of play materials in the therapeutic process. In this chapter we shall suggest desirable characteristics of the playroom and discuss materials which have been found suitable for non-directive play therapy.

While it is desirable to have a room set aside and furnished for the playroom, this is not absolutely necessary. Some of the therapy sessions described in this book took place in a specially equipped play-therapy room; some in the corner of a regular schoolroom; some in the corner of an unused nursery, the therapist bringing the play materials in a suitcase for each meeting. This is pointed out because it indicates the vast possibilities of utilizing play-therapy techniques with very small budget and space appropriations.

If money and space are available to furnish a special play therapy room, the following suggestions are offered. The room should be sound-proofed if at all possible. There should be a sink in the room with running hot and cold water. The windows should be protected by gratings or screens. The walls and floors should be protected with a material that is easily cleaned and that will withstand clay, paint, water, and mallet attack. If the room can be wired for phonographic recordings and provided with a one-way screen so that observations can be made without the child's being aware of the observer, so much the better, but this equipment should be used only for the further-ance of research and as a teaching aid for student ther-apists. The writer does not advocate that parents observe the therapy contacts or listen to the phonographic record-ings of the play sessions.

Play materials which have been used with varying de-grees of success include: nursing bottles; a doll family; a doll house with furniture; toy soldiers and army equip-ment; toy animals; playhouse materials, including table, chairs, cot, doll bed, stove, tin dishes, pans, spoons, doll clothes, clothesline, clothespins, and clothes basket; a di-dee doll; a large rag doll; puppets; a puppet screen; cray-ons; clay, finger paints; sand; water; toy guns; peg-pounding sets; wooden mallet; paper dolls; little cars; airplanes; a table; an easel; an enamel-top table for finger painting and clay work; toy telephone; shelves; basin; small broom; mop; rags; drawing paper; finger-painting paper; old newspapers; inexpensive cutting paper; pictures of people, houses, animals, and other objects; and empty berry baskets to smash. Checker games have been used with some success, but are not the best type of material for expressive play. Likewise, mechanical toys are not suggested because the mechanics often get in the way of creative play.

If it is not possible to secure all the suggested materials, a beginning can be made by furnishing a doll family and a few pieces of furniture in proper scale, including beds, tables, and chairs; nursing bottles; clay; boxes of paints, if it is not possible to have the large jars of watercolor; drawing paper; crayons; toy gun; toy soldiers; a toy car; puppets; a rag baby doll; and a telephone. These materials can be packed in a suitcase and carried about with the therapist.

All playthings should be simple in construction and easy to handle so that the child will not be frustrated by equipment which he cannot manipulate. Moreover, they should be durably constructed, designed to withstand strenuous handling in the playroom. The doll house should be made of light-weight wood, with removable and variable partitions, and should be furnished with sturdy wooden furniture that can be tossed about, bombed, and even stood upon, and still remain relatively intact. The doll family should be as unbreakable as possible, and outfitted with removable clothes. Very satisfactory doll families can be made from pipe cleaners, wrapping the pipe cleaners with cotton and securing it with adhesive tape to give them body. The heads can be made of little cotton-stuffed cloth balls. There should be mother, father, brother, sister, baby, and grandparent dolls to equip the child with all possible family symbols. The hand puppets— or mitten dolls, as they are sometimes called—can also be made out of cloth, using cotton-stuffed heads and yarn hair. The puppets, too, should include all possible family characters.

A large sand box serves as an ideal setting in which to place the doll house and family, the toy soldiers, animals, cars, and airplanes. Moreover, the sand is an excellent medium for the children's aggressive play. It can be thrown about with comparative safety. The dolls and other toys can be buried in it. It can be "snow," "water," "burying ground," or "bombs." It can readily keep pace with the most elastic imagination. If the sand box is placed flat on the floor and has a seat built part way around it, it is more accessible to children of all sizes than a sand table would be.

If the room is large enough, it is desirable to have a "stage" built into one end of it, with an elevation of about eight inches. This should be furnished with child-sized playhouse furniture, which should also meet the standards of durability, thus giving the children the advantage of having a playhouse unit as well as a stage for dramatic offerings. The slight elevation is not absolutely necessary, but does have the effect of setting aside the playhouse unit; also, it seems to inspire dramatic efforts. The possibilities of psychodramatics seem worthy of further research as a medium for therapy.

The materials should be kept on shelves which are easily accessible to the children. The writer believes that better results are obtained when all the play materials are in view and the child can choose his own medium for expression than when the therapist places certain selected materials on the table before the child and then sits quietly by, awaiting the child's non-directed play. However, some therapists prefer to use a minimum of materials and have observed interesting results with materials which they have selected for the child.

It is the responsibility of the therapist to keep a constant check on the materials, removing the broken toys, and keeping the room in order. If the room is used by several therapists, each one has the added responsibility of seeing that the playroom is left in order so that one child's play effects will not be suggestive to the child that follows him. For example, if the sand box is used as a replica of a home set-up by one subject, it should never be left in a state of chaos for the next play-therapy subject. The paints and clay should be kept clean and sanitary. If the paint colors become smeared, they should be freshly mixed. The nursing bottles should be kept sterile. All pictures and clay work should be removed from the playroom at the end of each session so that the room is always free from suggestive use of materials.

Because of the nature of some of the play materials, it is suggested that the child be provided with a coverall to protect his clothes; this may be furnished either by the parent or by the therapist. The child should feel free to use the materials in any way that he desires, within the few limitations that are set up, without being restricted by a fear of soiling his clothes.

4.
The Child

INTO THE PLAYROOM with its wealth of toys and play materials comes a child around whom the whole play-therapy situation is centered. What kind of a child is he and how does he come to be there? Tom and Emma and Timmy and Bobby are examples of the kind of child he is, and he is in the play-therapy room because some adult who must deal with him has found him to be a "problem child." In this chapter we shall describe problem children more fully and discuss the various types of problems which they present.

Tom and Emma and Timmy and Bobby and all the rest of them are real children, up to their ears in trouble most of the time—miserable, unhappy children who have not been given even a small share of the love, security, and happiness that one feels is the right of every child. They are fighting to establish themselves in a hostile world. They are striving to achieve status in their own eyes. They have courage and perseverance and fortitude, but they are problem children.

Tom fights, fights, fights, all day long. Emma devils those who would be her friends. Timmy and Bobby get sick because of the tensions within themselves. They get into trouble wherever they are. They alienate themselves because of their defensiveness. They have problems and they do not know exactly how to solve them. They drain

57

off some of their tensions by their aggressive behavior, but that very behavior generates more trouble for them. It is the misdirected drive for self-realization within them that seems to cause their maladjustment. It needs to be channeled into more constructive behavior. These children are examples of problem children who are often referred for play therapy by parents, matrons, teachers, physicians, or other agencies. The aggressive, disturbing, noisy child is the one most readily identified as the child with problems, because he is continually creating new problems, not only for himself, but also for those who are in close contact with him.

There are many other children who are just as desperately in need of help, but who withdraw from their miserable world and live a tenuous life on the outer edge of human relationships; and because they are quiet and are not a disturbing element, they are left alone. But these withdrawn children need therapy and benefit greatly by it.

There are the children who seem to be refusing to grow up and who cling to their baby ways. There are the nervous children who bite their nails, have nightmares, wet the bed, have tics, refuse to eat, and manifest many other types of behavior that indicate inner turmoil and anxiety. Play therapy offers these children an opportunity to work through their problems, to learn to know themselves, to accept themselves as they are, and to grow more mature through the therapy experience.

The handicapped child, also, benefits by a therapeutic experience if the handicap is a source of conflict and anxiety and emotional disturbance. In this book there is an account of a blind boy who was so helped. There is also the case of Ernest, a handicapped child whose recovery was blocked by an emotional disturbance that he was able to work through. There are cases on record of spastics being helped by play therapy. These handicapped children have within themselves the same feelings and desires of all normal children. Many times the handicap is a frustrating and blocking experience that generates almost intolerable tensions within the child. It is not uncommon to find the handicapped child living in a home where he receives no understanding, no feeling of adequacy, no sense of personal worth. To refuse to face the problem does not solve it. Everything that can be done for these children should be done. Some physicians are quite willing to work co-operatively with a play therapist in order to give the child all the help that is available in order to bring about maximum adjustment.

In general, play therapy provides the psychologist and teacher with a technique for understanding and helping those maladjusted children who are so often termed problem children—including those with behavior problems, study problems, speech problems, and even somatic problems, if referred by the physician.

Behavior problems include all types of behavior that might constitute problems of adjustment, including the very repressed, withdrawn, inhibited child, and running the gamut up to and including the very aggressive, uninhibited child.

Study problems are quite often tied up with emotional conflicts and tensions. Play-therapy sessions have proved helpful in untangling study problems by enabling the child to explore his feelings and attitudes, release his pent-up emotions, and, through the complete process of therapy, attain the psychological growth and maturity necessary for satisfactory school work.

Speech problems, such as stammering, stuttering, baby talk, repetitious language, garbled language, also seem to be corrected by play therapy. Even the non-talker has been known to begin verbalization after therapy has been undertaken. Speech problems, too, seem to be linked with the emotional life of the child. When there are snarls and tangles in the child's feelings, quite often they show up in a language difficulty.

Reading problems have also shown improvement when therapy has supplemented, or in some cases replaced, remedial-reading instruction. Many times the non-reader is quite obviously a disturbed child. At other times the disturbance is so slight that it is not considered a serious element in the reading disability, and yet play therapy revealed cases of tensions, fears, and anxieties that the children were able to work through and by so doing achieve stabilization.

There is a great need for more research in all of the areas mentioned. The evidence of the cases which have responded so well to this type of treatment points the way for more intensive research to investigate these areas more thoroughly and more scientifically. At the present writing, the field of non-directive therapy is so new that it is like virgin territory for those interested in research. The implications are tremendous and seem well worth following up.

There is no justification in waiting until a child is seriously maladjusted before attempting to secure some kind of help for him. It seems that there is an element of preventive mental hygiene in a play-therapy experience. Children who do not seem to be seriously disturbed respond quickly to such an experience. And the children enjoy the experience immensely. It is a play experience to them. The fact that it is self-directive removes every vestige of fear of the play-therapy situation, once the child has experienced a contact.

The children are not aware that they are problems—at least, the therapist does not indicate that in any way. Tom knows only that he is unhappy and defensive and alone against the world. Emma cannot understand the void that she feels in her heart because of the rejection that she receives. Timmy and Bobby feel the very ground slipping out from under their feet. All four are lone children against an unfriendly, unsympathetic world and constantly make their positions worse by their undesirable behavior. They are caught in a vicious circle which can be broken only by a realization of their own ability to function as individuals in their own right, and to express their feelings in a very graphic and dramatic manner in their play and in their creative activities.

One need only to observe the physical response of a child to realize that, when happy, he is happy all over. His eyes dance and sparkle. His step is light and carefree. His laugh is free and quick to come bubbling to the surface. When he feels loved and secure and successful, he goes forth courageously about this business of living, and life is a gay adventure that he rushes out eagerly to meet. He is fortified against the little ups and downs that make life interesting. He is prepared to live, secured by a satisfactory family relationship.

And when a child is sad and depressed, his figure droops, his movements are slow and heavy, his eyes mirror the unhappiness that is in his being. He is unhappy from the top of his head to the bottom of his feet.

Children respond quickly and whole-heartedly to any overture to reach out and help them. Even children who have been bitterly deprived are quick to react to this type of experience that accepts them, that provides release for their feelings, that opens the door of self-understanding so that they might enter into a new and complete self-realization.

Yes, Tom and Emma and Timmy and Bobby are real children. They were referred for play therapy and utilized the medium so offered to work out their problems of adjustment. Their complete cases are reported in this book.

5.

The Therapist

WITH THE CHILD in the playroom, not as a supervisor or
a teacher, and not as a parent-substitute, is the therapist,
whose personality qualifications and whose part in the
non-directive play-therapy relationship we shall now describe.

The therapist's rôle, though non-directive, is not a passive one, but one which requires alertness, sensitivity, and
an ever-present appreciation of what the child is doing
and saying. It calls for understanding and a genuine interest in the child. The therapist must be permissive and
accepting at all times. These attitudes are based upon a
philosophy of human relationships which stresses the importance of the individual as a capable, dependable human being who can be entrusted with the responsibility
for himself. Consequently, the therapist respects the child.
She treats him with sincerity and honesty. There is nothing brittle or surgary-sweet about her manner when
dealing with him. She is straightforward and feels at ease
in his presence.

The therapist does not patronize the child, hurry him,
or, in impatience, quickly do things for him that implies a
lack of confidence in his ability to take care of himself.
She never laughs *at* him—with him, sometimes, but never
at him.

She has a kindly patience and a sense of humor that

relaxes the child, puts him at ease, and encourages him to share his inner world with her.

She is a mature person who recognizes the responsibility that is entrusted to her when she undertakes to work with a child. She maintains a professional attitude toward her work and does not betray the child's confidence to the parent, teacher, or anyone else who might ask what he has said and done during his therapy hour. It is truly the *child's* hour, and the strictest adherence is maintained to the principle that what he says or does during his hour is confidential.

The therapist must like children and really know them. It is helpful if she has had some personal experience with children outside the therapy situation so that she has an understanding and knowledge of them as they are in their world outside the clinic.

Age and physical appearance seem to be immaterial. Nor does the sex of the therapist seem to be important. Some men therapists as well as women therapists have been very successful in working with children. The important element seems to be the underlying attitude toward the child and the therapy in the mind of the therapist.

The child is extremely sensitive to the sincerity of the adult. He is quick to catch the inconsistencies of attitudes and behavior in the adult. Therefore, it would seem advisable for the therapist to clarify his attitudes toward his therapeutic procedures and then move ahead with consistency and honesty.

A good therapist is in many ways like a favorite teacher. Usually the favorite teacher has earned that distinction because of her basic attitudes toward her pupils—attitudes that usually stress kindliness, patience, understanding, and steadiness, with the added discipline of placing responsibility and confidence in the pupil. The successful teacher or therapist may be young or old, beautiful or homely, smartly or indifferently dressed, but the attitude toward the child is one of respect and acceptance.

The therapist cannot assume these attitudes. They must be an integral part of her personality. Not until she fully realizes the significance of what it really means to be completely accepting of another person, and has sufficient understanding of all the implications of this term, is she able to be permissive so that the child can be himself, can express himself fully, and she can accept him without passing judgment.

While the non-directive therapists rôle seems to be one of passivity, that is far from the actuality. There is no severer discipline than to maintain the completely accepting attitude and to refrain at all times from injecting any directive suggestions or insinuations into the play of the child. To remain alert to catch and reflect back accurately the feelings the child is expressing in his play or in his conversation calls for a complete participation during the entire hour that the play therapy is in session.

Successful therapy begins with the therapist. She must have consistency in her technique. She must have the courage of her convictions. She must enter each new relationship with confidence and relaxation. A tense, insecure therapist creates a tense, insecure relationship between the child and the therapist. She must be sincerely interested in helping the child. She must be a friendly, dependable adult who brings more than her presence and a pencil and paper into the playroom. It is necessary for successful therapy that the child have a feeling of confidence in the therapist. Care must be taken to avoid an extreme relationship one way or another. A show of too much affection, too much concern, can easily smother the therapy and create new problems for the child. The crutches of a supportive relationship are just another thing that the child must get rid of before he is "free."

A therapist is not ready to go into the playroom with a child until she has developed self-discipline, restraint, and a deep respect for the personality of the child. There is no discipline so severe as the one which demands that each individual be given the right and the opportunity to stand on his own two feet and to make his own decisions.

The therapist is professional in her dealings with the child, keeps appointments with him as punctually as she would with the adult, does not break appointments unless it is absolutely necessary, does not terminate the contacts without considering the child's feelings and without informing him well in advance so that he will not feel rejected.

The therapist does not become emotionally involved

with the child, because when that happens the therapy bogs down and the child is not helped by the complicating circumstances. An emotional involvement is usually forestalled if she has assimilated the basic principles and attitudes. and is sure in her own mind what the limitations shall be, and what she will do if the child should behave in some unpredictable manner (which happens often). With sufficient self-confidence it is not likely that she will be "thrown for a loss" if the client becomes a challenging, amazingly resourceful creature who gets around her with subtle artistry. It takes steadiness, sensitivity, and resourcefulness on the part of the therapist to keep the therapy alive. If she feels bored and sleepy during the play-therapy contacts, then she should not work with children.

Since the therapist will find that it is very helpful to take notes on the activities and conversations that occur in the playroom, the necessary materials should be at hand. The therapist will find that a critical evaluation of the written account of each session in the playroom will improve his or her skill in handling the various problems that occur in the playroom, in developing insight into children's behavior, and in becoming more sensitive to the feelings and attitudes that the children express in their play. These notes and all records regarding the therapy hour should be kept confidential and when discussed for professional reasons should be disguised sufficiently so that no one is embarrassed in any way.

All that we have said concerning the therapist may be summed up by saying that she must be a person who can and will accept the word and the spirit of the eight basic principles which govern all her contacts with the child or, in group therapy, with the children. These principles we shall list and discuss in detail in Part Three. Before we proceed to them, however, it may be well to discuss briefly the rôle of an indirect participant in the play-therapy process—the parent, or, as is so often the case with these problem children, the parent-substitute.

6.

An Indirect Participant
—The Parent
or Parent-Substitute

WE NEED only to read through some of the cases presented in this book to realize what an extremely important part the parent—or the foster parent or the matron— plays in the course of the therapeutic process.

While the parent or parent-substitute often is an aggravating factor in the case of a maladjusted child, and while therapy might move ahead faster if the adults were also receiving therapy or counseling, *it is not necessary for the adults to be helped in order to insure successful play-therapy results.*

The reader will notice that many of the reports in this book are of children who were in situations where there was little insight on the part of the adults toward a better way of helping these problem children. In very few of the cases did the adults receive treatment of any kind, and yet the children were able to become strong enough within themselves to withstand very trying conditions. It seems as though the insight and self-understanding gained by these children brought about more adequate ways of coping with their situations, and, since the tensions eased, this in turn brought about a certain change in the adults. This follows through with the explanation of relative, dynamic reactions that are constantly shifting and changing in the light of new experiences. If the child becomes more responsible and more mature, then the adult feels less irritation and less need to nag the child.

When Tom ceased to fight and sulk around his home, when he became able to accept the little half-sister, when he showed signs of behaving in a more mature manner, then the step-father was able to accept him and, with the relaxed family relationships, the mother was able to consider Tom more fairly and constructively. They had progressed beyond the stage where they were each fighting for self-esteem and recognition. Tom no longer resisted the step-father. The step-father no longer resented Tom. The source of friction disappeared. When the family trouble cleared up, Tom did not feel the urge to take it out on the children at school. The insight into his own behavior that he achieved during the therapy experience helped him to modify his behavior in such a way that he was able to get along with the other children. When he had achieved status in their eyes, when they showed a certain amount of genuine appreciation of Tom as a person, when he became one of them, then Tom stopped being a "problem child."

In this case, as in all the others, neither Tom's parents nor his teachers were given any information as to what Tom was doing in his therapy hour. The parents knew that he was receiving some help, but the therapist never met the parents or had any contact with them. This indicates that there is no absolute need for concomitant therapy in such cases. However, it does not nullify the value of concomitant therapy. Had Tom's mother or step-father come in for counseling, it is quite possible that progress would have occurred more rapidly, and the parents themselves might have obtained insights that would have gone beyond their trouble with Tom and proved quite helpful to them.

This also seems to be true when worked the other way. If a parent receives counseling help and the child does not receive any therapeutic help, quite often the parent's insight is sufficient to bring more positive action in improving the relationship which sets off a chain reaction that in turn brings about a change in the child. One can see how much simpler and complete the therapy would be if both parent and child received help.

The case of Emma is also interesting in this respect.

The mother was not accessible for therapy—and may not have been willing to assume any responsibility for her part in the relationship. The therapist did not have any contacts with the mother. Certainly there was nothing done in a manipulative way to ease the situation. The matrons had decided to put a stop to the mother's erratic behavior when she created so much turmoil within Emma by her unkept promises, but this was not done until after the therapy was completed successfully. However, Emma had learned to adjust sufficiently to her mother's behavior, unpleasant and difficult as it was. The therapist likewise had no contact with Emma's teacher, and yet a report showed considerable improvement in Emma's attitudes and behavior while at school and indicated that she had made a more satisfactory adjustment there.

The case of Timmy and Bobby is another example of this same kind of situation. In fact, many of the children in this book are victims of parental neglect and rejection and mistreatment and *alone* they worked out an adjustment to these problems which are just about as difficult as any personal problem can be. It is this evidence that impresses the therapist with the strength within the individual to cope with his problems, unaided by environmental manipulation. This does not mean that certain environmental adjustments are not sometimes desirable and helpful. It merely indicates that the capacity within the individual to adjust to the conditions that he is sometimes forced to face is far greater than it is usually thought to be.

In the case of a handicapped child, however, it seems more helpful to have the active participation of the parents, particularly if the child is mentally handicapped and the parents have difficulty in accepting the fact. However, insight cannot be forced upon anyone. Unless the parent is willing to assume part of the responsibility in working through his problem, then it seems to be up to the child to do what he can. Very little has been done in this particular area to determine the effectiveness of therapeutic help for the mentally handicapped.

There are a few instances related in this book which indicate that the parent or foster parent co-operates willingly and sometimes effectively when consulted by the therapist, but there are just as many where suggestions were of no value at all. It seems fairly correct to say that the only suggestions that are ever followed with any degree of effectiveness are the ones with which the individual agrees.

There has been some play therapy done in schools where only the child was given therapy and the results in the attitudes and behavior of the child were very gratifying, not only in improved school relationships, but also in his home relationships. This adds a rather pertinent factor to the treatment of the problem child and indicates very strongly that curative forces within the child are potent.

PART THREE

The Principles of Non-Directive Play Therapy

7.
The Eight
Basic Principles

THE BASIC PRINCIPLES which guide the therapist in all non-directive therapeutic contacts are very simple, but they are great in their possibilities when followed sincerely, consistently, and intelligently by the therapist.

The principles are as follows:

1. The therapist must develop a warm, friendly relationship with the child, in which good rapport is established as soon as possible.
2. The therapist accepts the child exactly as he is.
3. The therapist establishes a feeling of permissiveness in the relationship so that the child feels free to express his feelings completely.
4. The therapist is alert to recognize the *feelings* the child is expressing and reflects those feelings back to him in such a manner that he gains insight into his behavior.
5. The therapist maintains a deep respect for the child's ability to solve his own problems if given an opportunity to do so. The responsibility to make choices and to institute change is the child's.
6. The therapist does not attempt to direct the child's actions or conversation in any manner. The child leads the way; the therapist follows.
7. The therapist does not attempt to hurry the therapy

along. It is a gradual process and is recognized as such by the therapist.

8. The therapist establishes only those limitations that are necessary to anchor the therapy to the world of reality and to make the child aware of his responsibility in the relationship.

The therapist realizes that non-directive therapy is not a panacea. She admits that, like all things, it, too, has its limitations, but accumulating experience indicates that the implications of this type of therapy are a challenge and an inspiration to those who are concerned with the problems of adjustment.

When a child comes for play therapy, it is usually because some adult has either brought or sent him to the clinic for treatment. He enters into this unique experience just as he enters all new experiences—either with enthusiasm, fear, caution, resistance, or any other manner that is typical of the way he reacts to new situations. The initial contact is of great importance for the success of the therapy. It is during this contact that the stage is set, so to speak. The structuring is demonstrated to the child, not merely by words, but by the relationship that is established between the therapist and the child.

Structuring

The word *structuring* is used in this instance to mean the building-up of the relationship according to the foregoing principles so that the child understands the nature of the therapy contacts and is thus able to use them fully. Structuring is not a casual thing, but a carefully planned method of introducing the child to this medium of self-expression which brings with it release of feelings and attendant insight. It is not a verbal explanation of what this is all about, but by establishing the relationship.

The relationship that is created between the therapist and the child is the deciding factor in the success or failure of the therapy. It is not an easy relationship to establish. The therapist must put forth a sincere effort to understand the child and to check constantly her responses against the basic principles and to evaluate her work with each case so that she, too, grows in her understanding of the dynamics of human behavior.

8.

Establishing Rapport

The therapist must develop a warm, friendly relationship with the child, in which good rapport is established as soon as possible.

THE THERAPIST meets the child for the first time. She is beginning the initial contact. Structuring has begun. What does she do? A smile is usually an indication of warmth and friendliness. A few words of greeting should establish rapport. So the therapist goes up to the child and smilingly says, "Good afternoon, Johnny. I'm glad to see you. Did you like that Mickey Mouse over there on the table?" Now Johnny should smile back and say, "Yes, he's funny." He might. But the very fact that Johnny has been recommended for play therapy is an indication that he might not act "according to Hoyle." He might very likely turn his back on the therapist. Then what? The rapport-seeking therapist is not easily discouraged. "Would you like to come over to the playroom with me and see all the nice toys?" "No." "Oh, come on, Johnny. There are paints and clay and toy soldiers. You like toy soldiers, don't you?" "No. And I don't want to come!" says Johnny.

The therapist might well pause here. In fact, she should have paused, perhaps, before she spoke. What about those basic principles which she is trying to convey to Johnny? She is trying to establish a warm and friendly relationship, but she is sacrificing some of the other principles. She is not accepting Johnny as he is. She is not reflecting his feelings. He said that he did not want to go with the therapist and see all the toys. Apparently, this therapist has not yet started to let the child take the responsibility to make choices. "Lots of children come up here and they like our playroom," says the persistent therapist. "We've got a big doll house and a whole family of dolls." She looks appealingly at Johnny. He steals a glance at her. She is trying to make him act like other children. She is coaxing him. She is warm and friendly enough, goodness knows, but at what expense. Johnny, who is resenting her more and more, begins to whine. "I don't wanta. Mamma, I don't wanta!" Mamma becomes active. "Now, Johnny, you go with the nice lady. She has lots of toys for you to play with." Johnny begins to whimper. "I don't wanta. I wanta go home." "Now, Johnny," says Mamma, "I am ashamed of you. Here this nice lady is offering you a whole room of play-things to play with and you act like this. The lady won't like you!" Mamma will enter into the structuring if the therapist doesn't look out. "The lady won't like you!" isn't a particularly good basis for establishing a therapeutic relationship.

What on earth should she do? Should she pick up the child and carry him over to the playroom and, when he howls his protests, reflect his feelings back to him? "You are angry because I picked you up and carried you over here. You don't like to be treated that way." That would get him into the playroom. However, all therapists are not Amazons and all problem children are not light-weights!

Perhaps she had better try getting him into the playroom under his own power. She might say, "Hello, Johnny. I'm glad to see you. Do you like the Mickey Mouse over there on the table?" Johnny turns his back. "Oh! You just don't feel like talking to me now. *You* don't *know* me." The therapist watches the tone of her voice. It must not sound like a reproof. But the therapist mustn't forget Mamma. She might say, "Johnny, look at the lady when she talks to you." Johnny whines, "I don't wanta. I wanta go home." Then the therapist says, "You don't want to have anything to do with me. You want to go back home. The playroom is over here if you want to look in before you make up your mind to go home." She leads the way. Mamma follows. Johnny tags along reluctantly. Then the therapist has an inspiration. "You had an appointment to talk to Mr. X, didn't you, Mrs. Johnny?" "Yes, I did," Mrs. Johnny says. "Well," says the therapist, "if Johnny doesn't want to stay in the playroom with me and play, he may wait in the waiting room for you." "Yes, Johnny," says Mamma, "would you rather wait in the waiting room? I'll be gone an hour." "I wanta go with you!" says Johnny tearfully. "You can't go with her, Johnny. She must talk to Mr. X alone. It will be either the waiting room or the playroom. It's up to you." More tears, and Johnny creeps into the playroom. Getting him there is half the battle.

The therapist must be ready for the Mamma who is not so co-operative—the one who has made her Johnny so dependent. She will want to go into the playroom with Johnny. What will the therapist do about that? Will she take the mother along, thinking that the therapy contacts will never materialize unless she makes that concession? Will she say, "Only children are allowed in the playroom, Johnny. Your mother will wait for you. She won't go away and leave you." Johnny cries. "Johnny doesn't want to leave his mother," says the therapist. "He is afraid to come into the playroom by himself." Mamma rushes in with reassurance. Johnny edges toward the playroom. The door is closed. Mamma waits outside.

Suppose Mamma wasn't ready to be separated from Johnny? Could there be much hope for therapy? There have been occasions wherein the mother went into the playroom and sat there during the play contacts and Johnny's willingness to let Mamma leave was considered a sign of progress. If it became an issue of Mamma's sitting through the play sessions or no play contacts, what should the therapist do? It seems that the therapist must permit Mamma to stay if she follows the basic principles. In fact, she might be able to clarify a good many of the feelings between Mamma and Johnny by having them both in the playroom. This is an untried theory, but it seems to have possibilities if it is the only way out. Mamma, at least, might gain some insight if the therapist handled the situation skillfully. Johnny might act out his complete dependence upon his mother by constantly asking her to do this or that for him. The therapist, alert for the attitudes and feelings, might catch some of them. "Johnny wants Mother to show him how to play with the doll." "Johnny wants Mother to tell him what to do next." She may even be able to reflect back some of Mamma's feelings. Perhaps Mamma is volunteering the suggestions to Johnny. "Don't do that, Johnny. Play with it this way." The therapist might help Mamma gain a little insight by saying to her, "You don't think Johnny could figure that out by himself. You like to tell him everything to do." However, such an experiment is not advocated for beginning therapists.

It is pleasant to note that most children go into the playroom readily. It becomes a source of great satisfaction to them. There is no serious problem involved in establishing a warm and friendly relationship with the children who go willingly with the therapist.

It might be well to voice the warning that the therapist can unwittingly inject subtle influence into the relationship in an effort to gain rapport. For example, the therapist says to a co-operative client, "My, what a nice big boy you are! Want to come over to the playroom and play? There are paints and clay and all sorts of toys." Once inside the room, perhaps he starts to paint, and he says to the therapist, "I can't paint so good." And she answers, "Why, I think that is a fine picture. And you did it all by yourself! And you don't think it so good." Finally she reflects the attitude the child expressed, but it is so discounted by the time she gets around to it that it doesn't do much good.

Then there is the case in which two brothers, aged four and five, were having a play-therapy session. One boy was painting and accidentally spilled some paint. He got the paint rag and wiped up the paint. The therapist said, "Bobby is careful. He wiped up the paint that he spilled." From then on, the contact became a display of how careful both boys were and the stock comment was, "Look, I'm being careful. See? I'm being careful." Finally, they identified the therapist.— "Look, *teacher*, I'm being so careful!" Unintentionally, the therapist had directed the behavior of the boys. Praise for actions committed in the playroom is not conducive to therapy.

The beginning therapist might examine the case of six-year-old Oscar. He was brought to the therapist by his mother. The father had been killed when Oscar was two years old. On the day the father was killed, Oscar came down with a bad case of measles. Oscar was sent out of town to a relative. The mother had a nervous breakdown and was in the hospital for three months. Finally, when she recovered her health sufficiently to go back to work as a private secretary, she took Oscar back into her home and hired a woman to take care of him. The woman was not satisfactory, and others came and went at surprisingly short intervals. Oscar had no sense of security at all. Some of the helpers mistreated him. He became one of the most maladjusted children imaginable. He was aggressive, belligerent, negative, insecure, defiant, dependent. He was a masterpiece of conflicting feelings. His mother, erratic and nervous, brought him to the psychologist. This is an excerpt from the initial contact.

Mother: This is Oscar. Heaven only knows what you can do with him! But here he is.

Therapist: Would you like to come over to the playroom with me?

Oscar: NO! Shet up! *(Yells.)*

Mother (also yelling): Oscar! Now you be polite. Stop that sass!

Oscar (louder than ever): No! No! No!

Mother: Well, you are! What do you think I brought you up here for? The ride?

Oscar (whimpering): I don't wanta!

The beginning therapist asks herself at this point, "Now what?" Cajole him into the playroom? "We have such nice toys over in the playroom. You're such a nice big boy now. You come with me and I'll show you what there is to play with." That is not accepting Oscar exactly as he is. He doesn't want to come. Or should she say, with a note of regret in her voice, "Your mother brought you all the way up here and you don't want to come into the playroom with me!" That is a reflection of feeling, but it also carries subtle condemnation. There is an implied "My, aren't you an ungrateful little brute!" If the therapist wants to reflect his feeling only, what should she say? "You don't want to come with me." The therapist tries that.

Therapist: You don't want to come with me.

Oscar! NO! (*Makes face at therapist and folds up fists.*)
Shet up!

Mother: If you don't go over there, I'll leave you here
forever.

Oscar (attaching self to mother, whimpering): Don't
leave me. Don't leave me. (*Sobs hysterically.*)

Therapist: Oscar is scared when Mother threatens to leave
him here.

[This is a recognition of Oscar's feeling, but condemnation
of Mother, who flares up.]

Mother: Well, I've got to do something. Honest to God,
Oscar, if you don't shut up and go with this lady, I *will* leave
you! Or *give* you away!

Oscar: You wait for me? (*Pitifully.*) You be here when I
come back.

Mother: Of course I will—if you behave.

*Oscar (transferring death-like grip from Mother's skirt to
therapist's skirt):* You wait?

Therapist: You want Mother to promise you that she will
wait.

Oscar: You promise?

Mother: I promise!

(*Therapist and Oscar go into the playroom. Therapist
starts to close the door.*)

Oscar (screaming): Don't shet the door! Don't shet the
door! (*Tears roll down his cheeks.*)

Therapist: You don't want me to shut the door. You're
afraid to stay here with me if we shut the door.

This is recognition of his feeling. He looks up, amazed,
and then nods his head. Now what? Does the therapist, after recognizing his feeling, disregard it and say,
"But when we come in here we shut the door," and
convince herself that this is a valuable limitation? What
purpose would that serve? To point up the fact that we
recognize feeling, but ignore it? Is she accepting Oscar
exactly as he is—fear of closed doors and all? Is she
showing the child what she means by letting him make the
choices and lead the way? Is she establishing an atmosphere of permissiveness to express his true feelings? Is she
maintaining a deep respect for the child? It seems that she

is forsaking all these principles if she closes the door. So what does she say?

Therapist: You don't want me to shut the door. You're afraid to stay here with me if I shut the door. Very well. We'll leave the door open and *you* close the door when you feel like it.

[This leaves the responsibility up to Oscar. It is up to him to make the choice. Oscar looks around the playroom. As he thaws out, he becomes aggressive.]

Oscar: I'll bust up everything in here!

What about limitations? Should the therapist say, "You can play with the toys in here any way you want to, but you can't bust them up." Or, "Other children use these toys, too, so you can't bust them up." That is not responding to Oscar's expressed *feeling*. That is succumbing to the trap of responding to content rather than feeling back of content.

Therapist: You're feeling tough now.
Oscar (glaring at therapist): I'll bust you up, too.
Therapist: You're still feeling tough.
Oscar: "I'll——(*suddenly laughs*) I'll——(*He wanders around the playroom and picks up the toy telephone.*) What's this?

This is another challenge to the therapist. Shall she say, "You wonder what that is?" or, "It is a telephone." It seems more conducive to progress in this session to answer the simple question rather than make an issue out of it.

Therapist: It is a toy telephone.
Oscar: I'll bust it up, too.
Therapist: You want to bust up the telephone, too.
Oscar (smiling like a little angel): Yeah, I just love to tear up things and bust people.
Therapist: You like to bust up things and hurt people.
Oscar (calmly): Yeah. Oh, look. Dishes. I'll play house. (*Begins to set the table, then picks up the telephone. Talking into telephone.*) Hello. Is that you, Mary? Oh, I'm home. I'm

getting supper. *(Aside to therapist.)* I am getting supper, ain't I?

Therapist: You're getting supper.

Oscar (back to telephone): Yeah, I'm getting supper. What we having? *(The tone of voice implies that Mary is asking him and he is repeating it. He turns to the therapist.)* What we having?

Therapist: You want me to tell you what we are having for supper?

Oscar: Yeah. Tell me quick.

Should the therapist quickly speak up with the menu? Or should she say, "What would you like?" or, "You do want me to tell you, don't you?" A menu would seem to carry on the play a little more expediently. The therapist quickly names some food. Oscar repeats it word for word over the telephone.

Oscar: What? You want to know have we got a doll house here? *(Aside to therapist.)* Have we got a doll house?

(The doll house is quite obviously there.)

Therapist: We've got a doll house.

Oscar: Have we got toy soldiers?

(Repeats this in aside to therapist, who answers, "We've got toy soldiers.")

Oscar continues this itemizing of all the toys in the playroom. The therapist responds to each aside question. What is Oscar trying to do? Of course he knows the answers to his questions. Then why does he continue to ask the therapist if what he sees before him is there? How else could Oscar establish rapport with the therapist? It seems that that is what he is trying to do. After he asks about everything in sight, he says over the telephone:

You want to know will I kiss the lady? *(Then to the therapist)* Will I kiss you, lady?

The therapist remembers the caution against too much display of affection that might smother out the therapy. Should she say, "You would like to kiss me." Or should she follow along on this, too?

Therapist: You want to know will you kiss the lady?
Oscar (grinning): I will.

He comes over and very gently kisses the therapist's hand; then, probably thinking of his old self, he rushes over and grabs the hammer and begins to pound on the peg-board set. The door is still open. Here is another challenge to the therapist. What about that door? The noise is terrific. Should she close it while he is busily pounding? Should she direct his attention to it and ask him if he thought he should close it? Should she keep faith with the little fellow and wait for someone who is bothered by the noise to come over and see that it is stopped? In this particular incident, no one was apparently bothered by the noise and it did not become necessary to close the door. However, if someone had come, it seems that it would have been a necessary part of the therapy to inform Oscar that the noise was bothering other people and that either the door must be closed or the noise stopped and to let him make the choice, being alert to reflect all the feelings he expressed at this point. It would be an injection of reality that would create this limitation to the permissiveness of the therapy situation. The following week Oscar closed the door voluntarily when he entered the playroom with the therapist. Had he not done so, the therapist would have waited until he did make the move to decide the issue himself. To suggest it would have been an attempt to hurry things along. The voluntary closing of the door might indicate a certain amount of progress in establishing the relationship. It seems to be a gesture of confidence toward the therapist as well as an indication of growth on the part of Oscar toward a new independence and an ability to make choices.

Application to Group Therapy

Although it seems that the relationship established between the therapist and the child in group therapy may be less intense than that established in individual therapy, the presence of other children who react in various ways to the situation seems to be advantageous in the development of rapport. One child, a little more expressive than the others, moves ahead. The timid child has the advantage of testing the security of the situation vicariously; that is, by watching someone else blaze the trail. Readiness for self-expression seems to be built up faster in the group situation for some children. Also, a child can retreat behind others if things get too much for him.

The first few minutes in the playroom usually seem to be a strain upon children. It is a new experience and they react to it in various ways, ranging from fear expressed with tears and near hysteria to bold exploratory activities.

The therapist must exercise caution to prevent focusing the responses toward one child at the expense of the others. She must make an effort to include the most backward child in the group, even though that child is ready for just a friendly smile.

The children do not appear to be as self-conscious during the first group contact as they sometimes do during the first individual contact because the presence of the other children in the room lessens the tensions and creates a more natural response to the therapist.

The children seem more ready to accept the therapist at an earlier time when in a group. Possibly they feel that there is safety in numbers. At any rate, the child in a group seems to develop a feeling of confidence in the therapist sooner than he does in individual therapy. This, of course, varies with each individual, but indications are that the group steps up the development of the desired relationship between therapist and child.

9.

Accepting the Child Completely

The therapist accepts the child exactly as he is.

COMPLETE ACCEPTANCE of the child is shown by the therapist's attitude. She maintains a calm, steady, friendly relationship with the child. She is careful never to show any impatience. She guards against any criticism and reproof—either direct or implied. She avoids praise for actions or words. All this calls for vigilance on her part. There are innumberable traps into which the unwary therapist might fall. The child is a very sensitive being and is apt to catch the most veiled rejection of himself on the part of the therapist.

When one stops to consider that the child has been brought into the clinic because the parent is seeking to change him, one concludes (and, it would seem, rightly) that the parent is rejecting some part, if not all, of the child. Thus complete acceptance of the child seems to be of primary importance to the success of the therapy. How can the child achieve the courage to express his true feelings if he is not accepted completely by the therapist? How can he avoid guilt feelings as a result of what he does if he does not feel accepted by the therapist in spite of anything he might do or say? Acceptance does not imply approval of what he is doing. This cannot be emphasized too strongly. Approval of certain negative feelings which the child might express would be more of a hindrance than a help.

Jean is brought into the clinic by her mother. Jean, aged twelve, is getting completely out of hand. She shows no respect for her mother, quarrels with her younger brother, will not have anything to do with the other children in her class at school. After introductions, Jean goes to the playroom with the therapist. The therapist attempts to structure the situation verbally. "You may play with any of the toys in here any way that you want to, Jean. There are paints, clay, finger paints, puppets." The therapist smiles at Jean, who stares back at the therapist in obvious boredom. The therapist waits for a few moments. Jean sits down and maintains her stony silence. The therapist, anxious to get things moving, speaks again. "Don't you know just what to do first? Oh, and there is a family of dolls over in the doll house. Do you like to play with dolls?"

Jean shakes her head negatively. The therapist pursues her quarry. "You don't like to play with dolls. Don't you see anything in here that you would like to play with? You may play with any of these things in here in any way that you want to." Jean still maintains the icy silence. Then the therapist says, "You don't want to play. You just want to sit here." Jean nods agreement. "Very well," says the therapist. She, too, sits down and silence descends upon both of them. But the therapist is tense. "Would you rather just talk?" she asks hopefully. "No," says Jean. The therapist taps her pencil on her barren notebook. She taps her foot. She looks a little annoyed at Jean. This silence is maddening. There is a silent battle going on between the two, of which Jean is surely aware.

The therapist says, after a long silence, "Jean, do you know why you are here?" Jean stares at her. "Your mother brought you up here so that you could get some help with the problems that bother you." Jean looks away. "I don't have any problems," she announces coldly. "Well, you have this hour to use any way you want to," comments the therapist. Jean sulks. The therapist very nearly sulks, too. Several minutes pass. Then—

Therapist: Did you go to school today?
Jean: Yes.
Therapist: Did everything go along all right?

Jean: Yes. (*More silence.*)

Therapist: You know, Jean, I'm here to help you. I want you to consider me your friend. I wish you would tell me what bothers you.

Jean (sighing): Nothing bothers *me!*

There is no doubt about it. The therapy is blocked. The relationship has not been established. Jean is acutely aware that she is not accepted here, either. Jean is resentful enough of her mother's attempt to change her to resist to the bitter end. What, under the circumstances, could the therapist do?

Sometimes the therapist feels that it might inspire activity if she gets out the clay and begins to roll it around in an inviting fashion. Then, perhaps, comment, "Would you like to do this, too?" The therapist, under the circumstances, might get a polite participation, but it is doubtful if the therapy would ever move out of that polite-resistance stage.

In the preceding case, the therapist is attempting to control the activity of the hour. It seems important to her that the girl *do* something. She is suggestive. She tries to push things along. "Don't you know what to do first?" implies a criticism of the lack of participation on the part of Jean. The therapist recognizes Jean's feeling when she says, "You don't want to play. You just want to sit there." But the therapist cannot accept this. She pushes harder. "Would you rather just talk?" "No." That is not accepted, either. That nervous, impatient tapping of pencil and foot! Then the therapist commits the unpardonable error of injecting the element of a threat into the therapy situation. "Do you know *why* you are here?" In other words, "You had better start doing something about yourself. There is plenty wrong with you or you wouldn't be here." She even drags in the word "problem," which Jean denies that she has. But the therapist doesn't accept her denial. She says, "I wish you would tell me what bothers you." She says, "You may use this hour any way you want to." Jean proceeds to use it for resistance and silence. The inconsistent therapist starts to probe again. "Did you go to school today?" And then, adding insult to injury, "I want you to consider me your friend." It just didn't add up.

The therapist was neither accepting, nor consistent, nor therapeutic.

The alternative suggestion that the therapist draw the girl into participation by more subtle means is equally as unaccepting. If the girl has been fighting for acceptance outside the clinic, why must she continue here? If it is obvious that she does not want to play or talk, why not be accepting and permissive to the extent of letting her sit there in silence? After explaining the situation clearly enough so that she understands that she might play with any of the things in the playroom, or use the hour any way she desires, the accepting therapist would go along with the child and, if silence was the order of the hour, then silence it would be. It would seem well to include in the preliminary explanation to the girl that it is her privilege either to play or not to play as she desires, to talk or not to talk, and, after the girl has made the decision, the therapist should abide by it. The therapist might busy herself with notes—or with doodling if she feels that she *must* do something. She should be on the alert to reflect any feeling the girl might express. A deep sigh, a longing glance out the window, might safely be reflected to her— "It is boring to just sit here with me. Perhaps you would rather be outside." At that understanding, Jean might relax a little. If she remained adamant, the therapist should remain equally accepting.

This brings up the question as to the length of time the child should be required to stay in the room, a question which is discussed in Chapter 15, "The Value of Limitations."

Acceptance of the child goes further than establishing the initial contact or getting the child into the room and functioning. After the therapy is well under way, the therapist must maintain an accepting attitude for all the things the child does and says. The process of nondirective therapy is so interwoven that it is difficult to tell where one principle begins and another ends. They are overlapping and interdependent. For example, the therapist cannot be accepting without being permissive. She cannot be permissive without being accepting. She cannot leave the responsibility to make choices up to the child that she does not respect. The degree to which the therapist is able to put these principles into practice seems to affect the depth to which the therapy can go. When a child is expressing violent, aggressive feelings, the therapist must be alert to accept those feelings, too. Silence, at such a time, might be construed by the child to indicate disapproval and lack of acceptance. The tone of voice, the facial expression, even the gestures used by the therapist, either add to or subtract from the degree of acceptance that is being put into the situation.

Application to Group Therapy

To apply this principle in a group situation the therapist is obliged continually to check responses so that one child in a group does not feel at any time that he is being compared or contrasted with any other member of the group. Such a feeling can be aroused quite unintentionally if the element of praise or criticism, either direct or indirect, is injected by the therapist's responses. Such a statement as, "John knows what to do, he is getting busy right away," could very easily be taken as criticism by the other members of the group if they happen to be enjoying the bliss of a few minutes of sheer idleness while silently evaluating the situation. Or when the child rolls a ball of clay, seemingly without intent to make something, a statement from the therapist such as, "You don't know just what to make, do you, Bill?" verges on criticism of the child's indecisive activity. It seems that the most worthwhile responses from a therapeutic standpoint are reflections of feelings and attitudes expressed rather than content responses. The tone of voice and the impartial scattering of responses does much to eliminate the feeling on the part of the child that he is being criticized by the therapist.

Indications are that the child's feeling of complete acceptance by the therapist is more easily established in the individual therapy contacts than in the group contacts because the element of comparison or implied criticism does not enter into the situation.

10.
Establishing a Feeling of Permissiveness

The therapist establishes a feeling of permissiveness in the relationship so that the child feels free to express his feelings completely.

THE THERAPY HOUR is the child's hour to be used as he wants to use it. The depth of feeling that he shows during his hour in the playroom is made possible by the permissiveness that is established by the therapist. To a certain extent, this depends upon a verbal expression of the permissiveness on the part of the therapist, but it goes farther than that. When the child and therapist enter the playroom, the therapist usually says, "You may play with these toys in any way you like for an hour." If the child is a timid child or one with such meager background experiences that he might not know how to use the materials, some therapists feel that it is advisable to take the time to point out and explain the use of the materials when they first go into the playroom. "The paints on this easel are used to paint pictures. Here are the large sheets of paper. Here are the paint rags. There is clay in this jar. You can work it like this and make anything you like out of it. These are finger paints. You wet the paper like this, put a gob of the paint down on the paper and then smear it around with your hands. These are the puppets. They fit on your hand like this. You talk for them—saying anything you want them to say. Here is the doll house. This is the family who lives in the doll house. This is the father. This is the mother. This is the baby. Now you may play with anything in the playroom in any way you want to. You will have an hour all your own."

During the first hour the child explores the materials and is very alert to the therapist's attitude. That is why words alone are not enough. Permissiveness is established by the therapist's attitude toward the child, by facial expressions, tone of voice, and actions.

If the child spills water deliberately and the therapist immediately wipes it up, the action more or less cancels the verbal expression of permissiveness.

If the therapist, thinking the child's problem is centered around family relationships, pushes the doll family toward the child with, "See the doll family? Wouldn't you like to play with them?" she is not granting permissiveness of choice to the child.

If the child picks up the ball of clay and rolls it idly between indecisive hands, the therapist will do well to refrain from commenting, "You don't know what to make." Such a remark might be taken by the child to indicate that the therapist is not satisfied to have the child roll the clay aimlessly back and forth. Permissiveness implies choice to use or *not to use* the materials according to the child's wishes.

The question often arises as to what to do with the child who comes into the playroom willingly enough and then stands or sits there shyly, not doing a thing, not saying a word. Is that conducive to therapy? The temptation grows to encourage the child to use the materials. Sometimes the therapist thinks that if she plays with the child some action will get under way. Then the therapist chooses the medium and entices the child to follow suit. This seems to be more a supportive technique than a non-directive one. The child continues to remain dependent upon the therapist and it is just another block that will have to be broken down later on during the therapy sessions. Then the change in technique will be confusing to the child, may cause resentment and consequent withdrawal from active participation. It seems that absolute permissiveness which is built upon complete absence of suggestion is more conducive to successful therapy. If the therapist says, "You may play with the toys any way you want to," and the child doesn't seem to want to play, then it would seem more consistent to let the child sit there doing nothing. If the therapist is friendly toward the child and accepts his silence and idleness, she is conveying to him that she meant what she said and he really can do as he likes. The child seems to realize that it is his responsibility to make his choice. He is on his own. It is up to him to initiate the course of action that he will follow. There is no one here to tell him what to do. There is security in the relationship, but not support. Sometimes it takes time for this feeling of his own self-sufficency to be accepted by the child. He may fight off attempts to help him gain independence and self-direction, but the therapist's supportive interference only delays the progress in the direction toward independence.

After a period of time has elapsed, the therapist might safely say in a quiet, friendly voice, "It's sort of hard to get started. You don't know just what you would like to do. Or maybe you would rather just sit here and not do anything?" The child might grin a response, might even nod agreement, and continue sitting there in silence. It seems more valuable to the therapy to sit out the hour with the child and to continue to demonstrate the sincerity of the words, "You may play or not play—as you like," than to try to direct the child's use of his therapy hour.

From the beginning session, the therapist lets the child know that she respects his ability to make his own decisions and she abides by that principle.

Sometimes this is the testing period on the part of the child. Children are skeptical of this attitude of permissiveness at first. They test it out. The child who sits in idleness may be testing out the therapist to see if she really meant what she said. Again, that idleness may be resistance—passive resistance to the change someone is trying to force upon him. The child resists all efforts to change him. If lack of participation during the play hour expresses his resentment against outside pressure, then it seems better to grant him the permissiveness to show his resentment in that fashion.

Permissiveness in the relationship extends far beyond the initial contact. It continues through every meeting with the child. It is a delicate thing to handle. It requires consistency on the part of the therapist to keep the atmosphere permissive. So many things can upset this feeling of permissiveness—sometimes quite unintentionally on the part of the therapist. There should be no attempt made to guide the actions or conversation of the child. That implies that there must be *no probing questions* directed toward the child.

For example, five-year-old May, who has been referred to the clinic for therapy because of a traumatic hospital experience, is playing with the family of dolls. She picks up the girl doll, places her in the toy wagon and pushes her across the floor. The therapist, thinking to capture the crucial experience says, "Is the little girl going to the hospital?" "Yes," says the child. "Is she afraid?" "Yes." "Then what happens?" asks the therapist. The child gets up, goes over to the window, turns her back on the therapist and doll family. "How much longer?" she asks. "Is the time up yet?" Thus the child wards off the probing. The child is not yet ready to explore the experience that has been so upsetting. She has not been accepted as she is. She has not been granted the permissiveness to open that door when she felt adequate to face what was beyond it.

The therapist is concerned with the *feelings* the child expresses. A child seldom goes into the playroom and straightway plays out his deep feelings. First there is a period of exploration, of testing, of getting acquainted. The child must have a feeling of confidence in the therapist if he is to share his feelings. He must feel so secure in this situation that he can bring forth his "bad" feelings as well as his "good" feelings and not be fearful that this adult will disapprove of him. This confidence in the therapist is built upon the therapist's consistency in applying the basic principles.

It is important that the child does not develop guilt feelings as a result of his use of the play-therapy contacts. Encouragement, approval, and praise are taboo in a non-directive play-therapy session. Such reactions on the part of the therapist have a tendency either to influence the type of activities or to foster feelings of guilt. The same is true of disapproval or negative criticism. The atmosphere must be neutral.

When a child comes into the playroom and begins to

paint, the therapist sits there watching him. She takes down a few notes. The child says. "I can't paint so good. This is terrible." Perhaps the picture is really very good. Should the therapist point it out to the child? Should she say, "You don't think your painting is very good, but *I* think it is." What the therapist thinks is of no consequence. Suppose she just says, "You don't think you paint very well." Suppose the child as a result smears the black paint all over the painting. Does that mean that he was so discouraged that he blacked it out? Or is he expressing a feeling of resentment against the therapist for not duly appreciating his work of art? Or is it the child's reaction against his lack of acceptance? If the therapist follows along with the child, he will bring his feelings out into the open in a recognizable form. It is important that the therapist does not get ahead of the child, also that she does not read into the situation something that isn't there at all.

The permissiveness that is most conducive to successful therapy is in direct proportion to the acceptance of the child. When he feels so securely accepted by the therapist that he can beat up the mother doll, or bury the baby in the sand, or lie down on the floor and drink from a nursing bottle even though he is nine, ten. or eleven years old, and yet can do these things without a feeling of shame or guilt. then the therapist has established a feeling of permissiveness. The child is free to express his feelings. He gives vent to his most aggressive and destructive impulses. He screams, yells, throws the sand all over the place. spits water on the floor. He gets rid of his tensions. He becomes emotionally relaxed. Then, it seems, the groundwork for more constructive behavior has been laid. He has gotten rid of the old feelings; he is ready for new ones. The experience brings to the child insight into his behavior. He understands himself a little better. He has gained confidence in himself. He is more capable of solving his own problems. He knows by experience that he can work things out for himself.

Application to Group Therapy

The group experience seems to accelerate the child's

feeling of permissiveness. Each child derives a feeling of security from the group. As one child in the group forges ahead, the others gain the necessary courage to pursue their activities by watching the successful manipulation of the environment by this member of the group. The period of testing out the situation is more or less shortened because each individual in the group evaluates the permissiveness of the situation both directly and vicariously. If Jimmy has the courage to pick up the nursing bottle and suck on it with obvious enjoyment, more reserved Fred is encouraged to try it. If May has the daring to beat up the father doll, perhaps Jean will gain the necessary courage to beat up the baby (if that is her feeling). A child who has been very inhibited in her actions and who is afraid of messing is sometimes inspired to try out the finger paints that seem to bring such joy to another member of the group. The children note the ready acceptance of each child's expression by the therapist and the freedom of expression seems to be contagious.

11.

Recognition and Reflection of Feelings

The therapist is alert to recognize the feelings the child is expressing and reflects back those feelings in such a manner that the child gains insight into his behavior.

So OFTEN during the initial contact the therapist's responses seem rather wooden and more a response to the content than to the feeling the child is expressing. The therapist and child are feeling their way and striving to establish rapport. The child is exploring the playroom. He picks up a doll. "What is this?" he asks. "A doll," responds the therapist. He points to the paints. "What's this?" "Paints. Children paint on that easel if they want to." "What's this?" and on and on. Some therapists, trying to catch feelings, have responded, "You wonder what that is," but it seems that such a response does more to bog down the therapy than help it along. It seems advisable to answer factual questions with a direct answer. Then the child can go on from there. It is quite often just an attempt on the part of the child to get acquainted with the therapist. What else do they have in common that they could talk about? However, the therapist should be alert to the feelings the child is expressing either through his direct conversation or through his play, which is the child's natural way of expressing his feelings.

Recognition of feeling and interpretation are two different things. However, it is difficult to differentiate between them. The child's play is symbolic of his feelings, and whenever the therapist attempts to translate symbolic behavior into words, she is interpreting because she is saying what she *thinks* the child has expressed in his actions. This seems to be unavoidable, and, at times, even seems to be advantageous. A cautious use of interpretation, however, would seem the best policy, with the therapist keeping the interpretation down to a minimum, and, when using it, basing it upon the obvious play activity of the child. Even then, the therapist's response should include the *symbol* the child has used.

For example, a six-year-old boy was brought to the clinic for play-therapy contacts because of his exaggerated feelings of fear and anxiety. He played with the family of dolls in the doll house. He took the boy doll out of the house and said to the therapist, "She is sending the boy out here where the quicksand is. The boy is afraid. He cries and tells his mother that he is afraid, but she makes him go anyway. And see! He is sinking down and down and down into the quicksand." The boy, showing much anxiety and fear, buries the doll in the sand. This child is certainly dramatizing his fear and his feeling of insecurity and lack of understanding. How should the therapist respond to this? It is very certain that this child is playing out the basic issue of his problem. If she follows the child she will say, "The boy is being sent out of the house and he is afraid. There is quicksand out there. The boy even cries. He tells his mother he is afraid, but she makes him go out anyway and he gets buried in the sand." The child is talking about "the boy" and the therapist talks about "the boy." She seems to be saying the child's words right back to him. Had the therapist said, "You are afraid and your mother doesn't pay any attention to your fears and that scares you still more," she is getting ahead of the child and interpreting his remarks. Perhaps the interpretation is correct, but there is the danger of thrusting something at the child before he is ready for it. When the child says, "I am afraid, too. And sometimes I cry, but my mother makes me do it anyway," then he is ready for the direct response, "You are afraid," etc. As long as he feels that it is necessary to use the doll as his medium, the therapist should use it, too.

When the therapist catches the feeling that is expressed and recognizes that feeling, the child goes on from there and the therapist can actually see the child gain insight.

This was evident in the first individual contact with Tom which was presented on page 29. In this contact Tom was granted the permissiveness to change from what had been set up as counseling contacts to play-therapy contacts. He had the choice of his medium for expression. His feelings were reflected back to him with sufficient clarity so that he gained enough insight to go on from a denial that he had problems to the fact that he thought everybody had them and that he had them, too. The permissiveness of the situation that granted him the right to go or stay, talk or remain silent, seemed to relax him and to reassure him that this was indeed his hour to use as he saw fit. It is interesting to note that during the latter part of the contact he once more returned to the original statement that he did not have anything to say, and when this was recognized and the therapist offered him a choice of coming back again or staying away, he took off his hat and coat and decided to stay.

In this case the acceptance of Tom, the permissiveness of the situation, plus the recognition and reflection of his expressed attitudes helped Tom to clarify his thinking and make a positive step toward helping himself.

Sometimes the child's verbalization and play seem to be in conflict. Such was the case with Jack. He was living in a children's home. His parents had been divorced and both had remarried. The father obtained custody of Jack's older brother. Jack felt very resentful of this—and especially the fact that he had not been permitted to bring his toys with him to the Home— "Especially the gun!" as he so often said.

One day Jack went home for a visit. He had been planning on this visit for a long time. He wanted to get his toys. He had been coming for play-therapy contacts for five weeks before the home visit. This was his first day back. Jack came into the playroom grinning broadly.

Jack: Well, I went home. *(He sat down at the paint table and drew a clean sheet of paper toward him, opened the box of paints, and began to paint, still grinning happily.)* I saw my father and my brother. And do you know why they hadn't come to see me?

Therapist: No.

Jack: Because they thought it would make me feel sad to see them and then have them leave me here. That's what my father said. And they took me on a picnic and we had ice cream and candy and a boat ride. I told my father I wanted to bring my toys back. I asked about my gun. And we went out in the country one day, too. *(All the time Jack was relating the story of his visit back home, he was painting a tiny green spot in the middle of the paper and all round the green spot a growing expanse of black. Finally the paper was covered over with the black paint.)* Yep, I went home all right. But I didn't get my toys. And my brother had broken my gun. And he had lots of his own toys. He has fun all the time. He stays there.

Therapist: You went home, but you were disappointed in your visit. [This statement is interpretation. The therapist is drawing a conclusion from what Jack has said.] You didn't get the toys you went after and your gun had been broken.

Jack: Yes. *(He got up from the table and went over to the shelf and got the nursing bottle. He brought it back to the table and sat down across from the therapist.)* I told him a thing or two. I told him I wanted my toys. *(He seemed very close to tears. He looked at the therapist.)* Me baby *(sucking on the nursing bottle).*

Therapist: Now you are a baby. You don't think they treated you very nice when you went home. [This, too, is interpretation, going beyond what the child expressed. In reality, it seems to be what the therapist feels about the home situation, but it was close enough to Jack's feelings to be acceptable by him.]

(Jack filled his mouth with water. He leaned over and spat it on the floor.)

Jack: Look. I spit on my home.

Therapist: You spit on your home.

(Jack jerked off the nipple and filled his mouth again and once more spat on the floor.)

Jack: I spit on my brother. I spit on my father. I spit right in their very faces. They wouldn't give me my toys. He broke my gun. I'll show them. I'll spit on them. (*Again and again he filled his mouth with water and spat it on the floor.*)

Therapist: You are very angry with your brother and your father. You would like to spit right in their faces because of the way they have treated you.

Jack: They broke my gun. (*He went over to the drinking fountain and filled the nursing bottle again and continued to spit on his father and brother.*) They had a new rug back home. Look. I'll spit on the rug. I'll get it all wet. I'll ruin it. And my brother's new suit! I'll spit on his new suit and I'll ruin that.

Therapist: You'll ruin the new rug and the new suit. You'll get even with your father and your brother.

Jack (violently): I hate my father! I hate my brother!

Therapist: You hate your father. You hate your brother.

(Jack sat down across from the therapist, suddenly very calm. He lowered his voice. He put the nipple back on the bottle and began to suck on it again.)

Jack: I didn't know how long I was going to stay when I went home. I didn't take enough clothes with me. I stayed longer than I had planned. I never know. They never tell me.

Therapist: You never know what to expect. You can't make plans for your visits unless they tell you how long you can stay. You didn't have enough clothes with you because they didn't tell you.

Jack (going over and getting the father doll. He bangs its head down on the table): That for you! There! There! There!

Therapist: You'll beat him up.

Jack (beginning to twist the father doll's head around): I'd laugh if his ole head came off. (*He laughed.*)

Therapist: You'd like it if his head got twisted clear off.

Jack: It would serve him right. He gave all my toys to my brother. He wouldn't let me bring them here. He broke my gun.

Therapist: You don't think he treated you very nice. He took your toys and gave them to your brother. You want them. You want your gun, too.

Jack (throwing the father doll clear across the room): I

didn't take enough clothes to wear and I had to wear dirty clothes. And I didn't get to bring back my toys.

Therapist: You had to wear old dirty clothes and you didn't get what you went after.

Jack: The dirty gypper!

Therapist: He gypped you out of what you think is yours.

Jack (picking up a small ball of clay): Can I have this clay?

Therapist: You would like to have it, but I can't give it to you. You see, it belongs in the room here. You can use it when you come here, but you can't take it out of the playroom.

Jack: But I want it.

Therapist: I know you want it, but you can't take it. All the children want to take something out of here. If we let them, then there wouldn't be anything left for you to play with when you come here.

Jack: Then we couldn't come any more?

Therapist: You could come, but there wouldn't be anything to play with.

Jack (pushing the nursing bottle toward the therapist): Fill this for me. *(The therapist did. She noticed that when Jack thought she wasn't looking at him he slipped a ball of the clay in his pocket. She handed him the bottle. He drank from it again.)* This doesn't come out so fast. Got a pin?

Therapist: No pin.

(Jack took out the large safety pin that was holding on his pants that were about four sizes too large for him. They almost fell off when he took the pin out. He jabbed at the nipple with the pin and enlarged the hole. Then he glanced down in disgust at his pants.)

Jack (angrily): Look at these clothes. They are a mile too big for me. I wish they would get me some clothes that fit!

Therapist: You don't like to wear such uncomfortable clothes.

Jack: Will you give me some of this clay?

Therapist: I know you want me to give you the clay, Jack. I know it would mean a lot to you if I gave it to you. You wanted to get your own toys and your gun and you didn't get them. Now you want me to give you this clay and I can't give it to you, because it has to be kept here. [This was definitely interpretation on the part of the therapist, and not a good thing to include at this point. It goes far beyond the boy's simple request for clay.]

Jack (sadly): Nobody will give me anything. [This is a reflection of what the therapist has said.]

Therapist: That makes you unhappy. [This was based upon the boy's tone of voice and facial expression.]

Jack: But if you gave things away, then we couldn't come here. *(He sneaked the ball of clay out of his pocket and put it back on the table.)* We could come here, but we couldn't play with anything because there wouldn't be anything to play with.

Therapist: That's right.

Jack: I put the clay back. See? Here is the piece I took.

Therapist: You wanted the clay and you took it but you didn't keep it. You want me to know that you put it all back.

Jack (turning his pocket inside out): See? Yes, I put it back. *(He tried to put the pin back in his pants, but couldn't get it in. Finally he jabbed the pin straight in and it stuck him. He swore.)*

Therapist: Having trouble with the pin?

Jack: I can't get it in.

Therapist: Want me to help you with it?

Jack: I wish you would. And I wish they would get me some clothes that fit.

Therapist: You don't like clothes that are too big for you.

Jack (emphatically): I certainly don't. *(He went over to the drinking fountain and emptied the nursing bottle. Then he came back and got the mop which always stood in the corner of the room and mopped up the floor.)* I made quite a mess today, didn't I?

Therapist: You think you made quite a mess today. *(Jack cleaned up the playroom.)*

In this case the boy progresses from a polite verbalization about his trip home to a violent display of his true feelings. It is interesting to note how he releases his feelings with deeper significance as he receives recognition for each feeling that he does express. The acceptance of Jack's negative feelings, the permissiveness to release these feelings in such a free way, the reflection of those feelings, all seem to help Jack gain enough insight to return the stolen clay, to end the therapy period on a more constructive note, although there was no evidence to indicate that he felt guilty about throwing the water all over the room. The water-throwing was a typical act of Jack's while in the playroom. The cleaning-up was something new.

Application to Group Therapy

When there is more than one child in the playroom the therapist's opportunities to reflect feelings are minimized. It is not possible to catch all of the feelings that are being expressed. The therapist must center her attention on individuals and at the same time scatter her responses so that no child feels neglected. This is not an easy thing to do. Sometimes a child will imitate another member of the group just to gain the attention of the therapist. If the therapist develops a sensitivity to the play of the children, she can detect when the child is imitating for attention. Her response should reflect the desire for the attention rather than for the activity. In the following example the therapist missed this point.

Delbert: I'm going to paint a picture for my mother.
Therapist: You want to make something for your mother.
Jenny: I'm going to paint a picture, too.
Therapist: You want to paint, too, like Delbert is.
Delbert: This is for my mother.
Therapist: You want to make something for your mother.
Jenny: This is for my mother . . . for *my* mother . . . for *my* mother.
Therapist: You want to make something for your mother, too.
Delbert: This is a machine gun for *my* mother.
Jenny: This is a bigger machine gun for *my* mother.
Delbert: Mine will be as big as the paper. My mother's big, big machine gun.
Jenny: Mine will be ever bigger than this paper. I'll put two together. I'll give my mother the biggest machine gun in the world.
Therapist: You both want to give something to your mother.

The therapist seems to have missed the feeling the children were expressing. Actually it was a contest between Jenny and Delbert; the fact that they want to make something for their mothers seems to have been secondary.

In some cases the addition of other children in the play contact brings out feelings and attitudes that could not show up in an individual contact. To illustrate this, the following excerpt is quoted. There were three children in this group, all four years old. Billy was painting a picture, when Carry and Evelyn began to quarrel and scream. Carry had found the big rag doll and Evelyn had jerked it away from her. Both girls called to the therapist for help. Evelyn seemed to be completely dependent on the therapist's help, but Carry seemed to be able to handle the situation by herself. The therapist did not intercede in any way.

Therapist: Carry found the doll and Evelyn took it away from her. Carry wants it back and Evelyn wants to keep it. Carry wants me to help *her* and Evelyn wants me to help *her,* too.

Billy (leaning over and speaking to the therapist): I'd like to play with the doll, too. [The therapist again recognized the problem, including Billy this time. Carry began to scream and cry for help. Then a real fight followed.]

Billy: Are you to make them stop? Are you going to spank them?

Therapist: You think I should stop them and maybe spank them. *(Billy stared long and hard at the therapist.)*

Billy: No. I don't guess you will.

(Carry went over to the box of blocks and selected the longest, most vicious-looking block in the box. She went back toward Evelyn and raised the block over her head to give Evelyn a mighty blow on the head.)

Therapist: You really are very angry. You want to hurt Evelyn bad!

(Carry immediately put down the heavy block, and Evelyn handed the doll back to Carry. She took the doll, immediately stopped crying, put it on the table beside Billy.)

Carry: You can have her, Billy. *(She started to paint.)*

12.

Maintaining Respect for the Child

The therapist maintains a deep respect for the child's ability to solve his own problems if given an opportunity. The responsibility to make choices and to institute change is the child's.

CHANGE IN BEHAVIOR, if it is to have any lasting value, must come from within the individual as a result of insight that he has achieved. When the therapist places the responsibility to change or not to change in the child's hands, she is centering the therapy in the child. Change in his behavior does not mean conformity through some kind of pressure, for conformity to certain set standards is no indication of adjustment. The therapist tries to help the child realize that he is responsible for himself. There is no pressure applied to bring this about. It is a part of the therapy structure. It starts with little things—material things in the playroom—and it spreads throughout the relationship. The child is given a chance to gain his equilibrium. He achieves self-confidence and self-respect. He builds up his self-esteem. This hour is his. He is on his own. Shall he play? And, if so, what shall he play with? He will be the one to make the choice, and anything he decides upon will be all right with the therapist. Shall he just sit here? It makes no difference to the therapist. She remains friendly, relaxed, and interested. She keeps hands off. She understands him. He can tell by the remarks she makes. She seems to know just how he feels. He looks about him. He has the privilege of selecting any toy he wishes to play with. Regardless of what he picks up, there are no objections from the therapist.

Take Bill, for example. He snatches up the mother doll. He turns her upside down. He takes her clothes off. There are no objections to his actions. Just the remark, "You want to take her clothes off." Not a very profound remark, certainly, but still in line with what he is doing.

   Bill: I'll beat her up. (*He grabs a big block and proceeds to beat her.*)

   Therapist: You feel like beating her up.

   Bill: Now I'll bury her in the sand. She'll smother.

   Therapist: You'll smother her in the sand now.

   Bill: Nobody will ever see her again. (*He buries her deep in the sand.*)

   Therapist: You got rid of her. No one will ever see her again.

   (Bill goes over to the shelf. He takes down a nursing bottle. He puts it to his lips. He glances at the therapist to see how she will take this.)

   Therapist: You want to drink from the nursing bottle. (*He tips it up a little higher.*)

   Bill: Me baby.

   Therapist: Now you're baby. (*He sucks contentedly on the bottle.*)

   Bill: Dis is fun.

   Therapist: Sometimes it's fun to be a baby.

   (Bill lies down on the floor, cooing and gurgling and sucking on the bottle. What matters here that he is eight years old? *Now* he is a baby! The therapist shows no sign of being bored by his baby play. He lies on the floor drinking from the bottle and being a baby for twenty minutes. He knows that the therapist will go along with him for as long as he wants to be a baby. He lives through this experience, relaxed, secure in his relationship. It makes no difference whether he is a cooing baby or a bloodthirsty young savage; he still is accepted completely. After he satisfies his desire to drink from the bottle and be a baby, he takes off the nipple and drinks the rest of the water.)

   Bill: I'm drinkin' beer, now. See? Like my dad.

   Therapist: You're not a baby, now. You're grown up. [This, too, is interpretation.]

   Bill: Yep! (*He lays aside the nursing bottle. He has made his choice. It is more fun being grown up than it is being a baby.)*

(Bill mans the gun and arranges the soldiers for a battle. Out come his aggressions. First this one and then that one are killed. Entire divisions are mowed down. He screams and yells bloody murder. The therapist continues to reflect his feelings.)

Bill (screaming): You dirty bums, why don't you do what I say? I'll kill you. I'll kill all of you. *(And he does.)*

Therapist: They wouldn't do what you said and so you killed them.

Bill: This block-buster is going to smash up their only remaining tent. But you just watch. This fellow is going to get away. See? Here *I* am. I'm going to sneak over here.

Therapist: The block-buster smashes up their tent, but you get away safely. Nothing happens to you.

Bill: He sneaks over here. Boy, is he afraid! Look at him shake. He thinks they are going to kill him.

Therapist: He *is* afraid.

Bill: Then they come around here, the enemy does, and they sneak up and they *almost* kill him, but just then he turns around and he lets them have it.

Therapist: They almost got him. But he turned just in time to save himself.

Bill (yelling): He yells "MOTHER."

Therapist: He calls his mother because he is afraid.

Bill (screaming): And when she comes out, he kills her.

Therapist: He kills his mother when she comes out.

Bill: Yep. She wouldn't do what he told her to do.

Therapist: He killed her because she wouldn't do what he told her to do.

Bill: Yep. But then he gives her first aid after, and then she is well again.

Therapist: He makes her well again.

Bill: Then she went to the movies with the boy and we saw *Red Rover Rides Again.* Did you ever see *Red Rover Rides Again*?

Therapist: Mother and the boy went to see *Red Rover* after the battle was over.

Bill: Did you ever see it?

Therapist: No.

Bill: Boy, it was neat. There's a kid in my room who has a Red Rover belt. It's mellow.

Therapist: You like Red Rover movies and belts.

Bill: Do you hear Red Rover on the radio?

Therapist: I'm afraid not.

Bill: Boy, it's neat. All you got to do to get one of these Red Rover belts is to send in ten box tops of Hunchy Crunchy cereals and ten cents and you get a belt. I'm going to send for one.

Therapist: You're going to try and get a Red Rover belt, too.

Bill: Yep. This kid's belt is brown and it's got sparklers all around it. It looks like this. (*He sits down at the table and draws a replica of the belt with the crayons.*)

The therapist goes right along with Bill as he changes from baby to adult to typical eight-year-old. He makes the choices. He brings about the change within himself.

The therapist believes that the child can help himself. She has respect for him.

Every child who comes into the playroom is confronted with this challenge to function on his own. What about the fearful child? The dependent child? The child who has never made an important choice on his own? Will he be overwhelmed by this experience? Will it be too much for him? Will he need support temporarily?

No more fearful or inadequate child than Jerry ever came in the play-therapy room. He was four years old, mentally retarded, phsyically undersized. He could not talk, was very poorly co-ordinated, and seemed to be absolutely lacking in self-direction. He was brought in for play therapy because of his unreasonable fears, because he was a feeding problem, and because the mother thought that Jerry might learn how to talk as a result of this therapy experience.

When the therapist first met Jerry, she saw a whimpering, insecure, bewildered little fellow who didn't know what it was all about. He muttered and staggered around in circles when the therapist reached for his hand to take him into the playroom. Jerry's mother had made arrangements to talk to one of the other psychologists for counseling help with her problems.

The therapist took Jerry into the playroom with misgivings. What on earth could this futile child do in the playroom? This case illustrates the *power* within the individual to become more mature *if* given an opportunity. Notes taken by the therapist reveal some interesting developments.

FIRST CONTACT

Jerry gazed around him at the toys in the playroom. Then he began to pick up the toys, look at them briefly, and drop them on the floor. He grunted and muttered, but said nothing intelligible. He picked out the army truck, smiled a very fleeting smile, dropped the truck on the floor. He lifted down the cardboard box containing the doll family. One by one he picked them up and dropped them down on the floor. Then he went to the box of blocks and repeated his activity, strewing the blocks aimlessly around the floor. During all this play, he grunted and muttered in a very subdued manner. His movements were nervous, quick, unco-ordinated. Things fell out of his feeble grasp and he made no effort to pick them up again. Then he picked up the hammer and began to pound on the peg-board set, but he could not control the hammer. After a very short interval of hammering, he pushed it away and took the toy knives, forks, and spoons and strewed them across the floor. Finally, everything in the room that he could handle was on the floor. Jerry got the little wagon and pushed it across the floor.

During this play, whenever he laughed the therapist said, "Jerry likes to do that," or, "Jerry thinks that is funny." Occasionally he would hold up a toy truck or a doll and grunt at the therapist. She would name the object that he held up. Jerry seemed to get a great deal of satisfaction out of this. He began to center his actions around that type of activity. He would hold up the toy, look at the therapist, she would name it, he would smile, lay it down, and pick up something else.

After a while he began to select the truck every other time. The therapist continued to repeat the names of the toys, especially "truck," the toy which he intermittently held up. Finally, Jerry said "truck" himself as he held up the toy. He seemed to keep his eyes closed most of the time and to fumble among the toys rather than to attempt any real play with them.

Finally he went back to the wagon and pushed it. The therapist said, keeping up with his activity, "Jerry is pushing the wagon," "Jerry is shooting the gun," "Jerry is smashing the trucks together." Then Jerry began to yell. He banged the trucks together harder and harder and yelled something that sounded very much like "Truck smash!"

Then a fire engine went by the building. Jerry immediately dropped what he was doing, whimpered, ran over to the therapist, and took her hand. "Jerry is afraid of the noise," said the therapist. Jerry suddenly smiled. He went over to the doll house, took all the furniture out of it, and dropped it down on the floor. He picked up the telephone, held it up to his ear, threw it down on the floor, went to the window, tried to look out, then picked up the truck again. The fire engine went back, with all its noise. Jerry again reacted the way he had the other time it passed. Again the therapist said, "Jerry is afraid of the noise."

Then Jerry took the therapist's hand and tried to convey some message to her. He said, "Do! Do!" very emphatically. "You want me to do something," said the therapist. Jerry pulled harder and repeated "Do!" He seemed to understand what the therapist said to him. Finally the therapist got up, Jerry led her over to the box of toys on the floor, and, by taking her hand and putting it down in the toy box and then putting a toy in her hand and guiding it over to his hand, finally conveyed the idea to the therapist that he wanted her to hand him the toys. The therapist did, one toy at a time, each of which he promptly dropped on the floor. He still tugged at the therapist's hand as though he wanted her to do something else. The therapist started to name the toys as she handed them to Jerry, and that was what he wanted. He began to smile. Finally he began to jabber and laugh and yell. Occasionally he would yell out, "Truck!" Then he got down on the floor, which was now covered with the toys, and pushed them around, laughing and shouting.

At the end of the hour, Jerry did not want to leave the playroom. He began to whimper. He yelled, "No!" But when the therapist started out the door, he went with her.

SECOND CONTACT (*two days later*)

Jerry seemed more fearful during this contact than during
the first one. Every time a streetcar went by, he whimpered
and showed signs of fear. At the end of the hour his mother
said that he had had his first streetcar ride on the way up to
the clinic that day and was so afraid of it that she thought
she was going to have to get off. However, she stuck it out
and, although he cried and whimpered all the way to the
clinic, they stayed on the streetcar.

Jerry continued throughout the hour to act out this fear.
He got out the wooden animals and dolls and pushed them
around. Quite by accident one of them remained standing
as he dropped it out of the box. Jerry looked at it and then
laughed. The therapist said, "Jerry likes to have it stand
up." Then he tried to make the others stand up, and was
delighted with the success he had. After he had stood them
up, he knocked them all over. He played with the dolls and
animals in that fashion for ten minutes, then went back to
his old trick of tossing everything down on the floor. He
spent most of the time doing that. Then he got the paint rag
and dipped it in the pan of water for the finger paints and
squeezed the water out of the rag for about five minutes.

Every time a streetcar went by, he whimpered and cried.
Each time, the therapist said, "Jerry is afraid of the noise."
At the end of the hour he went over to the window as a
streetcar went by, but he did not whimper or cry. He just
tried to look out. "Streetcar," said the therapist. "Car," said
Jerry, "car!"

THIRD CONTACT (*from here on contacts were at weekly intervals*)

A sand table had been added to the playroom equipment
since Jerry's last visit. He went right to it. The therapist
helped him climb in. He threw handfuls of sand for about
three minutes, then tried to climb out of the sand box. He
whimpered as though asking the therapist to lift him out.
The therapist said, "Jerry wants out of the sand box." Jerry
started to climb out by himself. The therapist gave the minimum amount of assistance.

He wandered over to the box of toys and began to take
them out of the box. He looked at the therapist and grunted.

She smiled at him and said, "Jerry wants to take the toys out of the box." Jerry turned his back to the therapist. He looked through the box of toys. He pulled out the truck. He held this up to the therapist. "Truck," he said.

Then he picked up a wooden cow and held it out to the therapist. It certainly looked as though he wanted her to name off the toys again. So once more that was the routine. Then Jerry very deliberately selected the truck, the cow, and the boy doll. One after the other he held these up. The therapist named them back to him. Then Jerry said, "Truck." "Cow." "Boy." Across the playroom he went with them, back to the sand box. He climbed back in by himself, and threw the sand around. He stayed in the sand box for about five minutes, then climbed out again, without assistance.

When the streetcars went by, he always went to the window, looked out, and whimpered. Each time the therapist reflected back his fear of the noise. He went over to the baby doll, picked it up, rocked it in his arms, then dropped it down on the floor.

He climbed up on the bench and pointed to the jar of blue finger paints. The therapist opened the jar, put some of the blue paint down on the paper. Jerry leaned over and looked at it. "See?" said the therapist. She showed him how to smear the paint around. Jerry began to whimper. "Jerry doesn't like it," said the therapist. Jerry really didn't. He got down from the table. Later during the hour, he went back and looked at it. Then he came over to the therapist and led her back to the table and, taking her hand in his, he pushed her hand down in the finger paint. Then very quickly he left it. He went to the peg-board set and pounded a few feeble pounds, strewed a few blocks over the floor, picked up the big doll, got the nursing bottle and held it to the doll's lips. He dropped the doll on the floor, put the nursing bottle in the doll cradle, and tried to look out the window. Then he got the truck and started to push it around on the floor.

FOURTH CONTACT

Jerry got into the sand table by himself. He found a little truck in the sand and spent ten minutes filling it with sand, pushing it around, emptying it, filling it again. After ten minutes of this play, he climbed out of the sand box by himself, went to the window and looked out, then took a few of the soldiers back to the sand table and climbed in again. The sand got in his shoes and he tugged at them and whimpered. The therapist took off his shoes and socks.

Every time a streetcar went by, Jerry lifted his head, but there was no sign of fear. The therapist said, "A streetcar" every time. Jerry nodded his head. Halfway through the hour he said "streetcar" whenever one went by.

He played in the box for another ten minutes, then climbed out again and went after the toy dishes. He took a cup and toy spoon back to the sand box and climbed in again. He poured sand into the cup and took it out with the spoon. Then he became hilarious. He threw big handfuls of sand and yelled and laughed.

Suddenly he got out of the sand box and, taking the therapist's hand, led her to the door. The therapist went with him. He went over to the waiting room, looked around. "You are looking for your mother?" asked the therapist. He turned and staggered back to the playroom and climbed back into the sand.

He began to bury the dishes and the truck in the sand and then took the therapist's hand and motioned to her to find them. She dug them out. He laughed. Then he got two trucks and banged them together, yelling, "Truck!" and "Bang! Bang!" and laughing. The bell rang indicating the end of the hour. Jerry jerked at the noise. Then he laughed.

The therapist put his shoes and socks on for him and he returned to the waiting room.

FIFTH CONTACT

When Jerry came into the playroom, he sat down on the floor, tried to take off his shoes and socks, couldn't quite manage it, and was given a little help by the therapist. He climbed into the sand box. He played with the dishes and little trucks in the sand box for a half-hour. Then he climbed out, got the big doll, wrapped it in a blanket, held it for ten minutes, laid it carefully in the cradle, climbed back in the sand box and played for the remaining twenty minutes. During this play, when he picked up any different toy, the therapist said, "Now Jerry is playing with the ducks," or, "Now Jerry is playing with the horse." Jerry made an effort to repeat the names. He said "Ducks" and "Cow."

Once during this contact, when a streetcar went by,

Jerry looked at the therapist and said, "Streetcar." He showed no signs of fear at any time during this contact.

At the end of the hour, Jerry got his shoes and socks and tried to put them on. With a little help, he finally managed.

SIXTH CONTACT

When Jerry came into the playroom, he sat down, took off his shoes and socks without help, and climbed into the sand box. He played there for a half-hour. Then he climbed out, got the doll, held it and fed it with a nursing bottle for ten minutes. Then he very gently laid the doll in the cradle and got the long building blocks and piled them in on top of the baby doll. He went to the doll house and spent ten minutes taking the furniture out and putting it on the table. When it was empty, he put the furniture back in it, but did not get it back in order. It was just a matter of filling the house up with furniture again. He then went back to the sand table and climbed in and played for the rest of the hour.

Not once during this hour did he seem to notice the streetcars or any other noises. At the end of the hour, he sat down on the floor and put his socks on without any help. He needed a little help with the shoes, but he made the effort to do it himself.

SEVENTH CONTACT

Jerry spent the entire hour in the sand box playing with the dishes, the trucks, and the toy animals. At the beginning of the hour, he took off his shoes and socks without help, and at the end of the hour, he put the socks on without help, but was still unable to get the shoes on.

EIGHTH CONTACT

Jerry spent the first half-hour on the floor playing with the animals that he had picked out of the toy box. He stood them up, pushed them around, and showed very definite organization of his play. Then he started to climb into the sand box, remembered about his shoes and socks, sat down on the floor and took them off by himself. He had on new shoes which had straps across the ankles rather than shoe-strings. He could manage these by himself. He climbed into the sand box and began to play with the toys he had selected as his favorites—the animals, the dishes, the trucks. He stayed there until the end of the hour, laughing most of the time. A fire truck went by during the middle of the hour, but he paid no attention to it. When it was time to go, he put on his socks and shoes without help. He could not buckle the straps, but otherwise he managed by himself.

This was the last contact the therapist had with Jerry. She felt that he could have been helped more by continued contacts and did not consider the case finished, but owing to the closing of the clinic it was not possible to see him again. The contacts were terminated by the clinic and not by the mother. The mother and child were referred to another clinic where both received further treatment.

The mother reported a noticeable change in Jerry's behavior after the first contact. He had become more self-assertive in his non-verbal fashion. Previously he had been very docile, and stayed where he was put, doing nothing but crawling aimlessly around the baby pen that she kept him in. He now tried to climb out of the baby pen. The mother let him out. Then she noticed other improvements as time passed. He tried to talk. He said a few words that all could understand. He said, "trucks," "streetcar," "ducks," and "cow." The mother volunteered the new words that he had picked up. Jerry must have said them at home, because the mother had no way of knowing what toys he played with and what words he said during the hour. She was very pleased when he started to try to take off his shoes and socks and to put them on by himself. She said he was eating better at home. He was more interested in things that went on around him. She said the most outstanding change in him was his increasing attention span. He played with his toys now with some purpose for quite a long time, whereas previously he had done little more than pick them up and drop them again.

Of course, the mother's attitude must be taken into consideration when trying to account for the change that had taken place in Jerry. Every time that Jerry was in for a play contact, the mother was seen by another psychologist for non-directive counseling. The mother gained a certain amount of insight into the problem of her relationship with Jerry. This influenced her attitude and her actions toward Jerry. She commented at one time that Jerry was much harder to handle now, because he seemed to be developing a mind of his own, but she guessed that that was all for the good and she should welcome the change.

Looking over this case, the reader might ask just what was it that happened to Jerry that brought about this change? Was it that in this play hour he experienced for the first time in his life a feeling of independence and self-sufficiency? Was it because in this experience he functioned entirely on his own and gained a feeling of self-confidence that gave him the courage to go a little farther? Did he gain insight into his own value as a functioning individual?

It is interesting to note the way he explored the materials at his disposal and finally centered on a chosen few, although they all remained in sight during his contacts. This is certainly evidence that even Jerry could make choices for himself when given an opportunity, as well as initiate change in his behavior. Apparently he found his independence much more satisfying than his former infantile dependence. He must have experienced a feeling of security in this relationship that enabled him to get over his fears and anxieties.

It seems as though Jerry received such satisfaction in being self-sufficient during this hour that he gained confidence to go ahead on his own. His tensions were cut down. He achieved a feeling of equilibrium that enabled him to get control of himself.

Application to Group Therapy

This principle is not weighted in any way in either the individual or the group experience. It applies at all times to each child, whether he is alone or in a group. The various personalities of the group members do not influence the principle. Even in a group in which one child is dominated completely by other members of the group, that child makes the choice to move out of the state of domination voluntarily. The dynamics of the group relationship sometimes brings into sharp focus immediate problems of the relationships of one individual with others in the group. The children in the group soon begin to interact. They discuss the attitudes and feelings of the other members. They are generous with their evaluation and advice. The individual reaction of each child to the other personalities is significant. It is quite possible to help the child achieve insight into his problem of social adjustment by reflecting back to him the feeling he expresses when playing with the others. Even though the group relationship seems to point up the problems and seems to hasten the development of insight, the responsibility to insitute change remains with the child.

13.

The Child Leads the Way

The therapist does not attempt to direct the child's actions or conversation in any manner. The child leads the way. The therapist follows.

THE THERAPIST consistently adheres to the non-directive policy. She asks no probing questions, except, possibly, "Do you want to tell me about it?" if the child initiates a discussion about something that has bothered him. She excludes all words of praise, so that he has no inducement to act in a certain manner in order to obtain more praise. She offers no criticism of what he does, so that he does not feel discouraged and inadequate. If he asks for help, the therapist gives it. If he asks for directions as to how to use any of the materials, she furnishes them.

The therapist offers no suggestions. The playroom and materials are at the child's disposal, awaiting his decision. The therapy period is his proving ground, the time in which he takes his own measure. If he attempts to make something out of clay, the therapist does not suggest that he make a certain thing that she specifies. Nor does she set up a prearranged selection of toys, hoping that the materials that have been laid out and are waiting will be taken over by the child.

One therapist, who felt that her group had problems centering around their family relationships, placed the doll house and family in the very center of the room and put everything else out of the way. The children came in, immediately saw the prearranged set-up, then sat down in idleness and asked how long they had to stay and would they have to come back again? By her selection of the material, subtle as it was, she had canceled out all of her previous structuring, had bewildered and confused the children by her attempt to direct the play, had betrayed their confidence in her, and had caused the children to make a quick retreat. She had become authoritarian to the children, as evidenced by their questions, "How long do we have to stay? Do we have to come back again?"

Prompting on the part of the therapist is just as futile. When the therapist says to a child, "Other children play with the nursing bottles. Wouldn't you like to try it?" she is trying to direct his activities. The children sometimes resent such prompting and become sullen. Sometimes in a group situation, the other children think they are expected to follow suit and enter into an activity for which they may have neither a readiness nor a need.

Unfortunately, many children have had the experience of being told that they can make a choice only to find that, unless their choice coincided with one already made by the adult in charge, their choice was null and void. As a result of many different kinds of experiences, children are wary at first of the permissiveness of the therapy session. This can be noted when a child tells a little friend about the therapy hour— "Honest, you never saw anything like it. You *really* can do what you want to!" Just as if it were unbelievable, but true.

The therapy hour is not just another recreation hour, or social hour, or school experience. It is the child's hour. The therapist is not a playmate. She is not a teacher. She is not a substitute mother. She is a very unique person in the eyes of the child. She is the sounding board against which he can try out *his* personality. She is the one who holds the mirror so that he can see himself as he is. The therapist keeps her opinions, her feelings, her guidance, out of the therapy hour. When one stops to consider that the child is in the playroom to become acquainted with himself, one realizes that the therapist's opinions and de- sires are not wanted. The child is stopped by the intrusion of the therapist's personality injected into the play. Consequently, the therapist keeps herself out of it. The child leads the way. The therapist follows.

This is illustrated in the following excerpt. Richard, aged nine, is in a private Children's Home. He has been recommended for play therapy because he is a daydreamer, a bed-wetter, and talks baby talk. Intelligence tests gave evidence that he was of average intelligence, and yet he was failing in all his school work. This excerpt is from his fourth session. It shows the use the child makes of the therapist when given the permissiveness to do so. It points up the difference between the rôle of the therapist and that of the typical adult with which the child is familiar.

Richard came into the playroom, sat down at the table and began to paint big blobs of color on the paper. He used orange and red paint. He grinned at the therapist.

Richard: I've been pulling weeds to earn some money. I want to buy my mother a present. I'm going to go home on my birthday and spend two weeks with my aunt. She lives near my mother and so I'll get to see my mother on my birthday.

Therapist: You are anxious to go and see your mother.

Richard: Yes. I'll get her something nice. I'll surprise her with a nice present.

Therapist: You'll take her a nice surprise.

Richard: Yes. I'll be gone two weeks. Maybe three. Gosh, it'll be good getting out of here.

Therapist: You'll be glad to get away from here for a while.

Richard: I'll be ten years old. I'm in fourth grade. My dad wants me to be in fifth grade, but I tell him I don't want to be in fifth grade. I like to fail.

Therapist: You like to fail.

Richard: I wrote and told my mother I was coming home for my birthday. I told her I would be five years old and I wanted five candles on my cake.

Therapist: You want to be five years old this birthday.

Richard: Father's birthday is in the next month. He is going into the army. He came to see me last month. Know what he asked me? He asked me if I wanted a little brother or a little sister. I said I didn't care. They are going to get one, I guess. (*At this point he paints black streaks across the orange and red blobs of color.*)

Therapist: You told your dad you didn't care if they did get another baby.

Richard: That's what I *said*.

Therapist: That's what you *said*, but you really do care.

Richard: You see my father and mother aren't any relation any more. They are divorced and father is married again. *(He sighs deeply and closes the paint box with a bang. He goes over to the shelf and picks up the nursing bottle. He sucks on it.)*

Richard: Me baby.

Therapist: You could be their baby. [Interpretation.]

Richard picks up the checker game and brings it back to the table and sits down across from the therapist.

Richard: You play with me.

(The checkers are placed on the board and a conventional game of checkers begins. Halfway through the game Richard tells the therapist what checker to move and where to put it.)

Therapist: You want to tell me what to do in this game.

Richard: Yes. Look. This is how I want you to play.

Therapist: You want to tell me what to do.

Richard: Yes. See. Don't move any of these ever. *(In that way Richard is sure to win the game and he proceeds to do just that. Then suddenly he sweeps all the checkers into a pile.)* This will be a new game. Pile them all up. You pile those all up. Red are mine. The black are yours. Now we will have a battle. *(Richard moves his men and then he moves the therapist's men. She eases out of the game and he takes over. He moves both sets of men, jumping them over one another.)* He is a big man. This one. He is a giant. He can do anything in all the world. *(He jumps over the therapist's men. He knocks some of them off the board.)*

Therapist: Whoever he is, he certainly is powerful.

Richard: He can do *anything*. *(Suddenly he stops this game. He arranges the checkers as though for an ordinary game, then places a red king over in the left corner of the king row on the therapist's side of the board.)* This is the little boy, see? He is lost. In fact his mother sent him away. She couldn't help it, see? There was no place for him and she had to work. *(Richard is very nervous. He moves his fingers quickly over the board and touches the checkers lightly.)*

Therapist: The little boy has been sent away from his mother.

Richard: This is the boy's father. This is his grandfather.

This one here is the other mother that the father married. And this is his aunt. And this one *(the checker in the opposite corner from all the other checkers)* is the boy's mother. Now these people—— *(He moves them out in between the boy and the mother.)* None of these people are going to let him get to his mother and this other mother won't let the father get to the boy and the boy cries, "Help! Help!" These soldiers hear him. They hurry out. They fight the father. The mother sneaks around this way. The father sneaks around that way. The other mother watches. Then—— *(Richard sweeps the father clear off the board. He goes rolling across the floor.)* Oh, no, you don't! *(Richard is yelling now, very excited.)* The mother is getting closer. This other mother goes at her. They fight. *(He messes the checkers up. Then he sweeps all the checkers off the board. They roll in all directions.)* Mother! Mother! *(Richard is crying. He stands up and wipes his eyes.)*

Therapist: You want to be with your mother. The father and mother both want to help the boy, but the other mother won't let them get close enough.

Richard (nodding his head in agreement): Yes. That's it. *(He walks over to the window and looks out with his back to the therapist.)*

Therapist: It makes you very unhappy.

Richard: I'll be with my mother on my birthday.

Therapist: You will like that.

(Richard gets the nursing bottle and sucks on it. He comes back to the table and sits down across from the therapist.)

Richard: It's nice to come here. (Sighs.) When I go home I'd like Ned to take my place.

Therapist: You want someone to come in your place when you go home.

Richard: Yes. I don't want there to be just a hole where I was.

Therapist: You would feel better if Ned came and sort of saved your place for you while you were gone.

Richard: Yes. Ned is a nice kid. Ned would like it. Can Ned come for me?

Therapist: Yes. If he wants to come.

Richard: Okay, I'll send Ned.

The reader will note that there was no attempt to direct this play. There was no attempt to question Richard about his statement that he liked to fail, or to correct him when he said he was five years old. The therapist did not point out to him that it wasn't nice to like to fail or to misrepresent one's age. There was no attempt to pry into the identity of the giant. The therapist let Richard lead the way. She followed along as best she could. She did not offer sympathy and support to Richard. She kept her feelings out of the situation entirely.

Application to Group Therapy

The child leads and the therapist follows in a group contact just as in an individual contact. One child in the group may attempt to direct the other children's actions and conversation, but such direction is not the same as direction by the therapist. The therapist, in such an instance, must check her responses so that they do not convey to the dominant child even subtle direction.

A strict application of the principle would rule out all probing questions on the part of the therapist, with the exception of one— "Would you like to tell me about it?" —which leaves the child free to tell or not tell as desires. There is sometimes a feeling on the part of the therapist that a little questioning at certain times might hurry up the therapy. In certain cases this might be true, but in other cases it causes the child to retreat and actually retards the therapy and because we cannot always predict the child's reaction, it is a risk that is better not taken. This principle calls for restraint on the part of the therapist. It is not always easy to let the child lead the way when he seems to be very close to the heart of his problem and yet seems to be skirting around it. However, experience warns that therapy cannot be hurried.

14.

Therapy Cannot Be Hurried

The therapist does not attempt to hurry the therapy along. It is a gradual process and is recognized as such by the therapist.

THE LAW OF READINESS operates in the therapy session. When a child is ready to express his feelings in the presence of the therapist, he will do so. He cannot be hurried into it. An attempt to force him to do so causes him to retreat. Quite often children pass through a period of seemingly uneventful play during the therapy hour. Such a period calls for patience and understanding on the part of the therapist. Some children are very slow to make use of the hour in what the therapist might consider a therapeutic manner. However, they may be going through a period wherein they are gaining the readiness to express themselves. If the therapist can just let them alone, let them take their time, she will be rewarded for her restraint.

The child lives in a hustle-bustle world. Things spin by him with bewildering speed. He is rushed here and rushed there. By nature he is slow. This world is a big place, and he needs time to take it all in. Everyone is familiar with the adults who cannot let the child do things for himself because "it takes him *forever!*" For example, the very common exasperation adults sometimes show at the fumblings of little children who cannot button up their coats "in a hurry" or who cannot tie their shoestrings "in a hurry"—who can't, in fact, do much of anything "in a hurry." The adults swoop down and do it for them. Tensions and frustrations are multiplied.

If the therapist is seeking to relieve tensions and pressures and to give the child a feeling of adequacy, she will not follow the "hurry pattern." She will recognize the value of giving the child an opportunity to gain his equilibrium. She will let the child take his time.

Here is at least one situation in the child's life where he is not hurried or prodded along. He can relax. If he wants to sit there and look, then he sits there and looks— for the entire hour if he desires to do so. If he begins to sift the sand through his fingers, seemingly a grain at a time, he does so to his heart's content. If he rolls the clay back and forth, back and forth, enjoying the feel of its pliable substance, then he does. If he wants to keep his mouth closed all hour, then he keeps it closed all hour. Finally, the child begins to notice that the usual pressure to hurry him along is absent. There is visible relaxation.

If the therapist feels that the child has a problem and she wants to attack the problem as soon as possible, she must remember that what *she feels* is not important. If the child has a problem, he will bring it out when *he* is ready. The problem of maladjustment is so complex that one cannot draw a simple circle around some singular experience and say, "This is it!" The personality of the child is such a complex mechanism that it is difficult, if not impossible, to isolate one causative element and say, "This is the thing that is causing all the trouble." The therapist does not know the child as well as the child knows himself. She cannot express the true feelings of the child as accurately as the child can. She may be able to reflect his expressed feelings. She may be able to make a rather accurate guess, but she cannot assume that she knows *all* the feelings of the child.

If the therapist thinks the child is not making any progress during weeks of therapy sessions, let her examine and re-examine her notes to see if she can spot something that has caused resistance to the therapy. Let her remember that change is a gradual process and that some children move at a snail's pace. Let her remember that therapy does not always bring about the desired results. It is not a cure-all. Let her remember that the child is living in a dynamic world of human relationships. The conditions which have created the maladjustment may be still operating. The child may not be able to combat the other forces that stifle his psychological growth.

The therapist should try to see things through the child's eyes, should try to develop a feeling of empathy with the child She should keep in mind the maxim that change cannot take place without the participation of the individual. and that worthwhile change comes from within. She should remember that growth is a gradual process.

It has already been pointed out that sometimes the *group* experience seems to accelerate the therapy. However, the therapist does not attempt to hurry it along. The intrusion of a probing technique is dangerous and unreliable. It might not do any obvious harm to the therapy, but there is the very real danger that it might cause retreat and destruction of rapport.

15.

The Value
of Limitations

*The therapist establishes
only those limitations that
are necessary to anchor therapy to the world of reality
and to make the child aware
of his responsibility in the
relationship.*

THE LIMITATIONS that are established in the non-directive
relationship are naturally very few, but very important. It
seems conducive to sound therapy to confine most of the
limitations to material things, such as limiting willful destruction of the play materials, damaging the room, and
attacking the therapist. Also, common-sense limitations
which are necessary for the protection of the child should
be included. There seems to be little or no therapeutic
value in spending a play period with the child hanging out
a high window or engaging in any activity that is dangerous to him. If he is to come out of the therapy room with
a feeling of security and respect for the therapist, he must
be treated in such a manner, while in the room with the
therapist, that these feelings are built up. This does not
mean that the therapist becomes supportive or protective.
It does mean that the therapist is convinced that, to be
effective, the therapy hour must not be so divorced from
an everyday life situation that there is no carry-over outside the playroom. She must keep in mind the fact that
successful therapy is release of feeling that goes on to
development of insight that brings about more positive
self-direction.

It is important for the therapist to realize that many times the child's activities while the the playroom would bring forth severe criticism if carried on outside the playroom. Also the therapist must face the fact that the child tends to feel guilty when he kicks the father doll, beats up the mother doll, or smothers a brother or sister doll. To protect the child from possible guilt feelings and to prevent the forming of any misconception in the child's mind as to what might be acceptable behavior, emphasis is placed upon confining the therapy to *play* therapy.

When the child's feelings and attitudes are expressed through his words and play, the experience can be looked at objectively, and both the child and the therapist can accept honestly and completely this verbal and symbolic behavior. If the verbal and symbolic element were removed, certain attitudes and impulses carried into action might not be accepted either by the child or the therapist. Consequently, the limitations that are necessary to achieve these conditions are set up as a prerequisite to satisfactory therapy.

The time element is the most obvious limitation. The appointment is fixed. The length of the play contact is determined and held to. If the appointment is set for one hour from ten to eleven and the child arrives at ten-thirty, the play contact ends at eleven. Certain circumstances, however, might modify even this limitation—if the late arrival was unavoidable. The child or the adult who brings him should realize that the time limit is very real. It does not seem advisable to extend the time at the request of the child. He must come eventually to realize the limits of time, and a consistent adherence to the time limit seems helpful.

The materials in the room are the mediums through which the child expresses his feelings. There are many different types of materials available. If the child feels aggressive, there are toys upon which the child can vent his feelings. His feelings are recognized and the therapist attempts to channel the actions toward the more suitable material.

Suppose the child picked up a heavy block and aimed it at the window. The therapist might say—and she had better speak quickly— "You feel like throwing the block through the window, but you cannot do that. You may throw it down over there, or you may pound on that log, or beat up the clay, but you must not throw it at the window." If the child gets angry because she is attempting to interfere with something that he wants to do, that feeling should be reflected back to him— "You are angry because I said you couldn't do that." If he glares at her and looks as though he would like to throw it at her, there is another feeling that she could recognize— "You are angry with me because I won't let you throw it any place except over there where it won't hurt anything or anybody." The therapist is helping the child to face the problem of adjustment to a realistic world. He will be stopped outside the clinic when he attempts to display such destructive behavior—and not with a reflection of his feelings. It seems as though it would be more of a help to the child to let him face the limitations that human relationships will force upon him than to let him give free rein to destructive *actions*.

When the child expresses his negative feelings against his mother or father or sibling, the mother, father, or sibling is not called into the room and the child permitted to beat her or him. He may use a doll. He gets rid of his feelings on the doll. He beats it. He buries it. He kicks it around. Why, then, shouldn't he get as much satisfaction out of using legitimate outlets for his other feelings? It is the belief of the writer that he gets more relief when his actions are channeled toward the materials that are in the room for that purpose than he would were he allowed to break all the windows in the room, smear the walls as far as he could reach, or throw, and attack the therapist.

Now, what about the child who breaks the limitation? Suppose he aims the block at the window and, although his feeling is recognized and he is told not throw it there, he does so anyway. Usually the recognition of his feeling is sufficient to bring down the block; but suppose this time it doesn't. The therapist should be alert to the possibility that he may not put the block down. She should try to prevent the throwing of the block if she can do so without engaging in a physical battle with the child. But if the block should go through the window, what then? Should she lecture the child? Put him out of the playroom? Or act as though she really didn't care? Such a situation would be a real challenge to the therapist. She could not temporarily shelve her basic principles. She would not reject the child because he disobeyed her. She would stay right there with her reflection of feelings. "It was important to you to throw it anyway. You wanted to show me that you *would* throw it."

It has been pointed out that the materials in the playroom should be as sturdy as possible. Certain materials, however, are breakable. The nursing bottles and the paint jars can be broken and often are—sometimes accidentally and sometimes deliberately. When they are broken accidentally, the therapist should get the glass out of the way for safety's sake as quickly and unobtrusively as possible, recognizing the fact that it was an accident. What should the therapist do when the child deliberately breaks something? Recognize the feeling that prompted the breaking, remove the dangerous glass if it were in the way, and continue the contacts without replacing the broken object? It seems that such a procedure would point up the child's responsibility for his acts. The therapist should exercise care in her attitude and response at such an occurrence so that she does not create feelings of guilt on the part of the child. If she is truly accepting of the child, he will not feel guilty even though he has broken one of the limitations.

Any attack upon the therapist should be stopped immediately. There can be no value in permitting the child to attack the therapist physically. There can be harm in such a practice—and not only to the therapist. The therapeutic relationship, to be a success, must be built around a genuine respect that both the child and therapist have for one another. A child needs a certain amount of control. He is not entirely self-sufficient. The control that is the outgrowth of a mutual respect seems to be far more conducive of good mental attitudes than any other method of control.

The therapy experience is a growth experience. The child is given the opportunity to get rid of his tensions, to clear the air, so to speak, of his troublesome feelings, and by so doing he gains an understanding of himself that enables him to control himself. Through his vivid experiences in the playroom he discovers himself as a person as well as new ways to adjust to human relationships in a healthy, realistic manner.

It is necessary that this experience be anchored to reality in some way. What better way can this be done than by the establishment of common-sense limitations? It is important that the limitations once agreed upon should be consistently followed. Consistency in the playroom is just as vital as consistency in any other relationship. It is the element of consistency that provides the child with a feeling of security. The consistency demonstrated by the therapist assures the child of his acceptance. The consistency of the permissiveness in the situation determines the depth to which the child can go in expressing his feelings.

When should these limitations be presented? Should the therapist explain them when the child comes into the room for the first time? Should she wait until the need for such an explanation arises? Some therapists believe that they should be presented when the child first comes into the playroom so that he will not feel frustrated and betrayed when he runs into a limitation. Others feel that the verbal expression of the limitations might serve as a challenge to a child and focus the attitudes around that. They feel that it might deter certain children from expressing violent or negative feelings for fear of incurring the disapproval of the therapist.

The writer believes that it is better to wait until the need for introducing the limitations arises. Children's everyday experiences usually prepare them for some restrictions upon their actions. If the limitations are kept to a minimum and are brought in only when the need arises, therapy seems to progress more smoothly.

For example, it seems important that a limitation should be placed upon the child's leaving the playroom unless it is necessary to do so. When a child leaves the room, comes back, leaves again, he is evading the therapy and attempting to turn it into some sort of game. In order to emphasize the child's responsibility in the therapy process, it is important that he should understand that, if he leaves the room because he feels bored or angry or stubborn, he cannot return during that particular session. The therapist should not mention this unless the child starts to leave the room. Then she should point out to him why he wanted to leave if she could catch the feeling and then explain to him that if he did leave he would not be able to come again until the next week, or whenever the next therapy period had been arranged. Unless this is done, it is quite possible to turn the therapy hour into a continual going-and-coming type of activity. When it is done, the child realizes that he cannot run out on his responsibility to face his problem unless he is willing to sacrifice the remainder of the play contact. If he is willing to do that, then there seems to be a real need for him to get away from it at this time—he is not ready for therapy. There are exceptions to this which the therapist should meet intelligently and realistically. A sensitive therapist will be able to differentiate between this type of behavior and a real need for the child to leave the room—for example to see if his mother is still there—or to meet some feeling of anxiety.

Care should be taken not to confuse a limitation with a pressure device. There is no desire on the part of the non-directive therapist to exert pressure to bring about change in the child. Any change that is worthwhile comes from within the child. Therefore, the therapist guards against using a limitation to bring a problem into focus. For example, a child who has become a non-talker is never told that he *must talk* when he comes into the room or else he must leave the room. The child who is a feeding problem is not told that he must eat if he wants to come into the playroom. The antisocial child is never told that he must play with the other children if he comes in with a group. These are not honest limitations. They are nothing more than pressure devices brought to bear upon the child who is already under too much pressure. They are, in essence, a bribe and are not worthy of a place in self-directive therapy. The child makes the choice to talk or not to talk. It is *his* problem, not the therapist's problem.

Summing up, it seems that limitations used with intelligence and consistency serve to anchor the therapy session to the world of reality and to safeguard the therapy from possible misconceptions, confusion, guilt feelings, and insecurity. It is the principle that serves as a device by which the child's participation, co-operation, and responsibility can be measured. It is the principle that calls forth all the tact, consistency, honesty, and strength of the therapist. The use of the limitations more or less indicates how far the therapy can proceed between therapist and child.

Application to Group Therapy

Limitations are kept to a minimum in group therapy as in individual therapy. However, they are a necessary part of any therapy and there is more need for the therapist to have a preconceived idea of the limitations to which she will hold the children in a group than there is when she is dealing with one individual. There must be consistency and assurance in the therapist's practice. In this way the children can accept the limitations in a more constructive manner than they would be able to do were the limitations inconsistent and presented to the group in an indecisive manner. Limitations can become a challenge to a group if clumsily handled. They can become a strong and positive help if they are introduced into the play situation naturally and sincerely.

The limitations in regard to destructive, dangerous, and aggressive behavior which were discussed in relation to individual therapy apply also to group therapy. The same applies to the discussion of the time at which such limitations should be introduced. One additional possible limitation is involved in the group situation, that is in regard to physical aggression toward members of the group. Regarding this limitation there are conflicting theories. Some think such aggression is valuable activity so long as the therapist can keep it under control and see that fair play is ever present. Others believe that there is more harm than good in physical attack and that it tends to involve the therapist in a rôle that calls for an assumption of authority and judgment which might at times appear as partiality to a certain member, or members, of the group. It is the opinion of the writer that the ruling-out of physical attack should be one of the limitations of group therapy; but that the introduction of this limitation should not occur until the therapist has evidence that a physical attack is imminent. A light shove or slap might be accepted with no ill effect by the child who receives it, and the introduction of a "limitation speech" from the therapist when such an act occurs might turn the entire attitude of the group into an undesirable channel. If this did happen, however, the negative attitudes should be handled by the therapist. For example, if a child lightly slaps at another who is doing something that was annoying to him, the therapist might reflect, "You didn't like what Jim did and you even slap him for it." If she adds, at this first incident, "But you can't slap him when you are here in the playroom," it might seem to the other children and to Jim that she was becoming protective of Jim. The group might split into factions for and against Jim and the situation might become a challenge to the children in the group to see how far they could go. If the limitation was not mentioned until after a second slapping incident, it would seem to be more acceptable to the group. The therapist would have to be careful to include all the children who had slapped if she felt it necessary to bring it up. For example, "First Bob slapped Jim, and then Jim slapped Bob, because they didn't like what each other was doing. From now on, let's leave out all slaps and pokes. Try to settle your differences of opinion some other way." The tone of voice would be very important in such a case. It should not carry criticism or disapproval. There should be the same acceptance of both children. There should be a calm, firm statement that presents the limitation in such a manner that it becomes a constructive part of the therapy.

PART FOUR

Implications for Education

16.
Practical Schoolroom Application

THE BASIC PRINCIPLES of non-directive therapy seem to have far-reaching implications for educators. The people who are closely associated with the schools today know that the primary need for the successful education of the children is sound mental health for all participants in the educational process.

A teacher whose mind is beset with anxieties, fears, and frustrations cannot do a satisfactory teaching job. A child whose emotional life is in conflict and turmoil is not a satisfactory pupil. If the school has available a therapeutic program, including both counseling facilities for the adults and counseling and play therapy for the children, the school is equipped to treat those individuals who seek help.

There has been marked progress made by the schools in developing techniques to cope with the problems in the mental-health area. There have been volumes written about selection of teachers, curriculum construction and reconstruction, and mental-hygiene programs. Again and again, emphasis is placed upon the old truth that an ounce of prevention is worth a pound of cure. Looking about for the prophylactic measures necessary to prevent serious maladjustment on the part of the pupils, the schools have incorporated in their programs some very admirable developments.

Progressive education places emphasis upon accepting the child as he is and encouraging self-expression. The progressive programs have been tried long enough to enable thoughtful students to evaluate the results. The evaluations indicate that, while progressive education has many advantages over the so-called traditional education, something has been lacking in both in regard to achieving sound mental health for all the pupils.

It seems to the writer that the most important single factor in establishing sound mental health is the relationship that is built up between the teacher and his or her pupils. This is as true in the kindergarten as it is in the high school. It is as true in a traditional set-up as in a progressive program. It is the permissiveness to be themselves, the understanding. the acceptance, the recognition of feelings, the clarification of what they think and feel that helps children retain their self-respect; and the possibilities of growth and change are forthcoming as they all develop insight. The amazing thing about this pattern is the many uses to which it can be put. It seems to be a prerequisite for desirable growth. The implications for this approach (which is the basis for a therapeutic approach) in educational practices are tremendous.

It is in the establishment of this relationship that the basic principles of self-directive therapy loom up into an important position.

A feeling of friendliness and warmth on the part of the teacher will establish the type of rapport between her and a child that will seem to individualize the instruction even though there are forty other pupils in the class. The teacher who has the well-earned reputation of never having smiled in class, nor of having deviated from the lesson plan at hand, is an object of pity and can scarcely be called an educator. It is in such a tense and rigid atmosphere that young nerves explode and emotional storms generate.

When tall, gangling, over-aged May, from the wrong side of the tracks, comes into the classroom, clothed in rags and embarrassment, her mental health is better cared for when the teacher gives her repulsiveness the same smile she might give the daughter of the president of the board of education than if the teacher looks down her nose at May and insultingly asks her why she doesn't *clean up*. In the latter situation, May will feel the freezing rejection. She will not be able to enter into any congenial state of rapport with the teacher. The teacher who seeks to establish good mental health creates warmth and friendliness with each and every pupil.

The teacher will accept each and every child exactly as he or she is. It is a common practice to accept Johnny's left-handedness or Marlene's crossed eyes. And no one expects crippled Jimmy to run races with the other children. Those physical differences are obvious enough to warrant a bit of special consideration. But what about the adolescent whose shyness is sheer torture, but who is "compelled to give a talk in front of the class or fail"? Or the immature first-grader who is put through the beginning reading paces because chronologically he is six; perhaps mentally he is six, but emotionally he is infantile? Or the eight-year-old boy whose family relationships have been so frustrating and who has been so deprived of any feelings of security or of belonging or of a feeling of success that his aggressions take visible and active form in school and he cries out, "I hate school! I hate you! I hate everybody!" Should the teacher accept him as a dynamic individual who is reacting understandably to a bad situation and say to him, "Sometimes you feel that you hate all of us—the school, me, everybody"? Or should she pit her authority against his righteous rebellion and say, "Not another word out of you! And you can stay after school today for your impudence!"?

The teacher will establish a feeling of permissiveness in the relationship so that the child feels free to express his feelings and to be himself. In a therapeutic situation the child expresses his feelings completely. In a schoolroom situation there would of necessity be limits placed upon *complete* expression of feelings. It is in this area that progressive educators have departed to the greatest extent from traditional education. Progressive educators have recognized the value of releasing the feelings of the child in some tangible expression—painting, clay work, creative writing, music, rhythms, drama, free play—all of these mediums are used as an outlet for the child's feelings. It was at this point, too, that many misconceptions of progressive education sprang up. The derisive term, "Let the little dears express themselves," became an insulting by-line for those people who lacked the understanding of child development to appreciate the value of self-expression.

When a teacher applies the basic principles of nondirective therapy to this free expression, she adds something of great importance to it. Free expression is not enough in itself to bring about insight for the child. The therapist-teacher is alert to recognize the *feelings* the child is expressing and reflects those feelings back to the child in such a manner that the child gains insight into his behavior. This can be done to a great extent in any classroom situation if the teacher has an understanding of her pupils and an insight into human behavior. If the therapeutic relationship has been established between pupil and teacher, many children may be helped to gain valuable insight into their problems before the problems become so unwieldy that they create serious maladjustment.

In the adolescent-aged group the feelings are close to the surface. So many, many times the English teacher occupies an enviable position in the school because her subject so readily lends itself to self-expression. For example, Angela, a sixteen-year-old girl, who submerged herself quite successfully in her large classes, handed in an autobiography which served as an instrument of help for her. In this particular class it had become a tradition for the pupils to write their autobiographies, with emphasis upon thoughts and feelings. Parents were encouraged to keep their influence away from the writings so that they would be strictly the child's own efforts. In fact, provisions were made for the children to write them during school time so that the manuscripts would not be influenced in any way by the parents. Several weeks were spent in the preparation of the papers. In this way the pupils had the opportunity to write under differing moods. It was understood that everything in the papers would be held in the strictest confidence by the teacher in charge. Angela poured forth her inner thoughts in her composition. She wrote in part:

I am miserably unhappy. All my life I have been unhappy. My mother doesn't like me. She likes my brother the best. But I think my father likes me. I *adore* my father. Whenever I can, I go places with my father. This makes my mother mad. She is jealous of me. I really believe she is. Sometimes she is cruel to me. Sometimes she even strikes me. I think I sometimes hate my mother. She won't let me grow up. She picks out all my clothes. She wants to know what I am doing all the time. She cross-examines me like I was a criminal. If it wasn't for my father, I would run away.

That was Angela's stormiest paragraph. Angela, tall, blond. extremely reserved. whose attractive mother was very active in the school's child-study organizations— Angela whose life had seemed so ideal and happy. who had everything that money could buy—Angela. the best-dressed girl in the class. She had never been interested in boys She seemed to mature slowly.

It was also customary to have a pupil-teacher conference following these autobiographies, going over them for literary merit and mechanical construction It was a wise teacher who handled Angela's composition. She did not give way to the "I-was-so-surprised-You-have-such-a-lovely-mother" reaction. She picked out the feelings and reflected them to back to Angela "You really are very unhappy. Angela. and you don't believe your mother likes you as well as she does your brother—is that it?" Angela, accepted for what she was. poured out more of her feelings and the teacher continued to go along with Angela. hoping that by this help the girl would gain some insight into her feelings and attitudes and would be able to work through her problem and achieve a constructive solution.

Angela wasn't the only one in the class who had troublesome feelings to release. Strangely enough. the students looked forward to the eleventh-grade English class under Miss X. It was an academic instrument that truly taught the pupils to know themselves.

In the first-grade class. tiny Charlene, a very bright little girl. whose ambitious mother has pushed her almost to the limit, waves her hand frantically when the teacher says, "Today let's write about some of the things that makes us angry. Who wants to dictate a story now?" And while the other children go about their business of being children, drawing, painting, modeling clay, playing in the sand, playing with toys, or whatever they have chosen to do, Charlene dictates her story with a glowering expression on her pretty face.

> My brother makes me so mad. He is always hitting me. And Eleanor, too. I get so mad when I have to throw flowers at weddings. I want to carry them, not throw them down on the ground. My daddy always scares me with his slipper. If I don't do *everything* everybody tells me to do! My big sister scares me, too. She slaps me right in the face. And John knocked me down, once. And there is so much work to do. I get so tired. Another thing that makes me mad —I can't write to 300. Only to 200, and mamma makes me write it all the time at home. I can't go out and play until I write to 300. 300 what? I never know. And the reader is too hard and too heavy. I'm so small I can't even reach into our sink and get a drink out of it without asking somebody to get me a drink. My mother always feeds me, too, like when we have chicken noodles and I don't like chicken noodles and she makes me eat them and when I won't she holds me and forces the spoon of old noodles down my throat and I just hate being me!

This is quite a vehement protest against the pressures that are bearing down on her. As the teacher writes down the words, she reflects the expressed feelings back to Charlene. "The big people at home scare you- -daddy with his slipper, and Eleanor when she slaps you, and you just hate being so much smaller than they are." Encouraged Charlene goes on, "And John knocked me down, once!" John is the faithful little boy friend and this is a grievous thing that he has done to Charlene. "And even *John* knocked you down once," the teacher says. Then Charlene complains about the school work—reflecting the pressure to which her ambitious mother subjects her. All through the dictation the teacher accepts Charlene's reaction, reflects back her expressed feelings. This is an outlet for her tensions. Given such an opportunity to get these feelings out in the open, there is far less chance for them to accumulate and become so far removed from reality that they cause serious blockings. Charlene would not be considered a maladjusted child, but the tensions, pressures, and repressed feelings could be a contributing factor to maladjustment. Prophylactic treatment has distinct value.

Other children in the same class also were eager to dictate their stories. There was nothing compulsory about it. If a child had something to say, here was the opportunity. Seven-year-old John had a story, too.

It makes me mad when my mother whips me and my brother does the same things I do and she doesn't whip him. When we go to the store I try to get my little brother lost in the store. He is littler than me and you know how big those big stores are? When I ask my mother and father for something and they won't let me have it I get so mad. Like when my cousin comes over and I ask for their cards so we can play a game and they say no. When they whip me I start crying. I just yell. Loud as I can, I yell. And they make me go to bed. Then I stop all of a sudden and I play with a marble or my dice that I have hidden in my bed and she said, "Listen. He's completely satisfied in there," and daddy says, "You get up, then," and I got to get up. Yesterday I made Joey so mad. He had a little bottle of water with a cork in it and he was hammering it up and down on the ground and I kept saying, "Hit it harder, Joey. Hit it harder!" and he did until finally it broke and he just cried! Then he got a bottle of bluing and I went outside when I first came home from school and I got a crock of sand and I kept saying, "Pour some in here, Joey," and he did and I kept saying, "More. Some more!" until finally he was all out of bluing and then I laughed at him for being such a fool as to let me get it all away from him and he cried and my mother *yelled* at *me* and *slapped me* and gave *him* some more bluing and I got mad. She said I was took-ing advantage of Joey, but I said Joey was a dumb squeak and she made me come in and sit on a chair and I got so mad and then I cried, too, *'cause she is nicer to Joey than she is to me.*

A reflection that John was unhappy because Mother paid more attention to Joey than she did to him seems as though it would be more help to John than to point out that he *was* taking advantage of two-year-old Joey. As John pours out his feelings his eyes shine. He smiles when he relates just how he got the best of Joey. His face sobers when the teacher says, "You wish your mother would pay as much attention to you as she does to Joey." Then he adds, as an afterthought, "I was the onliest child for a long time," and there is a wistfulness in his voice that indicates that John's feelings have been hurt by the little brother's advent.

Jimmy's story is very brief:

> Grown-up people make me sick. They're always whipping you. That's what *she* does to me. They make you go to bed early before it gets dark. My mom won't let me play in our yard 'cause she planted old grass seed, so I either don't play or I go away and play and then I get the devil.

And Carl scowls as he dictates:

> When I'm making something and have it half done and my dad comes down and says, "That's not the way to do it," and then he takes it and does it *his* way, I get so mad. He messes it all up and I don't want it then.

The theme varies. Sometimes the children are asked if they have anything to dictate about *Things I Am Afraid of*, or *I Wish I Was Somebody Else*, or *Things I Like and Things I Hate*, or *Things I Wish I Could Do*. The possibilities are great.

A wise teacher will take advantage of the veritable mine of materials in her classroom. Instead of having the children copy "cat-rat-mat-sat-fat-bat-hat," the children could be encouraged to write their own stories and express *their feelings*. Emphasis again is placed upon reflection of the expressed feelings back to the children, and complete acceptance of any feeling the children might express. There is value in catharsis—the outpouring of feelings; but the addition of reflection of feeling and acceptance is the added element that helps to clarify the feelings and helps the child to develop insight.

A second-grade girl whose mother had deserted her family wrote:

> I like my mother. I love my mother. My mother is very pretty. My mother is bad. Father says she is bad. But I *love* my mother.

Downtrodden Mike, aged seven, writes:

> My mother likes my brother. My mother does not like me. My father likes my brother. My father does not like me. Everybody likes my brother. Everybody does not like me. I hate everybody, too.

In this instance, "brother" is a blond, dimpled darling, aged two.

This joyous, second-grade youngster cries out with her clumsy pencil:

> I can write. I can write. I can write. I can write like my brother. I can write like my father. I can write like my mother. I will not be a baby again.

And the plaintive wail of seven-year-old Lynn is heart-breaking, even though it is so common.

> My mother wants me to go to school. My father wants me to go to school. Grandmother wants me to go to school. Grandfather wants me to go to school. Aunt Flora wants me to go to school. They all want me to go to school. They have a new baby at home.

The teacher can help these children by recognizing the feelings they are expressing and reflecting those feelings back to the children. It does help the child to achieve insight and understanding. It gets the feelings out in the open. It helps to prevent an accumulation of repressed feelings.

Art materials are also adaptable to this type of experience. Charlie, the eight-year-old "problem child," makes a clay coffin with a clay man in it. "I'll put a lid on it, too. I'll close it down tight. Now he can't breathe." The teacher comments, "You don't like him. You'll put him in the box and put the lid on so tight that he can't breathe." Charlie glances at the teacher. He presses the lid down even tighter. "He was so drunk last night and he beat me with his strap. Look!" He exhibits a black-and-blue mark on his leg. "You're getting even because he beat you up," said the teacher. "Yes," Charlie muttered. "I'll fix him." And Charlie did "fix him."

Henry drew a funny picture. It was shaped like a man, but it had the face and tail of a hog. He showed it to the teacher as she walked by. "This is a bad man. He said I ate like a hog. Now look at him. He is a hog himself." Henry retaliates for the insult someone had given him.

Instead of drawing forty identical landscapes or carrots or daisies, the children should be free to make their own pictures, express their own ideas and feelings. Even the child who sits there in passivity receives more help from the teacher who comments, "You are having a hard time thinking of something of your own to draw," than from the teacher who briskly says, "Draw a rabbit," or "Here, let me start you!" and sketches a beginning for the child who seems to lack initiative and who will never develop initiative until he is permitted to stand on his own two feet and initiate his own activity. Imposed activities do not foster self-initiative in anyone.

To illustrate further the way in which a child uses this art material for catharsis, and to demonstrate how the child progresses from very negative and destructive feelings to positive and constructive feelings, Ernest's painting experience is related.[1]

At this one time he painted four large pictures, quickly and dramatically. The first picture was a green and purple mountain. "Look," said Ernest to the teacher who was standing near-by, "it's a mountain. Everybody stay away from here."

"You want everyone to stay away from your mountain," the teacher replied.

Ernest nodded. Then he called two other boys over to him. "Come, Ronny. Come, Tommy. Help me." The two boys came over to him and watched while he painted an airplane flying over the mountain. Then he covered the airplane with a smear of red.

"Gee," said Ronny. "Look how Ernest blew up that Zero."

"Yes. Look!" said Ernest.

"They all died, I bet," said Tommy.

"They sure did," Ernest said. "That red you saw was fire and blood."

Ernest handed this painting to the teacher and painted

another picture of an airplane flying low over a purple mountain. He added something else to this picture.

"What's that?" Tommy and Ronny asked. There was no answer.

"It's a siren, I bet," said Ronny.

"It is not," Ernest replied.

"Then what is it?" asked Ronny.

"It is a sign of the enemy. It is a Jap sign."

"Aw," Ronny replied, "it is not."

"I ought to know," Ernest replied. "These are enemies. All these are my enemies." Once more he smeared the red across the airplane.

"Whose airplane is it?" asked Tommy.

"I am in there," Ernest said. "My enemies are all trying to hurt me. They are throwing fire at me." He handed this painting to the teacher.

"These enemies of yours are trying to hurt you," said the teacher.

"They *are* hurting me," Ernest said seriously.

He started a third picture immediately.

"This is another mountain. Help me. Here, Tommy. You do what I do. You, too, Ronny." The boys took brushes and imitated Ernest. They painted another mountain, using first white paint, then going over it with green, purple, orange, red, brown and, lastly, with black. Ernest again painted the airplane, smeared it with red paint. The boys made airplane noises and machine-gun noises. The picture became a smear. The paint was applied with free, swooping gestures. There was much laughter and shouting. Then Ernest cried out, "Look! Look! It blew up the whole world. It blew up the whole world and everybody in the world. And this airplane is on fire." The teacher standing beside them recognized the aggressive feelings. When this picture was finished, he handed it to the teacher and took another large sheet of paper. He cried out, "Let's make another mountain."

"A great big high mountain," said Tommy.

"Come on, Bill. Come on, Bobby. Come on, Anna. Want to help?" They did—following Ernest's directions, painting what he painted. Any observer of this activity could not fail to notice the children's intense reaction to this experience. It had great significance for them all. What it meant to each of them is a matter of conjecture, but it did have meaning for each participant.

"Isn't this a high mountain?" Ernest commented. "So very, very high. You know what this is going to be?"

"A very, very high mountain," said the teacher.

"White, then green, then purple, then red. Look, Anna, red. Now orange, then yellow, then blue. Oh, look! It is turning black!" exclaimed Ernest, with obvious delight.

"The colors mixed together like that turn black," said the teacher.

"It is smoke," said Ernest. "And it is dark. But look at the airplane. It is on fire. It is the enemy. See? I ruined them. See? There are no more enemies! And look at the mountain."

"Did you blow up the mountain, too?" asked Tommy.

"No. See? The mountain is safe. This is *my* mountain. It is all mine. Nobody but me can get up there!" said Ernest.

"The mountain is a safe place for you. It is all yours and nobody can get up there but you," said the teacher.

Ernest seemed very cheerful and happy. This last picture had more form and neatness than the others.

The following day Ernest painted another picture. A picture of a bright yellow sun and yellow flowers and across the picture in yellow he wrote, "Spring is here. Spring is here. The sun shines." Then, turning to the teacher, he said, "This is a happy, sunny picture. Remember the ones I painted yesterday? This picture is different."

"Yes. This is a happy picture," the teacher said. "Not a bit like the ones you did yesterday."

It seemed as though Ernest had painted something yesterday that had troubled him. He had achieved a certain amount of release from the painting experience and seemed to have achieved a feeling of security and relaxation. The pictures were graphic illustrations of the child's feelings, going from chaos and turmoil to orderliness and a more positive attitude.

Even a primary arithmetic lesson can give expression to some secret longings or to a child's feelings. They can make up their own problems, stories that use a growing number sense.

"I have twenty-nine marbles," says Joe. "Blue ones, red ones, and yellow ones. And I give away one marble. How many do I have left?"

"You're selfish," interrupts Jack, "keeping twenty-eight and giving away one."

"Well," says Joe defensively, "I might give Jimmy some."

"I wouldn't be like that," says Carl. "I have ten cookies and keep one and give away all the others. How many do I give away?"

"Nine," chorus the children. "I like you, Carl. You're my friend."

"I have *three hundred* marbles," Joe says again, "and I *keep all* of them."

"Joe is a pig," Jack says.

"I'm not a pig," says Joe. "I'll have marbles when you have given away *all* yours."

"Jack thinks it is selfish to keep all the marbles for himself," says the teacher, "but Joe thinks that if he keeps all of them, then he'll be sure and have some when he wants them."

"He might lose the whole bag," Carl says. "If he plays with them in school, maybe they'll all be tooken away from him."

There isn't just arithmetic here. In fact, some may say that there isn't any arithmetic at all. Place the combinations on flash cards, some say, and cut out all the foolishness. But the very nature of the child cries out against such stupid procedure. You cannot divorce learning from life. The child is a dynamic, forceful being. He should not be placed in a groove. Give the child an opportunity to function as an individual. Give him freedom and responsibility and a feeling of success.

A school curriculum that is worthy of a place in our educational system provides an opportunity to enrich the child's life far beyond the academic requirements. True education does not turn back to the critical needs of the individual. A teacher is more than a dispenser of facts and a tester of accumulated knowledge. It is not enough to hear lessons recited and to "maintain order" in a class-

room. Rather, it is the obligation of the teacher to develop
sufficient insight and understanding and interest in the
human beings that come before her so that they will all
know not only subject matter, but themselves and others a
little better. This does not mean that there is at any time
license or a lessening of educational standards. It is merely
pointing out the proved fact that the individual to be truly
educated must be considered a person entitled to respect
and understanding and the opportunity to develop to his
fullest capacities.

These examples have been related to demonstrate the
possibilities of releasing feelings when conditions are
created that are conducive to obtaining the child's confi-
dences. Any teacher who has admitted life into her classroom can recount examples of her own. There are many
avenues down which the pupils and teachers can travel
together which bring about this desired state of mental
hygiene that is a necessary foundation for growth.

The responsibility to make choices and to institute
change should be the child's as often as it is possible to
make it so. In a therapeutic situation this is a basic
principle. In a classroom situation it is possible and desirable, but, because of the limitations of a school situation,
must be modified.

In maintaining discipline in a classroom, these therapeutic principles are indispensable if it is the objective of the
teacher to carry along the educative process even through
the use of punishment rather than to use punishment as a
purely retributive act. If the rules of expected behavior in
a classroom are clearly and consistently drawn up and the
child is given an opportunity to act in the classroom like
an intelligent individual, this type of treatment becomes a
technique by which the child may develop self-reliance,
dependability, and initiative. What teacher has not at one
time or another had under her guidance the obstreperous
type of child whose outward aggressiveness creates a problem that demands immediate action? No thinking teacher
will stand idly by and watch the child either knock down
and drag out his opponent or behave in a similar fashion
without attempting to do something about it. "Bob is
feeling tough today. He thinks that if he uses force, he can
get to the head of the line. But our rules, Bob, say that

you will either take your turn fairly or get out of the line," one teacher might say. Bob then makes his choice. He either abides by the rules or he gets out. That either-or attitude is certainly not new. The added element is the reflection on the part of the teacher of the attitudes that Bob is expressing. Perhaps this borders on interpretation, but this seems obvious enough to risk it. If the teacher is wrong, Bob will correct her. Perhaps with a remark like this, "But *he* took my hat and he's got it under his coat right now." And the teacher comes back with the comment, "So you're trying to get even with Bill." And perhaps Bill and Bob both find themselves at the end of the line. Finding themselves at the end of the line may not have been the boys's direct choice, but the school rule was a limitation that they met realistically. They either kept the rule or they took the consequences. The teacher tried to bring into the situation an insight into their behavior.

Arguments and differences of opinion between children are easily controlled and settled in the same way. A teacher becomes an arbitrator, pointing out the way George feels and the way Malcolm feels, drawing into focus reasons for the conflict. When Malcolm picks up a vicious-looking stick and raises it to strike George, the teacher can effectively stop the blow if she remarks, "Malcolm is angry enough to try to use violence to settle the argument." Malcolm puts down the weapon and resorts once more to words. This has been demonstrated with therapy groups as well as in actual school situations. Therefore, it is apparent that it was the remark which stopped the blow and not the presence of the teacher as a symbol of authority, because in a group-therapy situation the therapist does not at any time become a symbol of authority. Anyone who really knows children is aware of the fact that a fight that is postponed by the voice of authority is usually completed when the participants are out of sight.

When a teacher respects the dignity of a child, whether he be six or sixteen, and treats the child with understanding, kindliness, and constructive help, she is developing in him an ability to look within himself for the answers to his problems, and to become responsible for himself as an independent individual in his own right.

Possibly the greatest contribution that educators can make to the younger generation is the type of guidance that places the emphasis upon self-initiative and transmits to the young people by living example the fact that each individual is responsible for himself. In the final analysis, it is the ability to think constructively and independently that marks the educated man. Growth is a gradual process. It cannot be hurried. It comes from within the individual and cannot be imposed by force from without.

It is the relationship that exists between the teacher and her pupils that is the important thing. The teacher's responses must meet the real needs of the children and not just the material needs—reading, writing, arithmetic.

It sounds so easy. An experimental teacher is anxious to try it out. The first day of school arrives. In comes the flock of little folks just starting to school; and, in this particular neighborhood culture, in come their mothers, too. Most of them greet the teacher, say good-bye to little Johnny or Mary, and take their departure. But maybe there is a little Oliver in the midst who tearfully hangs on to his mother's hand. The law says he is old enough to be in school now, but his feelings tell him that this is all a dreaful mistake. What should the teacher do? Drift over to his mother and say, "How do you do, Mrs. Oliver," and then dismiss her? Should she take little Oliver's hand (or try to) and speak to him very gently and understandingly. "Oh, you'll just love it here, Oliver. All the nice little boys and girls. You're a big boy now. You're not going to cry." (Oh, isn't he?) "Won't Oliver have a good time here, boys and girls?"

"Yes, Miss So-and-so!"

"Come look at the pretty picture books. See? Mary and Johnny are looking at the picture books. Come. You want to look at them, too." Then, in an aside to his mother, "We really prefer that the mothers not stay when they bring the children. Just to avoid this sort of thing, you know." Mother gets up and dutifully tries to desert her child. He howls. The teacher turns away with disapproval *par excellence*.

Or suppose Mrs. Oliver lived in the other end of town and the school set-up wasn't so progressive. In dragged

Oliver, tears and all. Teacher met him at the door. "You're in school now," she says, "stop that crying. If you don't stop this minute, you'll have to go home!" Oliver is an idiot if he doesn't increase his sobs. Mrs. Oliver takes the culprit home and confides in her husband, "I was so ashamed I could have cried. There were all those other children there. And Oliver acted like a little nut. Do you suppose we ought to take him to a psychologist?" Well, she ought at least to take herself to one!

Suppose Mrs. Oliver took him to still another school. The teacher in this school was going to try a very simple approach to this problem. Tearful Oliver is just the same; so is his mother. In they come. This teacher greets them, invites the mother in quite cordially. Oliver clings to her. "You're afraid your mother will leave you; but she'll stay with you until you want her to go." Mrs. Oliver blushes. "He's just such a baby," she says apologetically. "Some children are afraid when they first start to school. It is quite an experience for them," says the teacher. "Yes. I expect it is," says the mother. She notices the other children, already playing and adjusting to the situation. She can't help but wonder why they are getting along so much easier than her Oliver. In the meantime, Oliver has been assured. He is being accepted exactly as he is. This strange woman certainly hit the nail on he head when she said he was scared. There are some other children over there playing with some blocks. Maybe he might—— He looks about, fearful lest someone is lurking about to exert pressure. No one bothers him. The first thing anyone knows, Oliver is edging over to the group. Mother edges over to the teacher. "Should I slip away now?" she asks fearfully. "You wonder if you should slip away now that he isn't looking," reflects the teacher. "He might set up an awful howl," says Mother; "but do you want me to?" "You do as you really think you should. As far as I am concerned, you're perfectly welcome to stay, and it's perfectly all right to leave when you're ready."

Well, any mother who has kept her little Oliver so dependent will either go back and sit down or she will go over and say good-bye to him. She will not sneak out on him.

Yes, the therapeutic principles have implications for educators. They bring forth unbelievable results. Teachers are invited to try them out, if they haven't already done so many, many times.

One day a little first-grader said to his teacher, "I just love to hit people and bite them and scratch them and hurt them. I *like* to make kids cry!" Another teacher chanced to overhear this remark. She said later to the boy's teacher, "Now I've heard everything. Why, if that child stood there and told me that he liked to hit people and bite them and make them cry, I'd have told him what I thought of him!"

"But Pete was complimenting our relationship," said Pete's teacher. "He was telling me the most unflattering things that he could about himself. Soon he will be able to go on to more positive ways of thinking."

"You mean it's a compliment to have a child tell you exactly what he thinks?" said the skeptic, with more than just a trace of derision edging her voice.

The next day she stopped Pete's teacher. "Say, I tried that technique of yours," she said.

"What happened?" Pete's teacher inquired.

"You know that ornery, sulky Jacob in my room? Well, as he came in my room this morning, I reached down and grabbed him by the shoulder, and I said, 'Look here, Jacob, tell me just what you think of me.' And Jacob stared at me blank as ever. 'I mean it,' I said. 'I won't do a thing to you no matter what you say.' And Jacob growled and said, 'I think you're *crazy* if you think I'd tell you what I think of *you!*'" And Jacob's teacher laughed heartily. "Not so bad for a first try, is it?"

17.

Application to Parent-Teacher Relationships

THE SAME ACCEPTANCE of parents and a reflection of the attitudes and feelings that they express, plus an opportunity freely to express themselves are also important in establishing parent-teacher relationships. For example, the mother of six-year-old Robert had her share of troubles, in addition to having one of the school's most difficult problem children on her hands. She was an attractive young widow. One day she came rushing over to the school and said to the teacher, "I've just got to see you! Have you the time? I've got to talk to someone. I don't know who else to talk to like this." The teacher invited her in. "There is no use beating around the bush," said the mother, "I'm so mad I could die."

"Something has upset you," said the teacher.

"My boss told me today he was sick and tired of the way I worried about Robert. I come home at noon and I'm late getting back. And I worry so about him. He said that I would have to make up my mind to attend more to my work or else! Well, he did give my job to another girl. I thought she was a friend of mine. He transferred me over to the other office. Why, I've been the boss's stenographer for years! Now they tell me to come in for part-time work only. After all my years down there!"

"You're hurt at losing your job after all your years of work with that company," said the teacher.

"I was never so mad in my life," said Robert's mother. "I just walked right out and here I am. He was mad, too."

"You were both angry," commented the teacher.

"He said for me to put Robert in a Children's Home. He said Robert needed to be ruled by an iron hand. He said that Robert was ruining my life. What should I do? Should I put him in a Children's Home?"

"You don't know whether to put him in a Home or not," said the teacher. "You would like to have me tell you; but I can't answer that for you."

"He would get good care. I could get my old job back then," said the mother.

"You think that would solve the job problem," commented the teacher.

"Yes," the mother responded. She flung her arms around despairingly. "But I would just *die!* He's my whole life. I told the boss I would have to take a jug to bed with me and drown my sorrow and he's so strait-laced that he had a fit." She laughed.

"You thought you would shock the boss."

"I did, too. The Home that he wants me to put Robert in is over in S——. It is a nice place. He would get good care. They feed them well, and keep them clean."

"You would be sure that he was getting good care."

"And there wouldn't be this shifting about with the help all the time. He would get a chance to stay with the same person long enough to get acquainted."

"You think that staying with the same person would help him," reflected the teacher.

"Yes. But gosh! I'd miss him so. He's so afraid of new people and new places. He'd——" Her voice trailed off into silence.

"You think you would miss him and would remember how afraid he was of new people and places."

"Yes. My God! I'll just move over to S—— if I put him there. I'll show my boss. He can't do this to me. I'll stay near enough in case Robert needs me or gets sick or something."

"You'll get even with the boss. If he makes you give up Robert, you'll make him lose a good stenographer."

"Yes. I can get a dozen jobs. I've got A-1 training. Gosh, this hurts. I'm not young any more. I'm thirty-two. And I've got responsibilities."

"This really hurts you. You feel they really owe you something. You have given them years of good service and you're older now and have responsibilities."

"It's really because I was out last week when Robert had the measles. Oh, I can see *his* point. We have the catalogue to get out and the schedules are already made out and my absence did ball up the works. But to do *this* to me!"

"You think the punishment is more severe than you deserve—although you admit the boss does have a point."

"Yes. But tell me. Do you think Robert is getting any better? His behavior, I mean. I realize now that he can't learn to read and write and do arithmetic now. I don't worry about that any more. If he just acts better!"

"You think adjustment is more important right now than trying to force reading."

"Yes," said the mother. "He is better. I can see it. Even at home. And he's got so much to put up with, I'm so nervous. I make him nervous. It's really my fault that he acts the way he does. It wouldn't be right to put him away when it's really my fault and he is showing so much improvement."

"You can see a big improvement in him," said the teacher.

"My, yes! Don't you?"

"He is much better in school."

"It wouldn't be right to put him away in a Home. Not when he is trying so hard. He needs me and he needs a home."

"You don't think it would be fair to put him in a Home now that he is showing so much improvement. And you think he needs you. You think he would be better off with you."

"Yes." She held up a package that she carried in her hand. "See this? It's a rabbit. One of the girls at the office brought it down to me. The other girls pointed out that the office cat was missing. So I don't know. Maybe this is the cat!" She laughed. Then, after more small talk and thanks, she left.

A few days later, during the noon hour, the mother came back to the school, with smiles all over her face.

"I just came in to let you know I got my old job back."

"That's good," said the teacher.

"I told the boss what you said."

"What I said?"

"I told him that you didn't think it would be right to put Robert in a Home. He is so much better. And besides, it's been my fault that he acts like he does. He's been jerked here and there and never knew just what to expect. I told the boss that if Robert went to S—— I would move over there and get a job. I felt that Robert needs me and I know damn well that I need Robert. I couldn't do anything if I went around feeling guilty all the time."

The mother had summarized her own feelings and had reached her own decision. It is interesting to note that the mother had resisted the boss's decision to put the boy in the Home. Given an opportunity to get her feelings out in the open and to make her own decision in this case, she was able to state her case to the boss in such a manner that she not only kept her child but also regained her former job. This served as a starting point for the mother. She continued to use the teacher as a sounding board for her feelings and attitudes and achieved considerable insight into Robert's behavior, and continued to seek more constructive methods of dealing with him. She made a point of providing him with the feelings of security that he needed.

This type of help seems to be of more value than the usual teacher responses of either a dictatorial or a complete-agreement policy. There is a vast difference between complete agreement and an accurate reflection of the client's expressed feeling.

18.
Application to Teacher-Administrator Relationships

An examination of our present school systems would reveal an appalling number of indications of poor mental health among the teachers. Why is it that so many teachers show signs of frustrations and anxieties? The teachers would answer that quickly. It is because, in many instances, they find the teaching situations contributing factors to their maladjustments.

Teachers *are* human, even though cartoonists and wiseacres have considered them their stock in trade for years. (The teachers in the privacy of their pedagogical world are also quite apt in caricaturing their public—and have done so for years.) But there is a reason for the predominance of the very real problem of poor mental health among teachers. It has been attributed to a variety of reasons—large classes, heavy schedules, extra duties, pressures from administrators and taxpayers.

Although all of these factors are irritating and aggravating and nerve-racking, they do not seem adequate to cause all the trouble that is attributed to them. It seems highly probable that the causes for teachers' maladjustment are the same as those for the maladjustment of any other person. If it is true that all individuals have within them the one basic drive for complete self-realization, then it is quite possible that those circum-

stances which block this drive are the causes of the
maladjustment.

Perhaps the domineering, sarcastic teacher, who has
the reputation of being a hellion, is attempting to establish her self-esteem and self-realization at the expense of
her pupils because she cannot achieve direct satisfaction
of this drive in her professional relationship with the
administration. Perhaps the queer, timid little soul, who
acts like a scared rabbit and seems to be at every one's
mercy, can achieve self-realization only by withdrawing
into her protective shell and realizing her self-concept in
her dreams.

There is a definite need for each teacher to feel like a
person, to be treated with dignity and respect, to be
permitted to achieve her rightful status as an intelligent,
capable individual. In far too many school systems the
teachers are denied these fundamental needs. They are
told what to do and how to do it and when to do it.
They are driven by pressures from the higher-ups. There
are goals of achievement set for them. They are forced
to compete with one another and with outside school
forces. They are in many instances treated with a de-
plorable lack of consideration. One would never think,
in some situations, that the teacher was capable, intelligent human being who was worthy of the job that she
was hired to fill. In some communities the teachers are
told how to behave outside the classroom as well as
in the classroom, what to do in their spare time, what
church to attend, what vote to cast, what newspaper to
read, what kind of clothes to wear, what color of nail
polish to use, what cosmetics to leave off their faces.

They are forced to participate in many activities that
absorb all their spare time. They are assigned yard duty
and expected to be "out on duty" in any kind of weather
regardless of how they feel. They are assigned lunchroom
duty and deprived of even a free hour for their lunch.
They are given bus duty and required to stay for long
periods of time after school waiting for the last bus to take
its departure. They are told "to give school plays" and
battle through hours of rehearsals, costuming activities,
ticket-selling, and eventually play production.

They are called upon "to put over" paper drives,

popcorn sales, field days, and every other kind of activity the human mind is able to dream up. And through it all they are required to meet certain educational standards for their pupils and to maintain quiet and order in their classrooms.

On the one hand, they are compelled to overstimulate the pupils and, on the other, they are required to keep them calm and studious. All this seems to be a part of the colorful, dynamic atmosphere of some of the American schools of today—some, not all.

This might seem like enough stress and strain to cause even the stoutest one among them to break under it; but the significant fact remains that in many schools, even though there are all of these pressures of so many things to do and so little time in which to do them, there is not necessarily a correlation of poor mental health and an overcrowded program. There are some schools that do not have any of these "extras," and in an idle atmosphere some teachers are miserable, unhappy, maladjusted.

The teachers sometimes bring their problems with them—problems that have been built up definitely apart from the school situation; but some problems seem to be caused by the school situation, and it is the purpose of the writer to try and throw some light on the contributing cause and offer some constructive suggstions for the prevention or correction of them.

Teachers can and do carry extremely heavy loads— large classes, long hours, extra duties—and do it cheerfully and well *if* the morale of the school is good and if they are treated like human beings, given the permissiveness to express themselves, to utilize their capacities to the fullest, to participate in the school organization as a contributing member, to function as a *thinking*, dependable, trustworthy person. If they are permitted freedom of choice as to what they will do and say inside the classroom as well as outside the classroom, they will carry more adequately their responsibilities toward their pupils. If a teacher cannot be trusted to use good judgment in what she says and does when given this permissiveness to be herself, then she should not be employed as a teacher. If teachers are given the freedom to realize their self-concepts, the public will reap the reward of an enriching and stimulating contribution from the men and women who have chosen to live and work with young people.

The most important factor in establishing good mental health among teachers is the relationship that exists between them and the administrators. The principal is in a strategic position to offer real help to the teachers, the parents, and the pupils. Such help pays sufficient dividends to warrant further investigation in order to determine its effectiveness.

This country is a democracy, and democracy is a way of life. Therefore, it seems consistent to request a democratic procedure in school administration. No one person in any school system has all the answers. It is by planning and working together that each person comes to feel a sense of adequacy and fulfillment and, by helping to shape the policies and procedures, grows to feel a personal responsibility for them. These feelings have come from the experience of working together for the common good. They have come from within the individuals and have not been arbitrarily superimposed from without. Freedom and responsibility are balanced in a true democracy, and the freedom of a spontaneous creative intellect can do much to build up the schools so that they can be a true extension of a dynamic and functioning democracy.

"Yes," it is agreed, "democratic procedure in school administration is desirable and we are striving to attain it." And in a teachers' meeting what happens? Do the teachers actively participate in the planning? Do they set up their objectives and the criteria for the evaluation of them? Are they granted the permissiveness to express their true feelings about conditions as they exist and are their feelings accepted impartially? Is the teachers' meeting really a place for the co-operative airing of ideas? Or is it the usual kind, where the teachers sit in bored silence and dream away while the principal reads bulletin one, bulletin two, bulletin three, bulletin four, bulletin five, and so on until the meeting ends?

When something new in the way of educational practice is being considered for adoption, who decides the merits of it? Are the teachers given the opportunity to examine it, discuss it, evaluate it, and either accept or reject it? Or is it shoved down their throats?

When pressure is applied, as it is in many school systems, to "modernize" the school programs, then the tensions and frustrations are increased. Examine the usual "in-service-training" approach. The very nature of the approach usually blocks any desired progress. The impression is usually quite subtly conveyed that these teachers gathered together represent the prize group of old fossils on the public payroll. The pressure is put on like mad. Change! Change! Change! They hear it until they are blue in the face. In the more enlightened areas it is called "transition." "The schools are in transition. Why not you?" The teachers become panicky. Their feelings of security vanish. Their feelings of self-esteem and a sense of belonging disappear. And quite possibly they feel that no one loves them. They have theories and devices crammed down their throats and people think it strange that they choke on them.

Here, too, acceptance of them *as they are,* recognition of their feelings, and reflection of what they think and feel, help them retain their self-respect, and the possibilities of growth and change and self-direction in more positive ways are forthcoming as they develop insight.

How can this be accomplished? It has been mentioned before that the principal is in a strategic position to help the teachers work through their feelings. Suppose a school system decides to adopt a new type of reading instruction. The superintendent can make the decision and authoritatively see that it is carried out. Recalcitrant teachers can be punished effectively in several ways. They can be transferred to a less desirable school or class. They can be flogged with sarcasm and belittling words. They can be "coerced into co-operation." They can have the new system superimposed upon them and they can fight it every inch of the way. A keen superintendent or principal would realize that forced teaching would be most ineffective. Good teaching is the product of an enthusiastic and sincerely interested teacher. Those attitudes are not acquired by force.

Suppose that the superintendent felt that the new method was worth a trial. Suppose he wanted the best efforts of his teachers behind the project. Then it seems he might find it profitable to discuss the problem with the teachers frankly and honestly and ask for their co-operation participation in setting up the program, in following it through, and then in evaluating its effectiveness. If they are permitted to participate actively, to put something of themselves into it, to feel the responsibility that would go with their freedom to develop it, then their enthusiasm and interest would be there. And if any teacher felt antagonism toward the intrusion of this new element, the superintendent should not reject her for her disagreement or the expression of her negative feelings, but should accept her, give her an opportunity to express more of her feelings to him, and if he were able to do an adequate job of reflecting the emotionalized attitudes in back of her negativism, he might be able to help her achieve helpful insight and more satisfaction in her position.

The possibility of group therapy for the teachers is one which is well worth further investigation. This would call for a leader who had acquired skill in reflecting the emotionalized attitudes that were expressed by members of the group, a leader who would not express any personal feelings while he was leader, so that *one neutral person* would be present at each meeting. During these group sessions every member of the group should feel free to express his feelings completely, to get them out in the open where he could examine them for what they are, to objectify them, and gain some insight into the problems that cause them. The meeting should offer an opportunity to air any irritations that might be felt between teachers or between teacher and principal, any feeling in regard to the administration—in fact, anything that any member of the group cares to bring up. The success of such a meeting would depend upon the integrity of the members of the group, for each member must feel confident that nothing he says will ever be used against him. Such a condition is possible only in those school situations where the administrators are big enough and honest enough to face their problems squarely—where they accept the individual as he is, respect him, and grant him the right to be himself.

If this sort of relationship were established within the schools, it seems possible to predict that there would result a better state of mental health among the teachers than now exists in those places where the teacher is little more than a checker to be moved according to the whims of the administrators.

An administrator has an obligation to his teachers. The teachers have an obligation to the administrators. The obligation will be carried out most effectively if there is mutual respect and a togetherness in their efforts; if they extend intellectual and emotional hospitality to one another; if they strive to achieve unity of purpose.

PART FIVE

Annotated Therapy Records

19.
Excerpts from Individual Therapy Records

As we pointed out earlier, play is the natural medium for the child's expression of his feelings. Children bring forth in their play world the thoughts and feelings that they encounter in their relationships with other people. Words are inadequate and clumsy things for the child. He has feelings that he cannot put into words; but play is something that he can handle adequately.

The following examples, picked at random from case material, illustrate how closely related to the child's problem is his free play.

At the conclusion of each excerpt the writer has included the reason for the referral and a brief summary of the child's problem. This material is put at the end of the case material so that the reader may formulate his own hypothesis as he reads the material and then check it at the end to see how revealing the play is. It illustrates how the child plays out the problems that are close to him and in some instances manages to catch the expressed feelings in a graphic way.

DICKIE'S DEFENSE AGAINST THE WORLD

CASE OF DICKIE—AGE SEVEN—EXCERPT FROM FIRST CONTACT

Dickie gets out the clay and comes over to the table and sits down across from the therapist.

Dickie: Let's make something.

Therapist: You want to make something out of clay.

Dickie: I said "Lets." You make something, too.

Therapist: What do you want me to make?

Dickie (frowning, scratching his head): I want you to make a cat. You hide it back of a big rock.

Therapist (beginning to make a cat out of clay and also a rock to hide it behind): You like to boss me around.

Dickie: You do as I say. (*Therapist and Dickie make the clay figures. Dickie makes a rabbit and a pile of rocks to hide his rabbit.*) Now come on out and fight. (*Therapist edges her cat toward his rabbit. He immediately jumps his rabbit on top of therapist's cat and mashes it.*) There. That's the end of the old cat. Make another cat.

Therapist (making another cat): You ruined my first cat and now you want me to make another one.

Dickie: Yes. (*The therapist's cat again meets the same fate.*) Make another, and this time you have your cat jump on my rabbit. (*Therapist does, but just at the right moment Dickie's rabbit knocks the cat's head off and he pinches the rest of it out of the therapist's fingers.*)

Therapist: You like to get the best of my cat.

Dickie: Sure I do. I like to fight.

Therapist: You like to fight, too.

Dickie: Sure I do. And I like to get the best in a fight, too. You make a snake now.

Therapist: You want me to make a snake. (*She does so. Dickie makes one also. He reaches over and takes therapist's snake and measures it alongside of his. Then, very deliberately, he makes his snake longer than the therapist's.*) You want your snake to be bigger than mine.

Dickie: Yes. And it is going to knock your snake's head plum off. Here. Hide yours behind this rock. Mine is hiding here. (*Dickie has his snake protected by a large pile of rocks.*)

Therapist: You want your snake well protected.

Dickie: Now this time I'm going to let your snake kill my snake. Come on. Hssss. Sssss. (*The snakes are edged toward each other, but just as the therapist's snake is about to strike Dickie's snake, he drops a big ball of clay down on top of it and then pushes his hand down on top of the clay and mashes the therapist's snake. He laughs gleefully.)* I tricked you. I fooled you.

Therapist: You like it when you can trick me and get the best of me.

Dickie: Sure. Now you see if you can trick me. You really try and see if you can.

Therapist: You want me to see if I can trick you.

Dickie: Yes. You just see if you *can.*

Therapist: You don't think I can.

Dickie: No. I don't think you can, but you try it. *(The therapist and Dickie maneuver the clay snakes. The therapist's snake knocks Dickie's snake's head off. He springs up from the table and shouts at the therapist.)* Look what you did! Look what you did to *my* snake!

Therapist: You told me to try and trick you, and then when I did you didn't like it.

Dickie: No. I don't like it. Now you fix my snake's head back on. Now you give it first aid.

Therapist: You want me to fix it again since I was the one that knocked its head off.

Dickie: I want you to do what I say.

Therapist: You like to boss me around.

Dickie (laughing suddenly): This is fun. I really don't care about the old clay snakes. I'm just playing. *(He waits until the therapist has fixed his snake, then he picks it up by the tail and mashes it all up in a ball. Then he goes over to the shelf and gets the soldiers and begins another battle, with his back to the therapist this time.)*

Therapist: You're having quite a battle.

Dickie: Why don't you keep still?

Therapist: You want me to stop talking when you tell me to.

Dickie: Yes. Why don't you? *(Therapist does. Dickie peers around at the therapist and looks very pleased with his success at silencing her.)* Can I come back again?

Therapist: Yes, if you want to.

Dickie: I'm really just playing with you. You said I could play any way I wanted to.

Therapist: Yes. That's what I said. I meant it.

Dickie: I can say anything I want to say to you, too?

Therapist: Yes.

Dickie: I could even swear in here if I wanted to?

Therapist: If you want to.

Dickie (laughing hilariously): When can I come again? Every day?

Therapist: You may come every Wednesday at this same time.

Dickie: You're a grown-up lady and I can say anything I want to say to you *(laughs).*

Therapist: You think it's fun to say anything you feel like saying to a grown-up.

Dickie: Yeah. *(Grins.)* Shut up, Mrs. X [the house-mother's name]. *Shut up Mrs. X.*

Therapist: You would like to tell the house-mother to shut up sometimes.

Dickie: Shut up, Mr. M [the superintendent of the Home]. Shut your damn big mouth!

Therapist: You sometimes feel like telling Mr. M to shut his "damn big mouth."

Dickie: I'd like to, but I wouldn't *dare!*

Therapist: You would like to tell him that, but you wouldn't dare.

Dickie (sitting down across from the therapist): Know what?

Therapist: Hmm?

Dickie: I want to drink from the nursing bottle.

Therapist: There it is, over on the shelf. Drink from the nursing bottle if you want to.

Dickie: Know what?

Therapist: Hmm?

Dickie: I want to crawl on the floor and drink my bottle.

Therapist: You want to act just like a baby. Well, go ahead. *(As Dickie hesitates.)* You don't know whether you should or not.

(Dickie gets the nursing bottle, sits down across from the therapist and closes eyes and drinks from the bottle; then he gets down on the floor, lies down, sucks on the bottle with his eyes closed.)

Dickie: Me little baby.

Therapist: You like to be a little baby.

Dickie: Ummhumm. *(Lies on the floor, drinking from the bottle for the remainder of the hour.)*

COMMENTS

Dickie was referred for play therapy because he was "so immature," according to the house-mother's report, cried easily, and had temper tantrums. He was also enuretic.

Dickie had been placed in the private Children's Home four months prior to the beginning of the therapy contacts. He had not made a satisfactory adjustment to the new situation. His mother did not visit him often. She had remarried, after divorcing Dickie's father. The step-father did not want to be bothered with Dickie. Consequently Dickie had been placed in the Children's Home His own father never came to see him. In fact, he had deserted Dickie's mother when the boy was five years old. Dickie had been an only child. He had been kept by an old lady while his mother worked and had had no association with other children. As long as he played quietly, he could do pretty much what he pleased before he came to the Home. Now, suddenly thrown in contact with many other children, being regimented, and feeling deserted and insecure, Dickie took refuge in very immature behavior, occasionally giving vent to a temper tantrum when someone crossed him.

It is interesting to note how Dickie used this first contact. He seemed to be expressing his feelings against the too oppressive authority of the Home. He chose a plastic material that he could manipulate easily and could control in the matter of size and durability. He used the therapist in a rather unusual way, bringing her into his play as the symbol of adult authority which he could use to express the feelings that he would not dare express to the actual adults in control. It was interesting to see him fluctuate from the bossy, dictatorial child to the helpless baby.

Since this was Dickie's first contact, he wasn't sure about the permissiveness of the situation and the acceptance that he could count on. This is more or less indicated by his statement that he is "just playing," and later in the contact, after he asks if he can even swear, he wonders if he can come back again. Toward the end of the hour Dickie seems to get a little too close to his problem, when he tells the superintendent to shut his "damn big mouth." The therapist's reply here seems to be too strong for Dickie and he retreats way back to his secure baby world. The impact of his exact words repeated back to him seemed to be too much of a shock. His demeanor as he drank from the bottle was as relaxed and carefree as a baby. Immature behaviour might very well be Dickie's defense against a world that is too much for him.

The therapist's response also seems to have been inadequate when Dickie first mentioned the bottle. It seems that it would have been better had she reflected his feelings that he wanted to act just like a baby and had she not added the "go ahead," which was encouragement and support to a certain extent. The active decision should have been left entirely up to Dickie.

SHIELA STRAIGHTENS HER RIVAL'S HAIR

CASE OF SHIELA—AGE SEVEN—EXCERPT FROM THE FIFTH CONTACT

Shiela comes into the playroom, immediately picks up the nursing bottle and either holds it in her hand when she isn't sucking on it or sets it on the table within easy reach. She comes over and sits down at the table across from the therapist. She pulls the crayons and drawing paper toward her and begins to draw.

Shiela: Look, this is a clock. See, here are the numbers and here are the hands and here are the insides of the clock. doesn't like to have to wash it.

Shiela: Now you just watch this. *(She bends over the paper and draws a head with lots of long red curly hair.)* Write down here for me, "Mrs. B [the house-mother] said, 'I don't want to wash this awful hair.'" *(Shiela laughs as the therapist writes that down.)*

Therapist: The house-mother doesn't like her hair. She doesn't like to have to wash it.

Shiela (picking up the black crayon and streaking through the red hair): Look how dirty it is? Mrs. B said, "I don't want to wash this awful, dirty old red hair!" This kind of bushy hair ought to be red. Her eyes blue, huh? Shirley has red hair and blue eyes. She's pretty, too. And *she's* happy. But, *I'm* going to make her cry. I'm going to draw three of her and they are all going to be crying.

Therapist: Shirley has pretty red hair and blue eyes and she is happy, but *you* are going to make her cry three times.

Shiela: Yeah. You just watch me. (*Draws two more heads.*) Look at these tears. Aren't they big? Splash! Splash! Splash! Splash!

Therapist: You really are making her cry. You've fixed it so she isn't happy now.

Shiela: I'll say not. And now I'm going to take the curl out of her hair. See? (*She draws very straight hair over the curls.*)

Therapist: You wish she had straight hair.

Shiela: I sure do. It's straight now, though. See? And now, you look! (*She takes her red crayon and draws long red lines down the face.*) Ha! I scratched her face. Now when her mother comes she won't know her.

Therapist: You don't like having Shirley's mother come to see her. You've scratched her face and taken the curl out of her hair so her mother won't know her.

Shiela (bitterly): Her mommy came last night to see her and brought her a bag of candy and Shirley wouldn't give me any.

Therapist: Shirley wouldn't give you any of her candy and you didn't like that and you fixed her.

Shiela (smiling): Look here. (*She draws a brown ball in Shirley's hair.*) Chewing gum in her hair! (*Shiela is quite happy about it.*)

Therapist: You've put some chewing gum in her hair. You're spoiling those red curls.

Shiela: They aren't pretty now, are they?

Therapist: They aren't pretty now.

Shiela (laughing happily): Now write, "Cry, baby, cry, wipe your teary eye, point to the east, point to the west, point to the one that you like best," and then you write up here like Shirley says it—write, "I like Shiela the best!" (*Therapist does as she is asked.*)

Therapist: You really want Shirley to like you.

Shiela (sighing): Yeah! (*She picks up the bottle and sucks on it contentedly.*)

COMMENTS

Shiela was referred for play therapy because she was aggressive, jealous, quarrelsome, sullen, and antagonistic

to every suggestion. She had been placed in the private
Children's Home when she was four years old. Her
parents had been divorced. The mother had remarried
and had moved to another town and seldom came to see
Shiela. The father was in the navy and too far away to
come and see Shiela. She never heard directly from him,
although the matron at the home said that he did send
money to the home for them to buy "whatever extras
the children were allowed."

This is a rather simple example of how children will
use the play period to express the feelings that are close
to them. Shirley was a very pretty little girl with beautiful long red curls. Her mother came to visit her every
night and she managed to maintain a good mother-
daughter relationship even though she had been forced
to place Shirley in the Children's Home temporarily
after Shirley's father had died. Everyone loved Shirley.
She was a quiet, sweet, well-behaved little girl, inclined
to be smug and self-centered. On the other hand, Shiela
was a very unattractive child, with stringy, mouse-colored
hair, and hazel eyes. She was above average in intelligence, but was failing in school because of her troublesome behavior.

Her favorite toy while in the playroom was the nursing bottle. Every time she came into the room she
snatched up the bottle and sucked on it intermittently
during the whole therapy hour.

In the rather pathetic incident related above, the child
draws her antagonism for her rival in the Home. Her
jealousy was so close to the surface that she acted out
her feelings with the crayons—three times for added
emphasis. It may seem that jealousy over pretty curls is
a trivial thing, but to Shiela it was very important. It
seemed to do her good to get this feeling out of her
system, because she was able at the end of the hour to
express a positive feeling about Shirley. She said she
wished that Shirley liked her.

This example also illustrates the channeling of behavior into socially acceptable outlets.

THE CLAY MAN

CASE OF JOANN — AGE SIX —
EXCERPT FROM FOURTH CONTACT

Joann comes into the playroom, sits down at the clay table, plays with the clay. She is usually very quiet and does very little talking. Every time she comes in she plays with the clay and makes the same thing—a figure of a man carrying a cane. Each time, after he is finished, awful things happen to him. He is punched full of holes, beaten with a stick, run over by the toy truck, buried under a pile of blocks. The fourth time the clay figure emerges, the therapist says, "Here comes that man again."

Joann: Yes. (*Her voice is tense, determined.*)

Therapist: The man with the cane.

Joann: Yes. (*She begins to punch him full of holes.*)

Therapist: You're putting holes in the clay man.

Joann: Stab! Stab! Stab!

Therapist: You're stabbing him.

Joann (in small voice): Ouch. You hurt me. (*Voice changes.*) I don't care. I want to hurt you.

Therapist: The clay man is crying because he is hurt.

Joann (interrupting): I *want* to hurt *him.*

Therapist: You want to hurt *him.*

Joann (emphatically): I *don't like* him.

Therapist: You don't like him.

Joann: I don't like him. I hate him. Look. This hole went clear through him. It went in his front and out his back.

Therapist: He gets holes punched clear through him. You fix him.

Joann: Yes. I'll tear his head off.

Therapist: You'll even tear his head off.

Joann: I know. I know. I'll put him clear down in the bottom of the jar and then I'll put the clay in on top of him and he'll smother. (*She tears him into little pieces and gouges her thumb through the clay and carefully puts the pieces down in the bottom of the jar and then covers it with all the rest of the clay.*)

Therapist: You tore him into little pieces and buried him in the bottom of the jar.

(Joann nods—and smiles at the therapist. Then she goes

over to the baby doll, pretends to feed it, holds it tenderly in her arms, puts it to bed, sets the table, and plays house very quietly.)

This was the pattern of Joann's behavior while in the playroom. She always made the clay man, tore him up, got rid of him, and then played with the baby doll. This continued through the seventh interview and then she stopped making the clay man. She sometimes played with the clay, but made cats or toy dishes or candles. She was very fond of the doll and continued with this play.

COMMENTS

Joann was referred for play therapy because she seemed nervous, tense, withdrawn. What the real significance of this clay man was remained a mystery for a long time. Joann's father had been dead for three years, and she lived with her mother and a ten-year-old sister. There were no men in the family circle. However, her play seemed to indicate that she did have it in for some man. At the time of her play, identity of the man seemed unimportant. Joann never named him. The therapist did not pry into his identity, as it seemed important to Joann that she hide him behind anonymity. Finally Joann stopped making him. She showed considerable improvement in her attitude and behavior.

Later, after the therapy contacts had been terminated, the therapist met the mother, who told her that she was contemplating getting married again. "The only drawback," said the mother, "is the fact that he is a cripple and carries a cane. Joann acts as if she is afraid of him."

That seemed to be the explanation of the man with the cane. This man's intrusion into Joann's home must have been the reason for the terrible beating he always got at Joann's hands.

ERNEST PREPARES FOR HOSPITALIZATION

CASE OF ERNEST—AGE SEVEN—FIRST RETURN CONTACT

Ernest comes into the playroom and takes a quick survey of the equipment.

Ernest: Oh, paints! (*Looks in clay jar. Picks up telephone—moves it over to the table. Gets doll and cradle and brings them over to the doll house.*) Oh, what a nice doll house. I'll rearrange it. (*Does so, naming each article as he picks it up. He puts the two girls in the bed and throws the mother and father in the block box. He puts the rest of the children in the box. Then he gets the big, long wooden blocks and boards up the house, leaving an opening at each end.*) This is the back door. We can go in here and go to the icebox and get an orange or a cooky and come out again. See?

Therapist: There is food in this house.

Ernest: Yes. (*Picks up telephone.*) Hello. All right, I'll bring the baby over in just a little while. Good-bye. I'm going to paint a picture and write "closed" on it and put it on the house so nobody can get in. See. The house is all closed up. Nobody can get in.

Therapist: The house is all closed.

Ernest: I'd better board up the doors. (*Comes over to the house and blocks up the doorways. Paints a house with no doors and no windows. Fills in the background solid blue. Then he goes over to the soldiers and gets out the guns. He puts a machine gun by each door.*) I'll put this machine gun right here by the house and if *anybody* tries to get in, it'll kill them. See?

Therapist: You don't want anybody else to get in the house. They will get killed if they even try.

Ernest: Bang! Bang! Like that. (*He runs the policeman all around the floor, up to the therapist, up the therapist's arm, laughing all the time. He goes back to the paint table. He paints a picture of another house with no doors and no windows.*) Come over here. Write "CLOSED" up here. (*He points to the roof of the house.*) Paint it on with this brush. (*Green paint.*) Make it big. Now write, "This is my house. This is pretty, don't you think? Good-bye. Closed." (*Therapist does.*) I wish I had more paints at home. Army colors. So when I paint jeeps and stuff, I can make them the right color. Green and black sometimes I mix, but it isn't so good. Look. I put blue over my name, but it still shows. (*He goes back to the house.*) Now you lay down there and go to sleep. (*He places one of the boy dolls in the bed.*) Here somebody comes. I'm going to shoot. Bang! Bang! Bang! *(He runs over, gets the hammer and peg-board set, and pounds on it as hard as he can.)* This makes my arm tired. Three more pounds will get this one in. See? *(Hammers some more. He gets out box of soldiers and guns and boats.)* I'll get out all the boats and machine guns. *(Makes machine-gun noises.)* He's going to see that destroyer. See? It destroyed it! See?

Therapist: It destroyed the boat.

Ernest (getting paper and crayons): Know what this is going to be?

Therapist: No.

Ernest: Guess.

Therapist: An airplane?

Ernest: No, not an airplane. This is going to be purple—just purple. You were wrong. *(Laughs.)*

Therapist: You're tickled because I couldn't guess.

Ernest: I've got blisters on my heel. I don't have any corns. Why don't you have puppets here?

Therapist: You would like to have puppets?

Ernest: Yes, like at school.

Therapist (pointing out the puppets on the shelf): Over there.

Ernest: This is Doony the Clown. He's going to eat you up!

Therapist: Doony is going to eat me up.

Ernest: Shame on you, Doony. Biting *her!* *(Throwing Doony in the box.)* Get in there.

Therapist: You think Doony ought to be ashamed—biting his friend?

Ernest: Yes. Such a *good* friend. *(He gets the nursing bottle, puts bottle up to baby doll's lips.)* Drink this, baby. Do you hear me? You'll drink this if I gotta *force* you to.

Therapist: You'll force the baby to eat.

Ernest: Ah. There. See? The baby will eat.

Therapist: The baby *will* eat.

(Ernest smiles. Then he quickly jumps down after the toy ambulance. He makes sounds of the ambulance siren. He pushed the ambulance to the house, gets the girl doll, hides the doll in the box of blocks.)

Ernest: She is in the hospital. Where is the hospital? *(Looks around.)* Oh, here, under this table. *(Siren starts up again; he pushes ambulance under table.)* She is in the hospital now. *(Jumps up and gets the toy telephone.)* Pretend I'm talking to you. You *answer* this talk. Hello.

The child lives in a hustle-bustle world. Things spin by him with bewildering speed. He is rushed here and rushed there. By nature he is slow. This world is a big place, and he needs time to take it all in. Everyone is familiar with the adults who cannot let the child do things for himself because "it takes him forever!"

If the therapist is seeking to relieve tensions and pressures and to give the child a feeling of adequacy, she will not follow the "hurry pattern." She will recognize the value of giving the child an opportunity to gain his equilibrium. She will let the child take his time.

Occasionally some child in the group will do something that centers the attention of the group on that particular activity.
"Come on, Bill. Come on, Anna. Want to help?"

They did. Any observer of this activity could not fail to notice the children's intense reaction to this experience. It had great significance for them. What it meant to each of them is a matter of conjecture, but it did have meaning for each participant. Children understand one another. They speak the same language.

He is proceeding with caution—fascinated by the finger paint, and at the same time a bit fearful of it.

"I'm not afraid! I'll even throw this old duck clear across the room!"

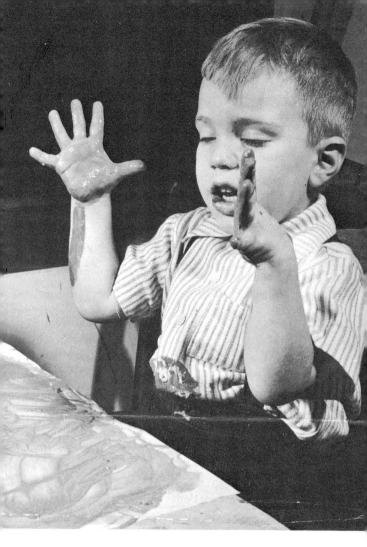

"Sometimes it bleeds! Look!" (*Indicates paper painted red.*)
"Look! Bloody! Like my throat!"

He smears his hands and arms through the finger paint. And as he pins his thoughts and feelings down on paper he feels, perhaps, more secure. After he has captured them on paper he can handle them a little better. This is his fear and his anxiety. Now he can see it—touch it—feel it. He is no longer at the mercy of some nameless fear for he can control it in this manner.

The group experience seems to accelerate the child's feeling of permissiveness. Each child derives a feeling of security from the group. As one child in the group forges ahead, the others gain the necessary courage to pursue their activities by watching the successful manipulation of the environment by this member of the group. The period of testing out the situation is more or less shortened because each individual in the group evaluates the permissiveness of the situation both directly and vicariously.

Here the little girl leads the way and shows the other children how to feed a baby. The boys, watching her carefully, imitate her.

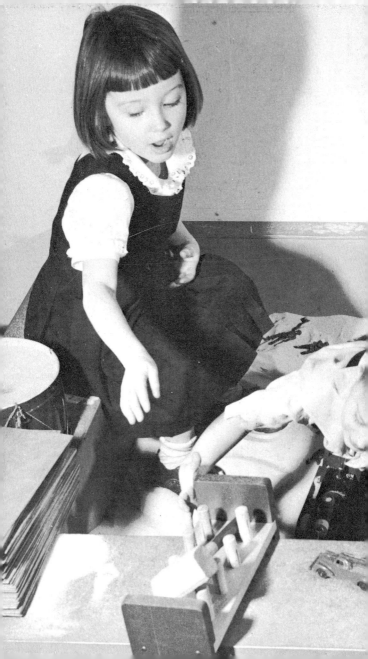

At times the children play together, share the toys, exchange ideas.

My little brother won't do it again!

Age 6

Age 5 — JEAN

Through her drawing, Jean reduced her older brother to a manageable size and rid herself of her feelings of anger against him. *Jean, age 5*

This perfect illustration of identification of father with son and mother with daughter was done in bright, clear colors. *Jonathan, age 8*

The background is gray, the border black, the figures inside black and dark-green. The largest figure was identified by an eight-year-old boy as "Mother," the middle figure as "my Stepfather," the third figure as "my Stepsister." The formless black on the right side of the painting he described as himself, "Not really anybody, but just me trying to get in there." *Boy, age 8*

"Since this is my last visit, I'll paint this for you. It's Central Park in the midst of a wonderful snow storm." *Eric, age 9*

Self-portrait. "The whole world is sad." *Nancy, age 13*

Also done by Nancy. "I can never be alone. I wish I could!"
Nancy, age 13

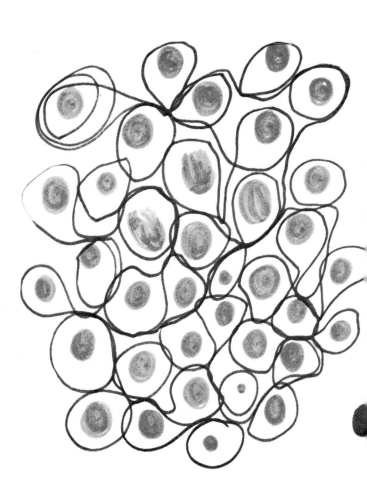

"And only one got free of it. Me!" *Freddy, age 7*

Siegfried

Colors are blue, green, yellow and red swirling around freely.
"Life! Life! Life! It's fun!" *Siegfried, age 7*

Richard entered the playroom tense and grim. "I want to do a painting." He varied the shades from deep red to lighter shades and from black to grey. When he finished, he scratched his fingernails across the wet painting with both hands. "Would you like to tell me about it?" "Yes, it's a picture of the assassination," Richard replied.
Richard, age 8

Therapist: Hello.

Ernest: How are you?

Therapist: Fine. How are you?

Ernest: When can I come back here again?

Therapist: You want to come back.

Ernest: I want to. When can I? Can I come next Tuesday?

Therapist: You would like to come next week.

Ernest: I want to come back. I like it here. When can I come?

Therapist: Just as soon as you get out of the hospital.

Ernest: Even if I get out tomorrow?

Therapist: Even if you get out tomorrow.

Ernest: Then I'll get out tomorrow.

Therapist: You'll try to get out tomorrow so you can come back here again before you go home.

Ernest (getting baby doll): Come on, baby. It's time for your formula. Now it's nighttime. Cover up. Go to sleep. *(Carries it over to the corner.)* She is in her bedroom. She is asleep. *(He gets out the clown puppet and has it shake hands with the therapist.)* Good-bye, Miss——

Therapist: He is saying good-bye to me.

Ernest: Yes.

Therapist: Good-bye.

Ernest: Good-bye. *(He throws the clown puppet into the box. He gets out the father doll.)* Daddy is going to hammer. *(He hammers again.)* Look at him pound things to pieces. Now the little girl is back from the hospital. She is all right now. The house is open again. *(Removes boards that had closed up the house.)* See? Everything is all right now.

Therapist: She has been to the hospital and is back home and everything is all right.

(Ernest places one doll in the dining room at the table and one in the kitchen at the table.)

Ernest: She is going to eat in the kitchen because she is a bad girl.

Therapist: Why is she bad?

Ernest: Because she throws up everything they feed her. Oh, look. *(Ernest throws the doll down.)* She fell down and broke her neck. That is the end of her. I'll bury her. *(He buries her in the box of blocks.)*

Therapist: That is the end of the little girl who threw up everything they fed her.

Ernest: Yes. She's dead. Now I'm going to change everything all around. This isn't going to be the kitchen again. Look. I'll move the piano out here. The lamp. This chair. *(Picks up the toy clock.)* What time does this say?

Therapist: Twenty minutes after eight.

(Ernest places the living-room furniture in the kitchen, the kitchen furniture in the living room, the bedroom down in the dining room, the dining room upstairs. In fact, he completely rearranges the furniture.)

Ernest (picking up other girl doll): Look. She broke her leg. The ambulance is going to come back after her. *(Siren noise. Ambulance comes. This doll is thrown into the box, too.)* She is back in the hospital again.

Therapist: She keeps getting back in the hospital again and again.

Ernest: Yep.

Therapist: Does she like to go back there?

Ernest: Yes. *(Then, quickly.)* No.

Therapist: She likes the hospital and she doesn't like the hospital.

Ernest: She is afraid.

Therapist: She is afraid to go the the hospital.

Ernest (getting baby of the doll family): She is going to a dance. *(Throws the baby up in the air.)* Look. She's afraid. She's gone. *(Throws her in the box of blocks.)*

Therapist: She is afraid, too.

Ernest (going over to the clay jar and getting out some clay): I'm going to make something. I'm going to make a donkey. *(He sits down and works with the clay.)* I'll make its head and its body and its tail. *(Sings as he works.)* I'm sticking it on to this paper. *(Reaches over and gets the gun.)* Bang! Bang! *(He gets the toy airplane and zooms it around. The airplane crashes into the house. Room by room the house is destroyed. Shouts.)* Everybody is dead! *(He upsets the house.)* Everything is destroyed! *(He picks up the house, turns it upside down, and shakes it.)* That is the end of the house! *(Yells.)* That is the end of the house!

Therapist: Everybody is dead. Everything is destroyed. That is the end of the house. You wanted to destroy the house and you did destroy the house.

Ernest (moving it clear across to the other side of the room): I destroyed it all. *(Chuckles.)*

Therapist: It makes you feel good to have destroyed it all.

Ernest: Yes. *(He goes over to the big baby doll. He*

brings it over to the therapist and places it in the therapist's lap.) Here. You feed the baby. You're the mother.

Therapist: You would like me to be the mother.

Ernest: I'll feed the baby. *(He gets the bottle, holds it to the doll's mouth. Then he takes the baby from the therapist, and puts it back in the cradle. Talking to the doll.)* There, now, baby, you go to sleep. Oh. Did you wet your bed? Nope. Oh! *(Excitedly.)* Take the baby to the doctor. The baby is sick.

Therapist: What is the matter with the baby?

Ernest: The baby has a sore throat. The baby is sick. Poor, poor sick baby.

Therapist: You feel sorry for the baby because it is sick. *(Ernest tries to put the baby in back of the box of blocks.)* You want to get rid of the sick baby.

Ernest (succeeding in cramming the baby in back of the box): I did! See? *(He gets out the soldiers and moves them over into the house, which he straightens up.)* The soldiers are going to take over the house. See? *(He plays with the soldiers and horses. He knocks over the soldiers and the box of soldiers and the house. He brings the horse over to the therapist and then goes back and stands the house up straight again and picks up the soldiers.)*

Therapist: There are five more minutes, Ernest.

Ernest (getting the puppet and bringing it over to the therapist): I'm coming over to say good-bye. *(Sticks his hand on the puppet.)* Ouch! He bit me. *(Laughs.)* When can I come back?

Therapist: You may come back another time when you get out of the hospital before you go back home.

Ernest (going back to his painting. He paints yellow over the "Closed" sign): I want to use red. *(Paints red all over the house.)* Blood!

Therapist: It looks like blood.

Ernest: Yeah.

Therapist: Our time is up now.

Ernest: Now we go to lunch and then I go to the hospital. *(Sighs.)*

Therapist: You're afraid to go to the hospital?

Ernest: I'm not *afraid.* I just don't want to go. But after I get out, we'll have a soda before I go home, won't we?

Therapist: You're not afraid; you just don't want to go. Yes, we'll have the soda.

COMMENTS

Ernest was brought in for play therapy in preparation
for hospitalization. He had been having therapy contacts
with this same therapist for several months at the beginning of the year. This was a return visit because he was
going to the hospital that afternoon. The problem that
confronted Ernest was his emotional upset at the
thoughts of the minor surgery that he was about to
undergo. He had had a constricted throat and had worn
a stomach tube for supplemental feeding at the beginning of the therapy. At the time of this contact he had
been eating in a normal way for several months; however, it was still necessary to have his throat dilated period-
ically. It was for one of these throat dilatations that
Ernest was entering the hospital. As a result of the
operation his throat was sore and there was usually some
blood in evidence. The preceding throat dilatation had
brought with it some very unpleasant complications and
Ernest suffered more anxiety than usual before this hospital session.[1]

Ernest's play brings out his concern with the problem
of eating, going to the hospital, being sick, dying, general destruction, saying good-bye to the therapist, and
hammering out his aggressive feelings. His play follows
a pattern. The baby, the food, the closed house, the
guns, the hammering, the hospital. He expresses his
fears and his aggressiveness through his play. At the
conclusion of his play period he says that he is not
afraid to go to the hospital, but he just doesn't want to
go. It is interesting to know that Ernest had less emotional reaction to this hospitalization than to any previous one. The following day he was out of the hospital
and came back to the clinic with a group of boys for
that other play contact which he had requested that he
have before he went home.[2]

Surely this case is evidence that the emotional life of
the child often is the basis for the play through which he
finds relief from his tensions.

[1] For complete case of Ernest, see Chapter 23.
[2] For an account of this group contact, see page 211.

SYLVIA CONTROLS THE GHOST

CASE OF SYLVIA—AGE FOUR—EXCERPT FROM SUBSTITUTE THERAPIST'S FIRST CONTACT

Sylvia had been in for therapy for some time prior to this contact. This contact was handled by a substitute because the regular therapist was unable to be there. Sylvia liked the finger paints. She spent a good bit of her time messing around with them. She used thick gobs of the paints and spread them over the paper with free, sweeping gestures. During this particular time Sylvia was smearing the blue and green finger paint around with both hands.

Sylvia: The water. The water. These are big waves.

Therapist: You've made the waves and the water.

Sylvia: Swish. Swish. Woooo.

Therapist: The waves make funny noises.

Sylvia: Give me black. Give me black. *(Therapist gives her some black finger paint.)*

Sylvia (changing her voice dramatically): Here comes the ghost!

Therapist: The ghost is coming.

Sylvia (forming a black shape in the middle of the paper): Wooooooo.

Therapist: The ghost goes "Wooooooo." The ghost is right in the middle of the water.

Sylvia (grinning up at the therapist): I like this.

Therapist: You like to do this. You like to mess with the finger paints.

Sylvia: Look. Look. I am the ghost that lives under the water. See?

Therapist: That is the ghost that lives under the water.

Sylvia: I am the ghost that flies in the open window at night.

Therapist: You are the ghost that flies in the open window at night.

Sylvia: It *scares* me.

Therapist: Your ghost scares you.

Sylvia: Yeah. *(She swoops her hands through the blue-green water.)* Go away. Go away!

Therapist: You are sending the ghost away.

Sylvia: Wooooooo. Wooooooo. *(Grins up at therapist.)*

Therapist: The ghost is saying "Wooooo."
Sylvia: The ghost is all gone.
Therapist: The ghost is gone now.
Sylvia: Find him.
Therapist (examining the paper): The ghost is not there.
Sylvia (shaking head emphatically): The ghost is not there. *Once more she smears the finger paints around in free, circular swoops and then she moves away from the table.)* Now I'll play in the sand.

COMMENTS

Sylvia was referred for play therapy because of fears and anxieties that resulted from a traumatic experience when, with no explanation or preparation by her parents, she had been taken to a hospital for minor surgery. As one manifestation of her tension and nervousness, she had pulled her hair out until she had a sizable bald spot.

The contact which we have described was handled by a substitute therapist because of the illness of the therapist who regularly saw Sylvia. According to the records, the ghost was a part of most of the play contacts. The ghost was not named. Perhaps it was just some nameless fear that she was working out. At this point in the therapy, Sylvia had overcome most of her fears and anxieties and had stopped pulling out her hair. Through her play, Sylvia brought forth her ghost and destroyed it at will. Finger paints, which were her own choice, seemed to be the perfect medium with which to express this ghostly visitor.

JEAN AND THE TOILETS

CASE OF JEAN—AGE FOUR—FIRST CONTACT

On the way to the playroom Jean pulls back and looks at her mother.

Jean (to therapist): Maybe I better not go with you.
Therapist: You think that maybe you ought not to go with me.

Jean: No.

Mother: But I have a little errand, Jean, and you said you would stay with the lady until I came back after you.

Jean: Yes, but maybe I hadn't better.

Mother: Now, Jean, don't be a baby.

Therapist: Even though you did promise, you're not quite sure you want to stay with me. You're a little bit afraid, maybe.

Jean (whispering to therapist): Maybe you haven't got a toilet.

Therapist: There is one right next to the playroom. Would you like to see it?

Jean: Yes. *(Therapist shows it to her.)*

Jean (nodding to therapist): All right, Mother. I'll stay. *(Mother leaves. Jean, looking around in playroom.)* Oh, now let me see. What will I do? What will I do? Paints. But maybe they would get on me.

Therapist: You're afraid they might get on your dress. There is an apron here.

Jean: Then I'll paint. Help me with the apron. Now hand me that black. *(She starts painting with the black paint. It runs down the paper.)* Oh, it's juicy. See? Oh! *(She is obviously bothered by the running paint.)*

Therapist: You don't like it to run.

Jean: No. *(She puts the black paint back and asks for the white. When that runs, she is through with the paints.)* Help me take this apron off. Wait. What is that?

Therapist: Those are finger paints.

Jean: Will they run?

Therapist: Not unless you make them run. *(Therapist shows her how to use the finger paints.)*

Jean: Give me some of that. *(Points to the black finger paint.)* Black. A whole gob. *(Then, without touching it, she pushes back from the table.)* No! No! No! It is too messy. *(She can't bear to touch it. She gets down from the table.)* Now take this off. *(Therapist takes off the apron.)* A doll house and a doll family. *(She goes over to the sand table where the doll house and doll family have been placed. She leans across toward the middle of the sand box, but she is so short that she cannot play with it in comfort.)*

Therapist: Would you like to get in the sand box, Jean? You could reach the doll house much easier then.

Jean (grinning): All right. *(Therapist lifts her into the*

sand box. As Jean's foot touches the sand she pulls it up.)
No! No! No! Take me out again. I don't want to get in it.
The sand will get in my shoes.

Therapist: Do you want to take off your shoes and socks?

Jean: No! No! No! *(Therapist puts her down on the floor.)*

Therapist: You would rather stay out here than take off your shoes and socks or get the sand in your shoes.

Jean (playing with the dolls and the house): Where is the girl? Where is the girl? This is the girl. This is the girl. She is with her mother. She is with her mother. *(Jean talks constantly and repeats everything she says.)* Come on in now and go to bed, honey. They go to bed—to bed—to bed. I can't figure it out. This is the table for the kitchen— for the kitchen—for the kitchen. The big girl goes to school every morning—every morning—every morning. There is a clock by her bed—by her bed. I'm going to fix the table— the table—the table. This is the mother. This is the papa. The papa. The papa. *(To therapist.)* I hear some children. Where are they?

Therapist: They are playing outside this building.

Jean: Oh, go to bed. Go to bed. She is reading in bed. This is the mother—the mother. This is the father—the father. They are reading in bed—in bed. Then pretty soon they will—they will—will—go to bed. Pretty soon. Pretty soon. Where is their house? House. House. I'm going to move them over in the house. They are going to live up here on this floor—on this floor. Do you suppose there will be enough room for them up here on this floor?

Therapist: You wonder if there will be enough room for all of them.

Jean: Yes. Yes. These are just rooms they sleep in.

Therapist: They just sleep up there.

Jean: Look. Look. Look. They are still reading. If I take these things out, there will be more room. They are not going to read any more. They are going to bed. Going to bed. Where's my mommy?

Therapist: You want to know where your mommy is. She has gone on an errand and will be back when you are through here.

Jean: Where's the bathroom?

Therapist: In the next room.

Jean: Let's go and see. *(Therapist takes Jean over to the toilet. She looks in and then says, "Let's go back now." They return to the playroom.*) There is a bathroom here, too. I'll put the toilet seat here in the girls' room.

Therapist: You'll put the toilet seat in the girls' bedroom.

Jean: Yes. And this little girl. She is four years old. She sleeps in the bathroom. She sleeps in the bathroom. In the bathroom. In the bathroom.

Therapist: The four-year-old sleeps in the bathroom.

Jean: I am four years old, too.

Therapist: You are four years old, too, just the same age as the little girl who sleeps in the bathroom.

Jean: Yes. Here is another toilet. That is near her, too. And the mother and father are going to come to bed. To bed. They have a nice room. See? They sure do have a nice room.

Therapist: The mother and father are coming to bed. They have a nice room.

Jean: They have a figgerator in their bedroom, too. A figgerator. A figgerator. (*She places the refrigerator in the bedroom of the mother and father.*) The children sleep in the next room. And they can come right through this door if they want to if they need their mother and father.

Therapist: The mother and father are handy in case they are needed.

Jean: They are asleep now. Asleep. Asleep. (*Turns and grins at therapist.*) I'll take my shoes and socks off now and get in the sand box.

Therapist: You'll get in the sand box now and play. (*Jean takes off her shoes and socks, and the therapist helps her get into the sand box.*)

Jean: I want a figgerator in the children's room.

Therapist: You want the children to have a refrigerator in their room, too.

Jean: Is there another toilet?

Therapist: Here is another toilet.

Jean: There is a toilet in the living room. There is a toilet in the kitchen. There is a toilet in the dining room. (*She rearranges the house. There is no organization to the rooms at all. The furniture is just placed in each room in haphazard fashion. The toilet seats are now in every room in the house.*)

Therapist: There is a toilet seat in every room in the house.

Jean: Father has to get up early—early—early. Here he is

in the living room. There should be books to read—books to read. Lamps, too. A radio. The mother is sleeping. This is the bathtub. I'm going to put a bathroom in the living room. This is the toilet seat. This is the bathtub. Someone might take a bath—take a bath—take a bath. This is the sink. The water is going to turn on. I'll put this in the kitchen. This is the kitchen—the kitchen.

Therapist: There are toilets all over the house.

Jean: The mother gets up and sits on a chair and eats her breakfast and has been to the toilet and then goes back to bed. The father has had his breakfast and has been to the toilet. The mother goes back to bed. She tells the father that she has been up and has had her breakfast and has been to the toilet and he says, "*Good! Good! Good! Good!*" *(She puts the dolls all to bed again. Then she climbs out of the sand box with help.)* I really do have to go to the toilet this time. *(Therapist takes her to the toilet. Back in the playroom again.)* Now I'll play with the telephone.

Therapist: You want to play with something else now.

Jean (over the telephone): Hello. I want something. Hamburger and everything and jelly. Huh? No. Yes. How are you? Fine. Oh, no. Just fine. My kids are in bed. The father is, too, I guess. Oh, I don't know. Jean is—— We've got a new baby. We got it three months ago. Why, yes. When are you going to come over? 'Safternoon? *(She goes over and gets the didee doll. It is wet. She turns suddenly toward therapist.)* Oh! Oh! Something has happened. She has a stomach. Look. She went to the toilet. Shame. Shame. *(Laughs.)* I don't have this kind of a doll. My goodness! See. She goes to the toilet.

Therapist: The baby goes to the toilet, too.

Jean (going over to the table and timidly picking up the nursing bottle): The baby drinks from a bottle like this.

Therapist: Baby drinks from nursing bottle like that.

Jean (laughing): I'm going to.

Therapist: You're going to drink from the nursing bottle, too.

Jean: The baby drinks from the nursing bottle and so do I. *(She laughs. She sucks on the nursing bottle.)*

Time is up. The mother is outside the door, waiting for Jean. Jean puts on her shoes and socks by herself and leaves laughing. When she meets her mother outside the playroom she brings her into the room and shows her what she has played with. The mother notices the many toilets in all the rooms.

Mother: Did you put all those toilets in there, Jean?

Jean: Yes.

Mother (to therapist): You know it's the funniest thing. Every time she plays with blocks or her doll house she wants to put toilets in every room. But I have broken her of that *at home.* I've told her and told her that it isn't nice and when she does that *at home* she has to stop playing.

Jean (gleefully): I drank from the nursing bottle, too.

Mother (looking quite pained): What! A *baby* bottle!

Jean: Yes. In *here,* I can!

COMMENTS

Jean was referred to the clinic because of her fears and anxieties about going away from home or leaving her mother. This was Jean's second visit to the clinic. During the first visit the therapist had given her a Stanford-Binet (L). At the beginning of the test the mother had to come into the testing room with the child. When Jean was halfway through the test, the mother asked her if she could go over to the waiting room until the test was finished and read one of the books she saw there. Jean permitted her mother to leave. The mother said later that that was the first time Jean had ever stayed with a stranger alone. Jean finished the test and scored an I.Q. of 138. She came back to the clinic three times after that. At the end of the third play contact, the mother said that Jean showed so much improvement that she did not think it necessary to bring her back again. She said that Jean would now go out and play with the other children in the neighborhood and stay out of her mother's sight for a long time. She said they really thought she was "cured" when she went over to a little neighbor's house for dinner alone one evening. And then another afternoon she went to another neighbor's house to take her nap. According to the case history given by the mother, Jean had established toilet habits at an unusually early age.

Jean reported during her second play contact that her mother had let her drink *milk* out of her baby brother's nursing bottle and had said that maybe she would get a "wetting doll" for Christmas.

During the second and third contacts she spent most of her time playing with the doll.

The repetition of words and phrases in her talk disappeared during the latter part of the first contact and was scarcely noticeable during the last contact. Jean's mother said that she repeated herself when she was upset about something. That, too, improved outside the clinic.

EDITH PLAYS OUT HER WISTFUL THINKING

EDITH—AGE EIGHT—EXCERPT FROM SIXTH CONTACT

Edith got out the box of paper dolls and sat down across from the therapist.

Edith: I know what I'll do. I'll play Home with the dolls. This one is Judy and this one here is Nancy. "Hello, Edith." Where is Edith? Oh, this one will be me. Isn't she pretty?

Therapist: The dolls are the girls here in the Home. And you are the prettiest one in the Home.

Edith: Yes. Boy, ain't I pretty!

Therapist: You *are* pretty.

Edith: And this one here is Ann. Ann is a old tattletale. I don't like Ann. *(She tears off Ann's head.)* Oh, look what happened to Ann? Her head come off.

Therapist: You don't like Ann because she is a tattletale and that's why you tore her head off.

Edith: She's a mean one. She sat right in back of me in school and all the time she bothered me and got me in trouble and she would always be tellin' me things and the teacher would make me come up in front and sit on a chair. And once I said the teacher stunk and Ann told her and the teacher slapped me.

Therapist: You think that Ann caused a lot of your trouble at school.

Edith: She does here at the Home, too. *(Plays with the dolls. Suddenly brightens up with an idea.)* This is inspection day. Here comes a man and woman looking for a little girl to adopt. "Children! Children! Get in your places. Is everyone here? This man and woman want to adopt a little girl. They want a little girl with yellow hair and blue eyes."

Therapist: They want a little girl that looks like Edith.

Edith (grinning): You just watch. "Children! Hurry! The lady wants to see all of you. Where is Mary?" "Mary is gone. She ran away." "Where is Jean?" *(She tears off Jean's leg.)* "Jean is crippled. She can't come. She's only got one leg." "Where is Betty?" *(She grabs up her pencil and stabs out Betty's eyes.)* "Betty ain't got no eyes. She can't see." "Where is Jim?" "Oh, he drowned today when we went swimmin'." Then the woman looks over and she sees this little girl. "Oh, who is that beautiful little girl over there?" "That is Edith." "Hello, little girl. Are you a good little girl?" "Yes, ma'am." "Are you good in school?" "Yes, ma'am." "Would you like to come and live with me in my great big house far away from here?" *(She pushes the dolls away from her. She walks across the playroom and gets the nursing bottle. She sits down across from the therapist.)*

Therapist: You wish someone would adopt you. You would like to get away from here.

Edith: Yeah. *(Sighs.)* Do dogs and rabbits have to take baths in water?

Therapist: Dogs do.

Edith: I read a story once about a horse who got stuck in the mud. Do you suppose they washed the horse?

Therapist: I suppose they did.

Edith (drinking from nursing bottle): Teachers are always lickin' kids. I just hate school.

Therapist: You don't like to go to school because you think teachers are mean to you.

Edith: I don't like anything in school. You don't have to go to school, do you? You're lucky. Of course I'm luckier than the first-graders who just started. They got to go two years longer than I do. *(Picks up another doll.)* This is Sara. She is in Girls' Cottage, too. She's the pet. She gets to lick all the pans.

Therapist: You don't like to have one girl be the pet and get to do all the extra nice things.

Edith (tears off Sara's head): No. I want to be the pet.

Therapist: You would like to be the pet.

Edith: I ought to. I've been here longer than the others. I can't remember not being here.

Therapist: You've been here longer than the others. You think that you have more right to be the pet.

Edith (sucking on the bottle): I wish I was a little baby.

Therapist: You would like to be a little baby.

Edith: Or a big lady like you.

Therapist: A little baby or a big lady like me—but not an eight-year-old girl.

Edith: Yeah. (*Long silence. She sucks on the bottle with her eyes closed.*) Will you get me one of these to take to bed with me at night?

Therapist: You would like to have a nursing bottle to take to bed with you. I can't get one for you, though, Edith.

Edith: Oh. I can drink on it here, huh?

Therapist: Yes. In here you can play baby as much as you like.

Edith (going over to the shelf, she gets the rattle, gets down on the floor and crawls): Dadadadada. Mamamama-mama. (*She lies down on the floor and closes her eyes and drinks from the bottle until the hour is up. Then she jumps up, puts the bottle on the shelf, grins at the therapist, says good-bye, and skips happily out the door.*)

COMMENTS

Edith was referred for play therapy because of her sulkiness, disobedience, and quarrelsome attitude. Edith's problem seemed to be the need for affection and security that she did not get in this Children's Home.

This excerpt from the child's play certainly displays wishful thinking. Edith lived in the constant hope that some day someone would drive up to the Home and adopt her. (Incidentally, three months after this contact someone did adopt Edith.)

In this instance, as in many others, the use of the nursing bottle seems to imply an escape on the part of the child back into the security of the dependent baby world. The nursing bottle seems to have more general appeal than any other bit of equipment in the playroom.

CONCLUSIONS

In view of these examples, it seems logical to conclude that children do play out the feelings that are very close to them when they experience the permissiveness of the therapy hour. Of course, every minute in the playroom is not pregnant with deep feelings, but those feelings do come out as the therapy progresses.

How, except through his play, could little Dickie say to any adult, "I don't like being bossed around by grown-ups. They make me feel inadequate and insecure. I will either boss them around or I will be a baby and be completely dependent upon them. And, since I cannot be a boss, then I have to be a baby." Perhaps these statements are interpretation on the part of the therapist, but she does not interpret or generalize to the child. She sticks to the feeling the child expresses as he expresses it. In the case of Joann, however, the therapist seems to get ahead of the child when she says, "Here comes that man again." Such a remark might have stopped Joann. Fortunately, in this instance, it did not have that effect.

And Joann, timid little girl that she was, couldn't talk out a hatred for an intruder in her world. But she can get rid of him in her own little play world. She can make him and then tear him apart.

Shiela could not have expressed her jealousy and her desire to be liked so vividly without her crayons and paper. She needs to get these feelings of jealousy out into the open where she can see them clearly. She needs to straighten her rival's pretty red hair, streak it up with black, even put chewing gum into it, and then make her cry. Why should Shirley be happy when Shiela isn't? Shiela will take care of that. Splash! Splash! Splash!

Sometimes the therapist wonders what the bugaboo is that bothers the child. "I am the ghost that lives under the water," says Sylvia, "I am the ghost that flies in the open window at night." She swoops her hand across the finger paint. How easily it skids across the paper, and the ghostly form spreads all over the picture. With the finger paint Sylvia could show how those ghosts pervaded everything, once they got in, and then how effectively they could be wiped away.

Jean has been trying to work out her problem for a long time. The incident reported from her therapy record points up the value of having recognition and acceptance of the child's play. It is not enough to have the child play. Children do that all the time. They live on

the borderline of fact and fancy and go back and forth
at will. Jean had been putting the toilets around in her
play until she had been forbidden to do so. It is noteworthy that she immediately brought forth the forbidden
play in the safety of the therapy room. It seemed a bit
unusual that she would draw her mother's attention to
the forbidden play. However, as she said, "In *here*, I
can." The case of Jean also points up the value of
waiting until the need arises before mentioning the limitations. Had the therapist said to Jean, "When we come
in the playroom we stay there; if we leave we cannot
come back until the next time," she might have frightened Jean away. It is in cases like this that the therapist
exercises intelligence in the procedure used. If this child
had wanted to go over and check up on her mother
during the remainder of the test, when the mother made
her first separation, it probably would have been more
helpful to let her go than to hold to hard-and-fast rules.
The therapist needs to keep the *values* of each therapeutic contact to the fore. The needs of each child are not
the same. What is a valuable procedure for one child
might be harmful to another. Flexibility and adaptability
and a sensitivity to each individual situation is necessary.

The case of Ernest reveals a child who is seething
with emotions and conflicting feelings. He plays them all
out until in the end he can honestly say that he is not
afraid.

Edith used the medium that represented destructible
associates. There are no limitations placed upon paper
dolls. They can be torn to pieces—and frequently are.
Many times pictures of babies, mothers, fathers,
schools, doctors, houses, animals, etc., are provided, and
the children are permitted to tear these pictures to
shreds if they so desire. Expression and release of feelings are channeled through the things they play with.

20.

Excerpts from Group-Therapy Records

THE FOLLOWING EXCERPTS serve to illustrate the various principles when applied in group-therapy sessions.

SHARON WANTS EVERYTHING THAT JANE HAS

Five-year-old Sharon wants everything that Jane has, just for the sake of taking it away from her. Jane picks up the doll, and Sharon tries to take it away from her.

Therapist: Sharon wants to take the doll away from Jane. *(Sharon agrees. That is exactly what she wants. Jane, however, hangs on to the doll. Sharon gets very angry and jerks at the doll.)*

Therapist: Sharon is angry because Jane won't give her the doll.

Sharon (screaming and yelling in rage): Gimme this doll. You gimme this doll.

Therapist: Sharon is very angry. She thinks if she screams and yells she can get it that way.

Sharon (tugging at the doll again and screaming): I'll break it!

Therapist: You want to break it if you can't have it.

Sharon: I will, too! *(But her anger is leaving. Then, when she is calmer she moves away from Jane and the doll.)*

Jane (in a matter-of-fact voice): You can have the doll

now. *(Sharon takes the doll. Jane goes after the finger paints.*
Sharon drops the doll and goes after Jane.)

Therapist: Jane gave you the doll, but you don't want it
now. Jane is going to finger paint and so now you want to
finger paint too.

The reader will notice that the therapist reflected
feeling rather than cited a limitation when Sharon
threatened to break the doll.

SARAH AND EDNA SAY GOOD-BYE

Sarah and Edna were two seven-year-old girls in the
Children's Home. They had been seen by the therapist
several times individually. One day Edna asked if she
could bring Sarah in with her because "Sarah is going
home and is never coming back and we want to come in
and play together." The therapist agreed to this arrangement.

Sarah brought the therapist two candy kisses. "These
are for you," she said, very shyly.

The following contact is group therapy, although
there are only two children in the group. It illustrates
the interreaction value of a group situation and shows
how the introduction of another child in the therapy
situation can bring with it valuable release of feelings.
Members of a group situation do not always play together as these girls did, but on this occasion the girls
were "saying good-bye" to one another.

Sarah's mother had been to see her the previous night
and had told her that she was going to take her home
"soon now." Sarah translated the "soon now" into
"immediately." The therapist did not know until several
days later that this was a common practice of the mother, full of promise but signifying nothing. Sarah lived in
high hopes for several days after each "promise," then
when nothing happened she broke into wild sobs; sometimes she even "got sick," then she became a "problem
child." The mother would visit her again and make the
same promises and let the bottom fall out of them again
and again. However, Sarah never seemed to question
her mother's sincerity and always believed that the

mother would keep her promise. Sarah's friends also believed that the mother was sincere and expected Sarah to go home each time the mother promised. It is scarcely any wonder that the girl was a "behavior problem."

Even had the therapist known about the actual conditions of the mother's promises, she would not have handled the contact in any other way and would not have injected into it any directive technique designed to get Sarah's reaction to a possible disappointment.

It might be well to say at this point that the Children's Home in which Sarah lived was a very modern institutional home and offered many advantages to the children. However, the children did not accept it as a home. Be it ever so humble or poorly managed, to the child there is no place like his own home. These children attended a public school and occasionally visited the private homes of their little school friends. This only pointed up their sense of difference and seemed to aggravate their problem.

The record of the contact follows.

Therapist (when Sarah gave her the candy): You want me to know that you like me.

Sarah: Uhuh. I'm going to marry you when I grow up.

Edna: Can women marry one another?

Sarah: Did you bring the nipple bottles?

Edna (persistently): Can women marry one another? Huh? Can they?

Therapist: You wonder about people getting married. A man and a woman marry one another. Two women don't.

Edna: Not even if one of the women dressed like a man?

Therapist: Not even if one of them dressed like a man.

Edna: I wouldn't want to get married then. I'm afraid of men.

Therapist: You're afraid of men.

Edna: Yes. Let's play with the dolls. *(Edna and Sarah sit down on the floor and begin to play with the dolls.)*

Sarah: This boy and this girl is going to get married. *(She puts a boy and a girl together.)* Put the mother and father together. Take off the father's clothes. *(Edna hands her the father doll and Sarah takes off his clothes.)* Look. He's made out of wood. Ha! Wooden father. Look, Edna. They already have a baby.

Edna: Put them to bed.

Sarah (putting the mother and father dolls to bed. She puts the baby in the little bed and then holds the big nursing bottle to the baby's lips): Poor little baby. Hasn't had anything to eat.

Edna: Give the poor little baby something to eat. *(She holds the bottle up to the baby doll's lips.)* Now let's go to grandma's. *(She puts the baby on the toy bus and takes it across the room.)*

Therapist: The baby has gone away.

Sarah: Yeah.

(They stop playing with the dolls and Sarah picks up the big doll. She holds it awhile. Then she puts it down and sorts idly through the paper dolls. Edna sits in the middle of the floor doing nothing. After a long silence, Edna gets up, goes over to the toy box and gets out a black mask. She holds it away from her.)

Edna: I'm afraid. Look. I'm afraid of this.

Therapist: You're afraid of the black mask?

Edna: Yes. I'm afraid of——

Therapist: You're afraid of——?

Edna: Something. I don't know. *(She shrugs her shoulders.)*

Therapist: You don't just know what you are afraid of.

(Edna goes back to the dolls and begins to play again. Sarah joins her.)

Sarah: The baby is going away again. Here comes the mother hurrying out. Where is the baby? Where is the baby? The baby is gone! *(Very dramatically. Then, changing her voice.)* The baby? I forgot the baby. I lost it. I left it downtown. *(Laughs.)* In fact, I threw the baby away.

Edna (in agitated voice): You threw the baby away? You are bad. *(She spanks the mother doll.)* How could you be so mean? You threw the baby away! *(She picks the tiny baby doll up in her arms and hugs and kisses it. Sarah throws the father on the floor.)* Why did you do that?

Sarah: The father is bad.

Therapist: The father is bad?

Sarah: I don't like the father.

Therapist: You don't like the father.

Sarah: No, I don't like him. *(She hands the father to Edna.)*

Edna: I don't want him. I don't like him, either. Take him away. Take him away. (*She tosses the father back toward Sarah.*)

Therapist: Edna doesn't like the father, either.

Edna: I'll take the baby away from these people. They don't like the baby. (*She takes the baby and its bed and places it clear across the playroom. Then she finishes drinking all the water in the nursing bottle.*) I like to drink out of the nursing bottle. I like to be a little baby.

Therapist: You wish you were a little baby.

Edna: Yes. I wish I was.

Sarah: So do I. (*She drinks from the bottle without the nipple.*) I like to drink out of the bottle. I like it in here. I'll never want to go out and play. Look, Edna, I'm drinkin' beer.

Edna: Oh! Are you? (*She laughs.*)

Sarah: I'm going home.

Therapist: You are?

Sarah: Yes. Tomorrow.

Edna: To stay forever.

Sarah: My mother is asking the judge today if she can have me.

Edna: Then I'll be left all alone.

Sarah: I cried all day Sunday.

Therapist: You did? You felt unhappy.

Sarah: Yes. I wanted to go home. I wanted to go away.

Edna: You're silly to cry. I wish I could go home.

Therapist: You would like to go home, too.

Edna: Yes. But you're nice. When you go, then I want to go. Let me come live with you?

Therapist: You would like to come and live with me.

Edna: Yes. Can I?

Therapist: I'm afraid that wouldn't be possible.

Edna (looking very unhappy): I want to.

Therapist: You would like to. It makes you unhappy because you can't.

Edna: Yes. (*She gets the toy soldiers and she and Sarah begin to play with them.*)

Sarah: None of these soldiers get killed, huh?

Therapist: You don't want them to get killed?

Sarah: No.

Edna· Neither do I.

Sarah· Where is the baby? (*She looks right at the baby.*)

Therapist: You wonder where the baby is.

Sarah: Yes. Where did the baby go?

Therapist: You just can't find the baby.

Edna: Oh, is the baby gone? The poor dear little baby. *(She runs over and grabs it up in her arms and kisses it.)* I love you, baby. I'll take good care of you. I'll let you come and live with me.

Therapist: You love the baby and would let it come live with you—if you could.

Edna: But you can't. *(Sighs.)* You can't even adopt me, maybe?

Therapist: I know how sad it makes you feel, but I can't even adopt you.

Edna: I know. You said you can't.

Therapist: I said I couldn't. I know you would like very much to come and live with me or go and live with your mother, but——

Edna: I haven't any mother. I never did have. Or any father, either.

Therapist: You never had a mother or a father.

Sarah (standing up very straight, exclaims ecstatically): I am going home! *I* am going home!

Edna (bursting into tears): I won't stay here. I want to go, too.

Therapist: Edna is very unhappy because you are going home and she must stay. *(Sarah puts her arms around Edna and asks her not to cry.)* Sarah dosen't like to see Edna cry. It makes her unhappy, too. *(Sarah is crying, too.)* You are so sad you are both crying.

(The girls cry it out. Sarah kisses Edna, Edna kisses her, and then they cry some more. Then Sarah takes off her little hair ribbon and gives it to Edna. Edna dries her tears, comes over to the therapist and asks her to put it on her hair. Therapist does. Then Edna sits down at the paint table and begins to paint aimlessly. Sarah sits down across from her.)

Sarah: I'll do what you do, Edna. Let's play.

Edna: Okay. *(She paints the paper solid black. Sarah paints her paper solid black. Edna pushes back her chair and accidentally spills the paint water on Sarah.)*

Sarah (angrily): Look what you did. On my clean dress!

Edna: I don't care. I don't care. *(She pushes the table deliberately toward Sarah. Sarah throws the remainder of the dirty paint water at Edna. The time is up at this point, but goes unannounced. Edna picks up her paint brush and stabs it in Sarah's direction.)* I'll smear you all up.

Therapist: Now you want to smear each other up because

some paint water was accidentally spilled. *(Edna drops the paint brush, hurls herself at the therapist, and cries bitterly.)* You are so unhappy because you two quarreled.

Edna: I got her nice new clean dress dirty.

Therapist: You feel badly because you accidentally got some of the dirty paint water on her dress.

Edna· I didn't mean to do it.

Sarah: You didn't mean to do it, honey. Don't feel so bad. *(Once more they twined their arms around each other's necks and kissed.)*

Therapist: Now you are friends again.

(The girls stand there and smile at each other through their tears. Edna goes over and gets the nursing bottle and sucks on it. Sarah sits down and looks at Edna. When they are told that the time is up they leave arm in arm.)

COMMENTS

Looking back over this contact, one notices the way in which the children reject the mother and father dolls and extend their pity to the poor little baby. Edna identifies herself with the baby by drinking from the nursing bottle and expressing the wish to be a baby. Sarah's confession of tears the preceding Sunday was probably a realization or her part that her mother really wasn't going to take her away. Edna tries to attach herself to the therapist, and when she finds out that she cannot do it, she seems to rebuke the therapist by saying to the doll, "I love you, baby. I'll take good care of you. I'll let you come and live with me." When the therapist reflects this back to Edna, she adds the "if you could" because Edna is not permitted to take the doll out of the playroom and she hoped to point out to her the element of limitations to her actions Whether she got the point or not is doubtful. Whether it was a good thing to do, is also doubtful. Edna attempted to arouse the therapist's pity by saying she never had a father or mother, or perhaps this is further rejection of her parents. Sarah's emotional announcement that she was going home climaxed Edna's feelings.

In retrospect, the therapist wonders if perhaps some of Sarah's tears were not for herself and her many previous disappointments.

An indication of the emotional content of this contact lies in the rapidity with which they went from extreme devotion to sudden and violent anger. This emotional fluctuation would not have been possible if the girls had come in by themselves. The reader will see the added impetus that the interplay of the children's personalities added to the therapy. The therapist did not announce the end of the hour for very obvious reasons. It would have been harmful to both the girls to dismiss them at the peak of the quarrel without giving them time to restore harmony. Edna's reversion to the nursing bottle following the quarrel is interesting.

RICHARD, JACK, AND PHILIP GAIN COURAGE FROM ONE ANOTHER

Another example of group therapy is included to show how the children in a group sometimes gain the courage to do things that ordinarily they might be a bit reluctant to do.

Richard, Jack, and Philip were eight and nine years old. They went to the same school, were in the same grade, and were very good friends. The therapist saw all three of them individually for several weeks before they were placed in the group at their request. Their problems were similar— bed-wetting, negativism, failure in school. Richard arrived first. While waiting for the others, he got out the checkers and asked the therapist to play a game with him. She did. During the play, Richard talked about school and the games they played at recess. He seemed very calm and relaxed. Then Jack came in. He sat down at the table.

Jack: Where's the nursing bottle? (*He reaches over and gets one.*)
Richard: Get me one. (*Jack hands him one.*)
Jack: Hurry up with that old game. (*The game is finished as quickly as possible.*)
Jack (sitting down across from therapist and pushing Richard off the chair): Let me play.
Therapist: You want to play a game of checkers like Richard did.
Richard (sucking on nursing bottle): Me 'ittle baby!

Jack (grinning): Yeah. Me, too. Play me a game of fast checkers.

Therapist: You want me to play with you.

Jack: Yes. Come on. *(Arranges the checkers.)*

Richard: He wants you to play with him because you just played with me.

Jack: Sure. You wanted to play with her, didn't you?

Richard: And because I did it, you want to do the same thing.

Jack: I like to do the same thing you do. I'm jealous. *(He laughs.)*

Richard: You're jealous all right. *(Laughs.)* So am I.

(The therapist plays the game with Jack and shortens it to a minimum. Richard and Jack talk back and forth about one another's attitudes. Therapist missed getting this in her notes because of the game, but it certainly was accurate evaluation of one another's motives. Finally, halfway through the game Richard gets down on the floor and begins to crawl.)

Richard: Me baby. Tum pway!

(Jack got up, left the game unfinished, and got down and crawled around after Richard. Richard lay down on his back and drank from the bottle. Philip came in and got a nursing bottle, too. The three boys spent the rest of the hour crawling around on the floor, talking baby talk, and finally squirting water on one another. They laughed and had a hilarious time. When the hour was up Richard said good-bye to the therapist and left. Philip and Jack poured the remainder of the water in their bottles on the floor and ran out. Jack came back in with the mop that stood in the hall and, with much giggling, mopped up the water and then he left.)

COMMENTS

This excerpt shows the suggestive element that is sometimes present in a group situation. One boy wants to do something because another has done it. Of these three boys only Jack had previously had the courage to pour the water on the floor. It may have been that the similarity of their problems caused the similarity of their actions in the playroom.

As pointed out in Chapter 3, checker games are not the best kind of material for expressive play, but this contact shows the possibilities of even this type of material when the permissiveness and freedom of the relationship are established. One of the disadvantages of this sort of game, when used in group therapy, is the possibility of the therapist's being drawn into the play with one individual and consequently centering the therapy around one child in the group.

21.

Complete
Group-Therapy
Record and Evaluation

THE FOLLOWING is an annotated case of eight therapy contacts for a group of behavior-problem boys who were temporarily placed in the same foster home for the summer. There were fifteen children in this foster home, ranging in age from three months to sixteen years. These therapy contacts were set up on an experimental basis, with the consent of the foster mother and the welfare agency. It was arbitrarily decided that there should be eight weekly contacts, each lasting for one hour. The boys were told before the first session that they could come to the playroom for one hour each week for a period of eight weeks. It was necessary for the therapist to go after the boys and take them home in her car because of the distance from their home to the clinic and because of their ages and handicaps.

There were five boys in the first contact. Timmy and Bobby we have met before, in Chapter 1. They were brothers, aged eight and seven years respectively. Saul was seven. Buddy, who was almost totally blind, was nine. Ernest was a temporary member of the group. He had had play-therapy contacts with this therapist all year. The day before this play contact he had had a throat dilatation in the hospital. He was waiting for his mother to come from another town to take him home and had requested one more play session before she came.[1]

Timmy and Bobby were described by the foster mother as "quarrelsome, noisy, disobedient boys, who cried easily, sulked often, had vomiting spells, and wet the bed." They had been placed in the foster home six months before these contacts occurred owing to the separation of the parents. The mother lived in a town about fifty miles from the city where the boys were "boarded out" and came to visit them at very irregular intervals. The father never came at all.

Saul was seven years old. According to the foster mother's report, Saul was "quiet and brooding, given to sulking spells." She also added that she didn't think he was "all there," and that he was "aggravating and unresponsive and didn't seem to understand a thing that he was told to do." Saul's mother was in a state hopsital for the insane. His father lived in a city approximately one hundred miles away from the foster home, but visited Saul at least once every month and took him down to this grandparents' home for short vacations. Saul was small for his age, very thin and pale. He had never played with the other children in this foster home. He would sit for long periods of time with this head buried in his hands, and whenever the other children came close to him he would either cry or spit at them. Saul had been staying in one foster home after another for several years.

Buddy had no known parents. He was a foundling who had lived in foster homes all his life. In the winter time he lived at the state school for the blind. He was described as "loud enough to drive anybody crazy; not able to say anything at all unless he was screaming at the top of his lungs." He seemed happy enough, but he continually teased the other children and got on their nerves because of the habit he had of suddenly making "loud, weird, blood-curdling noises." His near-blindness made him appear clumsy, and he was continually falling over things, stepping on the other children's toys and breaking them, dropping things, knocking things over,

[1] For the contact Ernest had the day before hospitalization, see page 182. For complete case, see Chapter 23.

and was a menace around the babies. The foster mother said many times during the pre-therapy interview: "I can't hardly stand Buddy, he is so much like a demolition bomb going off all the time."

The boys were told by the therapist that they would not have to come to the playroom when she called for them unless they wanted to come. They hooted at the idea that they would not want to come each week. The following is a complete report of the eight therapy sessions.

FIRST CONTACT

Therapist: You may play in here for an hour. You may play any way with the toys—just so you don't break them—or damage the room. *(The five boys came into the room, took a quick survey of the equipment.)*

Timmy: Machine guns! Machine guns! *(He makes noises for the machine guns.)*

Buddy: Oh, boy! Guns! Where is the gun? Boy! I'm going to shoot this—— *(Timmy hands Buddy the gun. Buddy makes loud machine-gun noises.)*

Ernest: I'm going to paint a picture. *(He goes over to the paint table and paints a sheet of paper yellow and blue and green.)* This is a rainbow. Is there any black in a rainbow?

Saul: A black rainbow! Yes. Put black in it.

Ernest: I don't think there should be black in it.

Saul: Look at all these things. *(He has a box of soldiers and animals.)*

Buddy (feeling the furniture): I'm going to play with these things—whatever they are.

Therapist: You can't tell what they are.

Buddy: I can guess.

Timmy (who has been rearranging the doll house): I'm fixing the place up, Buddy.

Buddy (picking up toy icebox): Here's a bar of soap. *(Others laugh. Buddy laughs, too.)* I can tell. It's a bar of soap.

Timmy: I'm going to fix up this house.

Saul: I'm going to—— *(Sits on the floor, buries his head in his arms. Others glance at him, then go back to their play.)*

Bobby: I'm going to get all these trucks out and play with them.

(Buddy has moved over to the box of blocks and begins to feel them, trying to identify them. Ernest is still painting his rainbow. Buddy takes out a long thin board and swings it around. It smacks Timmy, who is stooping over the house.)

Timmy: Don't do that, Buddy. You hit me.

Buddy (laughing): I hit you? Was that you, Timmy?

Timmy: That was me.

(Buddy tosses the board back into the box. Bobby lines up all the army trucks. Saul gets the toy cannon and shoots it aimlessly.)

Ernest (getting the baby doll): I'm the mother of this baby. Don't anybody touch this baby.

Buddy (accidentally bumping into the other big doll and beginning to feel it): This is a baby, too. It's a big one.

Bobby (having lined up the trucks, he then gets the ambulance and begins to knock over all the trucks, yelling): Bang! Accident! Accident! Somebody hurt over here!

Timmy (taking toy machine gun): I'll shoot *you*, Bobby.

Bobby: I'll run my ambulance over *you*.

Timmy: Bang! Bang!

(Timmy puts down the gun and turns back to play with the house. Buddy and Saul begin to crayon. Timmy leaves the house and begins to paint. Bobby explores the clay jar, but returns to the army trucks. He picks up the machine gun and shoots his brother Timmy.)

Therapist: You got even with Timmy, then. *(Bobby smiles, continues to play with trucks.)*

Timmy: What color is a house? What does a house look like? *(He turns to the therapist.)* What does *my* house look like? What color is it? I mean *my own* house.

Therapist: You can't remember what your own house looks like.

Timmy: No. Do you know?

Therapist: Mother R's house is gray.

Ernest: Mother R's house is dirty. *(Makes a face.)*

Therapist: You don't like the house to be dirty.

Ernest: It's a mess.

Therapist: You don't like it to be a mess.

Ernest (gets the baby doll again. Then he gets the nursing bottle and drinks from the bottle.): Look, fellows! *(The boys stop what they are doing and turn and look at Ernest in amazement.)* This is all right to do here. You can play baby here. You can play anything you like here. Now I'm playing baby.

Therapist: Sometimes you like to play baby.

Ernest (going over to the hammer. He bangs away on the boards in the block box. He gets the ambulance, pushes it around idly, watches Saul, who has found the box of dolls. Saul picks up the father doll): That's the father. *(Saul throws the father back in the box.)*

Therapist: You don't like the father. [This was getting ahead of Saul. It is too interpretive to be safe. "You don't want the father doll" would have been a better response. However, it was accepted by Saul.]

Saul (shaking head, no): Where's the mother?

Ernest: Here's the mother.

Saul (hugging the mother doll): Poor mother. *(He sighs deeply, places the mother doll in a chair in the doll house.)*

Therapist: You like the mother, but you feel sad about her. [This too is interpretive.] *(Saul buries his face in his arms.)* It makes you feel like hiding your face.

[This is interpretive, probably due to the fact that the foster mother had related the frequency of this mannerism of Saul's. The therapist is trying to explain it to Saul. This is a violation of the basic principles. "You feel like hiding your face," would seem to be more accurate, more helpful, and more acceptable.]

Bobby (getting the nursing bottle and giving it to Ernest): Here's baby bottle.

Ernest (takes it, drinks from it, cries like a baby, drinks from it like a baby; then he takes off the nipple and drinks from the bottle again): I'll drink it this way. It's more fun. I'm not a baby.

Therapist: It's more fun to act like you're grown up than to act like a baby.

Ernest: Sometimes.

Therapist: Sometimes.

(Bobby and Saul and Timmy and Ernest begin to draw with the crayons. Buddy has reached the paints and is fumbling around the jars.)

Buddy: Are these paints? Can I paint? I never painted. I'll paint.

Therapist (getting large sheets of paper in position for Buddy): Now you may paint. *(Buddy laughs hilariously,*

*paints streaks on the paper, starting with the first jar of paint
on the left and going from jar to jar.)*

Buddy: I'm painting!

Timmy (to Buddy and therapist): I made the house I
painted black and red. When it dries, I'll put black doors and
windows in it. *(Picks up hammer and peg-board and pounds
as hard as he can, then crawls over to the doll house again.)*
I'll play with the house again. *(He crawls over and gets a
nursing bottle, crawls back to therapist and hands the bottle
to her.)* Here. Put the nipple on this for me. *(Therapist
does.)*

*(Timmy crawls back to the doll house, holding the nursing
bottle and begins to play with the house. Saul begins to draw
a house. He colors the entire house black. Then Saul gets one
of the nursing bottles.)*

Saul: I want to be a baby.

Therapist: You would like to be a baby. *(Saul sucks on
the bottle.)*

*Buddy (finishing his picture and feeling his way over to the
corner of the room where the hammer set is located):* I
want the hammer. Where is it? *(Timmy hands the hammer
to Buddy, and pushes the peg-board out in front of him.)*

Timmy: Don't hit your fingers.

Buddy: I won't. *(Laughs. He begins to pound.)*

[Had the therapist remarked at this point, "Timmy doesn't
want you to hit your fingers," it seems possible that the other
boys might have adopted a protective attitude toward Buddy,
seeking what might have appeared to be praise from the
therapist.]

Timmy (now at the clay table): I'm going to make a
turtle.

Ernest: It would be nice if we could take these things
home.

[Ernest was familiar with the limitation about removing
materials from the playroom. It is interesting to note how he
seems to be structuring the play session for the other boys.
First he demonstrated the use of the nursing bottles. Now he
seems to be asking the therapist to state one of the limitations for the group. However, the therapist does not interpret
this time.]

Therapist: You would like to take them home, but the
toys all have to be left here because other children use the
toys.

Ernest: If we took them away there wouldn't be any left for them.

Therapist: There wouldn't be any left for them.

Ernest (hammering the peg-board viciously): I want to take them home.

Therapist: You still want to take them home, even though you know you can't. It makes you mad to know that you can't take them home.

Ernest: I'll break them.

Therapist: You would even like to break them up, because you can't take them home.

Timmy: It's against the rules to break the things. Anyway we can come back here every week. There wouldn't be anything for us, either, if we broke them up.

[Perhaps this was why Ernest threatened to break the toys. He knew that this was his last therapy session.]

Ernest (stares at therapist, then smiles): Okay! We are going to have a play this afternoon. Let's have it here. Okay?

Bobby and Timmy: Okay!

(Ernest gets a machine gun. Timmy gets the other machine gun. Bobby gets a gun. Sounds of shooting follow.)

Ernest: Clean up the room. Put away the crayons. We're going to have a battle.

Bobby (pressing the gun against Timmy's back): Bang! I blew up Timmy.

Buddy (at paint table): Is this red? I want red. Where is red?

Therapist (handing him the jar of red paint): This is the red.

(Buddy laughs and makes wide, sweeping streaks of red across the paper. The other boys glance at him. Bobby gets all the guns. Timmy hammers. Saul withdraws to the corner, gets out some soldiers, arranges them in two straight rows and builds a wall of blocks around them.)

Buddy: I made a flag. A *red* flag!

Timmy (getting the nursing bottle again): Look here, Bobby. You play with me now. You be the father.

Bobby: I'm baby.

Timmy: You be the father.

Bobby: Now if I'm going to play, I'll be the baby.

Timmy: Okay. Get in bed.

Bobby: Where is bed?

Timmy: Here on the floor.

Bobby: Oh, hell! All right. (*He lies down on the floor. Timmy feeds him the bottle. The water spills on Bobby.*)

Bobby: Dammit. You'll drown me. (*Timmy gets the baby doll, wraps it up in the blanket.*)

Ernest (with cannon): Now I'll shoot Miss—— (*Laughs and pretends to shoot the therapist.*)

Therapist: You would like to shoot me.

Timmy: I'll have to play with the clown and make the baby laugh—at least, make it stop crying.

Therapist: You don't like to have the baby cry.

Ernest (at therapist): Bang! Bang!

Saul (pointing to soldiers): They can't get out.

Therapist: They are all blocked in.

Ernest (shooting at therapist): Bang! Bang!

Therapist: You don't like to have me talk to the other boys.

[This was interpretation, based upon a thorough knowledge of Ernest's mannerisms, but nevertheless interpretation.]

Ernest: No. Bang! Bang! (*Shoots at each boy.*) Bang! Bang! Bang!

Therapist: You want to shoot all of us.

Ernest: I'm going to take this gun home and shoot Mother R, too.

Therapist: You want to shoot Mother R, too.

Ernest: You bet I do. And Bobby and Saul and Timmy and Buddy. Bang! Bang! Bang! Bang!

Buddy (messing with the paints): Shoot me, too.

Ernest: I did shoot you.

Therapist: Only five minutes left, boys.

Ernest: Bang! Bang! Bang!

Therapist: You want to shoot everybody.

Ernest: Clean up this playroom, you kids!

Therapist: You like to boss them around.

Ernest: Bang! Bang!

Timmy (grabbing up a gun): Bang!

Bobby (getting a gun and pointing it at the boys): Reach for it, all of you. (*The boys all drop their guns and hold up their hands—all except Ernest. He takes the little machine gun and fastens it to the doorknob.*)

Ernest: Nobody else can get in here now. If they do they will get shot.

Therapist: You don't want anyone else to come here after

you go home. [Again the therapist gets ahead of Ernest and interprets.]

Ernest: No. I'll shoot them if they do.

Bobby: Pretend we're Japs. Ready! Set! Fire! *(Sounds of gunfire.)*

Saul: I want to clean up the room. *(Saul and Bobby begin to pick up the toys. Timmy is at the doll house again. Buddy is still painting.)*

Bobby: Clean up, everybody.

Ernest (looking out into hall): If that man comes back to the door again and looks in here, I'll shoot him. *(The man does come and Ernest opens fire.)*

Bobby (grabbing nursing bottle): Next time I want to drink a whole bottle of water. Next time, I'll be the baby.

Timmy: Next time I'll be a baby, too.

Saul (looking in the doll house): Where's the mother?

Timmy: Here she is. *(Tosses mother doll to Saul. He puts the mother doll in a chair in the doll house.)*

Saul: There, Mother. You can stay there.

Therapist: You want the mother to be comfortable.

Ernest: No. I don't care what happens to her.

Therapist: You are mad at your mother.

[Interpreting again, the therapist goes beyond the expressed feeling.]

Ernest: I am—going home—pretty soon.

Therapist: And you don't want to.

[The therapist certainly was not reflecting feeling by this remark. She was finishing a sentence, going way beyond what the child was expressing.]

Ernest: No. Yes. There are horses and cows and my puppy.

Therapist: You don't want to go away from here—and yet you do want to go home and live on a farm and have all those animals to take care of.

Ernest: Yes. *(Stares at therapist.)* It might be better than here.

Therapist: It might be lots more fun.

Time was up. The therapist took the group back to the foster home.

COMMENTS

An analysis of the therapist's responses illustrates

several points. Out of thirty-three responses, twenty of them were directed toward Ernest, six were in response to Saul, three responses were to Timmy and Buddy, while Bobby received only one response. This is a very uneven scattering of responses. Too many of the therapist's responses in this first contact are interpretive and go beyond the feeling that the boys express.

Saul's behavior is interesting when compared with the behavior reported by the foster mother. There was no reluctance to talk in the playroom. Saul did not resist the other members of the group.

Buddy's behavior is also interesting. The placement of a boy with such a handicap in a group of boys without similar handicap was an experiment. It did not seem to have any negative influence. Buddy seemed delighted to be accepted as one of them. His pleasure in painting was quite noticeable. Buddy was the only member of the group who did not drink from the nursing bottle.

Timmy and Bobby were brothers. This raises another question: Is it advisable to have brothers or sisters in the same group? The first contact hints at sibling rivalry. Could sibling rivalry be worked out in a therapy group?

Ernest monopolized the therapy hour. His behavior seems to have been the result of a feeling of jealousy which was aroused because he had to share the therapist and because this was his last therapy session and he knew that the other boys were to come for eight weeks. However, Ernest seemed to be able to accept this and did not seem to be too disturbed about it.

An analysis of the play activities shows that the boys included reactions to home and to parents, desires to be a baby, and aggressive reaction in their play. The fact that the boys who drew houses colored them black may also be indicative of their feelings toward their homes. Although this is speculation on the part of the therapist, a study of the art work done by children during play-therapy sessions seems to support the theory that the colors which the children use in their drawing and paintings are significant. At the present writing, however, there is insufficient data to verify the theory.

SECOND CONTACT

The four boys enter the room eagerly. Buddy drops down by the house. He begins to feel each article in reach and name it. Saul, Timmy, and Bobby go over to the window sill where the nursing bottles (filled with water) are placed.

Timmy: Oh, look! Baby bottles. We can play baby.

Therapist: You would like to play baby.

Saul: Yeah. *I'm* the baby. *(To Timmy.)* You be the mother.

Bobby: I'm baby, too.

Timmy: Okay. I'll be mother.

Saul and Bobby (crying like babies): I want my bottle. I want my bottle.

Timmy (handing bottles to Bobby and Saul): Here, baby. Nice bottle.

(Saul and Bobby lie on the floor and coo and act like babies. Timmy stands at the table and squeezes water out in a cup, then drinks it.)

Bobby (getting doll family): I'm going to play with these and suck my bottle, too.

(Timmy asks therapist to put nipple on bottle for him. Therapist does.)

Timmy (lying down on the floor, sucking the bottle): I'm just going to be a baby.

Therapist: You would like to be babies again.

Bobby: Look. *(To therapist.)* He's eight-year-old baby. I'm seven-year-old baby.

Bobby: Uh-huh. *(Timmy and Bobby lie there on the floor, perfectly relaxed, sucking on the bottles.)*

Saul (crawling over to toy telephone): I'm going to call up daddy. Hello. Hello. *Hello.* Huh, nobody answers.

Therapist: Your daddy doesn't answer you.

Saul (sadly): No. He never does. I haven't seen him for about twenty years.

Therapist: You would like to see your daddy.

Saul· And my mummy. Poor mummy. She's been in a hospital for fifty years.

Therapist: You miss your mummy, too.

Saul (rolling over and clutching the bottle, whimpers): Mummy. Mummy. I want my mummy.

Therapist: You want your mummy. You miss her.

Saul: She's sick. She's in a hospital.

Therapist: It worries you because she is in the hospital and is sick.

Buddy (suddenly, and in a very loud voice): You know what? We made so much noise yesterday *she* put tape on our mouths.

Timmy (coming over to therapist): Yeah. See the mark. *(Shows therapist the red marks on his lip where the tape had been yanked off.)*

Therapist: You didn't like it when she put tape on your mouths because you made too much noise.

[The reader will notice the absence of any question to determine who "she" was.]

Buddy: No!

Saul: We can make noise here and no tape.

Therapist: You can make all the noise you want to in here—and no tape. *(All four yell at full lung capacity, watching the therapist.)*

Timmy (suspiciously): You ain't deaf, are you?

Therapist: You wonder if I'm deaf because I don't stop your noise. No, I'm not deaf.

[Thinking: Unfortunately, no one else in this building is deaf, either! The boys try it out again in unison and seem delighted with the results.]

Saul: We'll play policeman. Bang! Bang! Bang! Everybody is dead.

Therapist: You got rid of them all.

Buddy (going over to Saul, finds the cars by the touch system, bangs them together, laughing and shouting): Accident! Accident!

Bobby (painting a picture of an ambulance, dropping red paint down on it): It's an ambulance. See? Someone was hurt. Look. All bloody.

Therapist: an accident, an ambulance, and blood. Someone was hurt.

Bobby: I know *who.*

Therapist: You know who was hurt.

Bobby: I ain't going to tell.

Therapist: You know, but you don't want to tell.

Timmy: Somebody I know?

Buddy: Somebody I know?

Bobby: I ain't a-gonna tell.

Therapist: Bobby still doesn't want to tell who got hurt.

[Timmy and Saul sit at the table and pour water into cups and "eat it" with the tiny spoons. Buddy comes over to the table, fumbles for the baby doll in the cradle, picks it up, and gets the bottle with Timmy's help.]

Buddy· Where's bottle?

Timmy (handing one to Buddy): Here. This is yours, Bud.

Buddy· I'm the father. *(Runs his hand down Timmy's arm, feels the cup Timmy has in his hand.)* What are you doing?

Timmy: Pouring water into cups.

Buddy· Give me a cup. *(Timmy hands Buddy a cup. Buddy pours water from bottle into cup, does not spill any. He laughs gleefully.)* I can do it, too.

Therapist· You like to be able to do what Timmy does.

Timmy: I want to paint. *(Timmy paints. Saul and Bobby sit down and roll the clay around.)*

Bobby: I want some more water.

Therapist· You would like more water, but we can't get it now. There will be a bottle full for each of you each time; but no more.

Timmy: We can each have one bottle.

[Timmy accepts the limitation.]

Buddy: We oughta have so much water in here we could go wading.

Therapist: You would like to have more water, but there will be just one bottle for each of you each time.

Bobby: I want more water.

Therapist· You like to have your own way. *(Bobby squirts water on the therapist.)* You're a little bit angry because you can't get your own way. That's why you squirted water on me. Squirt the water on yourself—or on the floor, but not on the rest of us.

Bobby (stares at the therapist, grins, goes over to the clay table)· Okay. I'll made me a turtle.

Buddy (shouting with laughter): A turtle got to have water, too.

[Bobby makes a clay turtle. Timmy has painted a very strange picture, big, shapeless, blue gobs with lines going down to the green grass.]

Timmy· Look. Here's something floating through the air with a string on it. It came out of the bushes. Nobody knows what it is. *(Timmy paints it light blue first, then goes over it with purple. He paints odd shapes of white up at the top. Saul is watching him.)*

Saul: That must be a cloud.

Buddy: I wouldn't be afraid to break one in here. I wouldn't be afraid, but I won't.

Timmy: It's not a cloud.

Saul: It's a cloud if it's white. Nothing in the sky is white, except clouds.

Buddy (singing at the top of his lungs): Me want a hamburger.

All (singing): Me want a hamburger. Me want a hamburger.

Buddy (yelling): I want Bobby's head. (Buddy goes over and runs his fingers over Bobby's face. Bobby shivers. Buddy gently pokes at Bobby's eyes.) I want Bobby's eyes.

Therapist: You wish you had eyes like Bobby.

Buddy (singing loudly): Bobby on the ocean.
　　　　　　　　　　　　Bobby on the sea.
　　　　　　　　　　　　Bobby broke a milk bottle
　　　　　　　　　　　　And blamed it on me.
　　　　　　　　　　　　Ma told Pa.
　　　　　　　　　　　　Pa told Ma.
　　　　　　　　　　　　Bobby got a lickin'
　　　　　　　　　　　　Ha! Ha! Ha!

(The boys all laugh. Bobby sings it back, substituting Buddy's name for his own.)

Buddy (to Bobby): I'm not a-scared to throw paint on you.

Bobby (to Buddy): You better not.

Buddy (yelling at top of lungs again): I'm not a-scared to break up everything in here.

Therapist: You're not afraid to do or say anything in here.

Buddy: I'm not afraid!

Therapist: You're not afraid.

Buddy (giggling): In here.

Therapist: You're not afraid *in here.*

Saul: We found a puppy yesterday. Mother R says we can keep it if nobody claims it.

[Buddy hits Bobby with crayon box. Bobby ignores it, moves over to the doll cradle, picks up the doll, and hugs it tenderly. Buddy tries to take the doll from Bobby, who evades him. Buddy takes the box of crayons that Bobby had in his hand. Bobby lays the doll down and tries forcefully to retrieve the crayons. Buddy, loosing the crayons, goes back to the paint table.]

Buddy: Where is red? Show me red. *(Timmy, who is drawing an airplane with crayons, stretched out on the floor, gets up and hands Buddy the red paint. Buddy smears the red paint over the paper.)* I'm going to take this home. I'm going to hang this on the wall. I never painted before. *(He laughs hilariously.)*

Therapist: You like to paint—and to do the things these other boys do. It makes you happy. *(Saul is on the floor drawing on airplane. Bobby is playing with the house. Buddy steps back on Timmy's drawing and tears it.)*

Timmy: Look out, Bud! You *tore* my picture.

[Buddy laughs. He sits down on the floor, reaches out and gets the box containing the toy trucks. It is uncanny how he already knows just where everything is and can find his way around without stepping on anything. He sits there, feeling the cars. pushing them around. chuckling. Bobby and Timmy play with the doll house. Saul, Timmy, and Bobby keep the nursing bottles with them all the hour, saving some of the water. Buddy edges over to Bobby and Timmy.]

Buddy: Give me some of the furniture. *(He gets the box of furniture, takes out the pieces, feels each one, asks, "What's this?" "Is this a table?" He seems delighted when Bobby or Timmy or the therapist says yes. Then he goes back over the pieces, saying, "This is a chair." "This is a table.")*

Therapist: It makes you feel good when you know what they are without being told.

Buddy: I don't always have to be told. *(Giggles.)*

Timmy: How many more minutes have we got?

Therapist: Ten more minutes.

Timmy: I don't want the time to end.

Therapist: You would like to stay here.

[Timmy gets out the blocks.]

Buddy (to Bobby, who has been handing him the furniture, piece by piece): Don't give me too much stuff. I got enough now. Too much and I won't know what's here.

Therapist: If you don't have too many things you can remember what you've got.

Timmy: I'll play alone. I won't play with anyone else.

Therapist: You want to play alone now.

[Timmy builds a block tower. Saul has finished drawing his picture. Now he sprinkles it with water from the nursing bottle.]

Saul: It's raining. The sky is crying.

[Bobby has straightened up the doll house. Buddy reaches in one of the rooms, knocks over some of the furniture.]

Bobby· Oh, Buddy!

Buddy (laughing): Well, fix it again. *(Bobby crawls away from the doll house, lies on the floor sucking the bottle like a baby again.)*

Bobby: There are so many toys in here I don't know what to play with.

Therapist: You can't make up your mind what to play with because there are so many toys.

Bobby: I never can make up my mind.

Therapist: You always have trouble making up your mind.

Bobby: How many more minutes?

Therapist: Five more minutes.

Bobby: I'm going over here and make so much noise they will think the whole town is on fire. *(He gets the hammer and pounds the peg set with all his might. Saul and Timmy have taken out the soldiers and are having a terrific battle, yelling, screaming, making machine-gun noises. Buddy opens his mouth very wide and howls.)*

Therapist· You want to make all the noise you can now.

Bobby (taking nipple off bottle and coming over to therapist): Will you please put this back on for me?

Buddy (hammering away at the end of the peg-board set): Bang! Bang! Bang!

Bobby (to Buddy): You're pounding that on the wrong end.

Buddy: I don't care. It's the noise I like.

[Timmy fixes two chairs together to make a bed, lies down, drinks from the nursing bottle. Bobby builds a bed out of large building blocks, lies down like a baby. Buddy picks up the baby doll, hugs it, kisses it, puts it back in bed. Bobby crawls over, gets the blanket off the doll, puts it on the floor, lies down on it.]

Timmy· Mommy! Mommy! I want my mommy.

Bobby· I'm not mother. I'm baby, too. Doctor! Doctor! I'm sick. Oh!

Buddy (immediately assuming the rôle of doctor): Yes. I'm coming. *(He gets a piece of clay out of the clay jar.)* Here is medicine. *(He gives it to Bobby.)*

Bobby (wailing): I want my mommy.

Therapist: Bobby wants his mommy, too.

(Buddy picks up the clay jar, places it on top of his head, walks around the toy-strewn room.)

Therapist (she couldn't help it!): Be careful!

Buddy (shouting with laughter): You're afraid I'll drop it?

Therapist (meekly): Yes, I'm afraid you'll drop it.

Buddy: *I'm* not afraid to drop it.

Therapist: *You're* not afraid, but I am.

[Buddy laughs louder than ever, puts jar back on edge of table. Timmy reaches up and pushes it back to safety.]

Bobby: Time up?

Therapist (weakly): Yes. Time's up.

COMMENTS

In this contact the therapist scattered her responses equally among the four boys. Again Timmy, Saul, and Bobby pursue the baby play. Buddy does not join in during this contact, either. Buddy has a tendency to assume the more adult rôles. He is the one who offers to be the doctor, or who announces that he will be the father.

During this contact the boys test out the limitations. Buddy and Bobby have more difficulty accepting the limitations than do Timmy and Saul. When Buddy announces that he is not afraid to throw paint or to break everything in the room, the therapist wisely avoided the trap of repeating limitations. Instead, she reflected back to Buddy the feeling that he was *not afraid* to do those shocking things *in here.* Already the boys are realizing that this play situation is different. In the first contact, Ernest pointed that out to the boys when he said, "That's all right to do here. You can play baby here. You can play anything you like here." In this contact the boys make the observation that in here "You can make noise and no tape." Buddy feels the permissiveness of the situation and yet he argues against the few limitations. "We oughta have so much water in here we could go wading," and "A turtle got to have water," and then the direct threat to break the limitations. The therapist believes that the recognition of feeling did more to help the boys stay within the limitations than a defensive repetition of them, which might have served as a challenge to these boys.

Another thought-provoking element in these contacts is the ease with which the boys get along with one another. In the foster home, the mother said that there was constant agitation and fighting among the boys. She said that Buddy "got on the other children's nerves" and teased them unmercifully. In the playroom there is an unusual lack of conflict. They are very considerate of Buddy's handicap and help him find the things he asks for. He enters into their play and they accept him as one of them. In the playroom, Saul, too, is acting contrary to report. He is participating in the play, associating in a co-operative manner with the other boys, expressing himself quite freely.

One of the puzzling factors in Saul's case is his expressed attitude about his father. Saul's father had a record of faithful contact with his son. According to the case worker, the father-son relationship was good. This illustrates the possible harm of interpretation. During the first contact Saul threw the father doll back into the box. The therapist commented, "You don't like the father," and Saul apparently accepted it. Saul's expressed feeling for his mother is odd, considering the fact that he has not seen his mother for four years. During the first three years of his life the mother was not well, was given to fits of brooding and peculiar behavior. Before the mother had been placed in the hospital, she had attempted to kill Saul with a butcher knife, but was prevented from doing so by her husband. In spite of this past history, Saul cried out for his mother and seemed to brood about her.

Another high spot in this contact is Buddy's expressed desire for Bobby's eyes, followed immediately by his aggressive declarations, which were followed by his playful attack on Bobby, his affectionate treatment of the doll, and finally terminated in his painting and the statement, "I'm going to take this home. I'm going to hang this on the wall. I never painted before," and his obvious pleasure in being able to do what the other boys could do. Incidentally, the foster mother permitted the boys to put on the walls of their rooms any paintings or pictures that they made. Buddy's painting was prominently displayed.

Toward the end of the contact the therapist wondered if the "vomiting spells" that were a habitual part of Bobby's and Timmy's behavior could be caused by the longing for their mother. Bobby cries out, "I'm baby, too. Doctor! Doctor! I'm sick. Oh!" and then later, "I want my mommy."

The closing episode in this contact demonstrates what might happen when the therapist drops her rôle as therapist and becomes an ordinary person. She very nearly lost control of the therapy situation by the cry, "Be careful!" Buddy aptly reflected her expressed feelings. The warning and the expressed lack of confidence in Buddy served as a challenge to him. It was fortunate that it occurred so close to the end of the hour. Timmy's quiet, unobtrusive actions in helping Buddy place the jar with safety were more helpful than the therapist's outburst—but therapists are human, too.

THIRD CONTACT

When the therapist went after the boys for the third play period, Timmy was waiting on the curb. The others rushed down to the car. They had Charles with them. "Can Charles come with us?" they asked. Then Charles, a tall, quiet boy about ten years old, said, "I'd like to. Can I? You see, I'm the only boy left here when you take these other boys, and Mother R said to ask you if I could come, too." The therapist agreed to take him.

The foster mother said that Charles was a very quiet, reserved boy, who moped around the house most of the time, cried easily, and seemed to be always "in a fog."

After the therapist agreed to take Charles, Timmy asked her to come in the house for a minute and meet their mother. She had dropped in for a short visit just a few minutes before the therapist had arrived.

When the group went into the playroom, the boys, with

the exception of Buddy, made a dash for the nursing bottles and began sucking them. Charles picked up the toy telephone.

Charles: I'm going to call my mother. She works at—— I want to talk to her.

Therapist: You would like to talk to your mother.

Charles: Hello, Mother. I'm just a baby, Mother. *(Sucks on bottle.)* I'm taking my bottle now. You better come home.

Therapist: You want your mother to come home and take care of her baby.

[Timmy has taken out the wooden dolls and is playing with them. Bobby is painting a brown house. Buddy is feeling the new table and benches and easel that have been added to the room since the boys' last visit. Bobby has placed his bottle on the shelf of the easel. Buddy, in the process of feeling the easel, knocks Bobby's nursing bottle off and it breaks, scattering glass and water all over the floor. There was a good bit of conversation lost here while the therapist picked up the broken glass and mopped up the water. Bobby's face puckered up as though he was going to cry.]

Timmy: Now Bobby is going to cry.

Therapist: You think Bobby is going to cry because his bottle got broken.

Bobby: No. I'm not going to cry. *(He snuffs back his tears.)*

Therapist: You feel like crying, but you're not going to.

Timmy: Poor Bobby. He lost his bottle. I'll fix things for you, Bobby. I'll help you.

Therapist: You want to help Bobby.

[Timmy pulls out the benches and makes a bed, then he puts Bobby to bed and holds the bottle to Bobby's lips, puts his arm around him, treats him like a tiny baby.]

Therapist (to Bobby): You like to be the baby. *(Bobby nods agreement and closes his eyes. Timmy covers him with the baby blanket. Then suddenly, with a mischievous twinkle in his eye, Timmy takes off the nipple and pours some water right in Bobby's face. Bobby howls. Timmy laughs.)*

Bobby: You are mean to me.

Therapist (to Bobby): You think that was a mean trick to play on you.

Timmy (still laughing): Babies got to have baths, too. I just gave him a bath.

Bobby (mopping face dry with the blanket): Not only me, but the blanket.

Buddy: They have a new table here. And this is a bench.

Therapist: You've discovered what the new things are.

Buddy (jumping up and down and yelling): I like! I like! I like!

Therapist: You like it here.

[Buddy tries to give Bobby some water in one of the little cups. Bobby, entering into the baby play again, lies down on the bench and lets Buddy lift up his head and hold the cup to his lips. Buddy accidentally spills the water down Bobby's neck. Bobby pushes Buddy away roughly. Buddy falls against the easel. Then Buddy goes over to the corner, gets the colored doll, turns it across his knee, takes up a long thin board and paddles the doll.]

Buddy: This is Bobby. I'm fixin' him.

Therapist: You would like to paddle Bobby because he pushed you.

Buddy: Yeah. (*A few more whacks and he puts the doll down. He goes back to the window sill, picks up his bottle, empties some of it in the basin, and, with Saul's help, floats a toy submarine in it.*)

Buddy (to therapist): I want some more water.

Therapist: You would like some more water, but you can't get any more today.

Buddy: I know where I can get it.

Therapist: You know just where you could get it; but we said last time that there would be only one bottle for each of you.

Buddy (shouting): I want more water!

Therapist: Think if you yell loud enough you might get it.

Buddy: I ain't afraid to push out and get it.

Therapist: You're not afraid to——

Buddy (good-naturedly): But I won't.

Therapist: But you won't.

Saul: I'm going to play war.

Bobby (jumping up off bench): I'll play.

Buddy (knocks another bottle off the bench. This one doesn't break): Oh! Oh! I broke another.

Therapist: You think you broke another bottle.

Buddy: Did I?

Therapist: No. *(Long pause.)*

Buddy: I'm glad I didn't.

Therapist: You're glad you didn't break another.

[Timmy and Charles fill the house with wooden people. Then they suddenly scoop out everything.]

Timmy: A storm. A storm came and blew everything out of the house.

Therapist: The storm ruined the house.

Timmy (to Charles): Now let's fix it all neat. Give me all the pink things. They all go in one room. I like the house to be neat and clean.

Therapist: You want the house to be neat and clean.

Charles: I'm going to help you. *(Both the boys fix the house neatly.)*

[Buddy gets up, goes to the table, feels around, noting several things on the table, including the nursing bottles.]

Buddy (muttering): In my way. *(To therapist.)* Move these away for me. *(Therapist does.)* Are they all gone now?

Therapist: Yes. Everything is off the table now.

Buddy (muttering): I don't want to break them.

Therapist: You don't like to break things when you just accidentally knock them off.

Buddy (smiling): Sometimes I can't see.

Therapist: Sometimes you can't see them and they do get knocked off and you don't mean to do it at all.

Buddy (beginning to mark on the drawing paper odd, disconnected marks): I'm drawing.

Therapist: You like to draw.

Buddy: I can draw here. *(Sings "London Bridge." Bobby is drawing at the easel with crayons, drawing airplanes dropping bombs. Charles is still playing with Timmy at the doll house, carefully fitting out each room. Saul is drawing around the wooden animals. He is perfectly relaxed, carrying on a conversation with Charles and Timmy about his picture, the animals, the furniture.)* What are you doing, Bobby? *(Buddy is at the table, Bobby at the easel.)*

Bobby: I'm drawing.

Buddy: What are you drawing?

Bobby: A convoy.

Buddy: What am I coloring?

Therapist: What are you making, Buddy?

Buddy: I don't know. I can't see it.

Therapist: What do you want it to be?

Buddy (shrugging): I don't know. I'm just putting marks down here. Can I take this home and tack it up on the wall in my room?

Therapist: Yes. You would like to hang up the picture you draw.

Buddy (laughing): Oh yes! Oh yes! I would.

[Although the other boys looked at Buddy's picture at this time, not one remarked that it had no form or meaning. The colors he had used were black and red. The marks were rather short and squared.]

Buddy: Next time I'll draw, too.

Therapist: It's fun to come here and draw.

Timmy (referring to Buddy's picture): You know, that *could* be bolts and nuts.

Buddy (chuckling): A squirrel, too.

Timmy: Yeah. *(He goes back to the house. He pushes the army trucks up to the house.)* Here comes a convoy. Here are two little girls walking home. The daddy is with them. Then pretend—oh, pretend like a big storm came up when all these other people are in the house. [*These other people* are the mother, the grandmother, Mother R, the boys.] And the storm is a whopper and it comes plenty fast. *(He blows at the house. Charles helps.)* The daddy is going to be back there, too. *(He throws the daddy in the house. He is speaking rapidly.)* Everybody is in the house now and this terrible storm is coming closer and closer. *(He waves his arms wildly round the house.)*

Therapist: That awful storm is coming right at the house.

Timmy (claps hands twice): Pretend like it set the house on fire. And the fire just *rages* through. *(He sweeps his hands in room after room and violently scoops out the furniture.)* It burns all these people—and the funiture, too. It burns all these people—and all these—and the father and the mother—

Saul (who has crawled over and watched the destruction): Not the mother.

Timmy (glaring fiercely at Saul): Yes, the mother.

Saul (almost crying): Not the mother.

Therapist: Not Saul's mother. Timmy's mother.

Bobby: And my mother, too.

Therapist: And Bobby's mother, but not Saul's mother. *(Saul reaches in and gets the mother doll.)*

Timmy (yelling): You'll get burnt, Saul. You'll get burnt.

Saul (sobbing): I don't care.

Therapist: Saul has saved his mother. She is safe now.

Timmy: Come on, cat, you can get out. (*Timmy saves the toy cat.*)

Charles: The fire is over now. (*Obviously too much for Charles.*)

Timmy: No, it isn't. No, it isn't.

Therapist: Charles wants the fire to be out, but Timmy doesn't. (*Timmy picks up the house, turns it upside down, shakes it, leaves it.*)

Bobby: Was the fireman the only one saved?

Charles: Poor man. He was drunk, too. (*Charles upends one of the beds and places one of the wooden people on it.*) Look. The bed is standing up on one end and the man is standing on top of it. He is afraid of a mouse.

Therapist: The man is afraid of a mouse so he gets up on something, out of the way.

Charles: Everybody is afraid of something. (*Charles puts all the wooden people up on something—tables, dresser, bed, ice box, etc.*)

Therapist: They are all trying to get away from the things they are afraid of.

Bobby (hugging and kissing the baby doll): I'm a sissy because I like the baby doll.

Therapist: You like the baby doll and you think maybe you're a sissy because you do.

Bobby: I *wish* I was still a baby.

Therapist: You wish you were still a baby.

Timmy: You can be a baby when you come here. That's what we told Mother R. We like to come here because we can be two years old again.

Therapist: You like to come here and play baby.

Bobby: I like it here. I would like to come and stay here forever. (*He goes over to the easel, gets the yellow crayon, colors a picture all yellow. He has trouble with the thumbtacks, asks the therapist for help. She helps him. Referring to his picture.*) Clouds. See? Sunshine and hills.

(*Absolute silence reigns for five minutes.*)

Bobby (whose picture is finished now): I *could* get this down without help, but I don't want to tear it. Will you?

Therapist (taking it down for him): You want to keep this picture nice.

Bobby: For *my* room. I'm going to take it home.

[Charles is still sucking on his bottle. Then he gets the

hammer and peg-board set and whams away at it. Saul asks Charles to draw the "bomb-doors" on his plane for him. Charles does, quite willingly, then he goes back to his pounding, sucking on the bottle all the time.]

Charles: I'm going to build a house just for me.

Therapist: You want to build a house just for yourself.

Timmy (to Charles): How do you like being a baby again?

Charles: Okay. Soon I'm going to lay down on the floor and go to sleep.

Therapist: You would like to keep right on playing baby— even go to sleep.

Charles (lying down on the floor, sucking at the bottle): I'll sleep forever.

Therapist: You want to sleep forever.

(Quiet again descends. Timmy draws airplanes. Buddy, at the table, continues to make marks on his drawing paper.)

Timmy: This is fun.

Charles (sits up suddenly, reaches over and picks up gun): I wanta shoot somebody.

Therapist: Feel like you would like to shoot somebody.

Charles: I *wanta* shoot somebody.

Saul: Who you gonna shoot?

Charles: Anybody who makes me go home.

Therapist: You don't want to go home.

(Silence. The bell rings.)

Therapist: Five more minutes.

[The group ignores this remark. Buddy gets another sheet of paper, starts to feel around for crayons.]

Charles: You won't have time.

Buddy: Sure I will. Five minutes.

Charles (getting some paper for himself): Then I will. *(But he doesn't.)*

Buddy: Where is black? I want black. This will be a black picture. *(He makes disconnected marks on the paper. He holds the crayons up close to his eyes to try to determine the color. He sticks them so close he almost sticks them in his eyes.)*

Timmy: I hope Mother is still there when we get back.

Therapist: You want your mother to be there when you get back.

Bobby: Yeah. She got there just before you did and she wanted us to stay, but we said we wanted to come over here.

Therapist: You felt more like coming here than staying at home and visiting with your mother.

[Bobby goes over and wrecks the house which Saul has just fixed up.]

Buddy: I wish I could go to the dentist.

Therapist: You *wish* you could go to a dentist? (*More disbelief than recognition of feeling.*)

Buddy: Yeah. I had teethaches right in the middle of the night and it woke me up. I could get my aches rid of if I could go to a dentist.

Therapist: The dentist would help you.

Buddy: Yeah.

Therapist: Well, time is up, boys.

[Reluctantly and slowly they drag themselves out of the playroom. Therapist takes them back home.]

COMMENTS

The high emotional content of this therapy session demonstrates the fact that, even in a group, the children will use the therapy hour to release their feelings. The interplay of conflicting feelings did not seem to bother Timmy. The other boys in the group were interested in the play. After it was over there was unusually quiet play. Buddy's voice was calm and low. The usual yells and screams were not in evidence. Certainly this bit of play illustrates the depth of feeling that children who are deprived of a feeling of love and security are capable of expressing. Timmy saved the cat, but not the mother and father who had deserted him. So real was the play to the children that Saul was warned dramatically that if he rescued his mother he would get burned. Saul was determined to save his mother and was so emotionally disturbed that he cried. Charles, not yet ready to face such feelings, tried to terminate the play. It also seems significant that the brothers left their mother to come to the playroom with the therapist.

Buddy's punishment of Bobby after he was pushed against the easel shows how the play situation sometimes helps the child channel his feeling into a play outlet that is satisfying to him. Buddy paddled Bobby for pushing him, but he used the doll as a symbol for Bobby. Buddy once again tries out the limits. The writer feels that if the therapist had broken over this limitation, Buddy would have continued his search for something that would have had to be refused. Holding to the few limitations that are decided upon before undertaking the therapy seems to strengthen the therapy.

In this contact the boys again demonstrate how the playroom is accepted by them as a different sort of place. Here they can be two years old. Certainly the needs and problems of these children differ greatly, and yet they all are able to receive help through the group-therapy experience.

FOURTH CONTACT

Buddy, Timmy, Bobby, and Charles gave the therapist eighty-five cents to keep for them until the hour was over, for they were to go to the picture show for the rest of the afternoon. Buddy brought two sheets of writing paper with him. He gave these to the therapist and said that he wanted to write a letter to his mother and added that he hadn't seen her for five and a half years. The notes of this meeting are sketchy because of the therapist's participation in the finger painting—it was necessary to help the boys moisten the paper and then remove the dripping mess as carefully as possible and carry it across the hall where the paintings could dry.

Upon entering the playroom the boys as usual grabbed up the nursing bottles with shouts of "Me baby. Me big baby." They started to drink from the bottles. The therapist recognized their feelings of wanting to be a baby. Buddy did not drink from the nursing bottle. He held the bottle in his hand and grinned. Saul was not with the group this time. His father had taken him away from the foster home and had left town with the boy. Soon they discovered the finger paints.

Timmy: Let me. Let me. These are finger paints.
Therapist: You've worked with these before.
Timmy (sitting down at the table and reaching for the paints): I like to. I like to.

Therapist: You like to use the finger paints.
Timmy: Uh huh!

The therapist helps Timmy get started on finger painting, gives him the apron, a basin of water, some rags. The other boys stand around, commenting about the paint, wanting turns and aprons. All this time they were drinking from the bottles. The therapist tried to help Timmy fix the paper, spoon out the paints, tie the apron back, and reflect the expressed feelings that the other boys wanted turns, too, and were anxious to try out the new paint. Finally Timmy, selecting yellow and black without a moment's hesitation, was busy swooping his hands over the paper in free, expansive gestures, crying "Whee!" all the time. He ended the picture by circling through the paint with his arms and punctuating the work with his elbow in the center of the paper. While this was going on, Bobby and Charles were squirting water on one another. Buddy was standing quietly beside the therapist, asking frequently, "Will you write what I say? I want to write a letter to my mother." The therapist responded that Buddy wanted to write a letter to his mother and would like the therapist's help. She said that she would help him in a minute. After Timmy finished his finger painting, Charles took his turn. His painting was carefully done and had definite form.

Charles: This is going to be a flag. With stars.
Therapist: You want a picture of a flag on yours. *(Several times he made the same thing, rubbed it out, made it again.)*
(Timmy rushed over to the house. He grabbed it by the ends, turned it upside down, and threw it against the wall.)
Timmy: Fire! Fire! Eat up the house. Mess it all up.
Therapist: You want the house destroyed.
Bobby: So do I! So do I! Fire! Fire!
Therapist: Bobby wants the house destroyed, too.
Timmy (getting the mother doll, lifting up her dress, showing it to the other boys, and giggling): Look.
Therapist: You think it's funny to lift up the mother's dress.
Timmy (to therapist): I'll even take her dress off.

Therapist: You're not afraid to take her clothes off.

Timmy (removing the mother's clothes): Look. Look. Funny. Bah! She ain't got nothing on.

Therapist: You've taken off all the mother's clothes.

Timmy (pounding the doll): I'm beating her up. I'm pounding her to pieces.

Therapist: You're pounding the mother to pieces.

Timmy (trying to tear her in half): I'll pull her apart. I'll jerk her to pieces.

Therapist: You'll get even with the mother.

Timmy: I'll show her. I'll get even.

Therapist: You'll get even with the mother.

Timmy (pulling off the doll's removable arms): See there? *I* pulled off her arms.

Therapist: You pulled off her arms.

Timmy (throwing doll down on the floor): I'll slam her around good. I'll fix her.

Therapist: You'll fix her.

Bobby (picking up the doll and throwing it down): That'll fix the mean thing.

Therapist: You want to get even with the mean old thing, too.

Bobby (pressing his foot down on her head): I'll mash out her brains. *(Kicks her over into the corner.)*

Therapist: You mashed her head in.

Timmy (looking around wildly for something): Where is the man? Where is the father? I'll take off his clothes. I'll beat him up.

Bobby: Where is the father? We want the father.

Therapist: You wish there was a father here that you could beat up.

Timmy: I'd mash up his head.

Therapist: You'd mash his head.

Bobby: And tear him apart.

Therapist: And you would tear him apart.

Bobby: He's a mean, mean man.

Therapist: The father is a mean, mean man.

Timmy (painting the nursing bottle red): Blood. Look. I'll drink his blood. *(Drinks from bottle. Yells.)* *I* drink his blood.

Therapist: You even drink his blood. *(Timmy goes over and stands on the mother doll.)* You drink the father's blood and you stand right on the mother doll.

Timmy (laughing hilariously, goes over to peg-board and hammers on it with all his might): I'm one tough guy.

Therapist: You're a tough guy and you're pounding as hard as you can.

Timmy (pounding harder than ever. In fact, he split the peg-board in half and shattered one end of it): There now. I broke it.

Therapist: You hammered so hard you smashed it.

Timmy (defiantly): I'm glad I did.

Therapist: You're glad you broke it.

Timmy (kicking it under the table): I'll break the other one.

Therapist: You even want to break the other one.

[Timmy hammers on the other peg set—but not so vigorously. Finally he kicks it under the table, too. In the meantime Buddy has finger-painted, with Charles getting the colors for him. Bobby is painting wild streaks of color on the easel, crying out, "I'm blind. I can't see." Finally, after Timmy had kicked the second peg set under the table and the therapist could give some attention to Bobby, she commented on Bobby's remark.]

Therapist: You think it's fun to be blind.

Bobby (laughing and jabbing at the paper with the paint-brush): Can't see. Me blind boy.

[Buddy pays no attention to this. He quietly finishes his finger painting, then asks the therapist to write a letter for him. He thinks a long time between sentences as he dictates.]

Buddy: Dear Mother: How are you? I am fine. I want my money bank. I want my xylophone. I have five boys to play with. I have lots of fun here at Mother R's. I want my scooter—the one with the seat on. I want my wheel bike. I want to come home and see you some Saturday. We have cars and bikes and scooters at home. Mrs. C is going to get me a sailor suit. Buddy.

[As Buddy dictated the letter the therapist responded as best she could while keeping one eye on Timmy, who was finger-painting with the red paint, growling and muttering all the time. The therapist's responses included recognition of his wanting some of his toys and his money—and his desire to go home and see his mother. As Buddy finished the letter, the time was up and the therapist announced the end of the hour. As the group went down the hall, Timmy crawled like a baby.]

Therapist (to Timmy): You're a baby.

Timmy: Me little baby.

[He crawled all the way down the hall, down three flights of stairs, across the grass, across the street to the parked car. The therapist drove them to the picture show, but the theater was closed, so she took the boys home. When the boys found out that the show was closed, they calmed down. When they arrived at Mother R's and the therapist stopped the car, the boys just sat there, refusing to get out of the car.]

Therapist: You don't want to get out.

Boys: No. Take us back. We'll stay over there all day.

Therapist: You want me to take you back, but I can't. Other children will have their turn in the playroom this afternoon.

(Still they sat there. Finally, Timmy jumped out.)

Timmy: Come on, guys. Let's go raise hell. *(The therapist believes they did. Bobby and Charles followed Timmy. Buddy hung back.)*

Buddy (to therapist): Good-bye. Mail my letter for me, will you? I don't know the address.

Therapist: Will you go in and ask Mother R for the address?

Buddy: She isn't here. She went away. That's why we were going to the show. Nobody is here. *(Even Buddy was to "see the show," blind as he was.)*

Therapist: I'll get it from her the next time then.

Buddy (with a worried look on his face): Yes. Yes. We mustn't forget. Good-bye.

COMMENTS

When the therapist later tried to obtain the address of Buddy's mother, she learned that Buddy was a foundling, who had spent his life in an orphans' home, until he reached the age to attend the school for the blind. Apparently, Buddy's letter was wishful thinking. During this entire contact, he was very quiet, not once giving vent to the blood-curdling screams that were typical of his behavior. When he worked on his finger painting he worked quietly. He was the only one who commented on the smell of the paint. He worked slowly, using first his fingertips, feeling his way along. Then, as he got used to it, he swept his hands around with free movements.

His right hand went around in circles. His left hand usually moved up and down He used the fingers of his left hand, but the palm of his right hand.

Bobby worked with the brown, red, and blue paints. He made dozens of designs and piled the paint on thickly, squeezing it through his fingers. For his final design he scratched it on with his fingers like claws, making lines vertically and horizontally, spitting like a cat as he worked.

Timmy's behavior during this hour seems to illustrate the point that group therapy can and is used as fully by the individual in the group as in individual therapy. The boys in this group seem to be more troubled by their personal problems than by antisocial behavior. The manner in which they take turns, help one another, and play together demonstrates that The weakness of a therapist's responses in a group situation shows up in this contact. The activity got in the way of the responses during the first part of the hour. These boys seem to have accepted the therapist as completely as she has accepted them. They act out the complete permissiveness that they feel in the situation.

FIFTH CONTACT

The four boys met the therapist with enthusiastic shouts of "Guess what? Mother R lets us drink out of the babies' nursing bottles when we ask her. She says if *you* let us do it, it must be okay. *She* even let us drink *milk* out of them."

When they arrived at the playroom they again yelled for the nursing bottles, and Charles, Timmy, and Bobby grabbed them. Buddy did not show any interest at all in them. He said that he wanted to use the finger paints, sat down at the table, and started to work. The other three boys shouted about the sand table and the puppet theater which had been added to the playroom since their last visit. The therapist was about to explain the manipulation of the puppets when Timmy grabbed one of the puppets, went in back of the puppet theater, and thrust the puppet through the curtain.

Timmy (the puppet speaking): "Looky here. Looky here. I'm a crazy old clown. I'll blow the world up if you don't look at me." *(He continues speaking, but it is drowned out by the noise of the other boys, who are attacking the sand.)*

Bobby (throwing sand into the doll house): Look at this old house. I'll fix the old house up with ice and snow. I'll freeze the people.

Charles (also throwing sand in the house): We'll fix it so these people won't have any house. Look at this. *(He pours handfuls of sand on the mother and father dolls, completely burying them under the sand.)*

Bobby: They are all buried up in the snow. They will freeze hard solid. And *I don't care if they do!*

Therapist: The grown-ups are all freezing, but you don't care.

Bobby (crawling in the sand and sitting down): I am going to stay in here and build something for me. It will be *my* farm.

Therapist: You want to build a farm that will be all yours.

Timmy (coming over and crawling in the sand box, too): I'll build me something, too.

[Charles and Buddy came over to the sand table. Buddy ran his hands through the sand but did not seem very satisfied with it and went over to the easel and began to draw with the crayons and paint.]

Timmy: Come on. Let's fix up the house and then fix up the army over there and have a battle.

[Timmy and Charles put the furniture back in the house for a few seconds, but soon Charles picks up a handful of sand and throws it in the bedroom. Timmy picks up a handful and does the same thing. Again there is a terrific battle with the sand, with yells and shouts.]

Timmy: It's snowing! It's snowing.

[All the boys, except Bobby, put up the nursing bottles. Bobby gets three of them and takes them into the sand box with him. The therapist asks him not to get the water in the sand because it would ruin the sand. Bobby says "Okay!" and is careful. During the course of the hour Bobby drank the water in all four bottles, removing the nipple and drinking it "like a bottle of pop," as he phrased it.]

Charles: It's snowing. All the rooms are getting full of snow. People are getting buried in here.

Therapist: The snow is burying some of the people.

Charles: There are two people buried under this. Now four people.

Timmy: Now six people. This is killing off all the people.

Therapist: There won't be any people left.

Timmy: The father is here. He's freezing to death. He's dying.

Therapist: The father is dying.

Charles: They are trapped. See? They can't get out. (*He gets the baby doll and throws it over in the sand box. Then he wrecks the house, tips it over, throws sand at it violently.*) Take this thing out of here. No house. No *house*. No *house*. (*He took the house out of the sand box and put it on the other side of the room.*)

Therapist: You don't want the house there.

Bobby· There isn't any room in here for mothers or fathers or anybody. This is just for us.

Therapist: You don't want mothers or fathers or anyone but yourselves in there.

Timmy (loudly): This is our world.

Therapist: This is just your world.

[Buddy asks therapist if he can go out and get a drink of water. The therapist asks Buddy if he can wait until the hour is over. He willingly agrees and continues painting.]

Timmy: I'm going to get some blocks and we're going to build us a farm.

Bobby: How will you like that? We'll build things the way *we* want them.

Therapist: You'll build things the way *you* want them now.

[Bobby makes a garage for the cars, divides the animals.]

Charles: I only want animals in my world. I don't want any people. Animals and just one little boy who is a farmer boy.

Therapist: You'll just have animals in your world. No people except the farmer boy.

Charles (removing the furniture): And no furniture. No chairs. No beds.

Therapist: You don't want any furniture, either.

Bobby: Why did you throw away the daddy?

Charles: Because I don't like the daddy. I threw him away.

Therapist: Charles threw the daddy away because he doesn't like him.

Charles: He doesn't like *me*, either.

Therapist: He doesn't like you, so you don't like him.

Buddy: I want to take home some of these toys.

Therapist: You would like to, but you can't. They have to be left here.

Bobby: I would like to take some home, too.

Charles (throwing out certain toys): No army trucks. No guns. No fighting in my world.

Therapist: No fighting or guns or army things in your world.

Charles: Who wants the mother? *(He tosses the mother doll at Timmy.)*

Timmy: I don't. *(Tosses it back to Charles.)*

Charles: Take her away. *(Tosses her at Timmy again.)*

Timmy: I don't want the mother. (Throws it back at Charles.)

Therapist: Neither Timmy nor Charles wants the mother.

Bobby: Nor me.

Therapist: None of you want the mother.

Buddy (from easel): Nor me.

Therapist: Not Buddy, either.

Bobby: Smash her up. Kill her off. Get rid of her.

Therapist: You want to get rid of the mother.

[Charles hurls the wooden mother doll across the room. Charles, Bobby, and Timmy build barns and silos in the sand box with the blocks. Buddy is painting at the easel.]

Timmy (picking up a tank): We don't want this. Do you know why?

Bobby: No. Maybe there is something up in this box.

Therapist: You don't want the tank in there.

Charles (putting animals up on top of the silo): They are afraid, so they are up here.

Therapist: They get up out of the way because they are afraid.

Bobby (having built a garage out of blocks): I'll drive a car into the garage. Look. I'll run over the father.

Timmy: Goody!

Therapist: Now you've gotten rid of the father.

Timmy (to Charles, referring to the divided play areas in the sand box; each boy is building "his world"): Why can't Bobby and I come over and visit you?

Charles: You can.

[Timmy hammers the pegs out of the peg-board set to use for building blocks.]

Bobby: Where is the big house?

Therapist: Out here.

Bobby: Okay. Leave it out. I just wondered.

Therapist: You just missed it, hm?

Bobby: Yeah.

Buddy (coming over and sitting down beside therapist): I want to add something to my letter. Write, "I want some paints." And I don't know what else to ask for. Put that on the letter.

Therapist: You think you'd like to have some paints of your own.

Buddy: Yeah. And I don't know what else to say.

Therapist: You sort of thought I'd forgotten you were here, didn't you? [Interpretation.]

Buddy: Yeah. *(Laughs.)*

Timmy: Make a gate, Charles. We want to come and see you.

Charles: You can't come in here. The—— You are scaring my animals. I'll send my wild bear after you. Grrr. *(Chases Timmy out of his section with the toy bear, growling viciously.)*

Therapist: Charles doesn't want you in there.

Timmy: He ain't kidding, either. He really has a wild bear. Get out of the sand, Bobby. Then we'll have more room. *(He gets out and wipes up some of the sand from the floor with a clean, dry rag. Bobby says, "No." Timmy insists. Bobby gets out.)*

Bobby: Charles, don't get the bear after me.

Charles: This here bear takes care of me.

(Bell rings.)

Bobby: How much more time?

Therapist: Ten more minutes.

Timmy: Now pretend the Germans are here. Pretend they start bombing the whole place. *(He begins to throw the sand and blocks around in the sand box.)*

Bobby: No! *No!* Don't *do* that!

[Timmy continues to destroy what he has built and what the others have built. Bobby protests again.]

Therapist: Bobby doesn't want you to destroy what he has built.

[This response was not acceptance of Timmy, nor was it permissiveness. It was a reflection of what Bobby had said, but was directed to Timmy and therefore seemed more like intervention on the part of the therapist. It was a poor response. Timmy's reaction was inevitable.]

Timmy: You can't tell the Germans anything. (*Continues to bomb the place.*)

Therapist: You don't care how Bobby feels about it. You're going to do it anyway. [This response sounded too much like a reproof to be helpful.]

Timmy: Yeah. (*Continues to bomb the place.*)

[Bobby quickly leaves the sand box, goes over to the corner of the room, sits down on the floor, and buries his head in his arms as if he were crying. Then, as quickly, he jumps up—no sign of tears—and goes over to the puppet theater. He puts a puppet up before the curtain and makes the puppet talk.]

Bobby (the puppet): I don't like you. I'll murder you, Timmy. Well! Well! I've got to go to work again. Never know what to do. I don't know what I'll do. I never know. Oh, help! Help! Help! Well, here I go again. Oh dear! Oh dear! I can't wait 'til I come up here again." (*He puts the puppet down and climbs into the sand box again. He throws the big blocks around viciously. He gets the nursing bottle.*) I stole someone's bottle.

Therapist: You're getting even with Timmy. (*It was his bottle.*)

Bobby: Yeah. This is Timmy's. Have some, Charles. (*Charles takes a drink.*) Yes, it's Timmy's bottle.

Therapist: You want him to know you've got his bottle.

Timmy (coming to life and yelling): Hey, you!

Bobby (handing Timmy the bottle): Here you are, sir. Here you are. Do, please, control yourself. (*Timmy takes the bottle and grins at Bobby, who has a puppet in his hand again.*) I don't know what to do. I'll get you.

Timmy: I'll mash your head in. (*Bobby pouts.*)

Therapist: You certainly don't like the way Timmy treats you sometimes.

Bobby: No!

Timmy: Well!

Bobby: Next time I'll put on a puppet show and one of them will be Timmy and I'll beat it up.

Therapist: You can beat up the puppet, and get the best of it when you feel like that.

Bobby: Yeah. Timmy on the hoof is too tough.

Therapist: Timmy's too big for you, so you can take it out on the puppet.

Timmy (laughing): All right, Bobby. I'll put on a play with you. I'll play in the sand, too.

[Time was up. The therapist took the boys home.]

COMMENTS

In this contact the children play out their violent rejection of the parents whom they feel have rejected them. The play is shared by all the boys. Even Buddy, from the easel, cries out his rejection of the mother.

Buddy seemed to be a little neglected during this contact, but he painted during the entire hour. Once again, he was quiet and relaxed.

Charles brings out the same play of fear. The people are getting up on something because they are afraid.

It was interesting to note that the three boys in the sand box were able to divide it evenly and play together without conflicts during most of the hour.

SIXTH CONTACT

Charles, Buddy, and Bobby were the only ones who were waiting for the therapist this time. Timmy was visiting his mother, today, out of town. The three boys who did come rushed into the playroom and snatched up the bottles. Buddy immediately discarded his. Bobby got two of them. He then went over to the sand table and upset the doll house and lifted it out with the help of Charles.

Bobby: Get this darn thing out of here. We don't want no house.

Charles: No. No house. No people. *(Bobby climbs into the sand table and starts lining up the soldiers for a battle. Charles gets the puppets and goes behind the puppet stage.)*

Charles (with clown puppet): Oh, Mr. Clown. Hello. Howdy-do. Someone shot a hole in my house last night. Where's your bulldog? He tore my pants off. Well, that's enough for today.

Therapist: You think the puppets have talked enough for now?

Charles: Yeah. *(He goes over to the sand table and starts moving things around.)* Now I'll play in the sand.

Buddy (picks up the doll and cradle, puts it on top of his head, and walks around the room with it): I'm taking the baby for a ride. *(He puts it up on top of the easel.)* Now I'm going to paint—with the finger paints. Red. Give me red. *(Therapist helps him get the paper ready, puts out the red finger paint. Buddy works with both hands, slaps up and down, splatters it, laughs as he works with it.)*

Therapist: It's fun to work with the finger paints, isn't it?

Buddy: Yeah. It's fun to mess.

Therapist: It's fun just to mess.

Buddy: I ain't afraid to smear myself all up. I ain't afraid.

Therapist: You're not afraid to make an awful mess in here. *(Which is just what he was doing.)*

Buddy: That's why I like to come here. You ain't no "NO" person.

Therapist: You like to come here because I let you do pretty much what you want to do.

Buddy: Yeah. Now I wanta work with clay.

Therapist: I'll take your picture out of here now so it won't be in your way. *(Therapist leaves the room with the finger painting. Buddy, in therapist's absence, tries to get the clay by himself, but can't get the lid off the jar.)*

Buddy: The lid slips.

Therapist: The finger paint on your hands makes them slippery.

Buddy: Maybe I better wash them.

Therapist: They wouldn't be slippery then.

Buddy: The thing to do is wash them.

Therapist: You think that's what you should do.

Buddy: But you didn't tell me to go wash.

Therapist: You think I should tell you to go wash?

Buddy: I don't think you *should.* Lotta people *do.*

Therapist: Most grown-ups would tell you to. It seems strange that I leave it up to you.

Buddy: You're a funny person. *(He washes his hands in the basin, then begins to work with the clay. He hammers it with the wooden mallet on the glass table top.)*

Therapist: That's a glass top on the table, Buddy. If you hammer too hard, it might crack.

Buddy: Okay. I'll hammer on the bench, then.

Therapist: You could hammer as hard as you like on the bench. *(Buddy does.)*

Charles (arranging blocks in one end of the sand table— one big block in the center): Here's where a grave once was. A king—or someone important. And snow is falling on it. Here is the graveyard. See? And this is the snow—cold snow—falling, falling, falling. *(He sifts the sand down on the blocks.)*

Therapist: The snow is falling down on the graves.

Bobby: One of our men got killed. Here, Charles, bury him. Tombstone him, too. *(Charles does. Shakes his head sadly.)*

Charles: Now I'm going to start bombing this graveyard.

Bobby: This is a prison camp over here—and a—*(He can't think of the word and looks at therapist for help.)* What do you call them? They torture people, then finally they line them up and shoot them. What do you call it? Not a scout camp. Some kind of a camp.

Therapist: A concentration camp?

Bobby: Yeah. Timmy is in here.

Therapist: Oh, Timmy is in the concentration camp.

Bobby: Yeah. *(Charles starts bombing the graveyard with the blocks.)* Let's bury ourselves in here—all but our faces.

Charles: Okay. Let's. *(They bury the soldiers that way. Bobby takes some of Charles' blocks.)* No, Bobby. Don't take that.

Bobby: Yes. Let's divide the place.

Charles: Okay. I'll get some more blocks. *(He does. He arranges some more tombstones.)* My graveyard. And how the snow does fall on it. *(He sifts the sand down on the blocks.)*

Bobby (to therapist): I'm going to take the nipple off this. *(Does so, then he hands the two bottles to the therapist.)* Here! I don't want to be a baby any more. Put the bottles away. Where are the ducks?

Therapist: You don't want to be a baby any more.

Bobby: Nope. More fun to be big.

Therapist: It's a lot more fun to be grown up.

Bobby: Yeah.

Charles: See the bombs bombing my graveyard.

Therapist: Yes. The bombs are certainly bombing it. Who is buried in the graveyard?

Charles: Oh, the king and queen and the princess. In fact, everybody I know is buried there. They all died.

Therapist: Everyone you know is buried there and now they are being bombed.

Charles (quite seriously): Yes. The mother and the father.

Bobby: And you, too?

Charles: Yes. Me, too. No. Not me.

Therapist: Not Charles.

Charles: No, sir. Not me dead down there. *(He leans his head down on his folded arms and stares at the tombstones. He sighs; then sniffs.)*

Therapist: Makes you feel sort of sad.

Charles: Yeah. I was just thinkin'. Here these people are all dead, and can't fight back, and they are gettin' bombed.

Therapist: It doesn't seem quite right.

Charles: That's war for you.

Therapist: Yes.

[Charles continues to stare at the graveyard. Then suddenly he starts a violent bombing, using the biggest blocks available and screaming and yelling like a maniac. Bobby also begins a war in his corner. Buddy is modeling a boy on a bicycle—a very remarkable job. When he finishes that he starts crayoning a picture.]

Buddy (to therapist): This will be for you.

Therapist: You want to make a picture for me.

Buddy: Yes.

[Bobby suddenly jumps out of the sand box. He gets a puppet, gets behind the puppet screen and manipulates the puppets.]

Bobby: "Here I am, folks. Hello."

Charles: Oh, shut up.

Bobby: "I'm Mr. Clown. How are you out there?" *(He comes around the front of the puppet theater, tosses down the puppet, smears some purple paint all over the paper that is on the easel.) (To therapist.)* There! That's how I feel. All messed up.

Therapist: You feel all upset about something.

Charles: Like a blind man, are you?

Bobby: Yes. Like a blind man. Here. Take it away. Throw it out. Oh dear! Oh dear! Oh dear! *(Therapist throws away the painting.)*

Charles: I am so unhappy.

Therapist: You are unhappy?

Charles: Yes. *(Throws blocks wildly and screams.)*

Therapist: It helps to throw things and scream like that.

Bobby (crayons an airplane dropping bombs): What country are you bombing?

Charles: Japan. Here He-Ho is dressed up like Uncle Sam. Fooling people. See?

[Buddy comes over and climbs in the sand box. He throws the blocks wildly and yells and screams. Bobby goes over to the table and finger paints—first one all in red, second one all in blue, third one all in brown. He scratches it on with his fingernails—spitting and hissing like a cat, but talking to the therapist in an ordinary way about the colors he wants.]

Buddy (his blocks going wild): I'll show everybody I'm not afraid.

Therapist: You don't want us to think you are afraid of anything.

(Buddy hurls the largest blocks viciously against the sand table.)

Chalres: Don't knock those against the table. You'll break it.

Buddy: I ain't afraid to.

Therapist: You're not afraid, Buddy, but those big blocks might hurt someone. Use these smaller ones.

Buddy: Okay. *(He hurls the smaller ones up against the ceiling and they bounce all around the room. Charles, who wears glasses, looks a bit fearful.)*

Charles: Now you be careful, Buddy.

Buddy: I ain't a-scared. *(He hurls a handful of blocks skyward.)*

Therapist: Buddy, you might break Charles' glasses. Please don't throw any more.

Buddy: I ain't a-scared.

Therapist: We know you're not scared. That isn't the point. It might hurt someone in here.

Buddy: I ain't a-scared. *(But not throwing any.)*

Charles (yelling at Buddy): Well, do you want to *hurt* somebody?

Buddy (yelling back): No! I don't want to hurt somebody.

Charles (screaming at Buddy): Well, then.

Buddy (screaming back): Well, yourself. *(He tries to take Charles' blocks. They have a tussle. Both boys are now standing up in the sand table. Charles gets the best of Buddy, who sits down, grabs up the celluloid bulldog and a block and hammers the dog.*) I'll kill you, Charles. This is you, see? I'm beating you up.

Therapist: When you can't hit Charles, it helps to pound up the toy.

Buddy (throwing a handful of sand wildly): I'm mad! I'm mad! I'm mad!

Therapist: You *are* real mad.

Buddy (laughing): Nope. All over now.

Therapist: You got over it in a hurry.

Charles (gives Buddy the blocks he wanted and gets out of the sand table. He gets the felt doll father and uses that for a puppet in the puppet theater, holding it up by the feet): I'm the only man in town. Oh, how worried I am! Something almost killed me. Somebody is coming. I can hear their footsteps. Oh! Oh! (Groans.) Oh! (He comes around to the sand table and sifts the sand through his fingers.)*

Therapist: You're worried about something.

Charles (glumly): I'm all alone in the world. Just me and my graveyard. (*He starts arranging his tombstones again.*)

Therapist: Time is up for today, boys. (*No sign from the boys that they have heard.*) You would like to stay, but our time is up.

Buddy (jumping up in the sand table, holding the biggest block over his head menacingly): Look!

Therapist: No, Buddy. You feel like it, I know, because you don't want to go home. But come on now.

Charles: You could never come back again if you threw it.

Buddy: I ain't a-scared to.

Therapist: Buddy wants us to be quite sure that he isn't a-scared to do anything.

[Therapist and Charles and Bobby leave the playroom. Bobby goes into the washroom to clean up.]

Buddy (calling out to the therapist): Ain't nobody in here now but me. Now kin I throw it?

Therapist: Throw it in the box, but be careful of your toes. (*Buddy laughs, tosses it gently into the corner, climbs out of the sand table.*)

Therapist: It was fun getting to do it.

Buddy (laughing): You didn't want me to hurt my toes.

Therapist: No, I didn't.

Bobby: Timmy said to me, "I bet you wish you were going home today." But I said, "Today is the day we go to the University and I bet you wish you were going there."

And he said, "Yeah." Then he told Mom he wouldn't go with her, but she made him and then I had the laugh on him.

Therapist: Timmy thought you would feel badly because you didn't get to go home and it ended up by Timmy feeling badly because he couldn't come here.

Bobby: Yes. I even got sick and I threw up all I ate, even water, but even that didn't help. She still wouldn't take me.

Therapist: Even getting real sick didn't make your mother give in and take you along, too.

Bobby: No. She's a mean woman.

Bobby was very subdued all the way home. Again they all just sat in the car, silently refusing to get out. Buddy jokingly said, "Take us back, please. We'll stay there all day, thanks." The therapist recognized their desire to go back and just sat there, too. Suddenly they jumped out of the car.

Buddy: You just don't *make us* do nothing, do you?
Therapist: It's hard to believe, isn't it?
[They ran into the house.]

COMMENTS

In this contact Buddy evaluates the rôle of the therapist and concludes that she is a "funny person." This record also contains an illustration of Buddy's difficulty in making a choice—in this case to wash—but the choice is left up to Buddy. It also shows Bobby getting even with his brother by putting him in a concentration camp. Buddy also uses the channeled behavior by beating up the bulldog rather than Charles when he becomes angry with him.

Charles' behavior is interesting. According to his history, the father died suddenly two years ago and the home was broken up. The mother went to work, and Charles was placed in a foster home. At the end of the eighth contact, Mother R told the therapist that Charles had had an "unfortunate experience with a degenerate man" just the day before he joined the play group. This may have accounted for some of the fears that Charles expressed in a vague way.

The interplay of the members of the group is shown in this sixth contact. The boys make their choices as to whether to play together or to seek individual expression.

Bobby chose this day to hand the nursing bottle to the therapist and say, "Put this away. I don't want to be a baby any more." Later, he relates how he "even got sick" and "threw up everything" he ate and still *she* wouldn't take him along. In view of the fact that both he and Timmy have frequent attacks of vomiting spells, the therapist wondered if this might not be the explanation for such behavior.

The manner in which the therapist handled the limitations is worth noting. She tried to include recognition of feeling, but the firm adherence to the limitations was also there. The specific limitations were not introduced until the need for them arose.

SEVENTH CONTACT

On the way over to the clinic, Timmy told the therapist that he had been home with his mother. He said that she had taken him home because he had been sick most of the time since he had been in the foster home. Then he whispered to the therapist, "When we get over there to the playroom, I'll tell you why I get sick." He cast a furtive glance at Buddy, then continued his whispering. "It's because of Buddy—because he can't see and because he yells so much and makes such awful noises and because Bobby and me are having to stay here and our father and mother aren't any place near and so I get sick and I throw up what I eat." (The therapist reflected this back to him. He accepted it enthusiastically.) "I *know* that's why I get sick, 'cause before all this happened to me I didn't get sick at all."

When they arrived at the playroom they all grabbed nursing bottles; but Charles was the only one who kept one. The other boys almost immediately discarded them. The house had been taken out of the sand table before the boys arrived. It was in the room, however, available if the boys wanted to play with it. Timmy and Bobby and Charles got in the sand table and began to play with the farm animals and people—more just sorting through the toys than playing with them. Bobby handed Timmy the mother doll.

Bobby: Here, Tim. Take her dress off. *(Timmy does.)*

Timmy (to therapist): Look. A naked woman.

Therapist: The woman is naked.

Buddy (on the floor, taking off all the big baby doll's clothes): Look. The baby's clothes are all being taken off.

Therapist: You want to undress the baby.

(Timmy hits the mother doll with his fist.)

Timmy: This is mother. I'll hit her good.

Therapist: You want to hit the mother good and hard.

Timmy: I'll squash her.

Therapist: You'd like to squash the mother.

Bobby: Me, too. Kill her dead, Tim.

Therapist: Bobby and Tim both want to hurt the mother.

Bobby: Well, she hurts us.

Therapist: You would like to get even. *(Timmy picks up the long wooden block and pounds the mother doll vigorously)* You *are* getting even.

Timmy (grinning at therapist): Sure I are.

Bobby: Let me. Let me. *(He pounds it, too.)*

Therapist: You are getting even, too.

Charles: Give me a turn at it. *(They do, gladly. He hammers the doll viciously.)*

Therapist: You are getting even, too.

Timmy: We're going to have a battle.

Bobby: No! We're not.

Timmy: Yes! We are. For Charles.

Bobby: We will not.

Therapist: Timmy wants to have a battle and Bobby doesn't want to have a battle.

Timmy: We're not Americans.

Bobby: Yes, we are.

Timmy: Are we?

Buddy (having undressed the doll by the touch system): Is this everything that comes off?

Therapist: Yes.

Buddy (accidentally breaks the doll's foot off): What's this? *(As he finds the broken piece.)*

Therapist: The foot broke off just then.

Buddy: Did it? *(Laughs.)* I didn't know. I didn't mean to break it off.

Therapist: It was an accident.

Buddy: Can it be fixed?

Therapist: Yes. It can be glued back on.

Buddy: Yes. It'll fix.

Timmy (with the mother doll in the sand table): Oh, look! I don't have any clothes to wear. Mr. Daddy. Where are my clothes? *(Changing voice.)* You lost them! *(Feminine voice again.)* I lost them? *(Father's voice.)* You lost them all.

Charles: You ate them up.

Timmy (jerking mother's arms off suddenly): Oh, look! For goodness' sake! *(To therapist.)* Say, can we swear and cuss in here? *(Not waiting for an answer.)* God damn it. What happened to you? You ain't got no arms. You ain't got no heart. You're a— Every time we come here something happens to the mother.

Therapist: In the playroom something always happens to the mother.

Timmy: Yes. And it serves her right. She's a pig-headed, selfish, old thingamajig.

Therapist: The mother is selfish and pig-headed and what happens to her *here* just serves her right.

Timmy: Yes. Let's have a battle.

Bobby: I don't want a battle.

Timmy: Yes. There will be a battle and cold snow.

Bobby: NO. There won't be any snow.

Timmy: Yes! Yes! Yes! Snow. How about it?

Bobby: All right. A little snow. *(Timmy scoops up handfuls of sand and hurls them at Bobby—who certainly gives back what he gets. Finally some of the sand gets into Bobby's eyes.)* I'm not going to play in the sand with you.

Timmy: You're not going to play in the sand. All right. *(He throws more sand at Bobby.)*

Bobby: God damn you to hell! You want to boss everything—so I'm leaving.

Therapist: Bobby doesn't like to play with Timmy when he gets so bossy. *(Bobby climbs out of the sand table.)*

Timmy: See if I care! *(Yells.)* See if I care!

Therapist: Timmy wants Bobby to think he doesn't care.

Buddy: I want to undress the baby doll.

Therapist: You want to take off the baby's clothes.

Charles: He undresses all the babies he gets his hands on.

[Timmy and Charles get in a fight over the soldiers. Charles throws sand at Timmy and knocks over Timmy's cannon and two soldiers. Timmy knocks over all of Charles' soldiers.]

Charles: I didn't do this much to you.

Timmy: Well, when somebody does something to me I pay them back ten times ten times.

Charles: That isn't playing fair. *(To therapist.)* Is it?

Therapist: Charles doesn't think it's fair for Timmy to pay back ten times ten times, but Timmy thinks it's all right.

Timmy: You just bet I do. He ain't got guts enough to stand his ground.

Charles: Guts, huh?

Timmy (yelling): Yeah. You heard me. You ain't got the guts or you wouldn't let me get away with it.

Charles: Oh. You want me to knock the living hell out of you, do you?

Timmy: I didn't say that. I said you ain't got guts enough to.

Charles: It's the same thing. I'll show you my guts.

Timmy: All right. You show me!

Buddy (yelling): He ain't got guts enough. He ain't got guts enough. Guts! Guts! *Guts! (And ending in a peal of laughter.)*

Bobby (yelling, too, at full lung capacity): Guts! Guts! Guts!

[Buddy gets two big long blocks and bangs them together and laughs. Suddenly all the boys begin to laugh. The storm has subsided.]

Bobby (getting out the finger paints): I like to do this. Smear. Smear. Mess. Mess. I like it. This time I'm not going to tell you what I'm doing. I'll have you guess. *(To Buddy.)* You can have my bottle. I don't want it any more. *(Cleans up after finger-painting. Then he goes over to the sand table and pretends to mess it up. Timmy yells at him. Bobby yells back, then begins to crayon a picture of an airplane which ends in a scribble. He turns the paper over and draws another very neatly.)* This is an airplane.

Charles: Boy! That's neat.

Therapist: You like his drawing.

Charles: Yes.

Timmy: Charles drew a neat church at Bible School today.

Therapist: You think Charles drew a nice picture today, too.

Buddy (building with blocks): Look at this.

Timmy: Yeah.

Bobby: That's neat, Buddy.

Therapist: Bobby likes Buddy's building.

Buddy (seems delighted. He laughs): What are you doing, Timmy?

Timmy: I'm playin' here in the sand.

Buddy: You doin' something neat?

Timmy: I sure are.

Therapist: You can each do something the others like.

Charles and Timmy: Yeah! *(They seem surprised. There is quiet for a few minutes. Charles and Timmy begin bombing with the sand again. Therapist suggests care in regard to the fragile toy furniture.)*

Timmy: Okay. *(He picks out the furniture. Then to the therapist.)* Only in war real furniture, houses, and people are bombed, and you can't take them out.

Therapist: In real war furniture, houses, and people are bombed. But, because of the war, we can't replace any of the toy furniture here, so I ask you not to break it up.

Timmy: It's hard to get new real furniture, too.

Therapist: Yes, it is. You resent my asking you not to break the furniture.

Timmy: Sure. I like to break things.

Therapist: You like to break things and don't want me to stop you.

Timmy: One more time you said, and then we can't come any more. Why not break everything?

Therapist: You think if you're not coming any more you ought to be allowed to break everything.

Timmy: Then nobody else could come.

Therapist: You think if you break everything, nobody else can come. You don't want anyone else to come here, if you can't.

Timmy: If *we* can't come, why *should* anyone else be allowed to come?

Therapist: It doesn't seem right that others should come if you can't.

Buddy (gets the wooden hammer, smacks the hammer down on the bench, accidentally smashing a nursing bottle): What was that?

Therapist: You broke a nursing bottle.

Buddy (laughing): I didn't mean to.

Timmy: See what I mean? Always, always, he doesn't mean to do it. *He* makes me sick. *(He seems quite agitated.)*

Therapist: It really makes you sick—the accidents Buddy has because he can't see.

Timmy: Yes! Yes!

(Charles stands up, beating on his chest with his fists, yells "bloody murder!")

Buddy (yelling at the top of his lungs): Help! Help! Help!

Bobby (also at voice capacity): Help! Murder! Help! Somebody murdered me! People are after me! Killers are here! *(He jumps in the sand table, throws the sand all over the room, screaming "bloody murder!" He jumps down in back of the puppet theater, points the gun through the curtain, and in a quiet, deadly voice.)* All right. Stick 'em up! Bang! Bang! Bang! Everybody in here has been killed. Bang! *(To therapist.)* Bang! You, too, my fine feathered friend!

Therapist: You'd like to get rid of everyone in here. We all sort of stop you at times.

[This last remark should not have been included. It is pure interpretation, and without any justification.]

Timmy (getting the other gun): All right, Bobby. Bang! That fixes you.

Bobby (coming around in front of the puppet theater): All right. You want to get rid of me, do you? *(Screams suddenly, then pandemonium breaks loose. All the boys destroy as much as they legitimately can—the sand is thrown all over the room. They throw the small things that they can pick up.)*

Timmy (picking up a handful of sand and looking at the therapist with a twinkle in his eye): Right square in your hair this'll come.

Therapist: You'd like to throw it at me just because—? *(Therapist stops deliberately to see if he will finish the sentence. He does.)*

Timmy: Because *you* won't let us come back.

Therapist: Because I can't let you come back, you'd like to throw it at me.

Timmy (smiles, and sifts the sand gently through his fingers, kneels down in the sand table beside the therapist, and says in a voice of gentle wonder): How do you always know why I do what I do?

Therapist: You think I understand you pretty well.

Timmy: You really do. You must be magic.

Bobby (yelling): I want to murder somebody. The chief is going to beat himself to death. *(He jumps up on the table, opens the little window leading into the other room. All the other boys jump up and look.)* Just an empty room.

Buddy (screaming): I'm not a-scared of anybody in here. You look. I'll show you how a chief acts. *(He beats a long block against the wall.)*

Charles: How many more minutes?

Therapist: Five minutes.

[All the boys yell and scream. Buddy hammers the block against the wall. Then he throws the block into the sand table. Charles begins to draw. Timmy finger-paints. Bobby gets the puppets and handles them quietly. Charles picks up some drawing paper like a newsboy and begins to yell.]

Charles: Nazi! Nazi! Read all about the Nazis gettin' the hell knocked out of them! Extra! Extra!

Timmy: Extra! Extra! Hitler's got his guts kicked out of him. *(Buddy yells like Tarzan, and others take it up.)*

Therapist: It's a help sometimes to yell like that.

Buddy: Huh?

Timmy: Couldn't hear you.

Therapist (repeating in a louder voice): Sometimes you like to yell.

Buddy (to therapist): Sometimes you like to yell, too, huh? *(They all laugh—therapist included.)*

(Timmy comes over and puts black finger paint on Bobby. Bobby draws back, laughingly.)

Bobby: You dirty dog, you. Put black on me, will you? *(He sticks his finger in the blue finger paint and puts it on the end of Timmy's nose.)*

Therapist: You got back at Timmy, then.

Timmy: Yep. Oh, I don't mind. *(The bell rings. As the group leaves, Timmy smears his hands and arms with the brown finger paint. To therapist.)* Take a little nigger home, please. And thank you for a wonderful time. *(Charles and Bobby also thank the therapist.)*

Therapist: You really had a good time today.

Buddy: Today and every day!

[The therapist took them home.]

COMMENTS

During the seventh contact the boys were no longer interested in the baby play. They were more concerned with the release of their feelings of aggression against the mother doll, and against other people and one another.

It was very illuminating to hear Timmy discuss the reasons for his illness. During his visit home the preceding week, Timmy's mother and father discussed a divorce in his presence. There was apparently quite an emotional scene, which Timmy related to Bobby when he returned. Both boys were very much upset by their insecure position. Their reaction to the play situation, because there was only one more time for them to enjoy it, is rather typical. They were reluctant to terminate the play periods.

Timmy's wonderment at the understanding that he feels in the play situation is significant of the struggle he has probably put up for a little understanding.

At the conclusion of the hour the boys thank the therapist for a good time. This voluntary thanking seems to indicate the genuine feeling of release that the boys obtained through the therapy session.

EIGHTH CONTACT

Since this was the last contact, and since the boys had been asking all summer to come up the "tin stairs," the group came and went by way of the fire escape. When they entered the playroom, they walked up to the nursing bottles, but did not take them. Charles and Timmy climbed into the sand table. Buddy said he wanted to finger-paint once more. He asked for the blue finger paint and did a very nice finger painting, using free rhythmic motions. Bobby emptied all the nursing bottles into the basin and put the bottles on the shelf.

Bobby: I'm going to float a submarine.

Charles: Look! It's snowing. (*Sifts the sand down.*)

Timmy: Why can't we set up farms over here? Charles, let that be your farm. This side is mine.

Buddy: I like this kind of paint. Round and round, up and down, round and round, swoop, swoop, swoop. (*He hums.*)

Therapist: Finger-painting is fun.

Buddy: It's something I can do.

Therapist: It's fun to work with something you can really manage.

Buddy: Yes. Is it a pretty color of blue?

Therapist: Yes, it's a pretty color of blue.

[The other boys are all in the sand box playing together very nicely, talking among themselves. "This is my best horse." "This cow here gives me plenty of milk." "When you get your farm ready, I'll go visit you."]

Buddy: When I'm finished here, I'll pound and yell. To-day, I'll do all my favorite things.

Bobby: Say good-bye to the playroom—the nice playroom —the wonderful playroom. Say good-bye. Say good-bye.

Therapist: You really are sorry this is your last time.

Bobby: So sorry.

Timmy: Good-bye playroom. Good-bye sand. Good-bye paint. *(To therapist.)* Good-bye, my friend.

Therapist: You want to say good-bye to everything in here.

Charles: The snow is falling—the cold snow. Look, Timmy, take these soldiers. We'll divide them up.

Timmy (grinning): Half and half or ten times ten?

Charles: How do you want it?

Timmy: Ten times ten. But here, take these six and I'll take six. I'm afraid there is going to be another war.

Charles: It certainly looks like it. Look, you battle over there.

Timmy: I'll arrange mine.

Bobby (springing onto Timmy's army, throwing sand at them, yelling): Surprise attack! Surprise attack!

Timmy: Now you quit. Why can't you let me alone?

Bobby: Why can't I let you alone? Because I am *Saul*— the most powerful giant in all the world. *(Another vicious surprise attack—this time the sand gets in Timmy's eyes.)*

Timmy (yelling at Bobby): When I get mad you know what happens.

Bobby (imitating Buddy): I ain't a-scared of anybody in this room.

Timmy (laughing): Remember! I'm not a-scared of anybody in this room, either.

Buddy: I ain't a-scared of anybody in this room. *(He has finished the finger painting. Now he gets the hammer and pounds the peg-board set until it splits.)*

Charles: I'll have my own war. *(Does so.)*

(Buddy gets the baby doll, fills the cup with water from the

basin, and feeds the doll. Timmy comes over and takes the doll away from Buddy.)

Timmy: Look, Buddy. You feed the baby. It goes in it mouth. Feel. *(He takes Buddy's hand and places his finger on the doll's mouth.)* Feel. *(Buddy does.)* Now feel its pants *(Buddy does, then shrieks yith laughter.)*

Timmy: It wets its pants!

Buddy: Jeepers! He drinks. He wets.

Timmy: I know where it comes out at. It comes out his rear.

Buddy: Wish I could take it home, but I can't. Now I'll paint.

[Timmy pours water in the doll. It runs through. Suddenly he throws the doll clear across the room, then goes over and kicks it under the sand table.]

Timmy: I'll kill it! Babies! Babies! Babies! I hate the wet, screaming things. This one I'll kill.

Therapist: Babies annoy you. You can get rid of this one.

Timmy: Yes. See? I kicked this one.

Buddy: I ain't a-scared to paint anyone in this room.

Therapist: You want us all to be sure that you're not afraid.

Buddy: It's not because I'm afraid that I don't do it.

[Therapist should have reflected this remark back to Buddy.]

Charles: This is the mother, isn't it? *(He has the mother doll. He takes off her clothes and tears out her arms.)*

Therapist: That is the mother.

Charles: Now watch this. *(He begins to pour sand on the mother and as he does so he jabbers incoherently.)*

[Bobby buries soldiers in the sand. Timmy is painting. Buddy puts the brush in the wrong color. Timmy tells him what he has done and takes out the brush and washes it, then puts it in the correct jar.]

Charles (talking baby-talk): Something is happening to the mother again. See?

Therapist: She is getting buried in the sand.

Charles: Yeah. When I get through I'm going to jump on her.

Therapist: You'll fix the mother.

[Bobby pours sand on Charles' head.]

Charles: Bobby, I wish you wouldn't.

Bobby: Say please.

Charles: Please.

Bobby: All right. *(He gets the play dishes, arranges them in a circle around him in the sand, says it is a picnic, and talks to himself about the good food, the nice dishes, and the lovely picnic. Charles continues to pour sand on the mother.)*

Charles (imitating the mother's voice): Help! Help! I'm getting sand inside of me.

Bobby: It's snowed for one hundred and fifteen nights. Help! Murder!

Charles: Help! Help!

Buddy: Help! Help!

Bobby: The big, bad wolf will get us.

[Quiet. Charles buries the mother. Bobby and Timmy help. They use the little shovel and very quietly and seriously bury the mother. Bobby fills a little basket with sand, holds it up high, and sifts it down on the mother's grave.]

Bobby (whispering): Snow. Snow. Come down and bury the mother.

Charles: Like a blanket. It covers the mother's grave. It falls on my father's grave in winter. *(To the therapist.)* My father is dead, you know.

Therapist: Yes. Your father is dead and the snow falls down on his grave in winter—like a blanket.

Charles: He's up in Minnesota, you know.

Therapist: He's up in Minnesota, far away.

Charles: He's dead and I miss him. *(Sighs.)*

Therapist: You miss your father very much.

[Timmy and Bobby are sitting in the sand staring at Charles. Then once more all three begin sifting sand down on the mother doll.]

Timmy: Your father's got lots of snow on his grave.

Charles (fiercely): This is my mother's grave.

Bobby: Oh! Is this the mother? *(Throws sand on the grave.)*

Buddy (from the easel): I bet you don't know what this is.

Therapist: Want to tell us?

Buddy: I don't know what it is, but I'd like it to be a lumberyard.

Therapist: Then it is a picture of a lumberyard.

Buddy: Yes, and you can have it.

Therapist: You will give it to me.

Buddy: Yes. [He has taken every other picture home.]

[Timmy jumps out of the sand table and begins painting. He accidentally knocks over the white paint.]

Timmy: Look! Look! Oh, I spilled the white paint! Where's a rag? I'll clean it up.

Buddy: Spank him! Spank him!

Therapist: You'd like to have him spanked because he spilled the paint.

Buddy: Yes. Spank him.

Timmy (after "cleaning" it up): There! That helped some.

[Buddy goes over to Timmy, helps him "clean up." No results.]

Timmy: Let me color some more.

Charles: You color.

Bobby: One more finger painting. One more. It's such fun.

Timmy: Isn't it fun to do that—smear—mess—yell?

Therapist: You like to do that—smear—mess—yell.

Timmy: Doesn't everybody? Kids?

Therapist: You think everybody likes to mess and smear and yell.

Timmy: Do they?

Therapist: Sometimes they do.

Bobby: This is better than taking a nap.

Charles: It's better than going to a show.

Timmy: Maybe next summer you'll come after us again.

[Charles, Timmy, Bobby, and Buddy crayon pictures. This is the first time the four have done the same thing at the same time. Time is almost up. Therapist announces that there are only five more minutes. Charles and Timmy attempt to clean up the room. Timmy suddenly stops.]

Timmy: I'll wait on you in the waiting room. I don't want to clean up. In here, we don't have to do what we don't want to do and I don't want to clean up.

Therapist: You would rather wait over there than help. Go ahead, then. *(Timmy leaves.)*

Bobby: I don't want to help either.

Therapist: You don't have to if you don't want to.

Charles (continuing to help): I'll put these things straight. *(He picks things out of the sand table. Buddy continues to "help.")* Careful there, Buddy. Let me hand you the things. We don't want this grave bothered.

Therapist: Charles wants the grave to stay there. *(Bobby goes down to the washroom. Finally therapist says time is up.*

*Buddy lets out a terrific scream just before he leaves the
room, then he laughs hilariously.)*

   Therapist: The last scream, hm?

   Buddy: Yeah. In here.

   *Charles (at door turning around, looking back at the sand
table, and sighing):* Well, we *finally* got the mother buried
for good, didn't we?

   Therapist: Yes. You got rid of the mother.

The therapist took them home. She stopped in for a
talk with the foster mother, who said that Timmy and
Bobby had improved very much since they had been
coming over to the playroom until Timmy's visit home,
during which time the parents had discussed the divorce
in his presence. She said that since then they have
screamed and yelled so much that she has "almost lost
her mind." "Buddy also drives me wild," she said. He
screamed and yelled so much and was always falling
over things so that she could hardly stand to have him
around. Charles "was a lot better— a sweet child, but so
sad." She said that his mother never bothered much
about him, although she lived in the same town. In fact,
she said that none of the children's parents cared a thing
about them. They were all forsaken children.

Two weeks later the therapist stopped in to see the
children and the foster mother. The foster mother reported then that she could see a big improvement in the
boys' behavior—even Buddy's. She said the boys played
together without so many fights—that they played more
fighting games with the soldiers, but didn't fight among
themselves. She said that neither Bobby nor Timmy had
had any vomiting spells for the past two weeks. Charles
seemed more mature, didn't cry at all now, and seemed
much happier with the other boys.

During the eighth contact the reader will notice how
the boys had come to accept this as the last time they
could come to the playroom. There are evidences of
insights that the boys have gained through their play
experience. For instance, Timmy's ten times ten has
become half and half. Their sense of humor stands them

in good stead as they imitate one another's characteristic behavior when the tensions begin to grow.

The fact that Charles should discuss the death of his father when he was playing out the burial of his mother is thought-provoking. Bobby and Charles have adjusted to one another to the point where Charles can say to Bobby, "I wish you wouldn't do that," and Bobby respects his wishes. Timmy's reaction to the babies is understandable when one knows about the six very small babies in the foster home that got so much of Mother R's attention. Timmy observes that all kids like to mess, smear, and yell. The last act of the boys in the playroom dramatizes the freedom to make choices which the boys enjoyed in this experience. Two of them did not choose to clean up the playroom. Buddy gave one final yell.

The boys in this group accepted the play situation with its limitations in a very positive way and used it to release their pent-up feelings. That they had such intense feelings may be shocking to some readers, but a rejected child frequently becomes bitter and insecure and revengeful. The play experience helped these boys to get these feelings out in the open.

COMMENTS

A study of this group raises the question as to the length of the play contacts. When should they be terminated? Should there be any arbitrary time limit set up from the beginning? Were these boys really through? Or could they have profited from more contacts? It is the opinion of the writer that a time limit should be arbitrarily set up at the beginning of the contacts, with the possibility of an extension if time is available and if it seems that the children would profit by it. Such an arrangement gives the children and the therapist a minimum time in which to work and makes planning possible.

In this group Saul dropped out after the third contact. He was certainly in need of more therapy sessions, and had there been an agreement that he would stay for the eight weeks, results would have been more satisfactory. In regard to the other boys, had the situation permitted, they would have been given an extension of five more weeks. At the end of that time an evaluation of their behavior would have determined whether it would be necessary to extend the time five more weeks.

Having a definite time limit set at the beginning of the contacts has the further advantage of preparing the child for the discontinuance of the contacts. It seems unwise for the therapist to terminate them without adequate warning.

From the writer's experience, it seems advisable to set up the play contacts on five-week schedules, to be renewed if the therapy seems incomplete. Periodic check-ups help to determine when the child has received maximum help for the play sessions, as does also an evaluation of his behavior while he is in the playroom.

Such a planned program makes it possible for parents or agencies to plan for the children, prevents spotty attendance, and builds up a feeling of confidence in the situation. It might also help to eliminate the anxious parents' weekly inquiries: "How is he?" "Is he better?" "Does he have to come back?" Some parents expect miracles after one contact. A program of time arrangements might prevent pressure from such parents, both upon the child and upon the therapist.

Another factor that the writer believes to be important for successful therapy is the inclusion of individual contacts for those children who are having group contacts. Since the group experience seems to bring out types of behavior that are not possible in an individual therapy situation, it seems advisable that all should have the group experience. However, it also seems that the children who have been scheduled for group therapy would benefit by the individual contacts. The therapist, when dealing with the group of boys from the foster home, often wondered what might have been forthcoming if the group contacts had been supplemented by individual contacts. In cases where such a procedure has been tried, as reported in the next chapter, the results have been gratifying. Usually, the individual contacts have been terminated earlier than the group experience at the child's request. This request in itself may indicate a measure of growth on the part of the child who voluntarily leaves the individual experience and seeks satisfaction in the group experience. All of these statements, however, are based upon a limited number of cases. More extensive research is necessary to verify the theory.

Another problem which is raised by the group experience which we have reported is the matter of groupings. What would be satisfactory criteria for groupings? Is it wise to have both sexes in a group or is it more satifactory to have the boys and girls in separate groups? Is it advisable to include brothers and sisters in the same group? Should the age spread be carefully controlled? Experiments in groupings indicate that there are no hard-and-fast rules to govern them. Successful groupings have included both sexes, siblings, and wide age ranges. An alert therapist, constantly evaluating the behavior of the groups, should be able to spot any factor that seems to be harmful to a particular group and to make the necessary adjustment, either by forming another group to take care of any misfit or by transferring the mistfit individual to another group that would be more suitable. The inclusion of siblings in a group is sometimes necessary in order to help the children face the problem of adjustment to one another. However, if one sibling is the family "pet" and the other the rejected child of the family, it would seem inadvisable to have them in the same group because of the possibility of the favored child tattling on the other child outside the therapy room. On the whole, the element of intelligent common sense on the part of the therapist is the important factor in the initial organization of the group.

In regard to the part of the parent or parent-substitute in the success of the therapy, a problem which was discussed in Chapter 6, it may be pointed out that Mother R showed remarkable insight into the problems of the boys in her foster home. She had a good understanding of the children as well as a friendly interest in them. The fact that she permitted them to drink milk from the nursing bottles at home is indicative of her willingness to help the boys. It is also significant to note that, after she had accepted the boys' desire to behave as babies, they soon lost their desire to continue the baby play in the therapy room. A check-up revealed that, after a few days of the baby play at home, the boys abandoned it as no longer necessary. Mother R gave the boys freedom to express themselves; she accepted them as they were. And, although the noise did "get on her nerves," her sympathetic understanding that they were "forsaken children" helped her to extend to them warmth and friendliness which was the natural expression of this woman. It seems to imply that the basic principles, somewhat modified, are applicable in any situation that is centered around the adult-child relationship.

The group also demonstrates the fact that a handicapped child can be treated in a group with normal children. The therapist felt that Buddy gained insight as well as personal satisfaction from this group experience.

22.

Combined Individual and Group-Therapy Contacts

RESULTS from a very limited amount of research indicate that the possibilities of a combined therapy program which includes both individual and group sessions are well worth further investigation. In the course of such a program the child has the advantage of utilizing the therapy session to explore his feelings when he is alone and without the dynamic relationship of other members of a group, but he also has the opportunity to experience the same treatment in relation to other children. The group experience brings out problems of adjustment that are not possible in an individual experience, while the individual experience focuses the treatment more sharply upon the individual and eliminates the possible stimulation for activity that he receives in the group situation.

The program which is suggested to combine the two types of treatment is the arrangement of two sessions a week for the child, one of which would be a group session and the other an individual session. In such a program, the child would gain rapport with, and confidence in, the therapist earlier than he would if his treatment included only one type of therapy.

The child should be permitted to terminate either the individual session or the group session if he makes the request although it might be advisable to ask him to attend both sessions twice before making a decision so that he will be acquainted with the advantages of each experience.

The following case is an example of a combined individual and group-therapy program that terminated in group sessions at the request of the individual. The possibility of this choice was not presented to the child in the individual session, but when the request was made spontaneously it was granted by the therapist.

THE CASE OF EMMA

According to the record, Emma was seven years and eight months of age, had an I.Q. of 112, and was recommended for play therapy because she was "maladjusted, antisocial, and a behavior problem." She had been in the Orphans' Home for almost three years. Her mother and father were divorced. Emma had an older sister who also lived at the Home.

Emma's school record was poor. She disliked school and was a behavior problem while there. She fought with the other children, made faces at them, sulked when she was corrected, teased and tantalized the other children, talked back to the matrons at the Home.

She was not an attractive child. Her straight, mouse-colored hair hung down over one eye. Her eyes were green and hostile. She was continually wrinkling up her nose and twisting her mouth into a bitter, mocking smile. She was always on the defensive and resisted efforts to befriend her.

The Orphans' Home was a modern, country home supported partly by a religious sect and partly by the parents whose children were in the Home. There was a boys' cottage, a girls' cottage, and a nursery cottage. At this time there were about 125 children, between the ages of two to fourteen years, in the Home. Those who were of school age were taken by bus to a consolidated school six miles away.

When psychological services were offered to the Orphans' Home—services which included play-therapy sessions for the children recommended for such experiences by the social worker and the matrons—Emma was the first little girl named. The therapist planned to work with four little girls, seeing each of them for one forty-five-minute period per week, and having the four girls in for a forty-five-minute period of group therapy once a week. The same therapist also planned to see four boys under the same arrangement. Once a week the therapist met with a group of six-year-olds for a story hour. This story hour was also open to the children in the therapy groups if they cared to come, and they attended every meeting.

The "therapy room" was a corner of the kindergarten room, which was not being used at this time. There was running water in the corner which was used, and the toilet facilities were just outside the room.

The therapist who conducted this program was not experienced in play therapy, but had read extensive background material. She kept detailed notes of each child's experiences. The present account is centered around Emma's experiences during the play-therapy sessions which occurred during the summer vacation period.

Play materials were brought each time by the therapist. They included a baby doll, nursing bottles, clay, crayons, toy soldiers, a toy gun and holster, paper dolls, a toy bus, a train, scissors, writing paper, pencils, drawing paper of various sizes, a rattle, false faces, a black mask, a family of dolls and doll furniture, and paints. The paints were added after the sessions were under way.

First Contact—Individual

When Emma appeared for the first interview, she was told that she could come for forty-five minutes every Tuesday to play with the toys if she wanted to come. It was also explained that she could play with these toys in any way that she wanted to. The limitations were mentioned at this first meeting: She must stay inside the play area that had been marked off with chairs; she could not damage the walls or furniture; she could not take any of the toys out of the room. Otherwise she could do or say anything that she wanted to do or say while in the room

with the therapist and the therapist would not tell anyone what she did do or say.

Emma stared at the therapist. Then she smiled her
twisted smile and walked over to the drawing paper,
picked up a piece of it and the crayons, brought them
over to the table at which the therapist was sitting, sat
down across from her and began to draw. She seemed
very tense, and she certainly was silent. Not one word or
glance in the direction of the therapist was forthcoming
until the picture was finished. Then she glanced quickly
at the therapist and looked away again.

Emma: This is my house. This is where I live at 7 Blank
Street with my father and mother and sister. I have a sister
older than me.

Therapist: Does your sister live here, too?

Emma: Yes.

(Emma got up from the table, walked over to the bench
where the paper dolls were, and brought them to the table
where she had been drawing. Without a word she began to
cut out the dolls—the father doll first, then the dog, then
the little girl, then the big girl, and lastly the mother doll.
She began to cast more glances in the direction of the therapist. When she finished cutting out the family, she looked
up and grinned. Then she cut out an evening dress for the
mother.)

Emma (whispering): Is this *her* dress?

Therapist: Yes, that is the mother's dress.

(Emma continued cutting out dresses. She seemed completely absorbed with the task.)

Therapist: You like to play with the paper dolls.

Emma (making a face at the therapist): No, not very
well.

Therapist: Would you rather play with something else?

Emma: I would rather color, but you don't have a color
book.

Therapist: You wish I had a coloring book so you could
color in it.

Emma: Yes.

(Emma continued to cut out dresses for each paper doll
with the exception of the father. She picked him up and
stared at him. Then quickly she piled them in a neat pile
and put them away. She went back to the bench where the

toys were laid out and looked at them. She turned suddenly and looked at the therapist.)

Emma (shortly): May I have a drink? *(She pointed to the nursing bottle.)*

Therapist: You may do anything with the toys that you want to do.

(Emma picked up the nursing bottle and drank from it, keeping her back turned to the therapist. Then she picked up the baby's rattle and shook it. Next she played quietly with the soldiers on the horses. She kept her back to the therapist all the time and so the therapist was unable to see what she was doing with the soldiers, but there seemed to be some kind of a quiet battle going on between the two soldiers. First one, then the other was knocked down. She muttered something that the therapist could not understand. She seemed very upset about something. She scowled, glanced back at the therapist, picked up the bottle again and began to drink from it, glanced back at the therapist, drank from the bottle, glanced at the therapist.)

Therapist: You like to drink from the bottle.

(Emma immediately put the bottle down. She picked up the gun, took it out of the holster, whispered "Bang!" and put it back. Then she took the train out of the box and put it together. She pushed it along the bench for about two inches and then very suddenly crammed it back into the box. Then, still keeping her back to the therapist, she stood there and rubbed her hand along the edge of the bench.)

Therapist: Our time together is over for today, Emma.

(Emma came over to the table and stared at the therapist. The therapist smiled at her. Emma moistened her lips and smiled back with her lips only.)

Therapist: Do you want to say something, Emma?

Emma (whispering): Yes.

Therapist: What do you want to say? *(Emma twisted her hands together, made faces at the therapist.)*

Emma (whispering): I want to come back.

Therapist: You may come here by yourself every Tuesday, Emma. And you may come with a group tomorrow if you want to. *(Then Emma really smiled. She walked over to the door.)*

Therapist: Good-bye, Emma.

(No answer. Emma opened the door, went outside, looked back in, whispered "Good-bye!" and was gone.)

COMMENTS

The picture which Emma drew during this first interview was a very conventional type of drawing, consisting of a square brown house, with three windows and a door. There were blue, red, and purple curtains at the windows. There was a big tree beside the house. A bit of blue sky was across the top of the picture, and a smiling blue sun with yellow lines radiating from it was in the left-hand corner. There were five bluebirds flying in the sky. This is mentioned in such detail because, as time passed, the art work produced by this child became more and more expressive. This first picture seemed a typical, formal type of picture. It also seems significant that she volunteered the information that she lived in this house with her father and mother and sister, although the child has been in the Orphans' Home for nearly three years. However, it is a part of her history that the mother is continually writing to the children and telling them that she is going to take them out of the Home. The mother has called them up many times and told them to get their things packed and she will come after them and take them away. The children get ready to go and the mother does not appear. The social worker had attempted to stop this practice, but had been unsuccessful up to the time of this report. Occasionally the mother does arrive for a brief visit, but she seldom takes the children off the grounds with her.

The therapist's first response seems to be a very poor one. Emma had just expressed the crux of her problem—the broken home. The therapist responds with a question that takes the center of interest away from Emma and places it upon the sister. Quite naturally, Emma retreats. When Emma plays with the paper dolls, and contradicts the therapist when she suggests that Emma likes to play with paper dolls, the uneasy therapist tries to push Emma along with "Would you rather play with something else?" Emma names something that is not there. It would have been better in each instance if the therapist had followed along with the child.

The choice of uncut paper dolls for play-therapy material seems to be a poor choice, but in this case it seemed like good introductory material. The order in which she cut out the dolls is noteworthy. The fact that she cut out clothes for all except the father might be significant. At least it seems so in the light of what followed in later sessions when she played with the family of dolls.

Response by the therapist seems a bit meager in this interview, but it was a case of the therapist's not being quite sure of what to say and thinking that silence would be the best course to follow. Looking back over the interview, it seems that the therapist might have recognized the desire to drink from the bottle when Emma said, "May I have a drink?" rather than generalize on the permissiveness of the situation. When Emma apparently resented the comment from the therapist a little later to the effect that Emma did like to drink from the nursing bottle, the therapist might have recognized her resentment. Again, when Emma very quietly shot the therapist for her intrusion, the therapist might have recognized Emma's desire to shoot her. She might also have recognized the child's desire to come back again, rather then emphasizing the permissiveness of the situation.

SECOND CONTACT—FIRST GROUP CONTACT

The complete notes on this meeting are included because it offers a comparison of Emma's behavior with the behavior of the other children.

The group consisted of the four girls and the four boys who had had individual contacts with the therapist during the preceding week. The children were all behavior problems both at school and in the Home. The four boys were enuretic. The children in the group were Shirley-Ann, seven years, four months; Sharon, seven years; Edna, seven years, six months; Tommy, seven years, five months; Jack, seven years, seven months; Philip, seven years, three months; Dick, eight years, five months; and Emma.

(The four girls came into the room first. They squealed and giggled, made such remarks as "Look what I see." "I want a nursing bottle." "False faces!" "I want to be a ghost."

"I don't want anyone to know who I am." These remarks and others were made so rapidly that it was impossible to identify the speakers. Sharon got the nursing bottle and the rattle. She sat down on the chair beside the therapist and drank from the bottle and shook the rattle.)

Sharon: Me baby!

(Emma sat down across from the therapist and began to draw.)

Shirley-Ann: I'm going to be a baby. *(She put on the baby false face and got the nursing bottle.)* Da-da-da-da-da.

(Emma, who was so inhibited during the first individual contact, seemed much freer with the group. She, too, got a nursing bottle and drank from it, but this time she drank facing the therapist.)

Sharon: Miss X said the boys were coming over today, too.

Edna: Oh, I hope not. I'm afraid of boys.

(The four girls sat down at the little table. They began to play, but did not play together. Each one was following her own particular line of interest. Emma was drawing. Sharon and Shirley-Ann were playing baby, but not together. They were drinking from the nursing bottles. Sharon was crawling on the floor. Edna got out the paper dolls and was looking at them. Just at this time the boys came into the room. Tommy went over to the false faces and selected a girl-face. He put it on.)

Tommy: I want to be a girl.

Jack: I'm a black ghost. See? I'm a black man.

Philip: I want to be a girl, too. Girls get everything.

(He put on the other girl false-face. Jack got the gun, still wearing the black mask. The boys ignored the girls and the girls ignored the boys. They talked about going swimming and about the trip in the bus to and from the swimming pool. The therapist was included in their conversation. They were telling her about their experiences.)

Jack: I am a black man. I want to shoot you. I want to kill all of you.

(Suddenly Jack took off the gun and holster. Dick put it on. Then he began to shoot the other children. Philip and Tommy got the baby doll and began to fight over it in a playful manner. Tommy got it away from Philip and he hugged and kissed it and behaved exactly like a little girl with a doll, although Tommy is not a "sissy type." Suddenly Tommy became very bold.)

Tommy: I want to suck a nipple bottle. *(Shirley-Ann handed him one.)*

Sharon: Now Tommy is a girl.

Tommy: That's all right with me. I want to be a girl.

Dick: Dimmie dat baby bottle.

(Philip accidentally spilled some water on the floor and suddenly the entire group's attention was focused on that incident.)

Dick: He'll get the devil now for sure, won't he?

Therapist: You are afraid you will get in trouble for spilling the water.

Dick: You're darn right. I know it.

Therapist: You won't get in trouble for that in here.

(Edna put the gun and holster on, took out the gun, shot all the boys. She stood close to the therapist while she did it.)

Therapist (to Edna): You wish the boys were not in here.

Edna: I'm afraid of boys.

Therapist: You're afraid of the boys.

Edna: Yes. *(She looked frightened, although these boys did not even glance in her direction, let alone annoy her in any way. She put the gun down and sat as close to the therapist as she could get.)*

Therapist (to Edna): You like to sit close to me. You are afraid of the boys.

Edna: Yes. *(Whispering.)* They are so rough. They always hurt the girls.

(Dick sat down in the rocking chair and rocked and sucked the bottle.)

Dick: Mama. Mama. *(Sharon ran over to him.)*

Sharon: What you want, honey?

Dick (imitating a small baby): Wock me, mama. Wock me sleep. *(Sharon very gently rocked his chair.)* I'm 'sleep now.

Tommy: I'm going to be a bawl baby. *(He put on the crying mask.)* Look! I'm a baby that is crying. *(He lay down on the floor and cried like a baby.)* Waa! Waa! I want my mama. Mamamamamamama.

Dick: I'm dest a teeny 'ittle baby. Waaaa.

Sharon: I want to write a letter to my daddy and I want a nursing bottle. *(Then she, too, imitated a small baby crying.)*

(Emma drank from one of the bottles as she drew. Dick gave his bottle to Tommy.)

Dick: Here, baby.

Tommy: Dadadadada.

Dick (to therapist): At first I was afraid to suck from the bottles.

Sharon: So was I. I didn't think we would be allowed.

Dick: I thought I was too big to play baby, but I like to play like I am a baby.

Therapist: Even though you are big, you still like to play like you are a baby.

Dick: Yes.

Sharon: I like to play like I am a baby, too.

Tommy: I wasn't afraid. I'm not afraid of anything. I'm not afraid to do anything. I'm not afraid to say anything.

Dick: Add *in here* to that.

Tommy (laughing): All right, then. In here.

Therapist: You're not afraid to do or say anything in here and so you can do things you want to do very badly sometimes, but can't because of rules, and the other children, and things like that.

Dick: You ain't kiddin', lady.

Shirley-Ann: I was afraid to do the things I felt like doing the first day I came over here.

Sharon: I was, too.

Edna: I still am. *(The other girls laughed at her.)*

Sharon: Why should you be, Edna? She won't do anything to you no matter what you do in here.

Edna: I'm still afraid.

Therapist: You want to feel a little more sure of yourself before you do the things you want to do.

Edna (to therapist): You're nice. Some day, maybe, I'll— *(She did not finish her sentence. She reached over and very timidly patted the therapist's hand.)*

Dick: I never saw anybody like you before in my whole life. You don't care what we do or say. Everybody else always says "Stop that!" and "Shut up!"

Therapist: You feel that there are times when you can't always do and say the things you want to.

Dick: Yes. That's it. Too many crabs in the world.

Edna: Bring me eight bottles the next time you come.

(Emma finished her picture. It was a picture of a brown table with a bowl of fruit on it. The bowl was purple. There were six pieces of fruit in the bowl.)

Emma (standing up and making a sudden lunge at Tommy): Gimme that baby bottle. *(She chased Tommy. He ran from her laughing and squealing.)*

Sharon: When we come by ourselves we get to do just as

we please. We get to play with anything we want to play with. We get to suck the bottles all the time if we want to.

Therapist: You think it is nice to come all by yourself so you can do just what you want to do.

Sharon: Yes.

Dick: Lots of times it's that way. When you are all alone you can do things that you can't do when there are others around. *(He began to squirt water on the floor. Emma grabbed Tommy. She giggled.)*

Emma: I'll kiss you; that's what I'll do. Then what will you do?

(Tommy pulled away from her and handed her the bottle that he had. Emma returned to the table. Edna and Sharon and Shirley-Ann started to play with the paper dolls. Sharon had finished the letter to her daddy. She showed it to the therapist, folded it, put it in her pocket. She had written only Dear Daddy from Sharon on the paper.)

Therapist (to Sharon): You would like to write a letter to your daddy. I'll help you if you want me to.

Sharon: I can't think of a thing to say. Just *Dear Daddy.*

(Emma got up from the table again and went over to the bench. She got the rattle. As she passed Tommy she kissed him. Tommy slapped at her. Emma shook the rattle and drank from the bottle. Then she went back to the table and sat down. She held her hands up, shading her face from the others, but keeping the bottle up to her lips. The other children settled in small groups. The boys began to play with the soldiers. The girls played with the paper dolls. Emma sat apart from the groups, shading her face with her hands. Then the other girls asked her to play with them. Emma took the paper doll they laid before her. She got up from the table and took the paper doll with her.)

Emma (pretending to talk for the doll): I'm going away and I'm not ever going to come back again.

(She crawled under the sand table and stayed there sucking the bottle until the time was up. Then she crawled out, smiled quite sincerely at the therapist, freely said good-bye, and left with the group.)

Comments

In the group experience it is interesting to note Emma's behavior in relation to the other children in the group. She was either very withdrawn or actively aggressive.

The feelings expressed by these children in the group experience certainly imply that even in so large a group there is therapeutic value. The weakness in this contact does not lie in the children's response to the free-play situation, but in the inadequate responses of the therapist. In two instances, particularly, the therapist's responses are very poor. In one place she goes beyond the expressed feeling when she mentions "rules and other children and things like that." Tommy was doing a bit of bragging. The intrusion of the voice of authority was unnecessary and might have stopped the children's expression of feeling. The other poor response was in reply to Sharon's letter. The therapist implies a criticism of what Sharon has done by offering to help her write a letter.

In addition to these inadequate responses, the therapist remained silent at times when she should have made a response. An example of such a time is during Tommy's expressed desire to be a girl.

The manner in which the children imitated one another's play is interesting. When one had the courage to dramatize being a baby with such evident relish, the others also tried out the experiment. This seems to hasten the therapeutic process. It seems to break down the barriers of reserve that the children, individually, may have. The honesty of expression is also contagious. The therapist has less time to respond to individual acts in a group situation, but the children have a way of responding to one another themselves. The play between Sharon and Dick seems to be dramatized response to feeling. Emma's part in this session shows very clearly her relationship with the other children.

THIRD CONTACT—SECOND INDIVIDUAL CONTACT

(Emma came into the room and immediately got the nursing bottle and brought it over to the table and sat down across from the therapist. She drank from the bottle and smiled at the therapist.)

Therapist: You like to drink from the nursing bottle.

Emma: Yes. *(She took the nipple off and drank from the bottle that way.)* I like to drink this way, too.

Therapist: Sometimes you like to drink with the nipple on, then you like to take it off.

Emma: Yes.

(Emma began to play with the family of dolls. She put the bottle on the table within easy reach and looked at the dolls. She placed the mother and the big sister at the table. Then she placed the father and the boys on the floor. The mother doll was manipulated over to the stove and she moved the doll around. Her lips moved silently. Finally she looked at the therapist.)

Emma: Mother is cooking bacon.

Therapist: Mother is getting a meal ready.

Emma: Watch. *(She grinned at the therapist. Then she placed the mother at the table again.)* How long can I come here?

Therapist: I'll come out every week this summer. You may come as often as you like on your day. I will save this time every Wednesday for you. If you want to come, you may.

Emma: And on Fridays with the group. Don't forget that.

(Emma took off all the girl doll's clothes. She placed the doll in the bed. The mother doll came in and embraced the boy doll and kissed him. Then the mother was placed at the table again. Emma took off the father doll's trousers and placed him in bed with the girl doll. Then Emma brought the mother doll in to the bed. Emma jerked the girl doll out of the bed, dragged her by the hair over to the doll's clothes, beat the doll, then put all the doll's clothes on again. She dressed the father doll again. Then she put the father and mother at the table. She lined all the other dolls up in a sitting position facing the mother and father. Then she moved the mother and father and the table at which they were sitting away from the children. She placed the baby and the dog on a chair facing the children. Then the father was brought into the room again. He kissed all the children good-bye, ignored the mother doll, and was finally placed in a sitting position on the bed. Then the baby was placed in the mother's lap and she was placed in a chair, facing all the children. The father was taken off the bed, made to pat the dog, then was put back on the bed again. The dog growled at the mother and was placed under a chair. Emma picked up the bottle and drank from it with the nipple off. She looked long and hard at the dolls. Then she got up from the table, went over to the bench and got the drawing paper and crayons, and brought them back to the table and sat down beside the therapist. She began to draw.)

Emma: This is going to be a church. *(She drew silently for a while.)* I don't know how to make church windows.

Therapist: You want to put church windows in your drawing, but don't know how.

Emma: Yes. Can you tell me?

Therapist: Sometimes church windows have pictures in colors on them. Sometimes they look just like different-colored pieces of glass.

Emma: I'll make different colors. They are bigger than most windows, aren't they?

Therapist: Yes.

(Emma drew the windows, bent intently over her drawing. She finished the picture and handed it to the therapist.)

Emma: Here. For you.

(She then put the crayons away and sat down by the dolls again and looked at them. Then she laughed shortly. She got up from the table and went over to the soldiers and had a little battle with them. When told that her time was up, she came over to the table and grinned at the therapist.)

Emma: I'm coming back, and coming back, and coming back as long as ever I can.

Therapist: You like to come here.

Emma: Yes. *(She said good-bye and skipped out of the room.)*

COMMENTS

The picture which Emma drew was of a brown church, with a black door on which was drawn a white cross and her name. The windows were placed quite high and were of different colors. The bells were bright red, barred off with harsh black lines. The chimney was also bright red, rigidly marked off in bricks. At the top of the picture were printed the letters A B C E F D X Y in bright colors. We can only wonder just what the significance of the church was to Emma. Keeping in mind that the Home is a religious institution where religious instruction is stressed, we might *guess* that it indicated a sense of guilt on Emma's part, since it followed the play with the dolls which seemed to be a very disturbing sex play. Her manner during this play was very tense and vivid. The mother was a dominating, threatening person. The little girl was punished for her actions with the father doll. No one liked the mother doll. Even the dog growled at her. The therapist did not verbalize any of the actions being so vividly pantomimed by Emma, because she felt that it might cut off the play. Emma had told the therapist to watch. The therapist did just that. Possibly the therapist could have eliminated a feeling of guilt by recognizing some of the feeling that was expressed. At a later interview, Emma again played with the family in a similar manner. Then she verbalized her play. Perhaps the therapist exercised too much caution in refraining from comment at this experience, but at the time she felt that verbalizing the feeling expressed in this silent play would be premature.

FOURTH CONTACT—SECOND GROUP CONTACT

(The four girls came in together. The boys did not appear. Edna and Sharon got out the nursing bottles. Edna began to draw. Shirley-Ann sat beside the therapist and drew aimlessly. Then she got a soldier and a nurse and traced around them. Emma took Edna's bottle and drank from it. Edna did not say anything, but continued her drawing.)

Shirley-Ann (to Emma): You always take things from people.

Emma: So what? What if I do?

Shirley-Ann: You're not going to get any of my stuff.

Emma: Oh yeah? I'll tell on you. I'll tell what you did.

Shirley-Ann: Ole Emma always tells on people. Always. Always. She runs and tells.

Emma: Sure I tell. I tell on everybody.

Sharon (putting on the black mask): I like to wear false faces. I'll put on the black one.

(Emma handed the bottle back to Edna. She sat down at the table and picked up the father doll and held it in her hand.)

Emma (to Edna in a tiny sing-song voice): Please may I have the nursing bottle?

(Edna handed it to her. Emma took the bottle, removed

the nipple and drank the water that way. She hooted with derisive laughter. Shirley-Ann got out the clay. After about twenty minutes they finally got together and sat down on the floor to play with the clay together. Sharon dropped one of the nursing bottles and broke it. She looked at though she was going to cry.)

Shirley-Ann (consoling her): Don't cry. The lady won't scold you.

(The therapist reassured Sharon, then swept up the broken glass.)

Shirley-Ann: It's all right to cry if you think you are going to be scolded; but when you know you won't get scolded, then why cry? *(Sharon smiled at this bit of wisdom.)*

Sharon: I don't even have to say that I am sorry?

Therapist: You don't even have to say that you are sorry, Sharon. You don't always like to have to say that you are sorry for things you do.

Sharon: No, but I really am sorry that I broke the bottle. I really am.

Therapist: You really are sorry about this.

Sharon: Yes.

(The other girls did not work very well with the clay. They spent most of their time looking around and commenting about the trip out to the swimming pool that they were going to take that afternoon. They fumbled with the clay, but did not shape it at all. However, Emma made something. She had her back to the others and hid what she was making. Finally, Shirley-Ann came over to the therapist and asked her very intently if she would please send something over to China to help the people over there who are starving to death and who have no clothes to wear.)

Therapist: You are worried about the little children in China.

Shirley-Ann: Oh yes. They are starving to death. They are dying because they don't have any food to eat. We learn about that in Sunday School. Sometimes I cry about it at night. I feel so sorry. *(She looked as though she might cry again.)*

Emma (glancing over her shoulder with a wicked-looking grin): Yah! Send them garbage to eat and spit on them.

Shirley-Ann (horrified): Oh no! Don't you talk like that Emma Blank.

Emma (mimicking): Emma. Emma Blank. Well, that's

what Emma Blank *thinks* about them. And could I tell the teacher that?

Therapist: You want to say it here because you know you couldn't say it to the teacher.

Emma: Yes. She would kill me and send me over there for them to eat. (*Laughs.*)

Shirley-Ann: She would not. But she ought to. You are hateful, Emma Blank. Nobody likes you. (*Emma immediately tried to take the bottle away from Edna by force. A battle ensued.*)

Edna: Take that one over there. Not mine.

Emma: You take that one over there. I want yours.

Edna: I had this one first. You let his one alone. That is yours over there.

Therapist: Emma wants yours because she is angry at what Shirley-Ann said about her.

Emma: Of course I am. I'm mad at you all the time. I'm mad at all of you.

Shirley-Ann: Anyway, there is a bottle over there. Take that one. (*Emma went back to the clay.*)

Therapist: Emma wanted the bottle that Edna had—not just any bottle. (*Emma went back to the clay.*)

Emma (indicating the therapist): I don't fight with *her.*

Shirley-Ann: No. Of course not. You ain't that crazy.

Emma: I'm not afraid. (*Long pause.*)

Sharon: What are you making? (*Emma hid what she was making.*)

Emma: You sure wish you knew, don't you? Well, you are not going to see it.

(Their time was up and the girls got up to go. No mention was made by any of them that the boys had not appeared. Emma came over to the therapist and showed her the figure of a man that she had just made.)

Emma (grinning): See? He ain't got no clothes on.

Therapist: The man hasn't any clothes on. (*Emma rolled him up in a ball and tossed it on the paper with the rest of the clay.*)

Emma: Nobody will ever see him now, either. They don't need to know what I made.

Therapist: You don't want them to know what you made.

Emma (grinning): I hate their guts.

Therapist: You hate their guts.

(Emma laughed loudly. The other girls had said good-bye

and left. Emma called a cheerful good-bye and left the room hooting with laughter.)

COMMENTS

After the girls had left, the boys came in. They said that they did not want to come in with the girls. The therapist agreed to see the girls and boys in separate groups.

This group session illustrates the possibilities of the group interacting in such a way that insight is gained by certain individuals. Emma seemed to recognize the fact that when she approached the other girls in a courteous manner she met with more success than when she resorted to force. As time passed, this was more in evidence. She finally stopped trying to get her way by force. She expresses to the full in this contact her hostility to other children, to adults such as Sunday School teachers, and to the world in general, including those who are suffering. Emma's venom is the result of years of frustrating deprivation. She also expresses even more freely her interest in sex. The therapist could have been more alert to catch the expressed feelings rather than being merely repetitive.

Emma shows an important acceptance of herself when she admits that she wanted Edna's bottle only because she wished to attack Edna. This part was handled in a more satifactory manner by the therapist. Emma tentatively explores the possibility of using courtesy rather than force in getting her way.

In this contact one can see the dynamics of therapy at work. The interaction of the group, the acceptance of Emma as she really is by the therapist, the freedom really to express herself add up to signs of a more positive type of behavior. Although the other girls expressed shock at Emma's daring remarks, there was evidence that they, too, enjoyed them. Once again we have the man without clothes, which has figured in three out of four contacts. Emma seems to enjoy every minute of the interviews. She no longer shows any signs of tenseness. She loves this chance to "be herself."

FIFTH CONTACT—THIRD INDIVIDUAL CONTACT

(Emma came in, opened the paints, smiled broadly.)

Emma: Where is black paint? *(The therapist pointed out the black paint. Emma made an outline of a house. She put red paint on it. When the paint ran she made a face.)* Ug. Look. Black and red got all mixed up.

Therapist: You don't like that.

Emma: No. *(She painted a blue tree beside the house. She seemed very happy.)* Will you write *The Three Bears* for me so I can have it to read to my sister.

Therapist: You want me to write it for you because I wrote it for Edna yesterday.

Emma: Yes. That's why. Will you?

Therapist: Yes. You tell me what to write. Edna did.

Emma: Once there was three bears and they were stinkers. They made soup—bean soup again—and got too much pepper in it and went out for a walk. Along came Goldilocks. She was a lousy thief. She went in and wrecked the joint and ate the soup and the bears came back and found her and made soup out of her and she was much better than the bean soup. *(Emma laughed delightedly. She suddenly picked up the picture and the paint all ran together again.)*

Emma: Oh damn! *(Looked quickly at the therapist.)*

Therapist: You thought I would call you down for that, didn't you?

Emma: Ain't you? *(Grins. Therapist does not say anything. Emma laughs aloud.)* Well, I guess you ain't! *(Seems delighted. Painting.)* Damn. Damn. God damn.

Therapist: You like to swear. *(Emma nods and swears some more.)*

Emma: Can I go and change this paint water?

Therapist: If you want to.

(Emma changed the water and started another picture. She smiled as she painted her name in red. Then she painted B to baRRa in green. Then in blue she painted PATTY 515. She painted LAB in orange and U.S.A. in yellow, followed by a yellow V.)

Emma: Now what do you think of that?

Therapist: Umhmmm.

Emma: Know what it is all about?

Therapist: Want to tell me? *(Emma nodded vigorously.)*

Emma (pointing to the green): These are just letters.

They don't mean anything. Patty is my sister. She is eight. *(Very carefully she put this on the table to dry. This did not run. On the other paper she painted again in red E.B.P.B.)* P.B. is for my sister Patty. *(She painted a green house, a green tree, and green grass.)* Look. If I don't put much water on my brush, it doesn't run. *(She smiled broadly.)*

Therapist: That's right. You're glad you discovered something.

Emma: You know I never painted before like this. Never.

Therapist: And you like to do it.

Emma (laughing): I'm talking more, too. Ain't I?

Therapist: Yes, you are. You feel free to say whatever you feel like saying to me.

Emma: Uh huh. *(Then she painted over the green house with black paint.)* Here. You can have this. I want you to have it. *(Therapist accepted the picture.)*

(Emma started to paint a third picture. She painted a service flag on this paper.)

Emma: This picture is for me.

Therapist: You want to keep that one.

Emma: Yes. You guess what this one is.

Therapist: It looks like a service flag.

Emma: It is. *(She seemed quite pleased that the therapist should recognize it, but it was very well done in red, white, and blue. The star was gold.)* It is a service flag for my daddy. He is in the army.

(She painted an airplane above the flag and just as she was painting it an airplane swooped down over the building they were in. It flew so low that the children outside began to scream, "It's going to land." The matrons ran outside and began to scream. The airplane swooped down over the place three times. Some of the little nursery children began to cry. Emma painted on imperturbably, even smiling a little to herself. She turned the paper around toward the therapist and said, "Write airplane, right here." The therapist did. Emma then put away the paints, emptied the water, and came back to the therapist.)

Emma: Come on. Play with me.

Therapist: You want me to play a game of checkers with you.

Emma: Yes. Show me how. The other snots over at the girls' cottage won't let me play with them because I don't know how.

Therapist: You think it would help you to get along with

the other girls if you learned to play some of the games they play.

Emma: Yes.

(The therapist explained the game as they played it and showed Emma how to make the moves and take turns. Emma learned quickly.)

Emma: Now let's play another game and you let me win.

Therapist: You want to be sure that you win this game.

Emma: Yes. (*The therapist and Emma played the game and Emma won this one.*) Have we time for another game?

Therapist: Yes. There will be time for one more game.

(The game went along without much comment until Emma saw that she was losing it.)

Emma: I suppose you would be mad if you lost this game?

Therapist: You think I wouldn't like it if you won all the games.

Emma: Would you?

Therapist: I wouldn't care. You want to win this one, too; don't you?

Emma: Yes, you let me win this one, too. (*The therapist deliberately moved her men out in front of Emma's and Emma won this game.*) Now show me how to cheat so I can always win.

Therapist: You want to know how to cheat so that you can win every time you play checkers.

Emma: Yeah. See. That's what I said.

Therapist: When we started this game you said that you wanted to learn to play so the other girls would let you play with them. They won't play with you if you cheat.

Emma: They needn't know I'm cheating.

Therapist: You want to win so badly that you want to know how to cheat and you think they won't know. But they would know.

(Emma got up and walked over to the bench and got the nursing bottle. She drank from it. She looked around at the therapist with a sullen, angry expression on her face.)

Emma: I'll throw this down on the floor and break it.

Therapist: You want to break the bottle because I won't show you how to cheat. (*Emma nodded. She seemed very tense. She jerked off the nipple and drank the water.*)

Emma: I'll throw it down and break it.

Therapist: You'll throw it down and break it because I won't do what you asked me to do. (*Emma grinned suddenly and placed the bottle on the bench.*)

Emma: How can I go ahead and be angry if you won't get mad, too?

Therapist: You want me to get angry, too?

Emma: No. No, I really don't. Besides, if I broke this bottle you might not let me use it any more.

Therapist: You couldn't use a *broken* bottle.

Emma: No. My time is up, isn't it?

Therapist: Yes. You've only three minutes left.

Emma: Can't do much in three minutes.

Therapist: No. You can't do much in three minutes.

Emma: You ain't mad at me, are you?

Therapist: No, I'm not mad at you. You think I might be, but I'm not.

Emma: I'm going to take this picture. You can keep this one of our house. I wouldn't want that house around me. I wouldn't even go in it. Not even if you paid me, I wouldn't. Good-bye.

(Emma left quickly. She took the service-flag picture and the one with the letters painted around it, but she left the picture of the house.)

COMMENTS

In this interview Emma seems to have expressed very deep and important feelings. She also showed signs of having gained a little insight into her antisocial behavior. She takes the initiative to try to help herself by learning a game to play with the others. She showed other positive actions, too. She expressed a consideration for the therapist's feelings when she asked if the therapist would be "mad" if she lost the second game. She was accepting the limitation of time when she asked if there was time for another game. Emma also seemed to have taken the responsibility for herself when she evaluated her own behavior, "I'm talking more, too," and when she remarked about breaking the bottle ". . . if I broke this bottle you might not let me use it any more."

Some of the therapist's responses in this contact are superficial and consequently inadequate. However, Emma feels the depth of acceptance of herself, for she freely brings her most hostile thoughts and feelings to the surface. The therapist handled the cheating episode very poorly. Emma's antagonism toward the therapist at this point is proof of what happens when the therapist departs from the sound principles of therapy and falls into the usual adult rôle of mild moralizing and subtly attempting to dissuade the girl from cheating. Immediately Emma reacts in her "normal" manner and becomes antagonistic and sullen. Had Emma been permitted to be responsible for her own attitudes, this would not have arisen. The therapist might have said, when requested for aid in cheating, "You really would like to learn to cheat, wouldn't you? But I'm not going to teach you how." This response would have set certain limitations as to what the therapist would do, but it would not be an attempt to control the child's feelings or outside behavior.

The reaction to the airplane is also noteworthy. A few days later, Emma mentioned how very frightened she was when the airplane swept so low over the cottage, but there was no outward sign of any fear during the incident.

The paintings were also interesting bits to add to the study of this girl. One wonders just what was the full significance of that black house that she didn't want around her and wouldn't go into even if they paid her.

Emma was more relaxed than she was at earlier interviews. It is interesting to note how she returned to the nursing bottle when she became blocked by the therapist's clumsy handling of the cheating episode.

SIXTH CONTACT—THIRD GROUP CONTACT

(The girls met the therapist's car and insisted on carrying in the suitcase of toys and unpacking them. Emma snatched a nursing bottle.)

Emma: Today I'm not using the nipple. I'm drinkin' this here beer straight.

Sharon: I'm not going to use the nipple, either.

Shirley-Ann: Me will.

Therapist: Emma and Sharon don't want to use the nipples but Shirley-Ann does.

Shirley-Ann: Me be the onliest baby here.

Therapist: You want to be the only baby.

Sharon: Baby. Baby.

Emma: Dirty little stinky baby.

(Sharon, Edna, and Emma sat at the same table and began to paint. Shirley-Ann sat across from the therapist and drank from the bottle.)

Edna: I could hardly wait for you to come today.

Emma: Dirty, stinky little Sharon is gettin' her water all dirty. I keep my water clean.

Sharon: Hear her? Emma is braggin' again. She said I get my paints all dirty and she keeps her paints clean.

Edna (to Sharon): We are messy. Emma is the onliest careful painter. We're dirty messers. (*She shook her paint-brush and sprinkled some of the water on Sharon.*)

Sharon: You quit that! Lady, look! She's sprinklin' water on me.

Shirley-Ann: Well, it's good for you.

Edna: Look how this paint water changes color. Kids are just naturally messy.

Emma: If they get a chance. All except me. I'm very careful. I'm the carefulest painter in the whole world. I'm not a messy, stinky brat. I'm better than everybody else. (*Other girls jeer at Emma.*)

Edna: Listen to old brag-puss Emma.

Emma (with a very superior smile): Edna, use that red more sparingly. There is no sense in wasting it.

Sharon: You sure do like to boss.

Emma: I sure do. Another thing. The Japs I will kill tonight.

(Shirley-Ann put away the bottle.)

Emma: Are you putting away the bottle, Shirley?

Shirley-Ann: Yes.

(Sharon got up and began to jig around.)

Emma: Sit down there and paint, girl, before I konk you one.

Sharon: I can't sit down. I've got ants in my pants.

Emma: Oh! I got paint on the floor. And it is very nice to know that I don't have to clean it up. But I will clean it up.

Therapist: You don't like to be told to clean up after your work.

Sharon: Why if Miss X told her to do it she would have a fit. Emma is hateful.

Emma: Our lady doesn't think I am hateful.

Therapist: Emma is pretty sure that I don't think she is hateful.

Edna (to Emma): I'm going to paint just what you paint.

Emma: Go ahead. Be a damn fool if you want to.

Sharon: Oh, Emma! How you talk! You shouldn't!

Emma: Our lady said I could say what I wanted to say when I was in here.

Therapist: Emma wants to see if I really meant that. She wants to try it.

Sharon: See. Edna still has some water in her glass.

Emma: She ain't a hog like we are.

(Shirley-Ann looks at Emma's picture.)

Shirley-Ann: What is that anyway?

Emma: It's a picture of a bit stink. That's what it is.

Shirley-Ann: A big stink?

Emma: Yes. It's really a picture of a big stink. It's a toilet. See? And somebody has used it.

Sharon (as she began to paint, using the nursing-bottle water for paint water): You paint awful funny pictures. (Emma went over to Sharon.)

Emma: Will you let me use a bit of your paint water? Those girls took mine. See? (*As Emma dipped her brush into the water, after Sharon had nodded agreement, the color changed to orange.*)

Sharon: Oh, look! Orange juice. I'll drink the orange juice. (*She grabbed up the bottle.*)

Edna (going for some water, she called to Emma from the lavatory): You better come in here and help me, Emma. I can't do what I'm trying to do.

Emma: Oh, hell! Ask the bogey man.

Shirley-Ann: Oh, Emma! (*The girls laughed.*)

Therapist: Emma loves to shock the other girls with her words.

Sharon (to Shirley-Ann): Oh, look! You old slop. You are using all the green. You know we were having fun until you had to butt in. You're just such a mess.

(Emma spilled some paint. She quickly got the towel out of the lavatory and wiped it up.)

Emma: Miss X would raise hell if she knew. Look at this here towel! Ha! Ha! Ha!

Therapist: You don't think Miss X would like paint all over her towel.

Emma: Dear lady, Miss X will *die* when she sees it—I hope.

(The therapist decided to take the towel home and launder it before returning it to its proper rack. Emma jumped up and began to parade around the table singing her version of "Onward, Christian Soldiers.")

Emma:

> Onward, Christian soldiers,
> Marching war, war, war.
> If she knew what I just did,
> Boy, would she raise hell!

(The other girls laughed hilariously.)

Emma (imitating Miss X): Oh, my towel! My towel! Who put that paint on my towel? I will whip her. I will *kill* her. My towel! My *towel!* (*The other girls screamed and laughed at Emma's show. Emma grinned and suddenly sobered.*) Stop that foolish laughing this minute. Mind your manners. (*Again the girls hooted with laughter. Emma sat down across from the therapist. She grinned.*)

Emma: Why doesn't our lady come out here and stay?

Edna: Please do.

Therapist: You think it would be nice if I stayed here with you.

Shirley-Ann: Will you?

Emma: No, she won't. Who would stay here if they didn't have to? (*She glared at the other girls viciously.*)

Therapist (to Emma): You don't like this place.

Emma: I *hate* this place.

Shirley-Ann: It is a *good* place.

Emma: Bah! It is a hateful place.

Therapist: Shirley-Ann thinks it is a good place, but Emma thinks it is a hateful place.

Edna (whispering): I hate it, too.

Therapist: You don't want to say out loud what you think.

Edna: No. Somebody might tell.

Therapist: You're afraid if somebody told how you felt, you might get in trouble.

Emma: I'm not afraid. I tell them. I scream it out. I say I hate you. I hate this old place. I hate you all.

Edna (with great admiration): She does. She isn't afraid.

Therapist: Emma isn't afraid to say right out what she thinks.

Emma: I'm not afraid.

Edna: But she gets punished for it.

Emma: I don't care.

Therapist: You don't care if you do get punished, you say what you think anyway.

Shirley-Ann: It's a *good* place.

Emma: Good if you're a pet, maybe. But I ain't no pet.

Therapist: You think it might be a good place for some of you, but not especially good for you.

Emma: I don't hate everybody.

Therapist: Oh! There are some people you like.

Emma: I like our lady. I like Sharon. I like Edna.

Therapist: You really do like some of us.

Emma: Yes.

Edna (in amazement): You like me?

Emma: I even like you, squirt.

Therapist: Our time is up for today.

Emma: Hurry! Hurry! Let us help clean up. Let us pack up the toys.

(The girls hurriedly cleaned up the room and put away the toys.)

Emma (to therapist): Here is my last picture. See. It is a jail. And I'm in it.

Therapist: Oh, you've put yourself in jail.

Emma: You can have it. And this one, too. My big stink and me.

(The girls left together.)

COMMENTS

In this session the girls' personalities clash again and again and finally become compatible. It is very interesting to note the complete reversal of feelings on the part of Emma after she expresses her very negative feelings toward the Home and toward all the people there. To be able to announce voluntarily that she likes some of the people is certainly a sign of progress as far as Emma is concerned. She enjoyed the center of the stage and wins the admiration of the other girls by her daring remarks and venomous expressions. This contact seems to illustrate one of the values of group therapy. In an individual contact Emma could not have experienced the reaction of the other girls to her remarks. It seems highly probable that Emma was able to align herself with the others after they expressed either agreement or approval of her feeling about the Home. The exclusion of Shirley-Ann from the group that Emma says she likes might support this idea.

The use of the art material is again interesting. Perahps if the therapist had been more capable of reflecting the feeling Emma was expressing in that drawing of the big stink, it would not have been necessary for Emma to punish herself by putting herself in a pictorial jail.

Emma seems to have gained considerable insight into her behavior in this interview. The therapist, too, seems more relaxed. She has become "our lady" to the girls. In previous interviews she was without any identity. In succeeding interviews her name is changed by the girls in such a way that the relationship that is built up between her and the girls is more or less illustrated by the tag they attach to her.

It seems unlikely that Emma would have progressed so far in an individual contact. Since her problem is primarily one of social adjustment, the group experience seems to be the better medium for her.

SEVENTH CONTACT—FOURTH INDIVIDUAL CONTACT

(Emma entered the playroom, grinned at the therapist, and sat down at the paint table. She growled like a dog, went over and got the nursing bottle, removed the nipple, brought it back to the paint table, and sat down again.)

Emma: I don't know what to paint.
Therapist: You can't make up your mind.
Emma: Nope.
(She dipped the brush in the red paint and painted the letters USA on the paper. She painted an orange airplane and trimmed it in yellow. She blotted the picture with a paint rag, then outlined the USA in green paint.)
Emma: Did you know the boys had an Indian dance down in the ravine last night and one of the boys fell in the fire and got burned? We could hear them scream clear over to the girls' cottage. The boys were burning the weeds and this boy fell in when he was dancing around the fire. He fell right in the blaze and burned himself.
Therapist: He really got hurt, then.

Emma: Yes. His arms and hands and face. His hair, too.
Therapist: Hmm.

(Emma painted B U S in purple letters on the picture.)

Emma: What does this say?

Therapist: It says bus.

Emma (laughing): It does? I didn't know that. I just accidentally wrote it. So it spells bus, huh? B—U—S spells bus. *(She laughed again.)*

Therapist: You're pleased because you spelled a word.

Emma: Yeah, I'm gettin' smart.

Therapist: It makes you feel good.

Emma: Yeah. Can I take some of this paper over to the girls' cottage?

Therapist: I can't let you take any of the paper over there. You may draw on the paper while you are here, but I haven't enough to let you take it out of here.

Emma: May I draw two more pictures?

Therapist: Yes.

(Emma paints a big yellow cross on this paper, adds a black swastika, a black German airplane, a red E.)

Emma: Last Friday when I got over to the cottage, everybody was already inside at the table. I was late.

Therapist: You didn't like being late.

Emma: Why, I didn't care. Not one little bit. In fact I liked it.

Therapist: Oh, you liked going in late.

Emma: This afternoon we're having the first corn cobs from the farm. *(She pointed out the window in the direction of the corn field.)*

Therapist: You'll like that.

Emma: I'll say! I'm a hog.

Therapist: You like to eat.

Emma: I like to be a hog.

Therapist: Oh, you like to be a hog. *(Emma nodded her head vigorously.)*

Emma: I sure do. *(She grinned impishly.)* I'm a smart aleck, too. And a sassy, smarty-pants.

Therapist: Oh! You think you're a smart aleck, and you think you're sassy, too.

Emma: I'm the meanest brat here at this dump.

Therapist: You think you're the meanest youngster here.

Emma: I fight and I lie and I tattle.

Therapist: You fight and lie and tattle.

Emma: Yes. Remember that airplane that flew low over here that time?

Therapist: Yes.

Emma: That really scared the pants right off me. But remember how I played like I didn't care?

Therapist: You were really scared, but you pretended you didn't care.

Emma: Boy! Was I scared!

Therapist: You were really scared.

(Emma painted a swastika on a plane and hangar. She painted USA on the house. The paint ran and Emma painted the letters out. Then she painted a USA in green on the other house. At this point two little nursery-aged girls knocked on the door and asked if they could come in and go to the toilet. When they went into the lavatory, Emma grinned at the therapist.)

Emma: There they go. Always running into the bathroom. (When they came out again Emma scowled at them and made faces at them. They scampered out in a hurry.)

Emma: I can scare those little kids easy. I make a face like this, see? and I growl like this and they run and hide.

Therapist: You sort of like to scare them.

Emma: Yeah, I like to. *(She painted along in grinning silence.)* I don't suppose that I would have time to play a game of checkers, would I?

Therapist: You have only five minutes left.

Emma: I want to play a game of checkers and I want to crayon a picture. I want to do both at the same time. I don't know which one I would rather do.

Therapist: It's a little hard to make up your mind.

Emma: Yeah. I'll draw. That's quicker.

Therapist: Drawing doesn't take as long as checkers.

Emma: Watch this. *(She draws a large U S and fills in the U with black crayon.)* Do I get to take this over to the cottage with me?

Therapist: If you want to.

Emma: I get to come tomorrow with the group, don't I?

Therapist: Yes.

Emma: Know what? I would rather come with the group every time. I think it is more fun. Have the group twice a week, instead of me alone. Could we?

Therapist: You think it would be more fun if we just had group meetings instead of the way things are now?

Emma: That's what I think. I'm alone all the time anyhow. Here I have somebody that will play with me.

Therapist: You really like it because here the others play with you and you like that better really than being all alone.

Emma: And do you really want to know something? My mother is coming up to get me one day this week and there is going to be a band and some animals and I'm going to watch it. There will be big wild animals. And she is going to get my step-father to come and get me and maybe he will and maybe the lions and tigers will eat him up. There will be monkeys, too.

Therapist: You think maybe your mother will be up to see you this week. It will really be quite a celebration.

Emma: Yeah. A whole big band of music, too.

Therapist: With a band of music and wild animals and everything.

Emma: I'm really a whopping big liar. *(She grins delightedly.)* She *told* me she would come. Maybe she will. I think she will. She won't, though.

Therapist: She told you she would come, but you aren't sure that she really will get here.

Emma (hiding her face in her hands): You are *my* lady.

Therapist: You want me to be your lady.

Emma (whispering): All mine—nobody else's.

Therapist: You wish I would belong just to you.

Emma (getting up and closing the crayon box): I'll come back tomorrow. I 'spect the time is gone.

Therapist: Yes, the time is up for today.

Emma: Good-bye, dear lady.

(Emma very sadly smiled at the therapist as she edged toward the door. Then she suddenly made a face at the therapist, giggled, and ran out.)

COMMENTS

In this interview Emma certainly examines herself frankly. She is looking within herself and in many instances puts her finger accurately on her trouble-making actions. It is interesting to note that she includes some negative evaluations of her behavior. She still likes to shock the therapist. When she calls herself a hog, she wants to be called a hog. Generalities do not quite satisfy her. After she states that she likes to be late for meals and be a "hog," she admits that such remarks and actions are "smart-aleck and sassy." One can imagine Emma's reaction if the therapist had made these accusations. They would have served only to challenge her negative reactions. Finding herself accepted unconditionally, she can go on from there and say, "I'm the meanest brat here at this dump. I fight and I lie and I tattle." Then she tries to explain herself to the therapist, beginning with the plane scare and how her actions belie her feelings and how different her real attitudes are from her external behavior.

When Emma suggests that she likes to come with the others and play with them, she seems to be well aware of her needs. The strange aspect of this request was that each of the girls made the same request during their individual contact this same week. Whether they got together beforehand and decided that all should make the same request, the therapist did not know. However, she agreed to see the girls twice a week in group situations. This, therefore, was Emma's last individual contact.

Emma's reference to her mother's expected visit certainly points up the confused and conflicting feelings that thoughts of the mother's visit seem to create in Emma. The child seems to be seeking for a dependable anchor when she appeals to the therapist to be "my lady." However, she cannot remain contrite and civilized for long. She quickly puts up her defenses, makes her face, giggles, and departs in character.

EIGHTH CONTACT—FOURTH GROUP CONTACT

(The four girls were already in the playroom when the therapist arrived. When she came in, they squealed and yelled.)

Sharon: Yippee. I thought you'd never come. Come in. Come in.

(They came up to the therapist's car and took the suitcase containing the toys and the box of toys and opened them. They each grabbed a nursing bottle.)

Emma: Come on. Let's be babies. Me fill bottle.

Others: Me fill bottle, too. Me baby.

(They all drank from the nursing bottles and babbled like very small babies. Shirley-Ann got out the clay. Edna, Sharon, and Emma began to draw.)

Sharon: Where is the paint glass?

Edna: It's broke. Shirley-Ann broke it.

Sharon (to Shirley-Ann): Did you?

Shirley-Ann: Yes, but I couldn't help it. Could I? I really couldn't help it. Could I? Could I?

Therapist: No, you didn't mean to break it.

Shirley-Ann (to therapist): I felt awful bad about it, didn't I?

Therapist: Yes, you felt very bad about it.

Sharon: I broke one of the bottles once. I almost cried.

Emma (dryly): Ha! Ha! Ha!

Sharon: I did almost cry, didn't I? Didn't I?

Therapist: Yes. You almost cried.

Shirley-Ann (to therapist): Then *you* dropped one one day and broke it and we didn't feel so bad then.

Therapist: You didn't feel so badly after I broke one, too.

Shirley-Ann: Yeah. Everybody breaks things once in a while.

Emma (mockingly): Everybody breaks things once in a while.

Sharon (defensively): Well!

Emma (to therapist): Do you like us, Mommy?

Therapist: You sort of wonder if I like you, hm?

Emma: Well, do you?

Therapist: Yes.

Sharon: We like her for a mommy, don't we?

Shirley-Ann: I'm going to——

Sharon: I'm going to marry my daddy.

Shirley-Ann: Oh, you can't.

Emma: I'm going to marry a man made out of wax and melt him down and tear him apart.

Sharon: Oh, Emma!

Edna: I'm going to marry Jesus.

Emma: You girls argue about such things. *I'm* going to marry everyone. There won't be anyone left for you.

Edna: You're going to marry everyone? Even him? *(Points down toward basement.)*

Emma: Even him! I'd learn him.

(The three girls painted in silence. Shirley-Ann made strips of clay and pressed them down into the table.)

Sharon: Mary said for me to bring her some paper. We can't, though, can we?

Therapist: No. You may use the paper in here, but you can't take it out of here. There isn't enough for that. *(Sharon messes up her picture.)*

Shirley-Ann: You better come over with me, Sharon. I won't make you so nervous.

Sharon: Look at these paints. They are all smeared.

Shirley-Ann: Well, you did it.

Emma: Stop talking so much about such nonsense. You bother my mommy.

Sharon: She is *not your* mommy!

Emma (yelling): She *is* my mommy. You are jealous because she isn't your mommy. But she is *mine.*

Shirley-Ann: She is my girl friend.

Emma: I like her better than my real mother. My real mother is mean. I have a step-father who is mean, too. When I am ten and my sister is older, too, then my mommy is going into the army.

Sharon: Is she? My mommy works awful hard.

Emma: Anyhow, my mom is going into the army and I hope she gets shot, too. Bang! Bang! Bang!

(There was a sudden and violent argument over the paint water at this moment and Sharon and Edna alternately called to the therapist, "Look! Oh, Miss—— Look what she is doing. She did it.")

Emma (imitating them): Look! Oh look! *(In the ensuing argument the paint water is upset.)*

Edna (yelling at Emma): Get the rag and wipe it up, you great big jackass!

Emma (doing as she was bid): Control yourself. Don't have a nervous breakdown. Edna, you are a screwball.

(The therapist missed most of the girls' conversation at this point, but it was about a play that the girls were going to give at the girls' cottage.)

Emma: Nobody will like you, Edna, if you don't behave better.

Edna (coming over and standing close to the therapist): Mommy likes Edna, doesn't she?

Therapist: You want them to know that I like you.

Edna: You're my mommy.

(She goes back to the table and smears the paints; then she begins to draw.)

Sharon: I want to give you something, Mommy.

Emma: I want to give you something. too.

Edna: They know they can't, don't they?

Therapist: They want me to know that they would like to give me something.

Edna: I'll give you my picture. See? It's kinda pretty.

(Emma paints a red house and cuts it out.)

Sharon· She is taking all the red. Now I can't finish my picture. Edna just took it.

Edna: Well, it was just laying there.

Sharon: Now I can't finish my picture.

Edna: I don't care.

Sharon: I'm going to tell Miss N on you.

Edna: I'm going to tell her first. I'll race you over.

Sharon: Oh, Edna.

Emma: You want to tell Miss N everything.

Sharon: Well, she——

Emma: She disgusts you.

Sharon: Well, she——

Emma: You want everything for yourself.

Sharon: Well, I had it first.

Emma: And just because you had it first, you think you ought to keep it.

Sharon: Well——

Emma (mockingly): *Good* little girls *share* their things. Only hogs hog things all the time. Only hogs hog all the slop—except Sharon.

Sharon: I do not! I do not! I'm going to tell on you.

Emma: Now you're going to tell on me. Again you're going to tell on me. How many times this morning now are you going to tell on me?

Sharon (limply): Well, you tease so.

Emma: Oh, I tease. My *dear* child, I am *sorry (heavy with sarcasm. For several minutes they paint in silence. Then Emma pushes over her paint box mockingly.)* Do have some red paint, Sharon. *(Sharon looks at Emma suspiciously, but she very gingerly dips her brush into the red paint Emma offers her.)*

Emma (grinning wickedly): Oh, dear. I'm *so* nice! See, Mommy? I shared. *(The girls all laughed.)*

Therapist: Emma shared her red paint like a *nice* little girl. *(Emma hands the entire box of paints over to Sharon.)*

Emma: Do take them all, Sharon. My brush, too.

Edna (to Emma): And you just must take mine.

Sharon (to Edna): Here. You take mine.

(They continue to push the paint boxes around making a game of trying to *share* their things. Soon they are all laughing. When time is up, Emma leaves holding hands with Edna and Sharon.)

COMMENTS

In the first part of this interview, the girls were seeking reassurance from the therapist. Then they identified the therapist with their "mommy." Their feelings flare to the surface and they give vent to their jealousy and rivalry for the therapist's affection. This problem comes up quite often in play-therapy sessions. The child demands a show of affection from the therapist. It seems as though it would be much better if the therapist continued to reflect back to the child the feelings that he is expressing—his desire for the therapist to say that she likes him, his eagerness to belong to someone. This is especially true of children who are as emotionally deprived as these children. However, there seems to be little or no therapeutic value in entering into an emotionally supportive rôle that will only create other problems when that, too, has to be destroyed.

Emma takes the part of behavior critic in this interview and, with protective sarcasm, she attempts to become a peacemaker, which is certainly a novel rôle for Emma. The contagion of her act and the immediate lessening of the tensions was quite noticeable. Emma left this interview definitely one of the girls. This seems to point up the value of group-therapy experiences. The therapist might have reflected a little of the feelings that were expressed at the close of this session.

NINTH CONTACT—FIFTH GROUP CONTACT

(The girls entered in an uproar. They grabbed the nursing bottles and yelled at the top of their lungs.)

Shirley-Ann: I want to drink from the bottle.

Sharon: I want to be a baby.

Edna: I be a ittle baby and crawl on floor.

Therapist: You like to be babies.

Girls: Yes!

(The girls got down on their hands and knees and crawled around on the floor, jabbering like very small babies.)

Emma: Am I the only one who wants to paint? I want to paint a toilet.

Therapist: You want to paint a picture of a toilet.

Emma: Yeah. A used toilet.

Therapist: You want to paint a picture of a toilet that has been used by someone.

Emma: Yeah. But I want to——

(She walked over to the checker game and kicked the checkers. Edna and Sharon had begun to play the game on the floor. When Emma kicked the checkers and they scattered all over the floor, a violent argument followed. The two girls were not as angry with Emma for ruining the game as they were with one another. Each accused the other of cheating.)

Emma: Dirty little sneaks cheat. If you can't play fair, don't play.

Edna: Oh, shut your big mouth!

(Shirley-Ann and Edna went over to the window and looked out. The four boys who followed the girls in play therapy were outside the window. The two girls talked out the window to the boys about another boy who had run away from the Home. Emma continued to paint—a very strange picture of blobs of red and black and yellow without much definite form. When she finished it, she showed it to the therapist.)

Emma: Like it?

Therapist: Do you want to tell me about it?

Emma: It's about a little girl who went out for a walk and when she walked past the house of the wicked old man he rushed out and grabbed her and took an axe and chopped her all to pieces and this is her blood. Then the sun came up and the man went out and looked for another little girl. These here black marks are his footprints where he went around hunting. He had a knife this long. (*She indicated a knife about two feet long.*)

Therapist: The man was a very cruel man, wasn't he? So he chased the little girl and chopped her all to pieces.

Emma: Yes. He got blood all over him, too.

Therapist: This is the blood all over him?

Emma: Please, won't you be my mama? Won't you please take me away from here?

Therapist: You do wish I could be your mama, don't you? And you would be so happy to get away from here.

Emma: Yes. Will you?

Therapist: I know you wish I would, but it wouldn't be possible for me to do it. I can come here and see you on the days we have already set, but I couldn't take you away.

Emma: I didn't think you could. I want to go away, though. I hate it here. *(She got out the black paint and smeared the paint all over the paper. Then she called to Edna. Edna came over to her.)* Get me some clean paint water, Edna.

Edna: Okay. You come, too.

(Both girls went into the lavatory. They closed the door and were gone for some time. Finally the door opened and the girls came back.)

Emma: Edna did something terrible in there.

Therapist: You think she did something pretty bad in the toilet.

Emma: Yes. She went to the toilet and when she was finished, she looked in the seat.

Therapist: You think it was bad to look in the toilet seat after she had used it.

Emma: Oh, yes! Miss X says it is. We always try to look, and if she is there she says it is wicked.

Therapist: Even though she does say it is wicked, you still want to look.

Emma: We'll go to hell.

Therapist: You think you might even go to hell by doing that.

Emma: That's what she says.

Therapist: That's what she tells you.

Emma: Yes.

(She sat down across from the therapist. Then suddenly she went over to the shelf and got a picture book that the therapist had brought along to read to a younger group at the Home. Emma sat down again across from the therapist and looked at the book.)

Emma: Write, "There was an old woman who lived in a shoe."

Therapist: You want me to write that for you?

Emma: Yes. *(The therapist wrote it for her.)*

(The house-mother came out and chased the boys away from the windows.)

Shirley-Ann: Goody! Goody! They had to go away.

Emma: Quiet. *(She continued to read the book.)*

(Shirley-Ann started to paint. She smeared the red paint all around. Edna painted.)

Edna: Will you bring us something the next time you come?

Therapist: You would like to have me give you something.

Edna: Will you? The next time you come.

Therapist: I'll bring you something the last time I come.

Shirley-Ann: Goody! What will it be?

Therapist: What would you like to have?

Edna and Sharon: Baby bottles!

Shirley-Ann: Please do bring us a baby bottle. Then, when we act like babies, Miss X can make us suck it. And I'd let on like I didn't like it, but I would like it. I'd suck it and cry.

Therapist: You'd like to have a baby bottle, then.

Girls: Yes!

(The girls got the bottles again and played with them until the end of the time, crawling around on the floor and pretending to cry.)

Edna: Be my mommy.

Therapist: You would like to have a mommy of your very own, wouldn't you?

Emma: Mommy, look. See Emma's pretty smear? See Emma suck the bottle.

Edna: Look at me.

Sharon: My mommy is very pretty. She has red hair.

Shirley-Ann: Look at me. Look at me.

Therapist: You all want me to look at you.

Edna: Mommy, look. You are *my* mommy.

(The other girls took up the cry and the girls spent the rest of the time proclaiming that the therapist was their mommy. The therapist recognized their feelings. The four girls left together, shouting hilariously.)

COMMENTS

In this interview the girls introduce a problem by asking for gifts from the therapist. This is not an uncommon request and can become quite a problem if the therapist does not avoid the giving of gifts during the therapy. When the demands of the children are met, the therapy might very possibly turn into a series of demanding sessions, with the requests growing each time. The therapist, feeling that these children were very deprived, did promise to bring them something the last time she came. The request for the nursing bottles at this stage in the therapy indicates predominant attitudes which were now engulfing the children.

The sudden adoption of the therapist as their "mommy" is quite typical of such emotionally deprived children. It certainly seems to bear out the children's need for affection and security.

The toilet episode is important in demonstrating how ineffective were the teaching techniques of the matron. Her attitude toward the children's curiosity about the toilets served only to heighten their interest and make it something forbidden and therefore much more enticing. Even the threat of hell itself did not serve to lessen their curiosity.

TENTH CONTACT—SIXTH GROUP CONTACT

(The four girls came in and snatched up the nursing bottles. They talked baby-talk and crawled around on the floor, addressing the therapist as "mommy.")

Edna: Remember. Last time you said you would bring us something the last time you come. I'll want a bottle like this.

Therapist: I won't forget. You think you would like to have a nursing bottle. (*The others echo Edna's statements.*)

Shirley-Ann: You know what? Emma acts lots nicer now than she ever did.

Sharon: Yes. She doesn't fight us any more or tattle.

Edna: We like Emma now. (*Edna blushed and grinned at the therapist. Edna and Sharon begin to paint.*)

Emma (mockingly): Oh, I'm just as sweet as I can be.

Therapist: Everyone seems to think you are acting better, Emma.

Emma: I try to be good.

Therapist: You really are trying to be a good girl.

(Accidentally Sharon spilled some water on Edna's picture.)

Sharon: Oh, I'm sorry, Edna. I didn't mean to spill it.

Edna: Oh, look! It got on my dress. I'll get a lickin'.

Emma (getting a clean rag and wiping off the water): I'll fix it.

Sharon: It'll be dry before you go back.

Emma: Maybe you better go out and sit in the sun.

Edna: Oh, well. Let's get down on the floor and paint.

(The four girls got down on the floor and began to paint. Shirley-Ann drew a picture of a face. Sharon drew a house. Edna drew a strange-looking figure.)

Edna: This is Miss X.

Emma: Oh, let me throw water on her.

Edna: Go ahead. But don't get it on *me*. (*The two girls began to throw water on Miss X.*)

Therapist: You're getting her wet, too.

Edna: Now I'll spank her. (*She hit the picture with her paintbrush.*)

Emma: Let me throw this bathroom stuff at her.

Therapist: You're going to make her real dirty.

Emma: Now she'll stink, too.

(Sharon and Shirley-Ann came over and added their destructive genius to the activities. Soon Miss X was reduced to a big wet brown smear. Emma completed the destruction by jabbing her brush handle through the paper.)

Therapist: You got even with her.

Emma: That'll learn her.

Edna: How much time left?

Therapist: Ten minutes.

(The girls got clean pieces of paper and started to paint again. Emma accidentally smeared her picture.)

Emma (with disgust): Oh, look! I've ruined it. That won't look a bit nice. I've smeared it and I don't like to smear things.

Edna: You never like to smear things, do you?

Emma: No. Do you?

Edna: Oh, I don't mind. I don't mind at all. Mess-and-smear Edna. That's me.

Emma: Mess-and-smear Edna and mess-and-smear Shirley-Ann.

Shirley-Ann: I do not mess and smear. Do I Miss—? I don't. I'll——

Emma: You'll tell Miss N. Oh my! Oh my! And what will I do? You'll tell and I'll die!

Shirley-Ann: Well.

Edna: We're going to have a play over to the girls' cottage. Would you like to see it? Want us to give it for you next week?

Therapist: Yes. I would like to see it.

Edna: We made it up and Miss N said we could give it. She doesn't know what it is all about yet, either.

Emma: I'm in this one.

Edna: Emma is good.

Emma: Oh, I'm the *star!*

Therapist: You've got a good part in this play. That pleases you.

Emma: You wait. It's a good play. We're making it up. We'll give it next time.

Edna (to therapist): What are you writing?

Therapist: Some things that I want to remember.

Edna (looking at notes): It's scribbling.

Therapist: It's shorthand.

Edna: Looks like scribblings to me. There is a word. And there is another one. I can't read it, though. There is my name.

Therapist: Your time is almost up. That's what it says here.

Edna: Let's clean the place up and put the toys away.

Emma: I'll help.

(The girls cleaned up the play area and put away the toys.)

COMMENTS

This was the first time the four girls really got together in an activity. The high spot in this contact is the voluntary group approval of Emma's improved behavior. This acceptance by the others, with a feeling of being able to do something with them, seems to have impressed Emma very much. The girls show signs of admiring many of her abilities.

The group attack on the matron who might punish Edna brought some violent feelings to the surface. The girls all worked together cleaning up the play area. All these incidents seem to indicate progress for all the girls.

ELEVENTH CONTACT—SEVENTH GROUP CONTACT

(The four girls met the therapist and told her that when they started to give their play over at the girls' cottage, the matron had taken one look at it and had made them stop it immediately. The girls were very indignant about the affair, which they termed "dirty mean and unfair." The therapist then suggested that they might like to give the play in the playroom.)

Edna: We'll ask in the boys and the nursery kids.

Emma: You go get them, Edna. We'll get things ready.

(When the girls went into the playroom, they stopped in disgust. The playroom was a mess. The nursery children had been there the afternoon before and all the toys were flung high and wide. Bicycles were turned over; blocks had been scattered all over the floor; broken toys littered the room. The girls were quiet upset, but, without waiting for a suggestion, they set to work and cleared a space in the center of the room. Then they designated the area that was to be the stage and lined up chairs for the audience. The following is an account of what took place. Emma opened the play with a hula song and dance. This was followed by Shirley-Ann singing "Off We Go." Halfway through this song Emma cried out, "You forgot to——" An argument ensued between Emma and Sharon about what she was supposed to have done. The therapist could not catch the reason for the argument. Shirley-Ann continued to sing the song to the bitter end, although the argument grew in intensity until all the audience could hear was:)

Sharon (screaming): You better shut your mouth! Do you wanta ruin the play?

Emma (also screaming): Do *I* wanta ruin the play? What do you think you're doing? You wanta boss everybody.

Sharon: Sure I wanta boss everybody. You keep your big mouth shut.

Emma: Didn't we decide *she* would bow *before* she sang the song because she always *forgot* to bow *after* she sang?

Sharon: Sure we did. But we *didn't* decide that you would shoot off your loud mouth all the time she was singing.

(Shirley-Ann finally finished the song. Edna then stepped out front and sang "Be Honest With Me." Sharon and Emma suddenly stopped arguing, but the minute that song was finished, they started again.)

Sharon: You better take your turn first, girl.

Emma: You just want me to be first.

Sharon: Yes, and you're goin' to be first, girl.

Emma: I could leave, you know.

Sharon: I'm going to tell on you.

Emma: You're going to tell on me. Five or six times a day you are going to tell on me. Well, go ahead and tell.

(There was a sudden silence, then Sharon stepped out in front.)

Sharon: All right, then, I'll be first.

(She began to sing "In the Navy." When she was halfway through the song, Emma began to sing, "I've Been Working on the Railroad." Edna and Shirley-Ann talked to one another all during the song, but the therapist could not hear them because the two singers were now trying to out-sing one another. The audience seemed positively entranced by the performance, the therapist included. Finally Sharon finished her song and took Edna into the lavatory with her. Sharon looked out at the audience and yelled, "Now don't anybody look in here." Emma immediately went over, opened the door, said "Phooey. It stinks!" but went in. Shirley-Ann also went in. The sounds of a violent argument could be heard by the audience.)

"I tell you I get to be the killer."

"You always want the best part."

"I don't want to be the grandmother."

"You gotta be the grandmother. How can we have our play if there ain't no grandmother?"

"All right. I'll be the grandmother." *(Emma's voice.)* "But this grandmother is a killer." By this time the audience was all keyed up for the drama. Suddenly the door was hurled open and out dashed the actresses.)

Sharon (on the way to the "stage"): Somebody gets killed in this play.

Edna: Oh, don't tell them.

Sharon: Well! *(Then she began to sing the "Air Corp Song" and the boys in the audience began to laugh.)*

Sharon (stopping the song and yelling at the boys): You boys laugh, huh? Well, you better not laugh when we get killed.

Edna: You tell again and we'll put you out of the play. It's almost beginning now.

(They fussed around the table on the stage and it looked as though the play was finally going to start, but Edna came around in front again and sang, "Children Would You Like to Go?")

Sharon: Let's tell who we are.

Edna: All right. I'm Betty. I'm one of the sisters.

Sharon: My name is Minnie. I'm one of the sisters.

Shirley-Ann: Who am I? What's my name? (*She whispered to the others, then, after a lengthy conference.*) I'm one of the sisters, too. I ain't got a name.

Emma: I'm the grandmother.

Shirley-Ann (picking up a short, blunt stick): Use this to stab us with.

Sharon (glaring at Shirley-Ann): Don't you dare tell again, or I really will stab you.

Edna: Go to sleep. (*She went around and slapped each one of them.*) Hear me? I said go to sleep. (*Emma began to crawl up toward them.*)

Sharon: What is that noise?

Emma (ghostly voice): Just your imagination.

Sharon: I smell grandmother's feets.

(Edna went over to Shirley-Ann and stabbed her. Emma came crawling up to the bed.)

Emma (uttering a blood-curdling scream): For God's sake! One of my children has been killed.

Sharon: And you ain't kiddin'. (*She jumped up.*) Now we're going to have a dance hall.

(All four of them began to jive around. Edna sneaked up in back of Shirley-Ann and stabbed her. Shirley-Ann fell to the floor.)

Edna: I'm on the sixth step. I'm on the seventh step. I'm at your door. Ha! I have *you!* (*She stabbed Sharon. Emma ran and hid behind a chair. Edna chased her and finally stabbed her. Then she started again after Sharon, who had made a rapid recovery.*)

Sharon: You're not supposed to kill me.

Edna: I don't care. I'm killin' you anyhow.

Sharon: Then I'm the killer in the next play.

(All the actresses were stabbed and were stretched out in dramatic poses. Edna sat down at the table and pretended to smoke a cigarette. Then she stood up, wiped her hands on her dress, and grinned.)

Emma: Blood. Some of it got on me.

Sharon: Show's over.

(The audience applauded enthusiastically. The girls went into a huddle to plan the second play. In a few seconds the other play started.)

Edna: Go to the store and get me some liver. *(Sharon left the stage and returned with a package.)* Where did you get this liver?

Sharon: At the store.

(This question-and-answer pattern was repeated again and again with increasing insistence. At last the climax was reached.)

Edna: Where did you get this liver?

Sharon: Well, if you must know, I got it out of grandfather's grave.

(Then pandemonium reigned. Edna screamed, clutched her heart, tore her hair. At that moment Emma came in, bent over, shaking, and trembling.)

Emma (in a quavering voice): Give me back my liver. Give me back my liver. I'm coming after you.

Sharon (picking up a chair): One more step, grandfather, and I'll brain you.

Emma: I can't live without my liver. Oh! *(She sank down on the floor and expired dramatically.)*

(That was the end of the girls' previously censored dramatic offerings.)

COMMENTS

This report seems to illustrate the dynamics of conflict and struggle which eventually changes into something resembling a state of equilibrium. The personalities of the children were pitted against one another. The type of play that grew out of their imaginations is indeed startling. The aggressive nature of their dramatics is quite evident. The co-operation among the girls during the cleaning of the playroom and the setting of the stage was remarkable. The rivalry for the "best" parts seems to be an outgrowth of the deprived living conditions of the girls. The fact that they eventually were able to get together with sufficient give-and-take to put on the plays seems to be indicative of a certain amount of progress.

Twelfth Contact—Eighth Group Contact

(The girls came in and began to paint. Before they started, however, they spread old newspapers over the floor in order to keep it clean. Then they all got down on the floor together. They seemed very relaxed and quiet. They talked very quietly among themselves about the colors and commonplace things. They frequently called to the therapist. "Look, Mommy. See this pretty color, Mommy?" After about fifteen minutes of this group activity, Shirley-Ann left the group and got out the paper dolls. She played with them at the table. There was one violent clash between Edna and Sharon about who had dirtied the paint water.)

Emma: Let me show you some magic. Emma, the magician, will fix things for you.

(Emma then picked up the dirty paint water, went into the lavatory and emptied it, got clean water and brought it back to the girls. The other two girls laughed sheepishly at Emma.)

Edna: I don't want you to leave, Mommy.

Therapist: You would like to have this go on and on.

Edna: Yes. Soon the stinky old school will start again.

Emma: I hate school.

Sharon: I hate the mean old teacher. She's cross-eyed.

Emma: A cross-eyed monkey.

Edna: It's don't do this and don't do that and shut up your talking.

Sharon: Oh, look at Emma's picture. Isn't that good?

Edna: Boy! Emma can really paint. She's a real artist.

Emma (smiling broadly): You really like it?

Sharon: I wish I could paint like that.

Emma: Do you want this one, Sharon?

Sharon: Yeah. Oh, gee! Thanks. *(She accepted the picture happily.)*

Edna: Will you paint me one, Emma?

Emma: Oh, I suppose so. What do you want me to paint?

Edna: I don't care. Paint anything.

(Emma painted her a picture of a house. The picture she painted for Sharon was a vase of flowers. The girls were very pleased with the pictures.)

Edna: I'll give you some of my paper dolls, Emma, if you want them. I've got a lot of them. Do you, huh?

Emma: If you want to give them to me.

Shirley-Ann: I'll give you my orange if you'll paint me a picture of something.

Emma: What do you want?

Shirley-Ann: I don't care.

(Emma painted her a picture of an airplane. She smiled all the time she painted. She used only bright colors for these pictures—blue, yellow, red, green, and orange.)

Edna: What are you going to bring us, Mommy?

Therapist: What do you want me to bring you?

Shirley-Ann: Nipple bottle.

Edna: Yeah. Or a hair ribbon. I'd like a pink hair ribbon.

Sharon: I want a bluebird barrette—like Jennie's got. It's two little bluebirds.

Emma: When is your last time?

Therapist: We have two more meetings.

Edna: I'll cry when you go.

Therapist: You won't like it.

Sharon: I'll cry, too. I love you, Mommy.

Edna: Emma, what you want her to get you?

Emma: I don't care.

Edna: Oh, tell her something.

Emma (blushing): Oh, I'd like a bottle of perfume and a little comb. My comb doesn't have any teeth left in it.

Therapist: Edna wants a pink hair ribbon, Sharon wants a bluebird barrette, Emma wants perfume and a comb, and Shirley-Ann wants a nursing bottle.

Shirley-Ann: Or maybe I would rather have a package of drawing paper.

Therapist: You think you might like drawing paper better than the nursing bottle?

Shirley-Ann: I'll tell you for sure next week.

Emma: Here is your picture, Shirley-Ann.

Shirley-Ann: Thanks, Emma. It's pretty.

Emma: I like that picture you drew, Edna.

Edna: You did? But look how I smeared it.

Emma: Yes, but this little part up here isn't smeared.

Therapist: Emma has seen something nice in your picture, too.

Emma: We'll clean out these paints for you.

Edna: Let's do.

Sharon: I'll get some clean water for you.

(The girls cleaned out the paint boxes.)

Emma: My mother is coming today to take me away from here.

Therapist: She is?

Emma: She's coming today. I have all my things packed.

Edna: Oh, Emma! We'll miss you so.

Emma: Oh, I'm coming back. I'll only be gone over the week-end.

Therapist: That makes you very happy, doesn't it?

Emma: Yes. My sister and me. She's taking us both.

(The girls continued to clean out the paints and straighten up the toys in the box and suitcase. When the time was up, they left together, Emma in exceedingly high spirits.)

COMMENTS

In this interview the girls have achieved almost unbelievable social adjustment. Emma acts as peacemaker. The girls for the first time admire something that one of them has made. Emma is praised by the girls, and when they ask her to paint them a picture she does so very graciously. Emma even finds something to admire in Edna's picture. She was visibly touched by the girls' praise and by their offerings of gifts to her. They still have their negative feelings toward school, but they do not seem to be very disturbed about them. They have come to accept school as a very disagreeable place, but they have *accepted* it.

The change in their requests is interesting. It certainly seems to indicate growth on the part of the girls. They no longer need or desire the infantile symbols. They request more mature gifts. Shirley-Ann is not quite ready to make up her mind.

Emma once again prepared for her mother's visit, and, as it developed, the mother once again did not make an appearance. Emma was so disappointed that she flung herself down under a tree on the corner of the grounds and cried until she was really ill. She ran a temperature, became nauseated, and was sent to the hospital room for two days. The matron reported that the doctor had said that it was because the child was so disappointed over her mother's failure to keep her promise that she had become ill.

THIRTEENTH CONTACT—NINTH GROUP INTERVIEW

(The girls came hurrying into the room. They immediately unpacked the suitcase of toys and sat down on the floor together drawing, painting, cutting out pictures, and pasting. They talked about school's starting in a few days. After fifteen minutes of this type of activity, Edna and Emma went after the clothesline and clothespins. A very short argument over priority rights followed.)

Edna: I'm going to tell Miss N.

Emma: Tee-hee. She isn't here.

Edna: Well, when she comes back.

Emma: You like to tattle.

Edna: Well—— (*Emma backed away, giving the clothesline to Edna.*)

Emma: Take it. I'll find something else to do.

Therapist: Emma thinks she can find something else to do and is willing to let you have that.

Edna: I really wouldn't have told. You can play with me.

Therapist: Edna doesn't really mean it when she says that she will tell.

Emma: Did you know that my mother didn't come after me last week?

Therapist: She disappointed you again.

Emma: I hate my mother.

Therapist: You hate your mother for that.

Shirley-Ann: That's bad to say. It's a sin to hate people.

Emma (more determined than ever): I *hate, hate, hate* my mother!

Therapist: Emma still feels like hating her mother because she was so disappointed.

Emma: I got sick when they told me she wasn't really coming. I threw up. I couldn't eat anything. They put in the hospital for two days.

Therapist: You felt so badly about your mother not cmming that it made you sick.

Edna: She wouldn't even talk to anybody all that time.

Therapist: She felt very badly about it.

Shirely-Ann: My mother wouldn't do that to me.

Emma: I wished I would die. I *tried* to die.

Therapist: You didn't even want to live, you felt so badly about the whole thing.

Sharon: I'm going to paint a very pretty picture and paste this here and this here. Oh, stop talking about that mother of yours, Emma.

Therapist: You don't like to hear it.

Edna: I'm going to play with the doll family.

(Emma sat down at the table and took out a funny book that she had brought with her. She withdrew from the group and looked at the book. Edna settled down on the floor and took the clothes off the doll family. She hung the clothes on the line.)

Edna: Look. Her pants! *(The other girls laughed. Emma apparently did not notice.)* Oh, she's just a little girl. But she wets her pants. You girls come and visit my little home.

Sharon: We've got to finish our pictures. Our lady isn't going to come very many more times and we've got to finish up now.

Edna: Then come when you can.

Sharon (to therapist): You tell who you work for that you oughta come back more.

Therapist: You would like to have me come back.

Sharon: Yes, you tell him.

Emma: Oh, we'll be in school. Dumb, stinkin' old school.

Edna (to dolls): You go to bed. Drink from the nipple bottle, baby dear. *(She held the bottle up to the doll's face.)* Oh, you wet the bed. You're going away today. Today is Sunday. Lots of kids go home on Sunday. I'm going to wash your hair. See! Hold still. Put your head down in the bowl. Say, confound you! Hold your head still! Do you know what? The other kids are all going down to the river, but you're going home. You stop that crying. *(Yells.)* Oh, I forgot the baby. Your hair needs washing. *(She poured water on the dolls' heads.)* Stop laughing. Stop that silly giggling. *(She beat the doll.)* You hear me? You hateful baby. Stop that grinning. You hold this doll. *(She handed the doll to the therapist and asked if she could really wash the clothes or would it have to be made-believe washing. Therapist suggested that she just pretend to wash them because they wouldn't dry very soon. Edna turned back to the dolls.)* Won't you be good? Don't cry like that. Why do you cry?

Emma: She cries because she likes to cry.

Edna: You're not going home. The great big daddy. You need a whippin'. Look at his britches. *(She took them off and laughed.)* You're going to get in trouble. I'll beat you up. You are a mean old thing. Remember what I told you. *(She picked up the baby.)* Poor baby. I haven't seen you for a long, long time. *(She gives the baby to Sharon.)* Here! You take care of baby Edna. This is mamma. Where did I put those clothes? Oh, you mean hateful woman! *(She beat the mother doll.)* Look at this boy. All of his clothes come off. Everyone of you have been so naughty you can just stay in bed. *(She hung the clothes up on the line.)* I never saw such people.

Emma: I hope my mother doesn't lie to me again.

Therapist: You hope she doesn't disappoint you again.

Emma: Yes. She did. She said this Friday for sure. This Friday she is coming and I am going home.

Sharon: My mother disappoints me all the time. I want to go home and stay home.

Emma: I want to go home, too.

Edna: I'm going to get to go home in December.

Emma: Nobody likes us.

Therapist: You would all like to go home.

(Edna went into the lavatory.)

Shirley-Ann (to therapist): Did you send anything over to China?

Emma (violently): Who cares about China? Let 'em starve to pieces.

Edna (returning with spoonful of water): Castor oil for them. A spoonful a day because they ate green apples.

Sharon (to therapist): I'll bet you say no, to play with here but not to keep, but just the same I want to keep these paints and scissors.

Emma: Just because we can't have it, doesn't mean we don't want it.

(Edna started to paint—smears of red and black with no definite form to the picture.)

Therapist: Even if you can't have certain things, you still want them sometimes.

(Emma started to paint a picture.)

Therapist: There are only five minutes left.

Emma: I'll hurry. I want to take this over to the cottage with me.

Sharon: Why?

Emma: Because I want to give it to my mommy when she comes Friday.

Sharon: Next week is your last time here, isn't it?

Therapist: Yes.

Sharon: Then is when you are going to bring me something.

Therapist: Yes.

Edna: I want a pink hair ribbon.

Sharon: I want a bracelet.

Shirley-Ann: I want a box of crayons—a big box of all different colors.

Emma: I want perfume and a comb.

(Sharon walked over in the corner and looked back at the therapist with a pout on her lips.)

Sharon: I don't want to not have you come back.

Shirley-Ann: Neither do I.

Edna: It makes me mad.

(Sharon went over to the dolls and kicked the mother doll all around the play area. Edna went over and stood on the baby doll. Suddenly Emma jumped up and collected the doll family. She sat down on the floor and began to play with them. She began to talk and the words came out in a rush. She talked in a colored dialect.)

Emma: Heah me, ma. Take off your clothes. You can be just bare naked. You're not the boss around here. I'll put you in a mud pie. Your hair is lousy. One time you'll get your dress off. I'll pound your head some day. I'm made out of chewing gum. Get your britches off now. *(She held the doll up.)* See. Bare naked. *(The other girls laughed as they stood around and watched Emma's play.)* I'm runnin' out of clothespins. Oh, gee! That ole ma she sure is funny. Here, Puddentain, off come your clothes. *(She took off the girl's clothes.)* Oh, you bad girl! I declare, you is bare naked, too. Father, you oughta be naked, too.

Edna: Oh! The father is going to be naked, too.

Sharon: She tells everybody in her family to take off their clothes. There's a funny family.

Emma: Pappy, take off your pants. What a stinker you are. *(She twisted the father's head around and around.)* Oh, father, your body is coming apart. Father, stand on your head.

Edna: Keep your big mouth shut!

Emma: I can't get the damn fool's shirt off. *(Emma handed it up to the therapist.)* Take it off—or show me how. *(Therapist did.)* Now father is naked. He is a son-of-a-bitch.

Sharon: Oh, Emma! I hate to hear that. *(Emma smirked at her. She took off the little girl's clothes.)*

Emma: Another one plum naked.

(Suddenly the room became very quiet.)

Sharon: Gosh! How quiet it is.

(Emma started to sing.)

Emma (to therapist): I want a comb. My comb has one hundred teeth out. My mother has to buy me a new one, but she won't. She is old and gray and too ugly. And as lazy. *(She picked up the big boy doll.)* Take your pants off, boy.

Therapist: Now they all have their clothes off.

Emma: Naked. Bad naked people.

Therapist: You think they are bad people.

Emma (jumping up from the dolls): Let's have an argument.

Edna: No. Draw your mother a picture.

Emma: No. I don't want to give her anything. *(She tried to snatch the paste away from Edna and Edna howled. Emma drew back and waited her turn.)* Where are the scissors?

Edna: You can't have them. *(She tosses the scissors at Emma.)*

Emma: Nice girl, you ain't. *(She splashes some red paint on her paper. She reaches over and snatches the pencil out of Edna's hand. Edna flew at her in a rage. Emma handed the pencil back to Edna.)* Sorry, Edna. Please forgive me. *(She grinned at Edna.)*

Edna: Ask me for it and I'll give it to you.

Emma: I don't really want it. I just want you to play with me.

Edna: What?

Emma: Next time let's all go on a hike. We'll show you the farm.

Sharon: Oh, yes. Will you, Miss———?

Emma: We'll take you over the stile.

Edna: And show you the corn field.

Sharon: And the cow barns.

Shirley-Ann: We'll show you the haunted house back of the corn field.

Emma: Yes. The devil lives there.

All: Will you? Can we? Let's do!

Therapist: If you want to.

Emma: Let's ask the boys, too.

Edna: All right.

Therapist: Then we'll plan to go on a hike the next time, if it doesn't rain.

Emma: It won't rain. I won't let it.

Therapist: You think you can keep it from raining.

Emma: I'll keep it from raining.

Therapist: Well, our time is up now.

Girls: Good-bye, Miss—— We'll take you for a hike. We'll show you the place.

(They hurried away, and as they passed the boys' group waiting to come in, they told them about the plan.)

COMMENTS

In this interview the girls play together, with a semblance of harmony. The flare-up of conflict is quickly smoothed out.

Emma releases some bitter feelings against her mother and even connected her illness with her disappointment, which indicates some insight. The play with the dolls by both Edna and Emma dramatizes the feelings that were close to both girls. Emma's ability to forgive her mother and even consider giving her a gift is evidence that the child needs only a chance and she would be able to make an adjustment that would be satisfactory to all concerned. Edna is more vindictive. She gives the adults castor oil and punishes them for the slights she feels they have given her.

In this session, as in the last, the girls did not use the nursing bottles for baby-play. Their repeated requests for gifts were on more mature levels. It is interesting to note that the therapist had again become "Miss——" to the girls.

The manner in which they accepted the responsibility for the last session seems to indicate that the girls have grown very much in social adaptation and adjustment. There was a note of pride in their voices as they spoke of the things they would show the therapist when they went on the hike. They were considering the positive elements in this place that was their home. The inclusion of the boys also seems to indicate progress. This was an experience that they wanted to share.

FOURTEENTH CONTACT—TENTH GROUP CONTACT

The girls met the car. They had a little box wrapped

in scraps of wrinkled white tissue paper. They all exclaimed at once that it was for the therapist. They insisted that she open it immediately. Inside the box was a scrap of red velvet, a "lucky stone," a bit of blue chalk, a tiny empty bottle, and a scrap of white lace. They were obviously the girls' treasures which they had decided among themselves to give to the therapist. They accepted their gifts very quietly. They thanked the therapist and then asked if they could leave them in the car while they went on their hike. It seemed probable that this was out of consideration for the boys, who had agreed to join the group on the hike. The boys had not asked for any gifts. However, the therapist had brought along gifts for the four boys to offset any possible feelings of slights on the part of the boys when they found out that the girls had received gifts, for she had discovered earlier in the summer that the children flaunted their gifts in front of the others whenever the opportunity presented itself.

The girls led the way. They met the boys under a big walnut tree down by the creek. The children had organized their hike with amazing thoroughness. The therapist was "Miss——" to all the children on the hike. They pointed out the wild flowers, the haunted house where the devil lived, the large corn field, the cow pasture, the pigpens, the shed where the school bus was stored, the oriole nest in the big elm tree, the nest of the red squirrel, the hiding place for the little brown rabbit with the lame foot. The rabbit was there, and the children very quietly tiptoed around so that he wouldn't be frightened. They picked some of the wild flowers that grew along the path and gave them to the therapist. Then they came to the stile. The boys helped the girls over the stile. They were all very considerate of one another.

Finally the tour of inspection was completed. The boys said good-bye at the stile and the girls went back to the car with the therapist to pick up their gifts. The therapist gave each of the girls one of the boys' gifts and asked them to deliver them for her. The girls promised to do so. They stood in the driveway and watched the therapist drive away, calling good-bye to her, as she left.

COMMENTS—IMMEDIATE EVALUATION OF THE
THERAPY EXPERIENCE

The following week the therapist contacted the head matron and asked for a report on the children's behavior. The matron reported a decided improvement, especially in the behavior of Emma. She had become more agreeable and more co-operative. She now played with the other children "without constant friction and teasing," and had offered to help the matron with some of the work in the cottage, an offer which was considered phenomenal by the matron. The matron also reported that Emma had gotten ready to go with her mother the Friday following the last meeting and the mother had again failed to come after the girl. Emma's reaction to the disappointment this time was quite different from her former reactions. She did not cry or "get sick." She very quietly and grimly took her bag back to her room and said to the matron, "To *hell* with my mother. She's a bitch." The matron said to the therapist, "It took all my will power to keep from saying '*That* she is!'" When the mother called the Home and asked to talk to Emma after that, the matron had refused to put through the call and had explained to the mother that the officials at the Home had decided that they would not subject the child to a routine of disappointments again. They informed the mother that if she wanted to talk to Emma, she would have to come to the Home and that she was not to ask them to get the children ready to leave again until she appeared on the grounds ready to take the children with her.

Shirley-Ann's mother was planning on taking Shirley-Ann with her the following month. Edna was up for adoption. An elderly minister and his wife were very much interested in the child and the matron thought that Edna would be placed in their home for a trial period. Sharon's status remained unchanged.

As a final bit of information, the matron added, "And thanks a lot for stopping those girls' constant tattling on one another. They haven't bothered us with that for weeks now."

23.

A Teacher-Therapist Deals with a Handicapped Child[1]

THE FOLLOWING CASE is presented to show what a teacher-therapist actually did to help a handicapped child who was a pupil in her classroom. It is presented in the hope that it might encourage other teachers to think through the possibilities of a therapeutic approach to the problems in their own classrooms, and perhaps inspire some of them to try some of the techniques discussed in this book. Every class is found to have at least one problem case. Although the case of Ernest is a complicated one, it demonstrates the great value of the therapeutic procedure in the classroom—or at least available for referrals of special cases by the teacher who feels that she must teach the child how to live with himself as well as to read, to write, and to figure.

Since the material is detailed and complex, it seems wise to give at the outset a simple summary of the whole process through which Ernest lived during the seven months covered in the case account. This is not to prejudge the process, but to provide a pattern of thinking from which the reader is free to depart as he studies the detailed material. This summary is given in the following two paragraphs.

[1] This case was reported in the *Journal of Abnormal and Social Psychology*, April, 1945, under the joint authorship of Carl R. Rogers and the writer.

Ernest, a six-year-old rejected child with a constricted throat, was fearful, infantile, and unsocial. In therapeutic contacts with an understanding teacher he expressed a need for affection from his mother, and took the initiative in exploring the possibilities of living with her. He received rejecting treatment from his mother, and became violently aggressive, turning, however, to his teacher-therapist for emotional support. Gradually he assimilated his disappointment, adopted his foster family as his own, and even accepted the fact that his teacher would not substitute as his mother.

Parallel with this development, he gained courage to attempt the grown-up behavior of eating, and with many swings between infantile and mature reactions, he gradually pursued the more adult rôle, leaving behind nursing bottles, rubber tubes, and the neurotic use of his handicap. His new adjustment was severely tested by upsetting periods of illness and hospitalization, but he maintained the more mature way of meeting life which he had achieved.

Detailed comments on the therapeutic process, the technique used, and the stages of insight and growth are contained in parenthetical remarks throughout the report.

With this introduction, the case record, as it was kept by the teacher who acted as therapist, is presented. It has been edited only in the interests of brevity and of disguising identities.

Ernest started to school in September. He was six years, three months of age. He was short for his age, but he had a personal history that was long indeed. When Ernest was three years old, he drank lye and as a result was hospitalized. His father deserted his mother. The mother brought Ernest to D——, placed him in a hospital, and left town. Ernest became a state ward. The mother went back to her home in a small town about sixty miles away from D——. Ernest remained in the hospital for three years. During that time his mother came to see him only twice. Seeing her only once a year, Ernest forgot his mother, and when she paid her last annual visit he did not recognize her. Ernest underwent a series of operations and throat dilatations. This

September he was pronounced "surgically cured." However, he still refused to eat, and it was necessary to continue to feed him through a tube inserted directly into his stomach.

When Ernest entered school, he had been out of the hospital for only four weeks. He did not know how to dress himself. He was enuretic. He had had no association with other children. He had been placed in a boarding home with a very dominating middle-aged woman. The child and the foster mother did not get along. He refused to eat anything. He even refused to drink water. The foster mother felt that it was an attempt to "get back" at her. The doctors also thought that the problem was entirely psychological.

The first day of school Ernest was rather awed by the other children, by the size of the building, by the school activities. There were thirty-six other first-graders in the class. On this first day he watched the other children drinking from the "bubblers." These fountains fascinated all the children and they went through the motions of drinking gallons of water those first few days. Ernest, standing beside his teacher watching the other children, said, "It looks like fun." The teacher responded to the obvious desire on his part to join the others in drinking from the "bubbler." This brief contact went something like this:[1]

E. It looks like fun.

T. You think it would be fun to drink from it, too.

E. (nodding agreement): But *I* can't.

T. You don't think you could drink it.

E. No. It looks like fun.

T. You don't think you could drink it, but still you would like to.

E. I'd like to try.

T. You want to try it.

E. I used to drink from one of those things when I was in the hospital. I don't drink now.

T. You remember what fun it was. *(Ernest grins and goes over to the drinking fountain.)*

E. It might not stay down.

---

[1] Throughout this chapter *E.* will identify the speaker as Ernest; *T.*, as the teacher-therapist.

T. You think it might not stay down, but you still want to try. (*Ernest nods his head. He takes the handle and turns it up too high and jumps back.*)

E. It's a lot of water.

T. It looks like a lot of water to you.

E. I'll drown myself. (*He takes a drink, glances at the teacher, grins broadly.*) It stayed down!

T. Yes. It stayed down. (*He drinks again.*)

E. It stays down. (*He seemed quite delighted.*)

(Even in this first incident, both Ernest and the teacher exhibit significant attitudes. The teacher shows an accepting, non-argumentative, non-coercive attitude, being just as ready to accept his discouraged and fearful attitudes as his courageous ones. Untrained workers are prone to persuade—"I'm sure you can take a drink"—or to be supportive—"I'll help you and then it won't be so hard"—or to bring pressure to bear—"You want to be a big boy like the others, don't you?" It takes restraint and a therapeutic point of view to let the child know that he is accepted for what he is, not for what he is not.

Ernest, on his side, shows a willingness to be courageous in spite of fear, which is characteristic of the growth impulse. It is as he is sure that the teacher accepts both of his contradictory attitudes that he can venture to attempt a drink.)

He came back into the room and told all the other children that he "drank a drink." They accepted the fact with all the appreciation of the five-year-old. They did not know that Ernest was "different." They only knew that he was very proud of the fact that he had had a drink from the bubbler and they boasted about their drinks, too. Ernest had about five hundred drinks that day—or so it seemed. From then on, he had no trouble drinking water at school and retaining it. However, he still refused to drink at home.

Two days later, Ernest noticed a big red apple on the teacher's desk. It looked very good to him. The exercise of walking to and from school and all the school activities were increasing his appetite. The other children were eating apples and pears and oranges on the school ground at recess time, and Ernest began to entertain the idea of eating like the other children. Late in the afternoon of this second day, he sidled up to the teacher and said, "If you shared your apple with me after school, I would help you eat it." The teacher immediately recognized his desire to eat the apple and accepted his invitation to share the apple with him. After school that day, the teacher cut the apple in half and gave part to him. He ate the apple. Part of it he did spit up, but enough of it stayed down to give him the satisfaction of eating it.

The apple eating session went something like this:

E. It is a pretty apple.

T. It is a very pretty apple.

E. It is a beautiful apple.

T. It is a beautiful, red apple.

E. You will share your apple with me. You said you would.

T. You want to share the apple with me.

E. We'll share it together. *(The teacher cut the apple in half. Ernest picked it up almost with a feeling of reverence.)* It may not stay down.

T. You think it might not stay down, but you want to try.

E. I want to try. *(He bit into the apple.)* You eat that part.

(This desire to solve his problem is a good prognostic sign. In many instances a client will clearly show, in a first or second contact, whether or not he has sufficient motivation to overcome his difficulties.)

T. You want me to eat this part while you eat that part.

(Ernest nodded his head, so the teacher ate her half. Ernest smiled at the teacher, his eyes shining.)

E. This is a very, very delicious apple.

T. You think the apple is very, very good.

(Ernest nodded sincerely. As a matter of fact, the apple, like most beautiful apples, was as dry as sawdust and as tasteless. Occasionally he spat out part of it, but some he really swallowed. He talked about the games they had played that day, about a picture he had drawn. Then came this thunderbolt out of the blue.)

E. Say, what is your I.Q.?

T. My I.Q.? You want to know what my I.Q. is?

E. Yes, I would like to know.

T. How can I find out for you?

E. Get someone to give you a test.

T. Do you know what yours is?

E. Oh yes. It's 119. Some man came over to the hospital and measured it. The nurses told me it was 119. That's good too. The nurses said I ought to be proud of it.

T. Did they have one?

E. I guess not. They didn't know what theirs was, either. And Mrs. S. [the foster mother], hers is terrible.

T. You think hers is terrible. Why?

E. Well, I asked her what hers was when I first went there. She didn't know. I said, "Guess!" She guessed hers was 100. I told her mine was 119, and since it was bigger than hers, I didn't have to pay any attention to her. I was smarter than she.

T. You think you are smarter than she is.

E. (*generously*): I expect yours is about 119.

(Here is the first clear evidence of the positive affectional attitude which he is forming toward the teacher. The handling of this relationship as it deepens constitutes one of the most interesting issues of the therapeutic contacts.)

T. You think I am about as smart as you are?

E. I really do.

(By this time the apple was consumed in spite of the I.Q.—or because of it. Then the teacher took him home.)

The next week there was a popcorn-fritter sale at school. Everybody was eating popcorn. Ernest eyed the popcorn with interest. Then after school he asked the teacher for a piece of popcorn. She gave him one of the fritters and he ate it all and retained every bit of it. At this session he talked all the time about the popcorn and how very good it was. This brief session was fifteen minutes in length. At the conclusion the teacher took him home in her car and stopped in to see the foster mother. When the teacher related how he was becoming interested in eating in school, the foster mother expressed quite evident antagonism toward the boy and said that he refused to eat for her. She said, "I just told him the other day, 'I know you think it hurts me when you don't eat. But I don't care. You can always run around with a silly rubber tube in your stomach, if you want to. It doesn't hurt me at all.' Then he looked at me curiously and said, 'Is that the way you really feel about it?' And I said, 'I don't care what you do.' That seemed to get him. It's the same way with his bed-wetting. I am convinced that he just does it to get back at me.[1] I tell him so, too. He is a mean one, though. He lies and steals. And he is so stubborn. I stopped the feedings for a while, when the doctor told me there was no real reason why he couldn't eat. And he refused food until he actually fainted. Then I just started the supplemental feedings again. I don't know what to do with him. But if he can eat for you, why can't he eat for me?"

Then Mrs. S. related the I.Q. episode exactly as Ernest had related it to the teacher in regard to Mrs. S.'s I.Q. of 100. She was quite obviously "burned up" about his remarks.

When the teacher told her that he had eaten some popcorn and had retained all of it, Mrs. S. said, "Well, that is the limit! Popcorn, of all things! Why, I wouldn't even let him have that. Suppose he choked? Suppose he choked on any of the things given him? My God! what would you have done?" The teacher said that the boy's nurse had said that they were interested in getting him to eat, that there was no risk of choking—no more risk than with any other child; and that the more he ate or even tried to eat, whether it stayed down or not, the better off the child would be. Mrs. S. didn't like that very well. However she accepted the teacher's foolhardiness by commenting acidly, "Well, it's your funeral!" A few other minor points were discussed to clear the air. When the teacher left, Ernest came out on the porch and called after here, "I wish you would take me with you. I don't like it here." All of which did not help his situation in the foster home.

The following week the boy's state guardian came over to the school and asked the teacher for a conference. The teacher made an appointment for the following day and went down to his office to discuss the case with him. Her opinion more or less confirmed the guardian's suspicion that Ernest was poorly placed and consequently it was

---

[1] It is interesting to note that the foster mother, too, has some understanding of the attitudes which underlie Ernest's behavior. She cannot accept them, however, and hence the situation goes from bad to worse. For the teacher's handling of a situation identical in its dynamics, see comment on page 356.

decided that he would be placed in another foster home—in one closer to the school if possible. The following week he was placed in another home. The guardian came out to the school and told Ernest about it the afternoon before he was moved. And so there was another adjustment to be made by this youngster. Individual therapy contacts after school were started. So far as possible, feelings and attitudes expressed in school were recognized and accepted.

September 29

On September 28, Ernest was moved to Mrs. R.'s—his new foster home. The contact on the next day was after school and at Ernest's request. He was very much disturbed by the sudden move to the new home.

In this home the foster mother was in her sixties. Her husband was in his seventies. She had another foster son aged fifteen. Mrs. R was an excellent cook, and had specialized in boarding feeding problems. She was soft-spoken, had a very bad heart condition, and was extremely religious. She seemed to be very sympathetic in regard to Ernest and said, "If I can't help him, then I won't keep him. I'll ask to have him placed in another home. I'm more concerned about his welfare than the boarding money. And I will not stand in his way. But I am confident that Ernest can be cured. I don't know how you feel about this, but I believe God will help this child if we pray to Him faithfully."

In the after-school contact, the day after the move to the new home, Ernest stood at the "paint table" and idly stirred the paints for a few minutes. The teacher was sitting at a near-by table. These contacts were all held in the classroom and all materials used were always available during school time to Ernest and the other children. There was no marked-off area of limitation. He could use anything in the room. The only requirement was that he stay in the room. Materials in the room included clay, paints, all kinds and sizes of paper, a workbench, hammer, nails, saws, crayons, cowboy suit, gun, soldiers, airplanes, tanks, building blocks, set of dolls and furniture, and many other games and toys.

(Ernest looked at the teacher and then came over and leaned against her.)

E. I want to write a letter to my mother. You know she lives away from here, in ——. That's far away. You write what I say.

T. You want to write a letter to your real mother.

E. Yes. Say "Dear Mother."

(The teacher writes it on a piece of Ernest's writing paper which he handed to her. Remember that Ernest has not seen his mother for almost a year. He has seen her only four times during the past three years and the last time he saw her he did not recognize her.)

E. Now say, "I am getting along all right." I really am, aren't I?

T. You want your mother to know you are getting along all right.

E. Yes. When I get better, then I can go home to *my real* mother.

T. You want to get better so you can go home.

E. Yes. Tell her—*(pause)* Write, "I ate some lima beans last night. I ate some pork chops last night and mashed potatoes and gravy on them. And a glass of milk. This morning I had some cereal. And some orange juice. And *two* pieces of toast." Are you writing *all* this down?

(This is the first meal he ate. Very little, if any, stayed down, according to the foster mother.)

T. I'm writing *all* of it down.

E. "This noon I had some soup with carrots and onions in it. I had a piece of toast and a graham cracker." *(To Teacher.)* And it stayed down, purt near—for a while, that is. Some of it.

T. Part of it stayed down and you were glad it did. You *wanted* it to stay down.

E. *(nodding):* Yes. And some day it will.

T. Some day it will.

E. I want to write some more letter. Write, "I moved last night to Mrs. R.'s house." I really did. And Mrs. R. is a nice lady. She isn't like Mrs. S. I *like* this Mrs. R. At least, I *think* I do.

T. You moved last night and you really want to like this new mother.

E. Yes. Only she isn't a mother. I call her Grandma R. And I have a *grandpa* and a brother now. A big brother called—I can't remember his name, but he is *nice*.

T. You have a whole new family and they are nice people.

E. Write, "How are my sisters?" I have two sisters at home.

T. You have two sisters at home.

E. Write, "How is my puppy? I hope he is getting along all right. I hope I get to go home to your house some time." *(To teacher):* I wish I could go home.

T. You want to go home. Moving to a new home yesterday made you think about your own home. You don't know how things will be in this new home and so you wish you were home.

E. .(nodding): Of course I do. My pigs are down there and my puppy. I want to see my pigs.

T. You would like to see your puppy and your pigs.

E. Yes. Write, "Dr. B. is on a vacation now. Love for grandma and mother, Ernest." *(Ernest draws the teacher's arm around him and snuggles up.)*

T. You feel uneasy about your new home. You don't know any of those people yet.

(This is an excellent clarification of the attitude which Ernest has been expressing by his actions, and by such statements as "I like Mrs. R. At least, I *think* I do." It brings him to a clear recognition of the attitude in himself, in the next response.

It should be remarked that at the outset of the contacts, the therapist's recognition of attitudes is at a relatively superficial level, such as the recognition of his desire to drink, along with his fear of it. This is almost invariably true at the beginning of therapy, but as these superficial attitudes are accepted and recognized, the child becomes more free to bring out deeper and more dynamic attitudes. The therapist must be alert to understand and follow and clarify these deeper attitudes as they are expressed.)

E. I only saw them yesterday. Never not once before.

T. Of course, I can understand how you feel. Everything is strange.

E. Will you come home with me tonight and meet Mrs. R.?

T. You want *me* to know Mrs. R., too.

E. Will you? *(Teacher agrees to go home with him.)*

(In this interview the teacher-therapist begins to adopt a supportive mother rôle rather than maintaining the strictly non-directive rôle which she has played thus far. By befriending him as he goes home, by giving him gifts of food, by reassuring him the next morning about the foster mother, the therapist is definitely saying, "I will help you," rather than continuing to say, "I will help you to help yourself." There is room for difference of opinion as to the best technique. Ernest, as we shall see, has been accustomed to a very demonstrative affection on the part of the hospital personnel, and hence would regard this behavior on the part of the teacher as similar to the adult behavior with which he was familiar. It is also true that a first-grade teacher is necessarily considered a substitute mother by the children, who continually turn to her for approval and support. Consequently, it may be thought that the teacher's supportive rôle is only natural and sound. Yet the dependence which is created will need to be handled, as we shall see. Perhaps therapy would have proceeded just as satisfactorily if here, too, the child had been helped to face his own attitudes, rather than placing responsibility on another. The therapist might have recognized the boy's need by some such statement as "You would like it if I would stand by you when you go home to these strange people." And if he insisted on the teacher's accompanying him, to respond in an understanding way, "I'm not going home with you tonight, but I will be here tomorrow, and you can tell me all about it.")

On the way home the teacher and Ernest stopped in a drugstore and bought him an ice-cream cone. This was according to a pre-arranged plan with doctors, nurses, guardian and others involved in this case and according to the theory that every *attempt* he makes to eat will help his case whether it stays down or not. Very little, if any, stayed down, although he kept right at it and talked about how good it was. The teacher echoed his comments about how nice it was to eat things. She met Mrs. R. and talked to her for about an hour after Mrs. R. sent Ernest out to play. His nurse called for him and took him to the clinic to weigh and examine him.

The first thing he said to the teacher the following morning was, "Did you like Mrs. R.? Is she a nice woman?" The teacher responded, "You want to know what *I* think of Mrs. R. Well, I think she is a very nice woman." Ernest smiled. Then he became quite serious, and said, "Why, last night, you know what?—she *prayed* for me.

She asked God to get me better. Now I *will* get better."
The teacher's response was, "You are sure you'll get better
now."

Nothing he ate the following day stayed down. He
seemed quite bewildered by everything and did not have
anything to do with the other children.

The state guardian had told the teacher that they were
trying to establish a better relationship between mother
and child so that eventually he could go back home. To
date they had not been successful. The mother claimed
that she was financially unable to come up and see the
child. She lived with her parents about sixty miles away,
and the state guardian seemed to believe that her long
absence was due to low finances. He had said they would
continue to try to get her to come to see Ernest. Consequently, when Ernest asked to write her a letter, the
teacher thought this might be used as a device to better
the mother-child relationship. This was the first letter
Ernest had ever written to her. He got the idea of the
letter from the school experience of having the group
dictate a letter to absent schoolmates. When the teacher
mailed Ernest's letter, she included one of her own to the
mother.

Dear Mrs. F.——:
Ernest started to school this fall and is in my first grade.
He wanted to write a letter. I wrote it down exactly as he
dictated it to me. I am enclosing his letter.
He is a very nice little boy, does good work in school,
and has such nice manners.
If you answer his letter, he will get it if you address it
as follows: [The school address was given.]
Ernest moved to another home last night. He seems to
like it very well. He is beginning to try to eat.
The children all like Ernest. He is a good boy and has a
winning personality. He has mentioned you several times.
A letter from you would mean a lot to Ernest.
Sincerely,
Ernest's teacher.

October 6

Ernest received an answer from his mother October 4.
He stayed after school. The teacher gave him a Stanford-

Binet (Form L.) He immediately recognized the equipment as "I.Q. material," although "not the same kind" that he had had before. He was quite anxious to be tested, and asked the teacher if she didn't think his I.Q. would be good. The teacher assured him that she thought it would be. Strangely enough, he received a score of 119—the same I.Q. he had quoted so glibly. After he had finished this test, the teacher told him she had a surprise for him. During the test he had been quite relaxed, but when the teacher produced the letter and told him it was from his mother, he became quite upset.

E. I know it. I know my mother wrote it. Mrs. R. told me.

(Mrs. R. did *not* know about it and could not have mentioned it to him.)

T. You are so glad you don't know what to do.

E. Read it.

(He crawls up on the teacher's lap and she reads the letter to him. When Ernest becomes excited or emotionally upset, he spits up mucus, and several times during the reading of the letter he spat in the receptacle provided for him.)

T. *(reading):* "Dear Little Son:"

E. That is me. I am "dear little son."

T. You *are* glad she called you dear little son.

E. I am her little son. It's because I'm a boy she calls me dear little son. *(He gets down from the teacher's lap and spits up mucus.)*

T. You are excited to hear from your mother and so you have to spit up.

E. Read it again—from the beginning.

T. *(reading):* "Dear Little Son: Just a line to answer your letter rec sat sure was pleased to hear from you and to no you was getting along so good——"

E. I am getting along good, aren't I? This letter is to me from my mother.

T. You think you are getting along good, too. You are happy to hear from your mother.

E. When I'm better I'm going home. I have some pigs and a cow too. And a grandpa.

T. You would like to go home—and when you are better you can go home.

(Ernest spits up again. The teacher wondered if she should continue with the letter, since he was so excited, and decided to risk it.)

T. When you get excited, it makes you spit up.

E. When I'm better I'm going home.

T. When you can eat all your meals and not spit up, then you will be better.

E. What else did she say? How are my pigs and my grandpa?

T. (*reading letter again*): "that sure was a nice letter your sisters are just fine, and——"

E. I've got two sisters. I don't know them. How old are they?

T. I don't know. You wonder about them, don't you?

E. I'm the *only* boy. I have no brothers.

T. You are the *only* son.

E. (*grinning*): The only son. (*Nods head solemnly. Then pulls at the teacher's sleeve.*) Go on. Read more.

T. (*reading*): "and your little puppy is to and your pigs are great big hogs now."

E. (*laughing*): I've got great big hogs. My puppy was such a nice dog. Nice little puppy. Little brown puppy.

T. (*reading*): "We have still got a cow for you to your oldest sister are going to school. She is in the third grade. I am glad you are learning your books good honey——"

E. She calls me honey.

(The degree of emotional deprivation which this child has suffered is made clear by his responses all through this letter. It is this extreme deprivation which might be thought by some to justify the therapist in carrying a supportive rôle. Unless the therapist is ready, however, to *be* a substitute mother, with all that that implies in terms of continuing care, the supportive rôle will have to be abandoned at some time, with consequent pain.)

T. She calls you honey. You like that.

E. (*leaning back against the teacher and closing his eyes*): I got some hogs and a cow.

T. It's nice to know that you have some things of your own back home.

E. I'm going to milk the cow when I go home. What else does she say?

T. (reading): "I am glad you are learning your books good honey be a good little boy and go to school and learn to be a school teacher don't you think that would be nice grandmother said tell you she were just fine and for you to be good and learn to eat so you can come home——"

E. I'll learn to eat. And then I'll go home and see my hogs. And the cow.

T. You'll learn to eat because you want to go home and see those hogs and that cow.

E. I'll bet they're big. What color are they?

T. She doesn't say. What color do you think?

E. I don't know. *(Laughs.)* But not *blue!*

T. Not blue.

E. Are there black hogs?

T. Yes. there are black hogs.

E. Then they are black. *(During this talk he becomes very relaxed. Murmurs.)* What else did she say?

T. (reading): "Be good and learn to eat so you can come home and be with us honey I thought your little letter were affel nice and I sure do love to hear from you and it sure was nice you are eating so good I am glad to hear that Mother will be up to see you as soon as I can

Ans soon with love from Mother
To Ernest goodbye."

E. (still very relaxed): Yes. She really is coming up to see me. She said she would.

T. You are glad she said she would come up and see you.

(When the teacher finished reading the letter, Ernest was quite calm. The teacher quickly copied the letter and put it in with her notes.)

E. What are you doing? Are you answering the letter?

T. No. I'm copying it down, so when *you* answer the letter, I can read it to you again if you want me to. You can take *your* letter home and show it to Mrs. R. if you want to.

E. I can take it home? *(Surprise.)*

T. Yes. If you want to.

E. I want to. Now let's go get ice-cream cones.

October 11

(During this after-school session Ernest rolled a ball of clay around for a few minutes, then suddenly came over to the teacher.)

E. Let's write my mother a letter.

T. You like to get letters from your mother.

E. My mother is skinny.

T. She is?

E. Yes. Skinny as a toothpick.

(It is interesting to note the positive way he speaks of his home. In reality he does not know anything about home or relatives.)

E. Ready? Say, "Dear Mother. I want to milk a cow when I come home. I hope you get plenty of milk with your cow. I hope I get to butcher my hog when I get home!" *(To teacher.)* And I really mean that. I'll take a big knife as sharp as a knife and I'll cut its throat. *(He gets a ruler and whacks on the table.)* I'll kill the old hog. *(Squeals, becomes very aggressive.)*

(This is the first time that Ernest has expressed an aggressive attitude which seems to be directed toward his home. The teacher's response is scarcely adequate to the depth and strength of the destructive urge exhibited. "You'd really *like* to cut his throat" might have indicated more acceptance and would perhaps lead to further expression of some of the underlying attitudes.)

T. You want to kill the hog when you get home.

E. *(Nods head, bangs on table, and squeals. Suddenly puts down ruler.)* Say, "How old is my baby sister right now? How are you getting along with your work? I hope grandpa can bring you up to see me soon!" *(To the teacher.)* Maybe he will, too!

T. You do want to see this mother of yours.

E. Write, "Bring me a game when you come to see me."

T. You want your mother to bring *you* something.

E. Yes. Any kind of a game. I don't have any games.

T. You want your mother to give you something.

E. Tell her, "I have been drinking chocolate milk at school." *(Dictates rapidly.)* "I get graham crackers, too. I want you to come up and see how I work sometimes. With love to you and Grandpa and Grandma, Ernest."

(Ernest walked over to the table and got out the box of dolls. He arranged the doll furniture and then started to play with it. The mother was getting dinner at the stove. She called the children. The boy came in. The sister came in. Ernest began to talk for each doll.)

Boy doll: What will we play?

Girl doll: Let's play Ring Around the Rosy. *(Makes dolls do this. The other sister comes in.)*

Sister: Let's play London Bridge. *(They do. The play is very restrained and proper. The father doll comes home.)*

Father: What did you do today?

Boy: I worked hard. I baked a cake.

Father: Was it any good?

Boy: Oh yes.

Father: Where is it?

Boy: Over there on the stove. *(Father goes over to stove.)* Have some?

Father: Yum-yum. Good. Now you go out and play. *(Mother takes sister and goes out.)*

(Suddenly Ernest swoops the box down on them and catches them under it.)

E. (yelling): The giant has got you. The *giant* will eat you up. *(He pretends to be the giant and pretends to eat them.)*

T. The giant is going to eat the mother and the little sister.

(A better response would have been, "You like to be the giant and eat them up." Because Ernest has shown such a definite desire to see his mother, and to have evidence of her affection, it is easy to overlook the fact that his feeling is ambivalent. He is clearly hostile to his family, which has deserted him, as well as being eager to make contact with them.)

E. Yes. Just you watch.

(Father sends the other brother and the other sister out. Same thing happens to them. Then the father calls, "Ernest!")

E. (to teacher): He's hiding. See? He don't want to come.

T. The boy doesn't want to answer his father.

E. No. *(Sighs.)* But he has to. He is well-behaved. *(Changes voice to a very sweet tone.)* Yes, Father?

Father: Go see what happened to your family.

E. I don't know. The giant ate them, I guess.

Father: The giant? Oh, my goodness!

(Father runs out and is caught and eaten, then flung violently into the toy box. E. "Even you, little boy!" And the other boy, identified as Ernest, is also caught, eaten, and flung into the toy box. The flinging is done quite violently.

Ernest walks away from the dolls. He comes close to the teacher.)

(It seems entirely likely that the reason for this symbolic self-punishment and self-destruction is that the aggressive attitudes have not been adquately understood, and consequently have not been adequately clarified or accepted by the therapist. Had Ernest's hostility toward his family been clearly accepted, it is unlikely that he would have had to punish himself in this play.)

E. (to teacher): Do you suppose some of the lye I drank is still inside me?

T. You think maybe some of the lye is still inside you?

E. Yes. I have such an awful time. I haven't been able to keep all my food down. Yesterday only breakfast and lunch, but not dinner. And this morning my breakfast came up and my lunch. *(Pause.)*

T. It discourages you. *(Pause.)* Do you want to tell me about the lye?

(Here is a very good use of a non-directive lead, which helps the boy release some of his feelings about the initial injury. Those who are unaccustomed to non-directive therapy may note with some surprise that this is the first question which the teacher-therapist has asked, and even this is a very general question which simply emphasizes the permissiveness of the relationship. There is no probing in this situation, simply because probing defeats its own end. Most workers tend to overwhelm the child with questions, which tend only to create defensiveness.)

E. I thought it was milk. It was in a glass sitting out in the alley. You see, I thought it was *good* milk and I drank it. I guess some of it is still down there.

T. You thought it was milk and you drank it. Then it made you sick. Now you think the lye is still down there, because you still get sick.

E. Yes. That's what I think. *(Pause. Ernest stares at the teacher unhappily—quite dejected.)*

T. What does the doctor say?

E. He says it is all out now. He says I *can* swallow, and I *do* swallow, but it won't stay down.

T. Sometimes it won't stay down.

E. Yes. And sometimes it does stay down.

T. Sometimes it won't stay down and you don't like that; then sometimes it does stay down and that makes you glad.

E. Yes. Are we going to have ice-cream bars tonight?

T. You want an ice-cream bar?

E. Yes.

T. Think it will stay down?

E. I think so.

(They went to the drugstore and got Ernest an ice-cream bar. He ate all of it—no spitting up at all. The teacher remarked about this.)

T. You said *you thought* this one would stay down and it did.

E. (*Looks at the teacher curiously, then very solemnly shakes head in agreement.*) I told you it would (*very confidently*).

October 18

Ernest has his throat dilated about once every three weeks. He goes to the hospital for this treatment, takes ether, and is in the hospital, or in a bed at home, for at least a day. Previous to this treatment, he has been upset and in bed for several days. The nurse told the teacher he would probably be absent a few days. His throat is raw and sore following the treatment. The doctor says this treatment will probably have to be continued until Ernest if fifteen years old. The teacher is notified ahead of time as to what Ernest is going to have to face. She usually has to break the news to him. This time the nurse also told him. The following contact had been arranged to precede by one day the hospital treatment. The teacher wondered if Ernest would use therapy time to work out *this* problem. He did.

E. (*Goes to paint table and starts to paint blobs of red on a large paper.*) I'm going to the hospital tomorrow. I'm going to have my throat dilated.

T. You're going to the hospital tomorrow.

E. I'll bet you'll miss me.

T. You know I'll miss you.

E. Yes. You will! (*Hits paper with paintbrush and spatters the paint.*) It'll hurt! It'll hurt! It'll *hurt!*

T. You think it will hurt to have your throat dilated.

E. Sometimes it bleeds! Look! (*Points to paper painted red.*) Look! Bloody! Like my throat.

(Any doubt as to the easy and direct way in which children make use of symbolism in expressing their attitudes in play therapy should be dispelled here. The way in which Ernest uses the paint to symbolize his fears, and the toys to act out his hostilities, is so clear as to need no comment.)

T. You think your throat will be bloody like that.

E. Yes. *(Puts down brush. Tears up paper.)* I'll throw it away. I'll get rid of it.

T. You'll get rid of the blood on the paper.

E. Yes. *(He crams it in the wastebasket and gets in and tramps on it. Then he gets baby doll and beats it with his fist.)* Bad, bad baby! I'll beat you up. *(Does so. Then gets the hammer and pounds the doll's head—it was a rag doll.)* I'll hurt the baby's head. I'll hammer it to pieces. I'll make *it* bleed *(defiantly)*.

T. You'll make the baby's head bleed.

E. (getting gun): I'll shoot it. Bang! Bang! There I fixed it. *(Aims gun at the teacher.)* Bang! Bang! There! I shot you, too.—Not really, though—just pretend. *(Comes over and pats the teacher's hand.)*

T. You just feel like shooting everyone.

E. (screaming): I don't want to go to the hospital!

T. You don't want to go to the hospital, and because you have to go, you feel like shooting everyone. That's all right to feel that way!

(Very frequently the handicapped child (or adult) feels deeply aggressive toward the whole world which has treated him so cruelly. It is not surprising that Ernest, deserted by his family, frequently hurt by physicians, and facing still another ordeal, should feel so destructive. The counselor's response is excellent at this point. It should probably be classed as interpretation of attitudes already expressed, and hence can be accepted by the child. Note how bringing such attitudes clearly into the open, and showing real acceptance of them, dissolves the need for their expression. The child can almost immediately cease being destructive, now that his attitude is understood and accepted.)

E. (grinning): Bang! Bang! Bang! *(Then he gets the hammer and pounds the workbench.)*

T. It makes you feel good to pound the old workbench.

E. *(Drops the hammer, kicks it across the room. He comes over and sits down beside the teacher and puts his head in her lap.)* I'm tired now. Let's go walking.

T. You want to go out for a walk?

(They go out for a walk. Ernest talks about the hospital. They buy some candy, but Ernest doesn't eat it.)

E. I'll save it until later. I don't think it would stay down.

T. You'll wait until *you think* it will *stay down* and then eat it.

October 20

Ernest was absent only one day. This contact was to obtain his reaction to the hospital experience, if any. Ernest spends most of the time pounding the workbench and the baby doll. He laughs all the time.

E. I'm tough, I am. The doctor was surprised when I told him I was eating everything and everything was staying down.

T. You're pretty pleased about that.

E. You bet. He said, "You're tellin' me tall tales." I said, "Oh no! Not me!" And it didn't hurt me a bit.

T. The doctor was pleased, too. And it didn't hurt a bit this time.

E. I told the doctor I eat and keep it down because I like it at school—I like the kids—I like my teacher. I like where I'm living now. (*Laughs. Picks up doll and dances it around the table top. Sings.*) I like! I like! I like!

("I can keep it down because I like it at school." Ernest has a good understanding of the fundamentals of psychosomatic medicine.)

Throughout this contact the satisfaction the child has gained from mature and courageous adjustments is very evident. It is not accidental that in this situation his song should be of positive and outgoing affection. His attachment to the teacher-therapist is also evident, as well as his insistence on the reciprocal nature of that relationship.)

E. (*Goes out in the hall to get a drink. The teacher goes with him. Another teacher is there. She speaks to Ernest and he speaks to her in a friendly way.*) I'm staying tonight. Miss A. and I are going to play.

Other teacher (*teasing*): Are you staying with *her?* Why, she's no good.

E. (*suddenly becoming a raging fury, butting the other teacher with his head, hitting her with his fists*): Don't you dare *say* such things! I *like* her. She *likes* me. (*Other teacher laughs and walks away. They return to the room. Ernest gets gun.*) I'll shoot her. Bang! Bang!

T. You want to shoot her because she said I wasn't any good.

E. Yes. (*Runs around the room, pretending to shoot, knocks over chairs, laughs, comes back to the table, sits down, throws gun back over his head, doesn't look where it goes, sticks his fingers down in the paint jars. Smears the paper.*) I'm a messy mess.

T. You like to mess in the paint.

(*Ernest continues to smear the paint on with his hands. Finally he comes over to the teacher.*)

E. I'll go wash my hands now. (*Goes out and washes hands. Comes back.*) I ought to get another letter from my mother, shouldn't I?

T. You want another letter, don't you?

E. Yes. Maybe tomorrow, huh?

T. You hope maybe tomorrow you'll get one.

E. Yes. (*Sits down at table. Puts head down and peeks at the teacher and grins.*)

T. It's time to go now.

E. I want an ice-cream cone.

(*They go and buy ice-cream cone. He eats it all. No spitting.*)

October 21

Parents of many of the other children visited the room this afternoon. No one was there to visit Ernest. During the afternoon other children asked him if his mother was there. He replied, "Yes. She isn't." He wore the cowboy suit all afternoon and kept the holster and gun strapped to his side. (The teacher had a cowboy suit of Ernest's size in the cupboard. Ernest found it and began wearing it during school time after October 11. This soon became an indicator of his feelings. When he felt very upset and tense he became more aggressive, taking it out in wild cowboy play at recess.) As the parents were leaving, he shot each of them. The teacher responded to this with "You'd like to shoot the other mothers because yours is not here." Ernest agreed. When the children talked about their mothers and asked him about his, he pointed to the teacher and said, "She is my mother." The other children said, "Is she?"

Ernest replied, "Yep. So my mother is here, see?" When the parents left, he stayed for therapy.

(Ernest got the nursing bottle, filled it with water, drank from it, cried like a baby, made feeble, futile baby gestures.)

T. You like to play baby.

E. Yes. (*Lies down on two chairs which he fixed like a bed.*) Baby is going to sleep.

T. Sh. Baby is going to sleep.

E. (*closing his eyes. Drinks from bottle. Sits up*): Look. I'm drinking like a little baby.

T. Sometimes it's fun to play you are a baby. (*Ernest pretends to cry again.*)

(The visits of other parents—visible evidence of his own deprivation brings out all of Ernest's infantile desires, which are satisfactorily recognized by the therapist. A somewhat deeper, slightly more interpretative response at this point might have been even more helpful. For example, "Seeing all the other children with their mothers makes you feel like being a baby with your mother.")

(Having expressed his infantile attitudes symbolically, he then expresses them as dependence on the teacher, asking for her protection and care. She continues her supporting rôle, giving him the care he desires, and using the strength of her relationship to bring about more mature eating behavior.)

(Ernest gets up, goes over to the doll and pretends to feed it, then suddenly he hurls the doll across the room, puts the bottle down, looks out the window. It is raining a little.)

E. You'll have to take me home in your car because it is raining outside.

T. You don't want to get wet.

E. I'd get wet, then I'd get sick, then I'd be sad.

T. You don't want to get sick.

E. I would have to stay home from school and I don't want to. I want to come to school.

T. Maybe you want to go for a little ride in my car.

E. No doubt I would. (*He grins. They go out to the car.*)

T. I would get you an ice-cream cone, but if you were in the car you couldn't spit, so——

E. But I wouldn't *have* to spit.

T. How do you know you wouldn't *have* to spit?

E. I would see to it that I didn't.

T. What would you do?

E. I would swallow it and see that it stayed swallowed. It's up to me, you know.

T. It's up to you, Ernest.

(They buy the cone. He eats it. It stays down. The teacher-therapist takes him home a very roundabout way. When he gets out of the car, he says, "Do you see? It stayed down. I *can* make up my mind—'stay down there'—and it does."

Therapy would have been nearly complete at this point, except for the gradual breaking of the supportive relationship, had it not been for the family complications which followed.)

Following this contact everything he ate stayed down and he received no supplemental feedings for three weeks —until he went home for Thanksgiving.

October 27

At letter from Ernest's mother came. Ernest stayed in at noon to have this letter read to him. He made no interruptions—showed no emotional upset. The contact was shorter than the others. The letter was as follows:

Dear Little Boy:

Will answer your letter Rec. the other day and glad to hear from you and you are sure doing fine in school you can make good figures you can milk the cow when you come home and help butcher. We have a lot of chickens for you to feed and your baby sister is four years old and your oldest sister is eight. She is going to school every day and in the 3rd grade grandma said that she was just fine and looking for you home Ernest be a good boy and go to school and mother will be up to see you before long. You have an offel nice teacher it is nice for her to write for you so be a good little boy I may be up after you for thanksgiving. I can't think of anything will close ans soon from mother to Ernest

Goodby
with love Mother.

E. (brightening up about going home for Thanksgiving): She's coming after me for Thanksgiving. I'm going home.

T. You *want* to go home.

E. I want to *kill* the chickens. I want to pull off their feathers. I want to chop off their heads. Take their insides out!

T. You really do want to kill those chickens.

(The letter from his mother touches off in Ernest both his infantile desires and his deeply hostile desires. The latter he does not dare direct toward their real goal. A better response from the therapist at this point would have been, "You want to go home, and you want to kill things at home." This might have enabled him to express his hostility more openly.)

E. I want to write a letter to my mother. I'll kill off all our chickens. I want to suck a nipple bottle *(getting it)*. See? I'm a baby! *(Cries like a baby.)* See how much I can drink!

T. You wish you were a little baby.

E. Let's answer that letter. *(He begins to dictate.)* "Dear Mother: I want to kill a chicken when I get home and feed my hogs. I'm glad my baby sister is four years old. I want to clean the chicken when I get home. That will be a lot of fun. I want to clean up the house."

T. You really want to *help* your mother when you get home. You want her to know that.

E. (continuing to dictate): "I'm glad my sister is in the third grade. Why doesn't she write me a letter sometime? Tell my grandma I hope she comes up to see me, too. I hope you can have dinner with me on Thanksgiving day. On Christmas day I hope Santa brings me a sled. I hope the family can all come up on Christmas day and eat dinner with me, too."

T. You want to be with your family. You want to know them.

E. (dictating): "I do good work in school. I mind what my teacher says. I have a boy friend now. His name is Robert. [He is fifteen years old.] I have a girl friend, too. Her name is Miss L. [His Sunday-School teacher.] She bought me a painting set two weeks ago."

T. You like Robert and Miss L.

E. (nods): "I want a Mickey Mouse watch for Christmas. I can read a little bit now. My teacher gets me ice cream all the time. My teacher has lots of toys for us to play with. We have a good time in school. I wear a cowboy suit in school sometimes." *(To the teacher.)* Gosh, I miss my mother. She is skinny, like a pencil. Write, "I play at school. I wore a funny face on Hallowe'en and a cowboy suit. I paint pictures at school. I have fun at school when I work and play. We are building a playhouse. I drink chocolate milk at school. I eat fine. Love to mother and my family. Ernest."

(When Ernest finished dictating this unusual letter, he took the nipple off and drank the water. This time he went home alone. It was noon. He did not ask for ice cream and candy. He was very happy when he left.

Ernest's mother came after him for Thanksgiving. The state guardian arranged for the meeting to take place at school. Ernest was quite anxious for her to come. The teacher knew she was not to arrive until two-thirty, so, to offset Ernest's anxiety, she took the class for a walk to see some live turkeys. He was excited and nervous. Once after returning to school, he went over to his receptacle to spit, happened to catch the teacher's eye on him, and walked away saying, "No, I won't spit up, I won't do it" and didn't. The class got out the rhythm band instruments (which seem to be a good outlet for tensions). Ernest was an excellent drummer and never missed a beat. They had played one piece when his mother and legal guardian knocked on the door. One of the children answered the door and then called the teacher, who asked them both in and brought chairs for them. The teacher did not call Ernest, but remained non-directive, much to the surprise of Mrs. S. and the mother. She went back to the piano and Ernest looked back at the couple. He recognized Mrs. S. and concluded the stranger must be his mother. He finally put down the drum and went back to the woman, held out his hand to shake hands, and said, "My mother, I think?" She did not kiss him. She looked quite upset. He stayed beside her for a few minutes and she put her arm around him quite gingerly. Then he came back to the group.

(At no point in the case is the therapist's deep respect for the integrity of this six-year-old personality better shown than in this episode. Most counselors, even though psychologically trained, would be likely at this point to take the matter out of the child's hands. She leaves it up to him, with very constructive—and very dramatic—results. Ernest's understatement can be matched only by Stanley's "Doctor Livingstone, I presume?")

Ernest went home with his mother and stayed for the weekend. According to reports, his mother was gone all day Saturday, had a neighbor take him to the bus Sunday, and sent him back alone.

November 29 (First contact after visit home.)

E. (Bangs on workbench with hammer. Pushes box of nails off bench. They scatter all over the floor.). There, nails! That'll learn you! Fall on the floor, damn you! See if I care. *(Kicks the nails.)* I won't pick them up. I want the nails there.

T. You're feeling tough now. You want to act mean. Go ahead. Act that way.

(The recognition of feeling is good. The instructions to "go ahead" are quite unnecessary and could be harmful if continued. Such suggestions might encourage the child to bring out hostility more rapidly than he is ready to assimilate it.)

E. They are the God-damnedest nails. Itty-bitty baby nails. Mamma and papa nails. *(Sits down on the floor and runs fingers through the nails. Picks up a bent nail and holds it out to the teacher. Grins.)* Look at this ole bitch! Son-of-a-bitch if I ever saw one.

T. You've learned some new words that you want to show off.

(Beautiful handling of this situation by simple recognition of the attitude the child is expressing. Note again that the satisfactory clarification of an attitude, in an accepting atmosphere, immediately dissolves the need for symbolic expression. It is this that accounts for the fact that accepted catharsis, that is, outpouring of feelings, alters behavior. If the reader will refer back to comment on page 336 and its accompanying material, he will see how the foster mother handled very similar behavior in such a way as to make it worse.)

E. Mrs. R. has a fit. She says I'll go to hell. They are *bad* words.

T. Mrs. R. says they are bad words, but still you like to use them.

E. Yeah. My mother said Mrs. R. didn't have any kick coming about me. She says Mrs. R. gets paid to take care of me. And you get paid to take care of me. You just do your job. You *gotta* take care of me.

T. You think Mrs. R. and I just take care of you because it's our job and that makes you feel very unhappy. You want us to take care of you because you belong to us and because we love you.

(Ernest picks up a handful of nails and throws them clear across the room. He kicks the box across after them. Then suddenly he flings himself into the teacher's lap and cries as hard as he can cry.)

T. Just cry it out, Ernest. You were disappointed in your trip home.

(Again a clarification of the deeper feelings being expressed brings release.)

E. (crying harder than ever. Then, sobbing): Do *you* love me?

T. Yes. I love you, Ernest.

(Now the therapist is openly admitting her supportive rôle. Its risks will be evident later. It is a real question whether, even at this moment of deep discouragement on the part of the boy, a simple reflection of feeling might not have been preferable. The response might have been, "You're afraid your mother doesn't love you and now you wonder if I love you." The therapist tries to reassure, but reassurance always falls short of complete effectiveness. The problem of doubt and insecurity is within the child and cannot be answered by the counselor.)

E. Mrs. R. says she doesn't love me any more. She says I can't stay with her if I act like I do.

T. You don't think she loves you and doesn't want you to stay.

E. (Nods head vigorously. Then he tries to wipe away his tears.) You told me a lie.

T. I told you a lie? What was that?

E. You told me it was wrong to play with matches.

T. Well, it isn't safe. And if it isn't safe, it's the wrong thing to do.

E. My mother said it was a lie.

T. Tell me some more about it.

E. (climbing up on the teacher's lap): Know what I did when I went home?

T. No. What did you do?

E. I played with matches. I even smoked. I lit my mother's cigarettes for her. All day long that's all I did. And I learned how to spit up in the fireplace without getting burned and we had hog all the time and it was so tough I couldn't chew it—Mrs. R. is a better cook—and I went barefooted. Just in the house, you know. And grandma couldn't hear me and my sisters wouldn't play with me and my mother went away and left me and I came back all alone on the bus. Mrs. B. took me to the bus. And I—I—I—— *(Suddenly brightens up.)* You should see my hogs. Know how to call a hog?

T. I don't know any hogs to call.

E. (laughing): I got hogs and you haven't *any* hogs.

T. You've got something I haven't got.

E. (clapping hands gleefully): I have my own hogs. Some day I'll kill them and strew their guts all over the damn place. *(Laughs again.)*

T. That tickles you.

(The most constant error of the therapist in this case is her failure to recognize aggressive feelings as adequately as she does the other negative attitudes which the child expresses. The recognition here is very weak. Some such response as "You'd just like to kill them *good*" might be better. Note also how the hostile and infantile attitudes are always associated in the play.)

E. (Goes over and gets nursing bottle and chews the nipple.) Look. Baby again. Baby hungry.

T. (taking out chocolate bar): Does baby want some candy?

E. (Takes candy bar, then lays it back on the desk. Looks very despondent. Whispers.) I can't eat any more. Everything comes up. *(Tears come to his eyes.)*

T. It makes you feel unhappy because you can't keep it down any more.

E. (suddenly, with a display of depression that is certainly unusual for such a young child, bursting out with a torrent of words. Some of it was lost and unintelligible. The gist of it was): I don't care what happens to me. I don't care if I never eat again. I don't care if I die. I want to die. I hope I do die. *(He started to cry again.)* You're the only person I got. I want to go home with you. I want to go live with you. I want to die. I hate Mrs. R. She is a mean woman. I hate her. *(And on and on he went, flinging his face in the teacher's lap.)* If I eat I'll have to go home and I don't want to go home.

T. You don't want to go home and so you are not eating.

(When he cries, "I want to go live with you," he is demanding, with the thorough logic of the child, that the therapist live up to the supportive mother rôle she has taken. If she loves him, she should be willing to take him to live with her.

In this deep expression of all his desperate attitudes, he brings out the most significant insight that he has yet shown. After his disillusioning visit at home, he is clinging to his symptoms and to his disability in order to hold on to the little security which he has.)

(Finally the storm subsided. The teacher reassured him that she did love him and told him that Mrs. R. loved him, too, and didn't mean it when she said she didn't want him any more. When Ernest repeated, "Can I come live with you?" she explained that she didn't have a home that she could share with him after school, but tried to point out that he did live with her five hours every school day. Then, being foolish and unscientific, and sentimental about the whole thing, she offered to take him downtown some day to see Santa Claus. He immediately brightened up, smiled, said he was going to tell Santa to bring him a *real* machine gun. He jumped down on the floor and picked up the nails. Then the teacher took him home.)

(The risk of the supportive rôle is that the therapist cannot live up to its demands. Having assured him that she loves him, she is [quite naturally] not willing to live up to the full implications of the mother rôle. She is at least frank in facing the extent to which she is emotionally involved in the situation, which helps to insure a more adequate handling of the problem.)

The teacher had a long talk with Mrs. R., who said she did not intend to keep Ernest unless his behavior improved. She said he talked "terrible" to her—said she got paid to take care of him and she could just earn her money. She said he swore, and spat in the fireplace. She talked herself out about the terrible habits he had brought back and said she would not put up with him unless he improved quickly. The teacher tried to explain his reaction—told Mrs. R. that Ernest had said she was a better cook than his mother—and begged her to bear with him—to give him time and understanding.[1] Mrs. R. said she

---

[1] Here for the first and only time, the teacher-therapist endeavors to alter the child's environment. In this situation it was of great temporary help, and it was possible to carry on a bit of therapy with the foster mother without hurting the relationship with the child. In general, however, it is not easy for one worker to carry on both environmental treatment and individual therapy. It involves taking over responsibility for the individual on the one hand, and leaving him responsible for his own choices on the other.

would. When the teacher recognized the feeling that Mrs. R. was disappointed and discouraged because they were right back where they started from, she agreed and said that was really the thing that "got" her, but if it was such a temporary thing, then it wasn't very important. When the teacher left, Mrs. R. expressed her willingness to try it again.

A few days later, in the midst of a reading class:

E. (grabbing stomach and stomach tube and glaring at the teacher, who detects a twinkle in his eye): Oh! Oh! It's come out!

T. It has come out?

E. Yes! Yes! Oh, do something or I'll die!—*(very dramatic).*

(Here we find Ernest tentatively making another neurotic use of his disability. Again recognition of the underlying attitude resolves the superficial problem, and enables the child to look at the real issue—the satisfaction which he has gained by this means.)

T. You want me to get excited.

(Ernest laughs. The other children are definitely alarmed. The teacher explains to them that Ernest is only teasing.)

E. It didn't scare you, did it?

T. You wanted to scare me, didn't you?

E. You should have seen my mother. She was scared. I'd yell, "Oh! Oh! I'll die!" And she got so scared!

(He laughed heartily. The teacher guessed that he had gotten revenge on his mother a few times.)

He continued to wear the cowboy suit during school. At recess he tore around like mad and shot everybody on the school ground. This aggression gradually wore down.)

December 6

The teacher and a friend took Ernest Christmas shopping and Santa-seeing. He seemed almost completely overwhelmed by the experience.

When he did get to see Santa, he walked up to that old gentleman—looking like a little angel—and said, "I want a machine gun—a real one, see?—and a sharp axe—and anything you've got that will kill people. And I ain't

kiddin', see?" (His hatred for the world and for his rejecting mother is still strong.) Then he stalked away and
Santa almost pulled off his beard in astonishment.

Since Ernest seemed very tired, the teacher decided to
take him home after his talk with Santa. His remarks on
the way were very flippant and sarcastic. When the teacher's friend asked him a very ordinary question about some
candy the teacher had given him, he replied with a German word. "What does that mean?" she asked. "It means
you're damn nosey," he said. "Mrs. R. taught me that
answer to people who ask me questions."

During the days that followed his visit to his home,
Ernest was sulky, aggressive, defiant, and depressed. He
wore the cowboy suit continually. He stamped his feet as
he walked around the room. He scribbled his papers. He
colored everything a solid blob of color—either black or
red. He spent his play time throwing the blocks back into
the box. He avoided the other children. When they did
come near him, he pushed them away. The teacher recognized as many of his feelings as she could. There was no
pressure put on him "to make him conform." His school
papers were accepted as an expression of his feelings.[1]

The record of his milk-drinking was as follows:

November 29—refused to drink the milk.

November 30—drank one-half bottle; spit it all up.

December 1—took only one mouthful; spit that up.

December 2—drank one-half bottle; spit it all up.

December 3—drank one-half bottle; spit it all up.

Every time he spit up the milk, he was quite obviously
discouraged and depressed. His feelings were recognized
every time, with such statements as, "It makes you feel
badly because you can't keep it down," "You want to
keep it down, but you can't do it. You are upset about
something." Then:

December 6—drank one-third bottle; no spitting up.

December 7—drank one-half bottle; no spitting up.

---

[1] Throughout the therapeutic contacts, it is difficult to know how much
of the progress stems from the fundamentally accepting attitude of the
teacher toward the group and how much is due to the individual therapeutic hours. Certainly, both contribute to the child's development, and
the underlying principles are the same.

December 8—drank one-half bottle; no spitting up.

December 9 and 10—no milk was served. Ernest asked for it—said he "needed it."

December 10

Ernest asked to stay after school. He was very depressed. A report from Mrs. R. indicated that he was not retaining any food and was refusing most of it. He was losing weight. His behavior at school was petulant. He complained of being tired. When he stayed after school, he sat at the table with his head in his arms.

T. You are tired.

(No response. Silence. Then suddenly he jumped up from the table, went over to the "music box" and got the drum. He brought it back to the table and pounded on the drum with all his might. After ten minutes of this, he pushed the drum away and began to cry.)

T. You are very unhappy.

E. (nods): I don't care what happens to me. Maybe I'll die. I hope I do die.

T. You are discouraged because you haven't been able to eat. *(He cries harder than ever.)* Go ahead and cry it out, Ernest. Then you'll feel better.

E. (finally looking up at the teacher): I want to come live with you.

T. You are crying because you want to live with me. And you are tired and hungry. *(The teacher offers him some candy. He eats a piece and promptly spits it up. Again he cries.)* When you are upset like this you can't keep it down. Then you cry because you are so miserable.

(Ernest has faced many of his own problems. Now it becomes necessary to face the problem which has been created by the teacher, the matter of the supportive relationship. The teacher recognizes his feeling, but for the first time tries to evade an attitude which he has expressed. The moment we become emotionally involved with a client, the accuracy and helpfulness of our responses tend to decrease. This is one of the strongest arguments for a strictly nondirective approach, in which the attitudes are merely reflected to the client, and the counselor does not become involved.

In this instance the counselor's attempts to attribute Ernest's feeling to weariness, and to placate him with candy, are both unsuccessful.)

(Ernest goes over to the desk and gets a library book— *Three Little Pigs.* He looks through the book, listlessly. It seems as though he is not paying attention to the book. He stops at the page where the wolf's picture is. He gets up and thrusts the picture at the teacher.)

E. Eat her up! Catch her!

T. You want the wolf to eat me because I can't take you home with me.

(The teacher here reverts to a better handling, and clearly accepts the hostility toward herself which has been caused by her attempts to be something less than a complete mother. This recognition tends to dissolve the feeling, but the residue is clearly shown by his flinging the book across the room at the close of the story.)

(Ernest takes the teacher's hand and very lightly sets his teeth down on the edge of it.)

T. You would like to bite me. *(He grins. Then suddenly kisses the teacher's hand.)* But you think it would be better to stay friends.

E. Read me this story.

(The teacher reads him the story. He makes noises like a pig and a wolf all through the story. At the conclusion of the story he takes the book and flings it clear across the room. He gets a piece of chalk and scribbles on the board. When time is up, the teacher takes him home.)

From December 13 through December 17 Ernest drank all his milk at school and did not spit up any. There was improvement in his attitude and behavior. He started to do some of his work again and he played with the other children.

Christmas vacation came. Ernest did not go home. Then January 3, 4, 5, 6, 7 he had difficulty drinking the milk again. He drank only one-half of it, but retained what he drank. He ate candy and ice cream without spitting up.

January 7

Ernest was absent one-half day. He was again very

depressed. He said, "Maybe I'll die." The teacher recognized his feeling of depression and unhappiness.

January 11

Because of a tonsilectomy on this day, Ernest was absent from school for four days. The teacher called up on Sunday evening to inquire about him. He talked to her. He said he was coming back to school, that he was now "without tonsils and talked like a frog with the croup." Mrs. R. told the teacher that when Ernest was in the hospital she had taken into her home a twenty-one-months-old baby that was a feeding problem, another desertion case.

January 17

Ernest came back to school. He took the teacher aside and told her he was not wearing the tube. He said, "I went down in the dark. I said I won't do it again." He asked to stay after school. The report of this contact follows:

(Ernest got out the nursing bottle and crawled around on the floor and jabbered. Then he sat down on the floor and said:)

E. (to the teacher): Mrs. R. got 'nother baby when I was in the hospital. It isn't much of a baby. It doesn't amount to much.

(Life continues to deal this child staggering psychological blows, yet he shows an amazing ability to assimilate them in the therapeutic relationship.)

T. You don't think very much of it.

E. No. It's got water on the brain. And sores all over it.

T. It must be a pretty sick baby.

E. A sick baby, but not pretty.

(He went over to the box of pictures and sorted through them. He picked out all the baby pictures he could find and then tore them up into tiny pieces.)

T. You don't like to have the baby at Mrs. R.'s. You are jealous of the baby. *(Ernest turns suddenly and looks at the teacher. Then he tears up the remaining pictures, takes the*

Annotated Therapy Records

nursing bottle and sits down with it.) You would like to be
the only baby.

E. It is wrong to be jealous.

T. Someone has told you it is wrong to be jealous; but you
feel sort of jealous of that baby.

E. It's a hateful, foolish baby. Maybe it won't even live.

(The counselor's handling of this jealousy situation could
scarcely be improved upon. Note that when she clarifies both
of his contradictory attitudes, that he hates the baby, but
feels guilty about it, he is able to reveal his murderous
attitude more fully.)

T. You don't want Mrs. R. to keep the baby.

E. I'm the baby. *(He gets down and crawls.)*

T. You like to pretend that you are the baby.

E. Will you buy me some candy?

T. Will *you* eat it? *(He had spit up all his milk.)*

E. I probably won't be able to keep it down.

T. You don't think you will be able to keep it down. Then
why eat it?

E. If I don't eat you'll buy me things to eat. You'll try to
help me all you can.

("If I don't eat you'll buy me things to eat"—an exceedingly significant expression. Ernest has discovered a new use
for his disability, and is using it to hold on to the teacher.
Would not this have been partially avoided if the teacher had
been less supportive?

Since the issue has arisen, the teacher handles it well,
recognizing the boy's need, and using his attachment to her
to bring about mature, rather than immature, behavior.
From this date on, Ernest had no difficulty eating or retaining what he ate. Perhaps he had been using his disability to
hold on to his foster mother, the doctors, and the nurses, in
the same way which he used it to hold on to his teacher.)

T. You know I want to help you; but you think you can
get me to give you things to eat just as long as you have
trouble eating.

E. (nodding): You will.

T. You know I want to help you; but with things as they
are I can only give you money for things to eat *if* you eat
them.

E. Not to spit up?

T. Not to spit up.

E. Then I'll eat them.

(They bought a candy bar. He ate it—and retained it.)

January 19—After School

E. Will you buy me an ice-cream bar? I've made up my mind. *(He ate and retained the ice-cream bar.)*

January 20

Ernest drank all his milk; ate an ice-cream bar; no spitting up. His behavior is definitely improved. He shows an acceptance of the baby.

E. *(in class):* I have a baby to care for at home. He is beginning to sit up a little. *(Another time.)* I'm a big help to Mrs. R. I help her with the baby. I *understand* it. *(His feelings of liking to help were recognized.)*

(Gradually he is turning to a more satisfactory source of emotional support and security—the foster mother. The foster mother can realistically carry the mother rôle, where the teacher cannot.

It also seems evident that Ernest's full expression of his antagonism toward the baby has helped him to work out a more realistic and mature relationship with his infant competitor. He is also attaining a new sense of usefulness and achievement.)

From January 20 on, Ernest had no difficulty in eating or in retaining what he ate.

From January 31 to February 14, he was absent because of measles.

February 14, 15, 16, he was back in school, still eating, but very tired. He had headaches and earaches.

February 17, 18, 19, 22, 23, he was absent because of an ear infection, but he was still eating.

From February 24 to March 6, he was back in school, cheerful, friendly, and eating regularly.

February 28

(Ernest received a letter from his mother and sister. He stayed after school and listened as the teacher read it.)

T. *(reading):* "Dear Little Son

"Will drop you a few lines as thinking of you how are you fine I hope we have all been sick here just about ever since you went back grandma and grandpa had the flu and when they get well me and the girls had the measles and have been offel sick (Ernest laughed gleefully. "They had measles, too!") but we are all better now Ernest. We all liked our presents you sent fine. How are you eating now do you eat good how are you getting along and be a good boy and mind your teacher. Mother will be up to see just as soon as I can Mother can't come ever time I would like to for I don't have the money to go on but I will come ever time I can the girls said tell you hello for them and they would love to see you Ernest we have still got the hogs and chickens and cow and horse for you when you come home Ernest get your teacher to write me for you ans soon with love from Mother to Ernest.

love

Mother."

E. (shrugging his shoulders): We'll answer it some other day.

T. You don't want to answer it now.

E. No.

T. Here is another letter. This is from your sister.

E. I haven't got a sister.

(As Ernest finds security in the foster family, he is rejecting his own family as a source of security. This is probably a realistic adjustment to his situation, unless he is forced to return to his own home.)

T. You don't remember your sister?

E. I haven't got a sister. But read the letter.

T. (reading): "Dear Brother

"I will write to you how are you fine I hope for myself I am OK Ernest I missed two weeks and three days of school with the measles Flora Joan is sick now."

E. Who is Flora Joan?

T. Flora Joan is your other sister.

E. I don't have any sisters. I have a brother.

T. You think the boy at Mrs. R.'s is your only brother.

E. I don't have any sisters. Read what else she says.

T. (reading): "Ernest how are getting along in school fine I hope it is raining here and the wind is blowing Mother is feeling bad tonight Grandma and Grandpa said Hello for them and to be a good boy and mind your teacher how many Valentines did you get. I got 5 valentines so I had better to close ans soon from your sister."

E. She is *not* my sister!

T. You don't want her to be your sister.

E. I got thirty-seven valentines.

T. You got more valentines than she did.

E. What else does she say?

T. *(reading):* "to Ernest With Love."

E. *(very indifferent to the letters):* The baby is beginning to walk around the baby pen. He doesn't have sores on him any more. Mrs. R. says I am a very good helper.

T. You would rather talk about *your* baby.

E. We'll answer them some other day. *(He went home.)*

Ernest was in school February 29, March 1, 2, 3, and 6. He went to the hospital for a throat dilatation on March 7. Complications developed, due to a new anesthetic, and a high fever, followed by pneumonia, resulted. His life was in danger, his temperature as high as 105°, and the oxygen tent as well as sulfa drugs were used in combating his illness, which lasted ten days.

March 14

The teacher called Mrs. R. to inquire about Ernest. He came to the phone and said he expected to be back in school Monday. "I hope to come back to school long enough to at least get the whooping cough," he said. Mrs. R. laughed, when she took over the phone again, and said the doctor, too, thought he would be back again Monday. She said that through all this upheaval he seemed a bit fearful. She said she thought the throat dilatation was more severe this last time and that Ernest is a bit afraid when he eats, but he *is* eating. The stomach tube has been out nine weeks.[1]

April 20

Ernest has settled down to a rather ordinary existence. He has become a member of one of the "gangs" in the room and no longer asks to stay after school. His school work is satisfactory and his behavior quite acceptable.

[1] Note how real the gains have been. In spite of critical illness, pain, and weakness, he is still reacting on the grown-up basis which he has gradually achieved.

One April day, when the teacher made a home visit to Ernest's foster home, he very proudly brought in the baby for the teacher to see and displayed a genuine affection for it. Mrs. R. said he was "quite a help in looking after the baby."

During the latter part of April, a psychologist asked to give Ernest a Rorschach Personality Test. It was arranged for the teacher and an adult friend to take him to the psychological clinic for the test. As they passed "his old hospital," he asked if it would be possible to go in and see his "old home."

The teacher and her friend went into the hospital with Ernest, letting him lead the way. He entered by a back door, went up two flights of stairs, down three corridors, and finally came to the room he had been seeking. The door was open. There was another child in the bed in this room. Ernest looked in. "Someone is lying in my bed," he said, imitating one of the three bears. Then, in a very calm voice, "There is where I used to live."

He led the way down another hall until he came upon some nurses sitting at a table. He stood there and looked at them. One of them turned and recognized him. She held out her arms to him, hugged and kissed him and called to the other nurses, "Look who is here! How well you look! How much you've grown!" When she released him, he grinned at her. "You should go and see Mrs. P.; she will want to see you," said the nurse. "I intend to," said Ernest.

He led the way down to the medical clinic. The nurse there grabbed him up in her arms and hugged and kissed him crying, "My baby! Well, well! My baby!" When she held him off to look at him, he thanked her for the Easter card she had sent him and told her he had spent the fifty cents she had given him. She asked him how much money he would like for her to send him the next time. He replied, "I think fifty dollars would buy about all I would need." When she said she didn't have that much money, he said that when he grew up and got a job, then he would give her some money.

As he left the clinic, he said, "I want to say hello to Clementine." Clementine was big and black and shining. Ernest called a cheery "Hello, Clementine! How are you?" He smiled and waved. Then he said to his teacher, "Come on. Let's go now."

He led the way out of the building. "Well," he said, "that *was* my home. But it's more fun being out of the hospital."[1]

In order to pass the time before the appointment hour rolled around, they went to the museum. He was quite interested in the things he saw. When he was taken over to the psychological clinic, he went quite willingly with the psychologist for the test. Following the test, Ernest, the teacher, and her friend went to a cafeteria for lunch. He walked down the line and selected his lunch without any adult suggestions— —mashed potatoes and gravy, spinach, chocolate milk, ice cream and cake. He ate his lunch, carrying on a very mature conversation with the two adults about the things he had seen. He was completely at ease. At the end of the meal he figured up the cost of the three lunches and counted out the money which the teacher had put on the table. He got his hat and coat and handed them to the teacher. He smiled. "Here," he said, "me baby. Help me. Put them on for me."

"You like to act like a baby sometimes," said the teacher, helping him on with his coat. He squared his shoulders and said, "Then sometimes I like to be big. Like now. Let me pay the bill." He took the checks and the money and paid the cashier as they went out. Outside the cafeteria, he said quite seriously, "I've had a big day today. When I started to school I couldn't do this. I couldn't eat then. I had an old rubber tube for a stomach. This was fun. I like this."[2]

On the way back to his home, he stopped at the Five-and-Ten-cent store to spend the twenty-five cents his foster mother had given him. He bought a bubble-set.

When he arrived at his home he said to the teacher, "Do you want to come in and talk to Mrs. R.? Or do you

[1] When one deals therapeutically with children, it is often astonishing the use they make of situations to express symbolically the progress they are making. Here Ernest is obviously saying farewell to his invalid past.
[2] It should never be overlooked that the motivating force for all therapy is that it is more satisfying, more "fun," to be mature than to be infantile. It is this, and this alone, which makes it basically possible for therapy to take place. Ernest still likes to point out that he has infantile desires, but the mature impulses are now the definitely dominant ones.

want to say good-bye here, so I can go in and take a nap? Because I am tired!" The teacher said "good-bye here" and Ernest went in the house with his bubble-set.

Ernest seemed to have used the day to say good-bye to his infantile past, and now appeared to be dismissing his therapist. Since that time he has been a satisfactory member of the school group and has shown no need for further individual contacts.

FOLLOW-UP STUDY OF THE CASE OF ERNEST

At the close of the school year in June, Ernest was moved suddenly and unexpectedly to another foster home in a different part of the city. He was to stay in this foster home until he had received the periodic throat dilation, after which it had been decided by the state welfare department that Ernest should be returned to his mother and family. Earlier in the book an account of Ernest's summer therapy contacts has been related.[1]

One year later, reports from the physician and the state welfare department indicated that Ernest's physical and psychological adjustment had continued to improve. He had made a very remarkable adjustment to his family. His mother, sisters, and grandparents have become very fond of him. He lives on the farm and seems to enjoy it immensely. As the case worker stated it, "His remarkable energies seem to have been channeled into constructive behavior." He has had no further difficulty eating and has made satisfactory progress in all phases of his development.

A follow-up two years later indicated that Ernest was continuing to make satisfactory progress. It is no longer necessary to undergo throat dilations.

SOME QUESTIONS AND CONCLUSIONS IN REGARD TO THE CASE OF ERNEST

It was mentioned in the introduction to the case material that the experience with this case raises and partially

---

[1] See page 182 for the account of his play-therapy contact immediately preceding this throat dilation, and page 213 for the account of the play contact immediately following the brief period of hospitalization.

answers a number of questions regarding therapy. Let us consider several of these questions.

Is it possible for the same person to be both teacher and therapist, in dealing with a maladjusted child? The answer would seem to be affirmative, provided the teacher's rôle is much the same in both situations—that of an accepting, permissive person who is willing to grant children a large measure of free expression and individual choice. This description would not fit the majority of classroom teachers. If the teacher were more authoritative, a much sharper differentiation would almost certainly have to be made between classroom hours and therapeutic contacts. This arrangement can at times be successful, but the difficulties are real.

Can a maladjusted child be treated in a group situation? Here a combination of therapy in the group and in special contacts has been highly successful.

How does a handicapped child use his disability? Ernest exhibits a number of ways. He uses his disability to remain infantile, and to excuse his failure to grow up and take responsibility. He uses it to gain sympathy and affection; also to control others and to control the plans for his own future. We see in this case many of the types of psychological use to which wounded veterans will put their disabilities. We also see here the beginnings of several neurotic manifestations nipped in the bud by intelligent psychotherapy. With different treatment, this boy might already be well on the way to being a permanent invalid.

Why does the individual overcome these beginning neurotic tendencies? What, psychologically, happens within the individual in therapy? These questions will be of utmost importance in rehabilitation work. The answer seems to be, in Ernest's case, that he comes to accept within himself both his infantile needs and his impulses toward maturity. He denies neither, he represses neither. Both aspects are accepted by the therapist, and hence can be accepted by the boy. He no longer denies that he feels at times like a baby. He is under no compulsion to pretend that at all times he feels mature. Accepting both these aspects of himself fully, he does not need to make a concealed choice (a neurosis), but finds that the socially approved adult rôle has greater satisfactions. When freed from the need of being defensive and permitted to choose without compulsion, the great majority of maladjusted individuals make this choice.

Is an emotionally supportive rôle sound therapy? Here the case raises a question for thoughtful consideration, but does not answer it. It seems apparent that warm emotional support may give temporary help, but it creates fresh problems which also demand solution. Any attitude on the part of the therapist which creates dependence has the same result of creating a fresh maladjustment which in time must also be solved. Probably one of the most essential differences between therapy with Freudian leanings and non-directive therapy rests on this point. The Freudian view is that considerable dependence and much emotional involvement (transference) is a necessary condition for therapy, though this problem of transference must be solved before therapy is complete. Non-directive therapy maintains that such emotional dependence, whether brought on by supportive activities on the part of the therapist or by the taking of responsibility for the client, is a hindrance to therapy, and that improvement takes place much more rapidly if, throughout the process, the client's need for dependence is handled in the same fashion as are all his other needs and attitudes, namely, through assisting him to be conscious of these emotionalized attitudes. The case of Ernest does not give complete support to either of these viewpoints, but does give significant material for discussion.

These are a few of the issues which the case raises. There are others which will occur to each reader. Perhaps the outstanding contribution of the case is the indication of the results which may be achieved when the therapist's attitude is one of warmth, of acceptance of all attitudes, of permissiveness, and of reliance upon the capacity of the individual to work out an adjustment once he can become consciously accepting of the attitudes within himself.

Index

Acceptance, discussed, 20-21; and guilt feelings, 86; initial contact and, 89; group therapy and, 90; in parent-teacher relationship, 157; and teachers, 165
Adjustment, 12
Administrator. See Principal
Adolescent, in classroom situation, 141, 142
Adult, and child curiosity, 24; and child tensions, 126
Agreement, versus reflection, 160
Anxiety, illustrated, 98
Approval, 86
Art materials, use in therapy, 147
Attention span, 116

Behavior, kinds, 12; verbal, 129; destructive, 130. See also Maladjusted behavior
Behavioral responses, and habits, 11
Blocking, illustrated, 88

Catharsis, 146, 148
Change, behavioral, meaning, 106; therapist's rôle in, 127
Child, the, personality discussed, 12; rôle in play therapy, 16; attitude toward adult, 63; and therapist relationship, 74; rôle in group therapy, 84-85; attitude toward permissiveness, 93, 120; and "leading," 121; personality of, examined, 126; relation to

limitations, 130. See also Problem child, Handicapped child
Child-centered therapy, 40
Child-chosen therapy, 40
Choice, illustrated, 107-09
Classroom therapy, limitations, 152, 153
Client, the, rôle, 26, 27
Client-centered, 23
Concomitant therapy, 67
Condemnation, 80
Confidence, in group therapy, 85; in therapy structure, 106
Conformity, and adjustment, 106
Contacts, 99
Control, and respect principle, 131
Counselor, the, rôle, 26, 27
Criticism, 90

Decision, child, 16; in parent-teacher situation, 160
Disapproval, and play therapy, 94
Discipline, in classroom situation, 152
Drive, inner, 13, 17-18
Dynamics, change in, 11, 23, 43

Emotional involvement, in non-directive therapist, 64-65
Emotional relaxation, 16
Empathy, 127
Encouragement, in non-directive play therapy, 94
English, class subject, as form of therapy, 142-45

Environmental manipulation, 68
Equilibrium, 106
Evaluation, 118

Fears, illustrated, 109-17
Feelings (general), discussed, 94; recognition and, 103; negative, 130
Flexibility, of personality, 11
Free expression, in non-directive therapy, 142
Free play, 171
Frustrations, 126

Group experience, illustrated, 35-36, 38-39
Group therapy, explained, 25; problems of, 25; and "lead" principle, 124
Growth, described, 10; as related to change, 127
Guilt feelings, 39, 44, 86, 94; prevention of, 129, 131

Handicapped child, the, 58

Independence, and permissiveness, 92-93
Individual, the psychological needs of, 10; rôle in play therapy, 23
Individual contact, 105
Individual status, discussed, 20, 21
Individual therapy, 25; acceptance in, 90
Insight, 95, 99, 103, 118; in classroom situation, 142
Integration, and behavior, 13
Interpretation, 23; explained, 98; illustrated, 107

Limitations, reasons for, 128; time element as, 129; consistency of, 132; versus pressure, 133-34; in group therapy, 134; and physical aggression, 134-35; in schoolroom situation, 141

Maladjusted behavior, types, 13-14; defined, 20
Maladjustment, explained, 12; cited, 58
Mental health, in schools, 139, 140; teacher's rôle in, 141; of teachers, 161

Non-directive counseling, as a technique, 25-26
Non-directive policy, 119

Non-directive therapy, 15, 22; basic principles listed, 73-74; in classroom situation, 142

Organism, living, and personality, 11

Parents, and the maladjusted child, 66, 67; co-operation, 68-69; in teacher relationship, 157
Participation, and permissiveness, 93-94
Passivity, in non-directive therapist, 64; in pupil, 148
Permissiveness, 15, 73; how established, 91, 92; absolute, 92; and child-therapist relationship, 93-94; group therapy and, 95-96; child's attitude toward, 120-21; schoolteacher and, 141, 163, 164
Personality, discussed, 11, 12, 13; of child, 12, 126
Personality structure, theories of, 9, 10
Physical aggression, and limitations principle, 134
Play contact, 105, 116
Play materials, for play therapy, 54
Play therapy, explained, 9; defined, 16; rôle, 58
Play-therapy room, value of, 16; described, 53; materials, 131
Praise, in playroom, 79, 94
Pressure, 106, 126; limitations versus, 133; in a pupil situation, 144; in schools, 163
Principal, and teacher acceptance, 164, 165
Problem child, examples, 58
Progressive education, evaluated, 140, 141, 142
Psychodramatics, 55
Pupil, and therapeutic approach, 140

Rapport, illustrated, 76; group therapy and, 84-85; therapist's part in, 127; in schoolroom, 140
Readiness, law of, discussed, 125
Reality, 132
Recognition, illustrated, 81-82; versus interpretation, 98; group therapy, 104
Reflection, value discussed, 146; in parent-teacher relationship, 157, 160
Rejection, 141

Respect, 109; in group therapy, 117; and child control, 131

Responsibility, in child, illustrated, 77, 89, 93; and destructive behavior, 131

Rogers, Carl R., 26

School curriculum, and the individual, 151-52

Security, as expressed in playroom, 17; and limitations principle, 132; in pupil situation, 141

Self-actualization, need, 44

Self-concept, and self-realization, 13; and inner conflict, 13-14; of teachers, 164

Self-directed therapy, 26

Self-direction, permissiveness and, 93

Self-esteem, 106, 162

Self-expression, and progressive education, 142

Self-initiative, in classroom situation, 148; guidance and, 154

Self-realization, 13, 161

Self-respect, 106

Shame feeling, 95

Standards, social, 44

Structuring, defined, 74, 120

Supportive technique, 92

Symbol, 98; authority, 153

Teacher, frustrated, 139; and pupil relationship, 140, 141, 154; and recognition principle, 147; in therapy rôle, 152; and authority symbol, 153; maladjusted, 161; as a person, 162; problems, 163; and acceptance, 165; group therapy for, 166

Techniques. *See* Non-directive counseling, as a technique

Tensions, in group therapy, 85, 95; adult and child, 126; and growth experience, 131-32; in classroom situation, 144

Therapeutic approach, and educational practices, 141, 156

Therapist, general rôle, 9, 17, 55-56; requirements of non-directive, 62; basic attitudes of nondirective, 63-64; passivity in, 64; relationship to child, 74-75; rôle in group therapy, 85; as "sounding board," 120

Therapist-teacher, the, in classroom situation, 142

Therapy. *See* Non-directive therapy, Individual therapy, Group therapy, Self-directed therapy, Child-centered therapy, Childchosen therapy, Concomitant therapy

Therapy structure, 106

Threat, in therapy situation, 88

Toys, rôle in play therapy, 22; kinds suggested, 54; use illustrated, 110, 129

Verbalization, 99, 103

CASES

Angela, 142-43

Bill, 107-09
Billy, 105
Bobby, 6, 7, 14, 15, 68, 79, 209-66
Buddy, 209-66

Carl, 151
Carry, 105
Charlene, 143-45
Charles, 227-66
Charlie, 147

Delbert, 104
Dick, 276-80
Dickie, 171-76
Dibs, 24

Edith, 194-96, 198
Edna, 200-06, 276-80, 284-87, 292-95, 301-26
Emma, 5, 6, 7, 14, 15, 67-68, 271-326
Ernest, 148, 149, 150, 180-86, 209-18
Ernest, age 6, 328-70

Herby, 19

Jack, 99, 100-04, 151, 206-08, 276-80
Jane, 199-200
Jean, 40-47, 87-90
Jean, age 4, 188-94, 197-98
Jerry, 109-17
Jim, 135
Jimmy, 141, 146
Joann, 179-80, 197
Joe, 40-43, 45, 151
Joey, 145
John, 144-45
Johnny, 76-79

Lynn, 147

Martha, 40-43, 45-47

Mike, 146-47

Oscar, 79-84

Philip, 206-07, 276-80

Richard, 121-24, 206-07
Robert, 157-60

Sarah, 200-06
Saul, 209-34
Sharon, 199-200, 276-81, 284-86,

292-96, 301-26
Shiela, 176-78
Shirley, 178
Shirley-Ann, 276-80, 284-86, 292-
  97, 301-26
Sylvia, 187-88

Theda, 40-43, 46
Timmy, 6, 7, 14, 15, 68, 209-46,
  253-66
Tom, 3, 4, 7, 14, 15, 28-50, 67
Tommy, 149-50, 276-81